COOKING WITH SPICES

Carolyn Heal and Michael Allsop

16 colour photographs by Charles Pocklington
100 line drawings by Ann Collingridge

DAVID & CHARLES
Newton Abbot London North Pomfret (Vt)

To

I.L.J.E.

and

A.C.C.

British Library Cataloguing in Publication Data

Heal, Carolyn
  Cooking with spices.
  1. Spices
  I. Title   II. Allsop, Michael
  641.3′ 383   TX406

  ISBN 0-7153-8369-8

First published 1983
Second impression 1983

Typeset by Typesetters (Birmingham) Limited
and printed in Great Britain
by R. J. Acford, Chichester
for David & Charles (Publishers) Limited
Brunel House Newton Abbot Devon

Published in the United States of America
by David & Charles Inc
North Pomfret Vermont 05053 USA

Contents

Introduction   7
  Notable Dates in the History of Spices   11
  Hotness Scale   14

Spices A to Z

Ajowan	16	Cubeb	78	Papaya	143
Allspice	17	Cumin	79	Paprika	145
Amchur	20	Curry Leaf	82	Pepper	148
Anise	22	Dill	84	Pomegranate	152
Anise-Pepper	24	Fennel	89	Poppy	154
Annatto	26	Fenugreek	92	Safflower	159
Asafoetida	28	Galangal	94	Saffron	161
Badrang	30	Garlic	97	Salt	163
Bay Leaf	32	Ginger	100	Sandalwood	167
Calamus	37	Horseradish	106	Sassafras	168
Caper	38	Juniper	109	Screwpine	170
Caraway	40	Kokum	111	Sesame	172
Cardamom	43	Lemon Grass	113	Soya	174
Carob	45	Liquorice	115	Star Anise	178
Cassia	47	Mace	116	Sumac	180
Cayenne	49	Mahlebi	118	Tade	182
Celery Seed	54	Mastic	120	Tamarind	183
Chilli	56	Melegueta Pepper	122	Tonka Bean	186
Cinnamon	60	Mint	123	Trifala	188
Citrus	63	Mustard	126	Turmeric	192
Clove	66	Nasturtium	130	Vanilla	194
Cocoa	69	Nigella	132	Zedoary	197
Coconut	72	Nutmeg	134		
Coriander	75	Onion	140		

Spice Mixtures   199
Chilli Guide   223
World Map Showing Origin of Spices   228

Appendices
Taste – How It Functions 230
Useful Weights and Measures 231
Indian Vocabulary 233
South East Asian Vocabulary 245
Chinese Vocabulary 251
Japanese Vocabulary 254
Arabic Vocabulary 256
Glossary of Technical Terms 258
Botanical Index 262
Index of Botanical Families of Spices 265
Spice Suppliers 266
Further Reading 267
Acknowledgements 268
Index 269

Introduction

Awake, O north wind; and come, thou south; blow upon my garden, that the spices thereof may flow out. Let my beloved come into his garden, and eat his pleasant fruits.

Song of Solomon

Cooking with spices opens the gate to a new culinary world: the warmth of the Mediterranean, the delicate formality of Japan, the fire of Mexico, the infinite variety of China, the rich spiciness of India and the alluring colour of Thailand, Malaysia and Indonesia. We know of cinnamon, ginger and vanilla but what of zedoary, amchur and galangal? One takes the former for granted but ignores the latter more exotic sounding spices which are, in fact, readily obtainable.

But what are spices? Spices are the dried, aromatic parts of plants or extracts from those parts – berries, buds, bark, leaves, fruit, pods, seeds or roots. They share many characteristics: many contain common chemical constituents, most respond in similar ways during cooking and generally they come from the hot countries of the tropics.

Historically the quest for spices has benefited religions, caused wars, built empires and created wealth in some ways comparable to the quest for oil and minerals in recent history. Mohammed's interest in spices has passed into tradition. Having married into a wealthy trading concern, divine revelation inspired him to bring the word of God and the merchandise of his family to the peoples of Arabia, Africa and Asia. The Romans, whose appetite for exotic spices increased with their decadence, found unseasoned food most disappointing. They brought some 400 herbs and spices with them on their campaigns in Europe and Britain; many of these are now naturalised.

For 300 years from the sixteenth century, Europe enjoyed an explosion of imperial and mercantile power closely allied to new skills in navigation and ship building. European explorers discovered an amazing wealth of natural resources in exotic lands which their governments and merchants could purchase with trinkets or exploit with force. The bulk of this trade was spices. In a period of intense seafaring activity, the Portuguese established areas of influence in East Africa, Brazil and the Far East, trading in pepper, cinnamon and ginger; the Spanish, in America and the West Indies, traded in chilli, vanilla and allspice; and the English pursued these enterprises in all areas. The great navigators associated with the onset of these ventures were Vasco da Gama, Christopher Columbus, and Sir Francis Drake. The Dutch also founded an empire in those disputed regions and for decades the nations of Europe found a distant battleground for their commercial rivalries. America, in its turn, became a culinary melting pot, absorbing many traditions including British, Jewish, Dutch, Spanish, Italian and Scandinavian and enjoyed the prizes of successful spice trading.

Throughout this period and for hundreds of years before, spices were considered vital to sustain life – they were necessary to preserve food, make it more palatable when it was in a state of decay, provide medicines and sweeten foul air. European guilds of pepperers or spicers were founded as early as the twelfth century, whose members were later to become the apothecaries – forerunners of today's medical profession. (Some notable dates in the history of spices are given at the end of the Introduction.)

The well known spices have been in use in the West for many centuries, but British cooking suffered from the influence of Puritan beliefs when highly flavoured food, along with all other stimulating aspects of life, was renounced as evil, provoking lusts and passions. Recovery from this attitude has been slow but it is finally here with us. Ease of travel and shifts in world population are now giving us the opportunity to discover spices which have been in age-old use in their countries of origin. We hope this book will help to bring this fascinating world much nearer.

Seventy spices are described in Part I under the following headings:

Spice Description Spices are often bought in powdered form and are not recognisable as coming from seeds, roots, bark or leaves. These natural forms are described in detail, together with their bouquet and flavour, to aid recognition and encourage the use of whole spices which better retain their freshness and flavour. With each spice an 'H Scale' value is given denoting its hotness. The full range of the scale is on page 14.

Preparation and Storage Disappointment may occur if spices are not stored or prepared correctly. Some of the lesser known spices, although available, may not include instructions for use (tamarind and coconut for example) – an omission not likely to encourage would-be purchasers. Guidelines for preparation and storage are given for all the spices together with the correct amounts to use and warnings as to hotness and pungency.

Uses Diverse uses for each spice are given, with special emphasis on classic and international cookery.

Chemical Composition Spices acquire their aroma and flavour from the contained essential oils, bitter principles etc. The chemistry of these compounds is too complex to be dealt with here. However, we give a brief description of each spice's composition in sufficient detail to illustrate that some apparently different spices have common constituents; for example, the essential oils of both bay leaf and clove contain eugenol. The chemistry of spices is as fascinating as the spices themselves and those interested are recommended to read the books listed under 'Further Reading'.

Attributed Properties Herbal and medicinal applications and some modern uses of interest are noted. These illustrate the variety of uses to which spices have been put through the ages, all over the world. Some of the properties claimed may appear amusing and bizarre, if not dangerous; but in former times they were taken seriously and in some cases still have a place in medicine today. UNDER NO CIRCUM-STANCES SHOULD ANY REMEDY MENTIONED HERE BE USED WITHOUT PROPER MEDICAL CONSULTATION.

Plant Description Spices come from a great many different forms of plant life ranging from tiny shrubs to great forest trees. These are as varied as the spices themselves: pepper grows on vines; vanilla, so common in sweets and confectionery, is the fruit of a tropical parasitical orchid, and so on. Spice plants are described in sufficient detail to aid recognition but are not given full botanical descriptions.

Cultivation Although most spices are grown only in the tropics, others can be successfully grown in temperate regions; the umbelliferous spices are good examples. In the former case local methods of cultivation are described and in the latter instructions are given for home cultivation.

Remarks Here we give items of interest not mentioned in the foregoing sections. These include the origin of spices, historical notes and non-culinary uses.

Other Names Many alternative names of each spice are listed here, followed by the spice's name in the four major European tongues and finally by names from the rest of the world; these are mainly Asian. No attempt has been made to rationalise the multiplicity of spellings of the latter, but several versions the reader is likely to come across in shops, menus and cookery books are included.

Recipes There are one or two recipes for each spice, chosen for their traditional associations with that spice. With the more familiar spices, therefore, the recipes are usually simple and well known. Other spices provide recipes that may be new to many, although they are often in everyday use in their country of origin. All the recipes have been designed with Imperial weights and measures. These have been converted directly into metric and US systems. Metric measurements have usually been given to the nearest 5g or 5ml but may be satisfactorily approximated to the nearest 10. All spoon measurements are level.

Note: 1tsp cumin, ground,
means
1tsp of ground cumin NOT 1tsp of cumin seeds which are then ground.

Spice Mixtures Over fifty spice mixtures have been collected from all over the world and form a fascinating subject on their own. In most cases undimensioned proportions are given. For example, the proportion figures mean 'parts', eg teaspoons, grammes, whatever, depending on the quantity required or the available measures, and they can be scaled up or down as required. The same unit of measurement must, of course, be used throughout.

Chilli Guide In addition to individual descriptions of cayenne, chilli and paprika, a separate guide to the complex subject of chillies has been added. A statement of the diversity of chillies is given, a list of recognised species, a description of a method of determining the hotness of chillies, and finally a list of scientific and common names of many chillies.

Part II contains the following appendices:

World Map Showing the Origins of Spices This map shows the origins of spices where these are known. Controversy still exists over some of these origins, coconut being a case in point (some authorities believe it originated in Colombia and others prefer Melanesia). The cultivation of many spices is now centred far away from their places of origin and most have spread right across the globe.

Taste A brief explanation.

Useful Weights and Measures These tables give useful conversion factors and have been used throughout the recipes. Also included is a table showing various measures of spices.

Vocabularies Vocabularies of spices and culinary terms in the languages of India, South East Asia, China, Japan and the Arab world are included on pages 233–57. These will prove useful in translating cooking terms, menus and food labels. No attempt has been made to solve the problem of the varied spellings of many of these words. The Indian vocabulary includes words in several languages from the whole sub-continent and Sri Lanka.

Glossaries and Botanical Indexes Short definitions of technical words in the book are given in the Glossary of Technical Terms, only chemicals being omitted. There is a scientific botanical index as well as a family index which groups all spices by their families, and where appropriate some common relatives are cited.

Spice Suppliers A short list of suppliers is given to aid the search for the less well known spices.

NOTABLE DATES IN THE HISTORY OF SPICES

3000BC	Caraway seeds in use according to archaeologists' excavations.
c3000	Sesame is a medium of exchange in Mesopotamia.
2500	Cassia recorded in China 500 years after soya.
c2500	Spices first used in embalming of Egyptian mummies. Advisable, as bodies were often kept several days before handing over to embalmers, who are recorded as apt to violate fresh corpses.
c2600–2100	Labourers building the pyramids are fed on garlic and onions to keep them fit.
c700	Cardamom, citrus, pomegranate and saffron grow in the hanging gardens of Babylon.
c500	Anise cakes are eaten by Romans to aid digestion after a gluttonous meal.
80	One of the entrances to the great Egyptian spice trading port of Alexandria is known as 'Pepper Gate'.
44	Romans bring garlic, coriander, mustard and other spices to Britain.

42BC–AD37	Apicius – a Roman epicure – provides material for ten cookery books featuring herbs and spices. (When he had squandered his fortune on rich and spicy food, he poisoned himself rather than live on plain fare.)
AD25	Emperor Tiberius wears a wreath of bay leaves during thunderstorms.
25	John the Baptist eats carob beans in the wilderness
40	Hippalus the Greek discovers monsoon winds, thus quartering the time for the round voyage to the Malabar coast from Egypt, and so makes pepper a common commodity.
77	Pliny tells of the efficaciousness of cumin ground with bread and wine.
410	Alaric the Visigoth demands 3000lb of pepper tribute to withhold sacking of Rome.
500	Mayans use allspice to embalm their dead.
540	Nutmeg, already known in India, reaches Constantinople, and shortly will reach Europe.
1030	Avicenna – Arabian philosopher and physician – prescribes fenugreek for diabetes.
1180	Pepperers' Guild founded in London.
1298	The Doge hears Marco Polo's tales of the inordinate value of the salt coins bearing the seal of the great Khan.
1348	Spices are used as charms and medicines to ward off the plague.
1362	The mastic fiefdom of Chios is given to Genoese commercial interests by Turkey, the islanders retaining self-government.
1494	Columbus's crew discover capsicums in the Americas.
1519	The Aztec emperor, Montezuma, is defeated by Cortés, who finds vast quantities of vanilla beans which were used as currency.
1528	Portuguese gain the Moluccas or Spice Islands, giving them the monopoly of nutmeg, mace and cloves for nearly 100 years.
1547	Jamaican ginger successfully grown and exported to Europe.
1548	Capsicum annuum (cayenne, chilli, guinea pepper, pimento, red pepper) first cultivated in England, having been brought to Europe by the Spaniards.
1556–1605	The Mogul Emperor, Akbar, plants 100,000 mango trees.
1575	'Clusius', the French botanist, cultivates first calamus rhizomes.

1597	John Gerard, renowned English herbalist, mentions fagara (badrang) and mahaleb (mahlebi) in *The Herball.*
1605	Dutch capture Amboina and retain monopoly of cloves for two centuries.
1620	'Mayflower' lands mint at Boston, Massachusetts.
1629	Onions are first cultivated in the New World.
1634	Dijon granted licence to prepare mustard. Licence stipulates wearing of 'clean clothes and sober'.
1641	Dutch capture Moluccas from Portuguese, breaking their spice monopoly.
1646	Nasturtium enters Europe from Peru via the Philippines, Zanzibar and the Middle East.
1718	Connecticut Collegiate school becomes Yale College in honour of Elihu Yale who donates gifts and spices from India.
1760	Nutmeg 'mountain' burnt in Amsterdam to maintain prices.
1770	Cinnamon actively cultivated in Sri Lanka. Formerly Dutch traders had the monopoly and preferred to use the wild trees.
1805	First mandarin orange arrives in England from China.
1818	Cloves introduced to Zanzibar, still a leading producer.
1828	Dutchman, C. J. van Houten, invents method of treating cocoa to improve its solubility.
1837	Worcestershire sauce is invented – a secret recipe in which an important ingredient is tamarind.
1841	Edward Albius, a former slave, discovers how to pollinate vanilla artificially using a thin stick.
1841	First patent taken out on soap using coconut oil.
1843	Nutmeg established in Grenada – today's most successful producer.
1880	In the American Wild West a mixture of asafoetida, ipecacuanha, cayenne and mustard is used as an antidote for alcoholism.
1885	English edition of the *Ananga Ranga,* translated by Sir Richard Burton and F. F. Arbuthnot, mentions numerous spices.
1896	First patent for margarine using coconut oil.
1896	The Governor of Bombay gives locally produced curry powder his official seal of approval.
1915	Prohibition of absinthe in France gains popularity for many anise-flavoured drinks as substitutes.
1930	Mahatma Gandhi leads mass pilgrimage to seaside to

make salt in protest at the high British tax on salt in India.

1937	Professor Albert Szent-Györgyi – Hungarian biochemist – receives Nobel Prize. He discovers that capsicums have large amount of vitamin C, 3–5 times as much as citrus.
1961–69	Man orbits earth and eventually reaches moon with spiced food.
1981	Development of microwave seasonings include spices.
1983	Spices used in genetic engineering.

HOTNESS (H) SCALE

The scale below has been devised to relate the 'hotness' of spices. It is an arbitrary scale using a range of eleven values from 0 to 10.

10 Volcanic
 9 Incendiary
 8 Fiery
 7 Burning
 6 Hot
 5 Piquant
 4 Warm
 3 Medium
 2 Mild
 1 Delicate
 0 Neutral

Each spice has been given a value on the above scale. This perfectly illustrates the relative hotness of all the spices. It is unlikely that a level 10 will be experienced outside Africa or Mexico where the hottest chillies grow. In general, most spices fall in the middle range.

Spices A-Z
Spice Mixtures
Chilli Guide

Spices A-Z

Ajowan

Trachyspermum ammi
syn *Carum copticum, C. ajowan, Ptychotis ajowan*
Fam Umbelliferae

SPICE DESCRIPTION
Ajowan is a member of the parsley family, its seeds being used as a spice. These resemble large celery seeds. The seed is red-brown with light stripes; sometimes the darker parts are brown-green. Usually about 2mm (0.08in) in length, the seed averages 1.5mm (0.06in) in width at the widest part. Occasionally a minute stalk occurs. The dried seed is available whole or ground.
Bouquet Like a pungent crude thyme.
Flavour Crushed seeds have a pungent acrid flavour of thyme. Though harsh, it is not unpleasant and soon leaves a milder but lingering taste. Because it is more 'herby' than 'spicy' it is used less widely in the East than expected.   H Scale: 5

PREPARATION AND STORAGE
No preparation is required other than to crush the whole seed where the ground spice is required. For *parathas* and similar uses, lightly bruise the seeds first. Dried ajowan seeds keep indefinitely in airtight containers.

USES
The whole dried seed is extensively used in India for savouries, crisp fried snacks and *parathas*. Ajowan is particularly associated with lentil dishes and recipes using chick pea flour (*besan*), a good example of which is the savoury snack *sev*. It is occasionally an ingredient of curry powder. In Europe it is used as a substitute for thyme, but only in moderation as it is much stronger than that herb.

CHEMICAL COMPOSITION
The seeds contain 4–6 per cent of an essential oil, ptycholic (ajowan) oil, which in turn contains 45–55 per cent thymol. Only monarda (American horsemint) yields more thymol than ajowan.

ATTRIBUTED PROPERTIES
Ajowan, because of its thymol content, is a strong germicide, anti-spasmodic, fungicide, and anthelmintic. In the East, especially in the form of Ajwain or Omum water, it is used against diarrhoea and wind. The spice is probably used there for its medicinal properties rather than as a flavouring. In India the seeds are a household remedy for indigestion and asthma. It also has aphrodisiac properties, and the *Ananga Ranga* prescribes it for increasing the enjoyment of a husband in the flower of his life.

PLANT DESCRIPTION
A small annual, 30–70cm (1–2ft) in height,

resembling a sparse wild parsley, to which it is related, both being of the Umbelliferae family.

CULTIVATION

In India it is a cold weather crop and grown similarly to caraway. For home growing:
Sow: September for next year. March for same year.
Soil: Any well drained.
Aspect: Sunny.
Cultivation: Grow seeds in permanent position and thin seedlings to 30cm (12in) apart. Weed and water when necessary.
Harvesting: Cut stalks at ground level when seeds are ripe. Hang in bundles upside down in a dry place and seeds will fall off easily. Collect on paper and store in jars. Alternatively, put in a bag and beat. Sieve out dust and pick out stalks.

REMARKS

Ajowan is native to and grown largely in India, but is also cultivated in Egypt, Iran, Pakistan and Afghanistan. It is exported to the West largely for the extraction of thymol, but is now available from UK shops specialising in Asian foods. Some Indian authors call it 'lovage'. It is pronounced aj'o-wen.

OTHER NAMES

Ajave Seeds, Ajwain, Ajvain, Ajwan, Ameos, (Candy, True) Bishop's Weed, Carom, Ethiopian Cumin, Omam, Omum
French: ajowan
German: Ajowan
Italian: ajowan
Spanish: ajowan
Indian: ajvini, ajwa(i)n, javanee, yamani

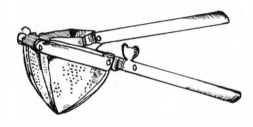

Potato ricer

Sev (colour page 103)

An Indian savoury snack ideal for serving with drinks. This recipe yields enough for 4-6 people when served with other savouries and nuts.

Imp	Metric	US
6oz chick pea flour (*besan*)	170g	6oz
3oz ground rice	85g	3oz
½tsp ajowan seeds	½tsp	½tsp
½tsp chilli powder	½tsp	½tsp
pinch turmeric	pinch	pinch
1½tsp salt	1½tsp	1½tsp
3tbsp *ghee*, melted	60ml	4tbsp
¼pt water	140ml	9½tbsp
oil to deep fry		

1 Sift chick pea flour and ground rice.
2 Mix in spices, seeds and salt.
3 Rub in *ghee* until well distributed.
4 Add water and knead well.
5 Heat oil until smoking and pass some dough through a potato ricer or rotary grater directly into the oil.
6 Deep fry on medium heat until golden brown and agitation ceases.
7 Remove *sev* with finely perforated spoon and drain on absorbent paper.
8 Repeat process until dough is used up.
9 Can be stored in airtight containers for several weeks.

Allspice

Pimenta dioica
syn *Pimenta officinalis, Eugenia pimenta*
Fam Myrtaceae

SPICE DESCRIPTION

Allspice resembles large brown peppercorns or small peas. Unripe berries are picked and sun dried until the seeds in them rattle. They vary in size between 4 and 7mm (⅛–¼in) in diameter, and are dark brown with a slightly wrinkled surface, which is rough to the touch because of the presence of many tiny oil glands. The top of the fruit has a small circular projection which is the remains of the calyx tube. The outer case contains two dark, hard kidney-shaped seeds. Allspice is available whole or ground.

Bouquet and Flavour: Said to be like a combination of nutmeg, clove and cinnamon or ginger, whence its name. However, clove seems to dominate, with some cinnamon and a trace of nutmeg. For these qualities allspice has been popular in Europe since the seventeenth century. There are peppery overtones which account for the other names: pimenta, Jamaica pepper. H Scale: 4

PREPARATION AND STORAGE

It is preferable to buy the whole dried spice and store in airtight jars, where it keeps almost indefinitely. Ground allspice, even when carefully kept, will not last very long. A good idea is to keep a separate pepper mill specially for allspice.

USES

Allspice is used almost throughout the world but it is particularly popular in European cookery. It forms an important ingredient in marinades, pickling spices and mulling spices. Many pâtés, terrines and smoked and canned meats include allspice. It enhances dishes made from root vegetables and a few allspice berries are often added to *Sauerkraut* and soups, eg Dutch pea soup. Game dishes, Scandinavian marinated raw herring fillets (*glasmästarsill*) and English spiced beef are all well known for the inclusion of the spice. Traditionally, allspice has been used in cakes, biscuits, fruit pies, milk and chocolate puddings and in particular Christmas pudding. In the United States it is used to flavour pumpkin pie, cakes and pickles; and in the Middle East, meat and rice dishes. Some Indian curries and *pilaus* contain allspice.

CHEMICAL COMPOSITION

The dried unripe fruits contain 3–4.5 per cent essential oil (pimento oil), 8 per cent or more tannin (quercitannic acid), cineol, moisture and fibre. The oil is yellow to yellowish red and is responsible for the spice's characteristic odour and spicy pungent taste. It contains 60–75 per cent of eugenol, which by treatment with alkalis and oxidation gives vanillin. It is used in medicine and commercially as an aromatising agent for liqueurs (Chartreuse and Benedictine), perfumery and soap. The oil is also distilled from the leaves of the allspice tree.

ATTRIBUTED PROPERTIES

Because of its eugenol content, allspice has attributes similar to clove. As a spice it is a digestive and carminative. The oil derivative is similarly used and is mildly antiseptic and anaesthetic. Certain anti-fungal and antibacterial properties of the spice have been reported.

PLANT DESCRIPTION

A tropical evergreen tree, 7–13m (22–43ft) in height, closely related to the clove tree. The tree, many branched, has smooth, grey aromatic bark; the leaves are dark green, elliptic, glossy, leathery, up to 15cm (6in) long. The fruit are formed on the ends of the smaller branches, which are broken off to collect the unripe berries: ripe ones tend to lose their flavour. The berries are green, turning to purple or red when ripe.

CULTIVATION

Allspice is cultivated only in the tropics and then as a wild, plantation or odd garden tree. Fresh seeds are planted in nursery beds or pots; after ten months they are ready for the field. Three seedlings are planted together 10m (30ft) apart and then reduced to one good plant. Fruiting starts in five or six years, full bearing comes at twenty years and the trees live to a very good age.

REMARKS

Allspice is the most important of the few spices native to the West. The tree is indigenous to the West Indies, South and Central America. Allspice is collected from the wild trees in these countries but also from plantations in the West Indies, notably Jamaica. A local drink in Jamaica is *pimento dram*, made from the ripe berries and rum. Allspice was used by the Mayans as an embalming agent and by other South American Indians to flavour chocolate. The spice was imported to Europe soon after the discovery of the New World. It has been introduced to the East Indies and other tropical countries. Its popularity in England caused it to be known as 'English spice'. Allspice is not a mixture of other spices and should never be confused with mixed spice. The name is applied to other aromatic shrubs, particularly the genus *Calycanthus* – Carolina allspice or strawberry shrub – but these have no connection with *Pimenta dioica*, the allspice of the kitchen.

OTHER NAMES

English Spice, Jamaica Pepper, Clove Pepper, Myrtle Pepper, Pimenta, Pimento
French: pimenta, piment poivre de la Jamaïque, tout-épice
German: Jamaikapfeffer, Nelkenpfeffer
Italian: pepe di Giamaica, pimento
Spanish: pimiento de Jamaica
Indian: kabab cheene, seetful
Tamil: vellai-milahu

Glasmästarsill (Glassblower's Herring)

Swedish sweet-sour herring fillets served as part of the *smörgåsbord*. Make at least five days in advance.   Serves 6–8.

Imp	Metric	US
2 large salted herrings	2	2
or 4 tinned *matjes* herring fillets		

Imp	Metric	US
½pt white wine vinegar	285ml	1¼ cup
¼pt water	140ml	9½tbsp
4oz granulated sugar	115g	4oz
1tbsp whole allspice	1tbsp	1⅓tbsp
2tsp white mustard seed	2tsp	2tsp
2–3 bay leaves	2–3	2–3
1 large onion	1	1
1 medium carrot	1	1
1½in fresh horseradish, thinly sliced	4cm	1½in
½in fresh ginger, thinly sliced	13mm	½in

1 Soak fish in cold water for twelve hours.
2 Bring vinegar, water and sugar slowly to boiling point together with allspice, mustard seed and bay leaves, stirring until sugar dissolves.
3 Allow to cool. Remove allspice, mustard seed and bay leaves and reserve.
4 Drain, dry and bone fish discarding heads and tails. Slice diagonally into 1in (2½cm) pieces.
5 Place a layer of fish in 1 quart (1 litre) glass jar and cover with a few slices of onion, carrot, horseradish and ginger. Sprinkle with some mustard seeds and allspice and top with a bay leaf.
6 Repeat until jar is full.
7 Pour on pickling liquid, seal jar and refrigerate for at least five days.

Pumpkin Pie

A traditional American dessert.   Serves 6.

Imp	Metric	US
8oz shortcrust pastry	225g	8oz
3 eggs	3	3
4oz sugar, brown or white	115g	4oz
½tsp allspice, ground	½tsp	½tsp
½tsp cinnamon	½tsp	½tsp
¼tsp nutmeg	¼tsp	¼tsp
¼tsp salt	¼tsp	¼tsp
15oz pumpkin purée	425g	15oz
½pt milk	285ml	1¼ cups
whipped cream		

1 Line a 9in (25cm) pie plate with the pastry and flute the edge.
2 In a bowl, lightly beat the eggs and mix in sugar and spices.
3 Beat in pumpkin purée and then milk and whisk together.

4 Pour into pie case and bake for 40 minutes at Gas Mark 6, 400°F, 200°C, until set and brown. Serve warm with whipped cream.

Amchur (Mango)

Mangifera indica
Fam Anacardiaceae

SPICE DESCRIPTION

The spice amchur is unripe or green mango fruits which have been sliced and sun dried. The name comes from Hindi *am*, mango. The spice is either whole or ground and sometimes seasoned with turmeric. The dried slices are light brown, rough surfaced and 5–10cm (2–4in) long, 2–3cm (¾–1¼in) wide and a few millimetres thick. Ripe mango slices are also dried and are orangey brown. Amchur powder is finely ground but with a slightly fibrous texture. It is beige in colour.
Bouquet: Sour-sweet, warm and slightly resinous.
Flavour: Slightly sweet and acidic.

H Scale: 1–2

PREPARATION AND STORAGE

Carefully cured mango will yield good quality amchur in both whole and ground forms. However, it is advisable to buy fresh quantities as and when required. Otherwise, store in airtight containers away from light.

USES

The use of amchur is confined chiefly to Indian cookery, where it is used as an acid flavouring in curries, soups, chutneys, marinades and as a condiment. The dried slices add a piquancy to curries and the powder acts as a souring agent akin to tamarind but, of course, needs no preparation. It is particularly useful as an ingredient in marinades, having the same tenderising qualities as lemon or lime juice. However, where, for instance, three tablespoons of lemon or lime juice are required, one teaspoon of amchur will suffice.

Chicken and fish are enhanced by amchur and grilled fish on skewers, *machli kabab*, is well worth trying.

CHEMICAL COMPOSITION

Amchur contains starch, protein and minerals. It is a good source of vitamin C, with some A and B_5. In ripe mangoes the starch is converted to sugar and vitamin A predominates. The gallic acid of wild mangoes has mainly been removed from cultivated varieties. The terebinthine trait results from terpenes present.

ATTRIBUTED PROPERTIES

The mango tree is so old and of such popularity in India and the Far East that it is not surprising that every part of it yields some specific or other. The leaves, the bark, its resin, the flowers, the fruit, the seed, all are utilised. The unripe fruit is acidic, astringent and antiscorbutic and in the dried condition, amchur, is particularly useful for the latter purpose. Of the mango's other uses and properties, its dyeing quality is of interest. In India, cattle are fed on mango leaves and their urine is used as a yellow dye, the active principle in this being xanthone. Needless to say, the fabric treated thus has its own special bouquet.

An evergreen tropical tree, 10–40m (30–130ft) in height, very long-lived (over 100 years), with a dense overhanging canopy. The trunk is greyish-brown, rough with many branches. The leaves are dark green and shiny. Tiny, five-petalled cream to pink flowers occur on branchlets. The flowers open at night and in the early morning. The fruits are sweet, medium-sized rounded oblong drupes, with thickish green to orange skin over sweet orange flesh, sometimes fibrous, around a large flat stone. The ripe fruit flavour varies from delicate to resinous, and its size, according to variety, from small to quite large, 7–15cm (3–6in) long.

CULTIVATION

Mangoes grow in tropical regions with marked wet and dry seasons, the dry period being necessary for good flowering and fruiting. Biennial cropping is usual. Mangoes will grow on a wide variety of soils provided the climatic conditions are correct. Usually propagated by seedlings, the trees are planted 9–12 metres (30–36ft) apart, but inter-cropping is carried out only in the early years. Many trees grow in the semi-wild state.

REMARKS

The mango tree is native to the India-Burma-Malaysia region and is one of the oldest cultivated fruits. In India it has grown for over 4,000 years; the various uses of the fruit are probably as ancient. After the European explorations during the sixteenth and seventeenth centuries, it has spread to all parts of the tropical and sub-tropical world, especially Africa. The mango, apart from its place as a fresh fruit, is most famous as a chutney or pickle ingredient. (Do not confuse it with mangosteen, which is a South East Asian fruit and is quite different). Amchur is an interesting by-product now appearing more frequently on the shelves of Asian food shops in Europe. The mango retains a special place in Hindu mythology and ritual. Lord Gautama the Buddha was presented with a mango grove and the Mogul Emperor, Akbar, (1556–1605), ordered a huge plantation of 100,000 mango trees to be planted. The dried seeds of the mango are ground into a flour in time of famine. The mango tree is a member of the family that includes the cashew and pistachio nut.

OTHER NAMES

Amchoor
French: mangue (mango)
German: Mango (mango)
Italian: mango (mango)
Spanish: mango, manguey (mango)
Indian: aam( )choor, aam( )chur, amchoor, amchur; aam papar (dried mango sheets); a(a)m (mango)

Amchur Fish Kebabs

Delicious fish kebabs, spicy and aromatic. Choose fish that is firm enough for skewering, such as cod, snapper etc. Makes 8 skewers, 4–5 pieces per skewer.

Imp	Metric	US
2lb fish, white	1kg	2lb
Marinade:		
1tsp amchur powder	1tsp	1tsp
1tbsp *besan* (chick pea flour)	1tbsp	1⅓tbsp
½tsp chilli powder	½tsp	½tsp
½tsp cloves, ground	½tsp	½tsp
3tsp coriander, ground	3tsp	3tsp
1tsp cumin, ground	1tsp	1tsp
2 garlic cloves, crushed	2	2
1tsp ginger, ground	1tsp	1tsp
1tsp pepper, black, ground	1tsp	1tsp
1tsp salt	1tsp	1tsp
1 cup yoghurt	1 cup	1 cup
4oz *ghee* or clarified butter	115g	4oz

1 Wash and skin fish. Cut into skewerable pieces, about 40mm (1½in) across.

2 Mix together all the marinade ingredients. Add more yoghurt if too thick.

3 Gently immerse fish pieces in the marinade so that each piece is completely covered. Leave for up to one hour.

4 Melt the *ghee*. Skewer fish pieces and coat with melted *ghee*.

5 Grill under medium heat until a nice

brown, basting constantly with the juices and marinade remnants.

6 Serve with plain rice and hot *sambals*.

Anise (Aniseed)

Pimpinella anisum
Fam Umbelliferae

SPICE DESCRIPTION
The spice consists of two tiny seeds, each 2–4mm (0.08–0.16in) long, ovoid with five fine light ribs against a grey-green background when fresh but brown when stale. The shape and lines make the seed reminiscent of a minute mandolin. Some seeds retain the fine stalk that passes through the centre of the fruit. Anise is available whole or powdered. Beware of adulteration with caraway seeds which are longer and thinner.

Bouquet Sweet and fragrantly aromatic.

Flavour A mild liquorice taste predominates. The lingering, spicy sweet flavour is similar to fennel.   H Scale: 1

PREPARATION AND STORAGE
The seeds do not remain viable beyond two to three years. They should be bought in small quantities as they soon lose their flavour, turning from grey-green to brown as they get stale. Keep in dark airtight containers. The seeds are easy to crush so avoid the powdered form. If to be used, as in India, to sweeten the breath, roast lightly beforehand.

USES
Aniseed can be used in much the same way as fennel to flavour cream soups, fish, poultry and root vegetable dishes. However, it is associated mainly with cakes, biscuits and confectionery (aniseed balls) as well as rye breads, and occasionally in Bengal and Bangladesh curries. Many Indian and Chinese dishes calling for the addition of aniseed very probably refer to star anise, a plant of a different family (see pages 178–80). The French liqueur *anisette* is nowadays mostly made with star anise. Numerous alcoholic drinks and cordials are flavoured with anise, particularly French *pastis*, Pernod and Ricard, Greek *ouzo* and *mastikha*, Spanish *ojen*, Turkish *raki*, Italian *anesone*, Arab *arrak* and Egyptian *kibib*. Lobster flamed with Pernod instead of brandy makes an interesting change. Add some whole fresh leaves of anise to green salads or a few, finely chopped, to omelettes.

CHEMICAL COMPOSITION
The fruits contain between 2–6 per cent of a fragrant essential oil which in turn contains 80–90 per cent anethole. Anise oil is obtained by distillation from anise or star anise. Oils, protein (20 per cent) and other substances (methylchavicol) also occur.

ATTRIBUTED PROPERTIES
Anise, used since ancient times for its carminative and sweetening properties, spread from the Middle East through Greece to Rome and the rest of the world. It is a mild expectorant, anise oil being used in modern cough mixtures and lozenges. It is also antiseptic, antispasmodic, soporific, anti-diarrhoeic and a cure for hiccups (a few seeds taken with water). In India the seeds are chewed to sweeten the breath and also made into a sweet-scented toilet water. It is well known that dogs are attracted by anise. The seeds are used to lay drag hunt trails and also by anti-blood sports movements to put hounds off the scent. Many pet foods contain anise.

A tender annual growing up to 60cm (2ft), with two leaf forms. The lower leaves are broad, coarsely toothed and more or less triangular in shape; the upper leaves are divided, narrow and tapering. The flowers are yellow-white, growing in compound umbels, producing small fruit which split into two seeds, aniseed. All parts of the plant are aromatic.

CULTIVATION

A long hot summer is needed for the seeds to ripen in northern climes and pot growing is not recommended.
Sow: March–April in permanent position.
Soil: Light, dry loam. Add lime if necessary.
Aspect: Sunny, south facing, sheltered.
Cultivation: Thin seedlings to 20–30cm (8–12in). Do not transplant. Keep carefully weeded.
Harvesting: Cut flower stems as seeds change colour to grey-green. Hang upside down in a dry place and collect seeds on paper below. Store in dark airtight containers.

REMARKS

Anise is native to the Levant, Egypt and the eastern Mediterranean, where it has been in use since ancient times. It is now grown commercially worldwide in warm, temperate and Mediterranean-type climates, the main areas being Spain, Greece, Egypt, Mexico and India. It has been used in Britain since the fourteenth and fifteenth centuries, notably in old English comfits and sweets. To aid digestion the Romans enjoyed anise-spiced cake after a heavy meal. Anise-flavoured sweets, such as aniseed balls, are very popular with children, as is marzipan similarly flavoured. With the prohibition of *absinthe*, anise-flavoured drinks were substituted. The name Pernod, once synonymous with *absinthe*, is today similarly associated with *pastis*.

OTHER NAMES

Aniseed, Sweet Cumin
French: anis
German: Anis
Italian: anice, anici
Spanish: anís
Greek: anís
Chinese: paat-kok, pa-chiao (cf Star Anise)
Indian: saunf, sompf, souf, suara
Tamil: vendhyam

Anise Cakes

Small, German biscuit-like cakes, quick and easy to make.   Makes about 16 cakes.

Imp	Metric	US
3 eggs	3	3
4oz caster sugar	115g	4oz
4oz self-raising flour	115g	4oz
1–2tsp aniseed, well pounded	1–2tsp	1–2tsp

1 Beat eggs until thick and foamy.
2 Add sugar and beat well.
3 Add sifted flour and aniseed and mix to a smooth dough.
4 Drop heaped teaspoonfuls of mixture on to buttered baking sheets, spacing well apart.
5 Bake for about 10 minutes in a fairly hot oven, Gas Mark 5, 375°F, 190°C.

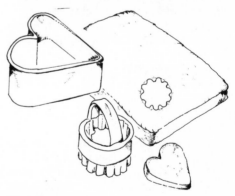

Marzipan

Add 1tsp crushed aniseed and 3tbsp Pernod to marzipan made from ½lb (225g) almonds, and form into decorative shapes.

Anise Liqueur

Add 30g (1oz) aniseed to a bottle of three-star brandy and leave for fourteen days, agitating every two or three days. Make a syrup from 1lb (455g) sugar and 1pt (570ml) water. Strain the brandy into the syrup, bottle and cork. Ready to drink.

Anise-Pepper (Szechwan Pepper)

Zanthoxylum piperitum
syn *Xanthoxylum piperitum*
Fam Rutaceae

SPICE DESCRIPTION
Anise-pepper is the dried, rust-red stalked berries of a tree of the prickly ash family. They are approximately 4–5mm (3/20–1/5in) in diameter and resemble tiny beechnuts. The rough skin splits open to reveal a brittle black seed approximately 3mm (1/8in) in diameter. However, the spice consists mainly of the empty husks. Anise-pepper is available whole or ground. The ground dried leaves known as *sansho*, and the whole leaves, either pickled or vacuum-packed, known as *kinome*, are both Japanese spices.
Bouquet The berries are warm, pepper-like and slightly pungent with citrus overtones. The leaves have a citrus fragrance with a hint of lychee.
Flavour When the aromatics are released, either by heating or moisture, the taste of the berries is hot, mildly peppery and acrid, producing a tingling sensation on the tongue. The leaves are milder and more lemony. H. Scale: 3

PREPARATION AND STORAGE
Remove any stalks from the berries and roast gently before crushing in a pestle and mortar. If a fine powder is required, sieve in order to remove the husks. Once ground, store in airtight containers and use within a short space of time. Buy the ground leaves in small quantities as their flavour will deteriorate.

USES
Anise-pepper, originating from the Szechwan province of China, is associated mainly with dishes from that region where the cooking is hotter and spicier than in the rest of China. Duck and chicken dishes in particular feature anise-pepper. Szechwanese-style roast duck is an interesting variation of the famous Peking duck, served in the same manner with sauces and pancakes, but having been seasoned with coarsely ground anise-pepper, ginger and fresh coriander leaves. An unusual hot sauce to pour over cold chopped chicken is made as follows: dry-fry a heaped teaspoon of whole anise-pepper for about a minute, pound and stir into three tablespoons of melted chicken fat and four tablespoons of soy sauce. In Szechwan, where this peppered chicken is famous, a further teaspoon of cayenne pepper is added. *Hua jiao yen* is a mixture of salt and anise-pepper, roasted and browned in a frying pan and served as a condiment to accompany deep-fried chicken, duck and pork dishes. Anise-pepper is often used in recipes in conjunction with ginger and star anise as these seem to have a special affinity with one another. In Japan the dried and powdered leaves of the prickly ash (*Z. piperitum*), known as *sansho*, make noodle dishes and soups mildly hot and fragrant. The fresh leaves, *kinome*, are used to flavour vegetables, especially bamboo shoots, and to decorate soups. Anise-pepper is an ingredient of Chinese five-spice powder and *shichimi togarashi*, a Japanese seven-flavour seasoning (see Spice Mixtures).

CHEMICAL COMPOSITION
The bark and berries of *Zanthoxylum* species contain volatile oil, resin, sugar and gum. The fruits and seeds contain 2–4 per cent essential oil which has citronellal, geraniol, limonene, phellandrene and sanshol. The essential oil of the leaves has citral, citronellal and geraniol, whence the leaves' citrus-like aroma. All species differ slightly in the amounts of these chemicals but the make-up is essentially similar.

ATTRIBUTED PROPERTIES
The berries of *Zanthoxylum* species are

carminative and anti-spasmodic. The bark of the prickly ash (Z. *americanum*, Northern; Z. *clavaherculis*, Southern) is known as 'Toothache Bark'. Generally, the berries are stronger than the bark; root-bark, berries and zanthoxylin appear in the United States Pharmacopoeia. The bark and berries are highly stimulative and used as a febrifuge, anti-rheumatic, blood purifier, digestive and for many other conditions. In the powdered form, the bark was famous in the United States as a toothache remedy and was also used for healing wounds.

PLANT DESCRIPTION
A small deciduous tree with pinnate leaves. The branches, bark and main stem are covered with sharp, spiny prickles. The American species produce black and dark blue berries in clusters at the ends of the branches; the Asiatic varieties have red berries, up to 5mm (⅕in) in diameter. The dried berry capsules are dimpled and split open in two or four sections, exposing small dark seeds in light coloured compartments. Some varieties of *Zanthoxylum*:

Z. *alatum* China and Himalayas. Fruit: Indian and Chinese condiment.

Z. *americanum* American Northern prickly ash. Herbal remedies, bark etc.

Z. *clavaherculis* American Southern prickly ash. Herbal remedies, bark etc.

Z. *limonella* see Badrang (page 30).

CULTIVATION
The tree grows wild and if cultivated needs little attention. The deciduous varieties require a temperate climate and will thrive on hill slopes.

REMARKS
Anise-pepper is uncommon in the West, but is available where there are oriental communities. Recipes from Chinese cookery books tend to omit it because of its rarity. However, this will no doubt change as its properties become appreciated. It is believed to be important in the Chinese south-west province of Szechwan because of the Indian cultural influence there during the first millennium BC; the province is the largest in China and borders on Tibet and its mountainous region. *Zanthoxylum* (or *Xanthoxylum*) species occur throughout the temperate belt including China, Japan, the Himalayas and North America. They all have similarities, are highly aromatic and all parts of the plant are used in herbal remedies in the West and cookery in the East. In Japan the wood of the prickly ash is used for pestles and mortars which impart some flavour to the substances being ground. The wood is also used for tobacco pipes in northern Japan. It would appear that the spice was named anise-pepper because of the resemblance of the dried open fruit to star anise. The name 'Fagara', below, relates to trees which grow under the main forest trees, some of which have husked seeds like the Fagaceae: oak, chestnut, beech, etc.

OTHER NAMES
Chinese Brown Pepper, Chinese Pepper, Fagara, Japan Pepper, Pepper Eyes, Suterberry, Szechwan Pepper, Toothache Tree, Yellow Wood
French: poivre anise
German: Anispfeffer
Italian: pepe d'anice
Spanish: pepe di anís
Chinese: chuan-chiao, chun-chiu, chun-tsin, fa(ah)-jiu,-jew, fa-chin, fa-chiu, hua-chiao, hua jiao, hwa jiao, ta-liao ('Great Spice')
Japanese: kinome (fresh leaves), sansho (powdered dried leaves)

Szechwan Duck
Crispy but tender pieces of duck from Szechwan ('four rivers'), served with spring onions, dips, steamed buns or pancakes.

Serves 4

Imp	Metric	US
1 duckling, 3–4lb (1.4–1.8kg)	1	1
1tsp anise-pepper, ground	1tsp	1tsp
¼tsp cinnamon, ground	¼tsp	¼tsp
2tsp five-spice powder	2tsp	2tsp
pinch red colouring powder	pinch	pinch
1tbsp salt	1tbsp	1tbsp

Imp	Metric	US
2tbsp sherry	40ml	2tbsp
1tbsp soy sauce	20ml	2tbsp
2tsp anise-pepper, whole	2tsp	2tsp
2 garlic cloves, bruised	2	2
2tsp ginger, grated	2tsp	2tsp
1 spring onion, chopped	1	1
2 star anise, whole	2	2
2tsp cornflour	2tsp	2tsp
1 egg white	1	1
1tsp flour	1tsp	1tsp

1 Dry duck inside and out.
2 Mix spices from anise-pepper to salt with sherry and soy sauce and coat all parts of the duck. Leave for 2 hours.
3 Place duck in a steamer with whole anise-pepper, garlic, ginger, spring onions and star anise. Steam for 2 hours or until done.
4 Allow to cool for 10 minutes. Wipe off any remnants of marinade and dry with paper towel.
5 Mix cornflour, egg white and flour and rub this over the outside of the bird.
6 Deep fry in a *wok* at 350°F, 180°C for 6 minutes turning frequently.
7 Cleave into 8 or 10 pieces through the bones and serve hot with *hoisin* sauce.

Japanese Steak (colour page 85)
Steak with finesse.   Serves 4

Imp	Metric	US
4 rump steaks, 8oz (225g) trimmed	4×225g	4×8oz
oil		
8oz bean sprouts	225g	8oz
1½tbsp *shoyu* (Japanese soy sauce)	30ml	2tbsp
sansho		

1 Sear the steaks in hot oil and cook to rare. Remove and keep hot.
2 Reduce heat slightly and gently fry the bean sprouts adding the *shoyu* last.
3 If available, warm a Japanese sizzler, cover with a bed of bean sprouts and place the steak on top. With a sharp knife cut the steak into ½in (12mm) slices retaining the shape of the steak.
4 Pour over the *shoyu* sauce from the pan, sprinkle with *sansho* and serve with salad.

Annatto

Bixa orellana
Fam Bixaceae

SPICE DESCRIPTION

Annatto is a red seed which imparts an orange to red colour and a slightly peppery flavour to food. The seeds come from heart-shaped fruit containing many seeds in a deep-red pulp. The pulp is removed and the seeds dried. They are oxblood red, pyramidal, 3–5mm (⅛–³⁄₁₆in) long, angular with slight depressions and a marked cleft. A red skin covers a thin inner white skin, which in turn contains a hard ivory-coloured core. Annatto seeds are available whole. An orange food colouring made from the pericarp is also available as an alkaline solution, which is used in home dairy butter and cheese production. 'Good arnotto is of the colour of fire' (Yeats, *Natural History*, 1870).
Bouquet Slightly peppery with a note of nutmeg.
Flavour Sweetish, peppery and etheric.

H Scale: 2

PREPARATION AND STORAGE

Annatto colour and flavour can be imparted to food either by adding seeds directly to the cooking liquid or by frying them gently in oil for a minute, covering the pan as they will jump, then discarding them and using the coloured oil. For stocks and cooking rice a few seeds may be infused in hot water, stirring until an orange hue is obtained. A useful proportion is one teaspoon of seeds to four tablespoons of fats or oils. Store the seeds in airtight containers. Should annatto seeds be difficult to obtain, substitute two parts paprika and one part turmeric, but this will, of course, affect the flavour of the dish.

USES

Annatto is best known in the West as a food dye for colouring confectionery, smoked fish, butter and cheeses such as Cheshire, Leicester and Edam. However, it is well worthwhile trying to obtain annatto seeds for home use as they give a marvellous natural colouring effect to all sorts of dishes. Thus it is a useful substitute for saffron, although the flavour it gives is only very slightly like that spice. In the Caribbean and Latin America, especially Guatemala and Mexico, it is used extensively to give dishes a bright and exotic appearance. A famous Jamaican dish is salt cod and ackee served in a sauce of onions, capsicums and annatto. The seeds are also particularly associated with Filipino cookery, having been introduced to the islands by the Spaniards during the seventeenth century. Several well-known Filipino dishes using annatto are: *ukoy*, shrimp and sweet potato fritters; *pipian*, a chicken and pork dish with a sauce cooked in oil, flavoured and coloured with the seeds; *kari-kari*, a colourful oxtail and vegetable stew. This unusual spice merits new consideration in our kitchens.

CHEMICAL COMPOSITION
Annatto is an important dye. The colouring principle is the ester bixin, a red resinous carotenoid. It is a permitted foodstuff dye in the EEC (No. E1606). The seeds contain carbohydrate, oil and protein.

ATTRIBUTED PROPERTIES
The name Annatto is applied to both the seeds and the dyestuff. Formerly it was used as a medicine, but now only as a colouring agent for medical preparations such as ointments and plasters. In Africa the fruit pulp is used as a febrifuge and astringent, being considered useful in dysentery and kidney diseases. In India the pulp is utilised as an insect repellent.

PLANT DESCRIPTION
An erect tropical tree or shrub, 2–10m (6–35ft) in height. Authorities disagree about the maximum height, varying between 5 and 10 metres. The leaves are shiny, broad and heart-shaped, sometimes with reddish veins. Attractive pink flowers with clusters of stamens occur in panicles.

The fruit capsule is heart-shaped, two-valved, with opposing clefts. It is reddish-green, drying to brown, and covered with numerous short, red prickly spines which serve as a protection against animals. The capsule contains many small seeds, each about 5mm (1/5in) in length, enclosed in a red pulp which is the main source of the dye.

CULTIVATION
Because of its flowers, the shrub *Bixa orellana* was highly regarded in colonial gardens and much used for hedges. It is commercially grown for the dye product annatto and for its seeds as a spice. For tropical cultivation:
Sow: Seed or cuttings in late summer.
Soil: Loamy or sandy loam.
Aspect: At altitudes below 1,000m (3,000ft).
Cultivation: Compost as required. Prune out deadwood in individual plants or trim hedgerows.
Harvesting: The fruits are collected when ripe, then macerated in water. The dye settles and is collected and dried into cakes. The seeds are washed and ready for use. This is, strictly speaking, a commercial undertaking.

REMARKS
Annatto, *Bixa orellana*, is indigenous to tropical America and the West Indies, but

is now cultivated throughout the tropics. It is most important as the source of the red and orange dyes which are also called annatto. These dyes are used in country weaving and industrial textile manufacture but their most common application is in the dyeing of oil or fat-based materials, such as butter, cheese, polishes and ointments. Edam cheese is a classic example. The Caribbean is the historic centre for annatto dye production, two forms of dye-cake being most common: the Spanish, which is hard and brittle; and the French, which is bright yellow and soft. The latter exudes a noxious smell owing to a curiosity of preparation whereby urine is used to assist fermentation of the pulp. Annatto, being so useful and handy, was seized upon by the South American Indians to create vivid war paint and today it is still used for adornment. The natural colouring agent annatto is perfectly harmless in dyeing, cosmetics and cookery.

OTHER NAMES
Achiote, Anatta, Anatto, Annato, Annotta, Annotto, Aploppas, Arnotta, Arnotto, Orellana, Orlean, Orleana
Dutch: roucou
French: rocou, roucou
German: Annatto
Italian: anotto
Spanish: achiote, achote
Argentine: urucu
Caribbean: bija (Sp.), bijol (Sp.), roucou (Fr. Du.)
Indian: latkhan, sendri
Philippines: achuete

Annatto Chicken and Pork (colour page 51)

This is a version of Filipino *pipian*, golden, spicy and nutritious.   Serves 4–6

Imp	Metric	US
8oz chicken meat, boned	225g	8oz
8oz pork shoulder	225g	8oz
4tbsp peanut or corn oil	80ml	5⅓tbsp
1tsp annatto seeds	1tsp	1tsp
½tsp chilli powder	½tsp	½tsp
1 garlic clove, crushed	1	1
1 onion, minced	1	1

Imp	Metric	US
1tbsp tomato purée	20ml	1⅓tbsp
4oz peanut (groundnut) butter	115g	4oz
½pt chicken stock	285ml	1¼ cups

1 Trim chicken and pork; cut into 1in (25mm) cubes.
2 Heat oil in pan. Add the annatto seeds, which will 'pop' as they fry. (Cover pan at this stage).
3 When the annatto seeds have subsided remove them quickly.
4 The oil is now red and aromatised. Add the meat pieces and fry until all are nicely brown and sealed.
5 Remove the meat pieces, keeping warm.
6 In the same pan add minced onion, tomato purée, chilli powder and crushed garlic, stirring continuously and adding stock gradually.
7 Now stir in the peanut butter.
8 Return the meat to the sauce and simmer for ½–¾ hour.
9 Serve with rice.

Asafoetida

Ferula assafoetida
Fam Umbelliferae

SPICE DESCRIPTION
Asafoetida is the sap from the roots and stem of several species of giant fennel which, when dried, becomes a mass of hard, resinous gum. Greyish-white in colour, it darkens with age to yellow, red and finally dark brown. It is available in tears, blocks, pieces or ground to a powder. The powder, crystalline in appearance, is sometimes mixed with a considerable amount of flour and dyed dark brown.
Bouquet Most pungent and unpleasant, smelling strongly of rotten onions.
Flavour Unbelievably nasty and lingering if one is unwise enough to taste it on its own: like concentrated fetid garlic. However, used in minute quantities it enhances food with its onion-like flavour and its fetid smell disappears in the cooking.   H Scale: 0

PREPARATION AND STORAGE
Use in minute quantities, adding pieces directly to cooking liquid, frying in oil, or steeping in hot water. The flavour can also be imparted by fixing a small piece inside the lid of the pot. It is absolutely vital to keep asafoetida in airtight containers or the nauseous smell will quickly permeate a room. In its area of origin it is sometimes used as a salt substitute.

USES
Although used very occasionally in France, it is used mainly in India, particularly in vegetarian dishes, and there probably to prevent flatulence. Recipes from western India often mention asafoetida. Pickles, lentil and vegetable soups and thin soups prepared with tamarind are enhanced by minute quantities of the spice. A Kashmiri dish of lamb cooked in yoghurt and spices contains a peppercorn-size piece of asafoetida. Some *poppadums* include asafoetida. Fish, both fresh and salt, seems to be particularly suited to the addition of the spice, but it must be stressed that only very little at a time should be used as it can be quite overwhelming. The Romans introduced asafoetida to England and there have been many references to it in the past, although nowadays it is hardly known in English cookery. Oliver Goldsmith wrote 'I am for sauce strong with assafoetida, or fuming with garlic' (*Citizen of the World*, 1762).

CHEMICAL COMPOSITION
Asafoetida is a gum-resin with essential oils, constituents being 25 per cent, 62–69 per cent and 4–6 per cent respectively. Its evil smell is due to contained sulphurous compounds. The asafoetida of commerce is sometimes adulterated besides containing impurities. It also contains ferulic acid, minerals, moisture, mucilage, tannins and vanillin.

ATTRIBUTED PROPERTIES
Because of its vile odour asafoetida has been used since time immemorial for a great variety of purposes. Its main properties that have been exploited are carminative, expectorant and anti-spasmodic. Formerly it was used in hysteria: presumably the shock of its noxious smell calmed the most hysterical patient. Today it is prescribed in pill, tincture and spirit of ammonia forms, chiefly for flatulence and bronchitis. In India it has many uses for diseases of the alimentary canal and the respiratory system, and as an anthelmintic enema. The Romans brought it to Britain and later, in 1398, John of Trevisa remarks, 'Some stynkynge thynges ben put in medycynes, as . . . Brymstoon and Asafetida'. In the American Wild West a mixture of asafoetida, ipecacuanha, cayenne and mustard was recommended as an antidote for alcoholism.

PLANT DESCRIPTION
Giant perennials of the fennel family grow wild in Afghanistan and Iran, to a height of 1½–3m (5–10ft). The stems are finely reeded with soft centres that exude, when cut, the white gum from which asafoetida is formed. The stem leaves are tripartite, toothed and sheathed. The yellow flowers, in umbels, rise from the wide sheathes of the lower leaves. The roots are thick and pulpy and also yield a similar gum-resin to that of the stems. All parts of the plant have the distinctive fetid smell.

CULTIVATION
The plants grow wild in great profusion in West Central Asia, particularly eastern Iran, Afghanistan, Kashmir and northern Pakistan. The most suitable climate is continental with extremes of temperature, and only modest rainfall is required.

REMARKS
The giant fennels, members of the Umbelliferae family, the ferulas, from which asafoetida is obtained, have been used for centuries by the inhabitants of their native regions as a spice-condiment and a vegetable. As a vegetable the unopened heads of the plant, the stalks' central pith and roasted root are favoured.

The obnoxious odour is dispelled by cooking. The plants grow profusely in some areas in dense forest-like systems and the masses of yellow flowers in summer are a feature of the otherwise barren landscape. The name derives from the Persian *aza*, mastic, and Latin *fetida*, stinking. Other species are: *F. foetida*, *F. narthex* which grows to a height of 1½–2½m (5–8ft) and *F. rubricaulis*.

OTHER NAMES

Asafetïda, Assafetida, Assafoetida, Devil's Dung, Devil's Durt, Food-of-the-Gods (Persian), Giant Fennel Gum Asafetida, Laser (Roman), Laserpicium (Roman), Persian Silphium, Stinking Gum
French: assa foetida, férule perisque
German: Asafötida, Stinkender Asant, Teufelsdreck
Italian: assafetida
Spanish: asafétida
Afghan: kama-i-anguza (plant)
Burmese: sheingho
Indian: heeng, hing, hingu
Tamil: perunkaya(m)

Spicy Potatoes (colour page 189)

A spicy potato dish good on its own with rice or *chapatis* or as an accompaniment to a main curry.   Serves 4

Imp	Metric	US
1lb potatoes, peeled and quartered	455g	1lb
1tbsp *ghee* or mustard oil	1tbsp	1tbsp
good pinch asafoetida, ground	good pinch	good pinch
good pinch ajowan seeds	good pinch	good pinch
1tsp turmeric, ground	1tsp	1tsp
good pinch chilli powder	good pinch	good pinch
2 onions, finely chopped	2	2
8oz canned tomatoes, blended	455g	8oz
½tsp salt	½tsp	½tsp
½tsp sugar	½tsp	½tsp
water		

1 Boil potatoes for 5 minutes. Drain.
2 Heat *ghee* in saucepan to frying temperature.

3 Add asafoetida, then ajowan seeds, then turmeric, then chilli powder, stirring constantly. Add onion and fry gently for 3 minutes.
4 Add potatoes and fry for a few minutes, turning frequently.
5 Add tomato blend, salt and top up with water, if necessary, for a good consistency. Stir well.
6 Cover and simmer until potatoes are cooked – about 20 minutes.
7 Serve with rice or *chapatis* or as a side dish to a meat curry.

Badrang

Zanthoxylum limonella
syn *Z. budrunga, Z. rhetsa*
Fam Rutaceae

SPICE DESCRIPTION

Badrang consists of the fruits of a tropical tree of the prickly ash family, like anise-pepper. In the dried form, the tough brown pericarp is rough textured, shaped like a cloven sphere some 6–10mm (¼–⅜in) in diameter. Within is a solid seed, 'involved in a thin and blacke filme' (Gerard). This spice is unlikely to be found whole in the West. The bark is also used as a condiment.
Bouquet When bruised, the shell yields a mild fragrance of orange peel.
Flavour The shell is bitterly citrus, like pith and peel, the seeds more peppery.

H Scale: 4

PREPARATION AND STORAGE

The shells and seeds are very difficult to grind down to a powder at home. A pestle and mortar or a blender will, however, render them into a usable crushed form. Keep airtight.

USES

In India, both shell and seed are used to add zest to main courses and desserts, and are said to enhance fish curries in particular. The fruits, bark and leaves of other species are used similarly throughout the Far East. Like so many minor spices, badrang is often described as a 'pepper substitute', although this seems a peculiarly Western concept, the worldwide importance we attribute to pepper deriving from Europe's long search for, and subsequent pervasive use of, that spice. It might well be said that pepper itself is an international substitute for those local flavourings.

CHEMICAL COMPOSITION

As with many minor spices, the chemistry is incompletely explored. However, it is likely to be similar in many respects to that of anise-pepper (*Z. piperitum*).

ATTRIBUTED PROPERTIES

The bark and fruit are attributed with stomachic properties. Gerard (1597) affirms: 'It helps concoction and bindes the belly'. Mullilam oil, an orange-scented, steam-distilled extract from the fruits, is reported to have a variety of medical applications. The bark of the related *Z. americanum*, prickly ash, is useful in toothache.

PLANT DESCRIPTION

A tropical deciduous tree of the prickly ash family, *Z. limonella*, syn *Z. budrunga* and *Z. rhetsa*, reaches 35m (115ft) in height. Among the many allied species are *Z. bungei* (Chinese pepper) and *Z. aromaticum* (Japanese pepper – also another name for *Z. piperitum*, anise-pepper).

CULTIVATION

Badrang thrives in the Indian *ghats* and the monsoon forests of Assam and Meghalaya (NE India, formerly part of Assam). The related species named *Z. piperitum* and *Z. alatum* are also found in the Orient and India.

REMARKS

Badrang and its related species cover between them a large area of India and the Far East, and are members of a vast motley of minor spices which are important as local condiments but are practically unknown in the West. Occasionally, however, one of these rarities finds its way into a commercial spice mixture or curry powder as an exotic token, much like trifala.

OTHER NAMES

Fagara
Indian: badrang, vadrang

Egg Curry

A quick-to-prepare vegetarian curry.

Serves 6

Imp	Metric	US
1tbsp *ghee*	20ml	1⅓tbsp
½tsp fenugreek, ground	½tsp	½tsp
½tsp salt	½tsp	½tsp
6 eggs, hard boiled	6	6
1 onion, chopped	1	1
½tsp badrang, ground or juice of half a lemon	½tsp	½tsp
½tsp chilli powder	½tsp	½tsp
½tsp coriander, ground	½tsp	½tsp
½tsp turmeric, ground	½tsp	½tsp
2 tomatoes, chopped	2	2
½pt coconut milk, thin	285ml	1¼ cups
1tsp *garam masala* (page 210)	1tsp	1tsp

1 Heat the *ghee*. Mix salt and fenugreek, prick the eggs with a thin skewer and rub them in this mixture, then lightly fry the eggs and reserve.
2 Add the onion and fry until golden. Now add the remaining spices and tomato and fry for a few minutes.
3 Stir in the coconut milk. Cook for 5

minutes then add the *garam masala*, stir well and cook for a further 5 minutes.

4 Halve the eggs, lay them in a warm dish and cover with the sauce. Serve with rice and *chapatis*.

Bay Leaf

Laurus nobilis
Fam Lauraceae

SPICE DESCRIPTION
The leaf of the bay tree is oval, pointed, leathery and smooth, 2.5–8cm (1–3in) long, 1–4cm (½–1½in) wide, shiny, dark green on top and lighter green underneath when fresh. When dried the bay leaf is olive green in colour and matt in texture. Available both whole and ground.
Bouquet Warm, slightly resinous and quite pungent when broken and the aromatic oils are released.
Flavour Slightly bitter and strongly aromatic and is therefore used sparingly.

H Scale: 2

PREPARATION AND STORAGE
Dried leaves should be bought when whole and green as broken brown leaves will certainly have lost their flavour. They may be crushed and distributed in dishes for extra strength. Ground bay leaves must be bought in small quantities and used quickly. The strength of flavour of the whole leaf will be retained for at least two years if stored in airtight containers.

USES
The bay leaf is one of the most valuable flavourings in cookery and is used throughout the world. Perhaps its pride of place is in *bouquets garnis* which are used in European cookery. It is also an important ingredient in marinades, pickles and *courts-bouillons*. Many soups, stews, casseroles and *daubes* are flavoured with bay, as are other dishes of fish, meat, poultry and sauces. It is an ingredient of whole pickling spice. Sweet custards and creams sometimes include bay, making it truly ubiquitous. Bay salt is not salt flavoured with bay leaves as might be supposed but is sea salt, possibly so named as it was originally imported from the Bay of Biscay coast.

CHEMICAL COMPOSITION
Bay leaves give a volatile oil of complex structure containing eucalyptol, eugenol, geraniol and pinene. These are responsible for its bouquet and flavour-imparting qualities which have been known and used, practically and mystically, from antiquity. The berries contain 25 per cent of a fixed oil which includes the ester of lauric acid (dodecanoic acid) and 1 per cent of the aromatic volatile oil.

1. *Tabbouleh (page 126); 2. Falafel (page 77); 3. Hummus bi Tahini (page 173); 4. Dolmades (page 125); 5. Armenian Boats (page 181); 6. Yoghurt with Sumac (page 181)*

ATTRIBUTED PROPERTIES

Bay leaves and berries have, in the past, been used for their astringent, carminative, diaphoretic, digestive, diuretic, emetic, emmenagogic and stomachic properties.

The oil, Bay Oil or Oil of Bays, *Oleum Lauri*, is used for liniments in bruising, rheumatic and skin troubles. Culpeper says 'A bath of the decoction of the leaves and berries, is singular good for women to sit in . . .'. The insecticidal properties derive from the lauric acid content and the leaves were once used to keep away moths.

PLANT DESCRIPTION

An evergreen shrub or tree, wild or cultivated mainly in Mediterranean-type climates. It can grow to 18m (60ft) in warm areas but in the British Isles to 8m (25ft) at the most. The leaves are strong, coriacious and shiny, deep green on the upper side and paler on the underside, ovate-lanceolate in shape with slightly uneven edges, usually 2.5–8cm (1–3in) long and 1–4cm (½–1½in) broad. The flowers are white to yellow, small, in clusters, blooming inconspicuously in April and May. The fruits are small, red-blue single-seeded berries, about 12mm (½in) long, turning black.

CULTIVATION

The bay, a hardy, can be grown as a garden tree or shrub, tubbed or indoors, to provide an all-year-round supply of fresh bay leaves. Young trees bought from garden centres should be planted out in March or April. However, it is possible to grow them from cuttings.

Propagation: Take cuttings of shoots, about 10cm (4in), in August-September and place in peat and sand in a cold frame.

Plant: May–June in tub or bed.

Soil: Any garden soil.

Aspect: Sunny and sheltered.

Pruning: No pruning is necessary for shrubs but trim tubbed trees two or three times in summer and remove suckers.

Harvesting: The leaves can be collected at any time for immediate use. Clean well. To preserve the leaves, collect and lay out between two sheets of paper until dry. Store in airtight containers out of light.

REMARKS

The bay tree, *Laurus nobilis*, is indigenous to Asia Minor, whence it spread to the Mediterranean and then to other countries with similar climates. Some authorities believe the tree was first cultivated in Britain in the sixteenth century but others mention earlier periods. The latter seems more likely in view of its historical associations with Rome. Bay, or laurel, was famed in ancient Greece and Rome. In Greek the word for laurel is *dháfni* from the myth of the nymph, Daphne, who was changed by Gaea into a laurel tree to escape Apollo's advances. Apollo, denied for once, made the tree sacred and thus it became a symbol of honour. Heroes, emperors and poets wore wreaths of laurel leaves.

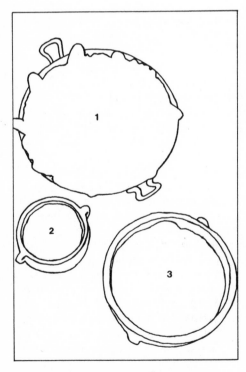

1. Paella (page 162); 2. Pomodoro Sauce (page 56); 3. Osso Buco (page 66)

Extending the idea, it was believed a laurel tree brought safety, especially from the deities responsible for thunder and lightning. It is said the Emperor Tiberius always wore a laurel wreath during thunderstorms. Today, grand-prix winners are bedecked with a laurel wreath. The ideas of honour and glory continue: we have poet laureate (Apollo was the God of poets), *bacca-laureat* (degree of bachelor, from corruption of *bacca-lauri*, the laurel berry) and such expressions as 'rest on, look to, your laurels'. It is said the Delphic priestesses pronounced their oracles with a bay leaf in their mouths. Always remember that it is the bay of *Laurus nobilis* that we use in cookery and not any other. Two of the others are: bay rum, a cosmetic oil from the West Indian *Pimenta acris*; and cherry laurel (*Cerasus* or *Prunus laurocerasus*), the common laurel, which is highly poisonous. Its almond-like flavour and bouquet is nothing else but cyanide. Maybe it is not coincidental that Daphne du Maurier's heroine Rachel succumbed to poisoning by laurel infusions.

OTHER NAMES
Apollo's Bay Leaf, Bay, Bay Laurel, Grecian Laurel, Indian Bay, Laurel, Noble Laurel, Poet's Laurel, Roman Laurel, Royal Laurel, Sweet Bay, Sweet Laurel, True Laurel, Wreath Laurel.
French: feuille de laurier, laurier franc
German: Lorbeerblatt
Italian: foglia di alloro, lauro
Spanish: hoja de laurel
Greek: dháfni

Daube Provençale (colour page 156)

Pieces of beef cooked slowly with wine and herbs. Serve straight from the oven accompanied by puréed potatoes and a green salad.   Serves 6–8

Imp	Metric	US
3½lb topside, cut 2½in square, ¾in thick (65, 20mm)	1½kg	3½lb
8oz green streaky bacon, diced	225g	8oz
3tbsp olive oil	60ml	4tbsp
2 large onions, sliced	2	2
3 carrots, sliced	3	3
2oz pork rind, cut in ½in (12mm) squares	55g	2oz
1 bouquet garni: thyme, bay leaf and parsley with	1	1
2 strips dried orange peel	2	2
3 garlic cloves, bruised	3	3
½pt red wine	285ml	1¼ cups
¼–½pt beef stock	140–285ml	½–1¼ cups
salt		
freshly ground black pepper		
1tbsp freshly chopped parsley	1tbsp	1⅓tbsp

1 Heat the oil in a large pan or the casserole in which the meat is to be cooked.
2 Lightly fry bacon, onions and carrots until slightly soft. Set aside.
3 In the same oil brown the meat, and set aside.
4 Put half the bacon, vegetables and pork rind in the bottom of the casserole, arrange the meat on top and cover with the rest of the bacon, vegetables and pork rind.
5 Add garlic, bouquet garni with orange peel, salt and pepper.
6 Pour on the wine to cover, adding stock if necessary.
7 Bring to simmering point and cover casserole with foil or greaseproof paper before attaching lid.
8 Cook in a slow oven, Gas Mark 2, 300°F, 150°C, for 3–4 hours.
9 Sprinkle with parsley and serve from the casserole.

Calamus

Acorus calamus
Fam Araceae

SPICE DESCRIPTION
The rhizome of a marsh plant, about 2cm (¾in) in diameter, pale grey-brown, wrinkled and scarred. The inner matter is white, porous and woody. Calamus is sold powdered and in peeled, unpeeled or candied pieces.
Bouquet Sweet and aromatic.
Flavour Aromatic, pungent and bitter.
H Scale: 2

PREPARATION AND STORAGE
Calamus deterioriates quickly, so buy the powder in small quantities and store in airtight containers. The root may be ground in a blender.

USES
Candied calamus roots were once popular as a sweetmeat in Britain and the United States, and the leaves were used to flavour

milk for custards, creams and puddings. The immature leaves may be eaten as a salad. Indian and Arab sweet dishes and stewed fruit are sometimes flavoured with the ground root. Some oriental beverages are spiced with calamus, but its main use today is in flavouring gin.

CHEMICAL COMPOSITION
The root yields 1.5–3.5 per cent of a bitter essential oil, containing the aromatic principle, asaryl aldehyde. Calamus also contains choline, the bitter principle acorin, gums, resin and tannin.

ATTRIBUTED PROPERTIES
An aromatic bitter stimulant, carminative and tonic, calamus is given as an appetiser and digestive in tincture or in infusion. It is good in dyspepsia, colic wind and hoarseness. In India it is considered of great medicinal value, being used for ulcers, diarrhoea, bronchial catarrh, haemorrhage and many other afflictions. With saffron and mare's milk it is given to hasten labour.

PLANT DESCRIPTION
A fragant perennial herb, reaching 1.5m (5ft) with long slender leaves with no stalk. Its tiny yellow flowers are borne on a spadix 5–10cm (2–4in) long.

CULTIVATION
The plant is propagated by root cuttings, thriving on river banks or very moist soils. Local Indian varieties can reproduce by pollenisation. Roots are gathered when two to three years old.

REMARKS
Probably native to India, calamus grows wild throughout the northern hemisphere, especially in British and European marshes and river banks, having first been cultivated in Europe by Clusius in the Vienna botanic gardens (c1575), from where it rapidly spread. It was known to classical and Arab doctors and is still used in folk medicine. Today the oil is used in the cosmetic and perfume industry, and in

Biblical times it was a component of anointing oil. The root is one of the botanical substances commonly used to flavour gin; however, the amount of calamus added remains a secret.

Sweet Cane, Sweet Flag, Sweet Grass, Sweet Sedge
French: calamus, roseau, rotin
German: Kalmus
Italian: calamo aromatico
Spanish: cálamo
Indian: bacha, vacha

Fruit Compôte

A sweet fruit compôte with a subtle flavouring reminiscent of cinnamon, ginger and nutmeg.   Serves 4–6

Imp	Metric	US
2 apples, peeled, cored and sliced	2	2
8oz cherries, stalked and stoned	225g	8oz
8oz pineapple, fresh, chunked	225g	8oz
2 peaches, peeled, stoned and quartered	2	2
1 mango, peeled, stoned and sliced	1	1
1pt water	570ml	1¼pt
8oz sugar	225g	8oz
1tsp calamus root, ground	1tsp	1tsp
2tsp lemon juice	10ml	2tsp
cream		

1 Prepare fruit as described above.
2 Heat water with the sugar until dissolved.
3 Add calamus and lemon juice and simmer for 5–10 minutes.
4 Add all fruit except apples and simmer until the fruit is just soft.
5 Transfer to oven dish. Lay apples over the top and sprinkle with a little calamus. Cover and bake in a moderate oven, Gas Mark 3, 325°F, 160°C, until the apples are tender.
6 Serve with cream.

Caper

Capparis spinosa
Fam Capparidaceae

SPICE DESCRIPTION
Capers are the unopened flower buds of the caper bush. Olive green, sometimes mottled pink, they are round and tight when tiny, becoming progressively more 'bud'-shaped. The finest capers should have a small part of the stalk attached. In France they are classified as follows:
1 *Nonpareilles* – finest and smallest, approximately 3mm (⅛in)
2 *Surfines* or *superfines*
3 *Fines*
4 *Mi-fines*
5 *Capucines* or *capottes* – five to six times larger than *nonpareilles*

Capers are usually pickled in salted wine vinegar and bottled. However, where the caper is a commonplace ingredient, it is dry salted and sold loose.
Bouquet Rather sweet and aromatic, but acidic due to the vinegar and the development of capric acid during pickling.
Flavour As the bouquet, with an aftertaste somewhat reminiscent of goat's milk cheese.   H Scale: 2

PREPARATION AND STORAGE
No preparation is needed other than to drain the capers and chop or pound according to the recipe. If kept covered with pickling liquid, capers will keep almost indefinitely.

USES
Capers are used throughout the Mediterranean and especially in Provence where the *nonpareilles* are produced. An important ingredient of cold sauces such as *tartare, ravigote, rémoulade* and *tapénade* to accompany fish and salads, they are also included in *salade niçoise* and *pan bagna*. They are an essential accompaniment to steak tartare. So often associated with fish, they can be added to black butter sauce to serve with skate. The term *grenobloise* refers to fish cooked *à la meunière* with

capers, lemon and anchovies. From Italy come the famous *salsa verde, vitello tonnato* and various pizzas and antipasti. Moving north, we have our own boiled mutton with caper sauce. Other northern European countries, especially Germany and Scandinavia, use capers in both meat and fish cookery. They are included in the manufacture of Liptauer cheese. When making Indian chutneys, capers and Worcestershire sauce can be substituted for tamarind.

CHEMICAL COMPOSITION
Capers contain the bioflavonoid rutin, which was formerly classed as a vitamin P (P from 'paprika' and 'permeability'). With vinegar, capers produce capric acid (decanoic acid) with its characteristic goaty smell.

ATTRIBUTED PROPERTIES
Capers are an appetiser and digestive. Since ancient times, caper poultices have been used to ease swellings and bruises and this led to the belief that rutin (see Chemical Composition) had properties affecting the permeability of the blood capillaries, such as reducing their fragility; clinical evidence is inconclusive.

PLANT DESCRIPTION
A bramble-like shrub 1–2m (3–6ft) in height. In the wild state it grows in stony surroundings in Mediterranean areas. Similar conditions suit the cultivated variety. The trailing stems carry thick, shiny oval leaves, with stipules, which are spiny in the wild variety. Pretty, white pink-veined flowers on long stalks grow from the leaf axils. The flowers are followed by small pear-shaped fruits containing many seeds. 'Capers' are the unopened green flower buds, the tighter and smaller the better. The fruits also are sometimes used, as are stems, leaves and spines.

CULTIVATION
Capers either grow wild or are cultivated in plantations. In northern climes it is possible to grow them in a hot greenhouse from cuttings. To obtain the best capers they must be harvested each day when the buds are the right size.

REMARKS
The caper bush is typically Mediterranean, growing from Spain to Jordan. Caper buds have been used for thousands of years by the peoples of this region. They are mentioned in the Bible and in Greek and Roman literature. *Caper* is the Latin for he-goat and Ovid refers to 'the smell under the arm-pits'. Also Sir John Suckling, who invented the game of cribbage, wrote in 1641 of 'The Capers which will make my Lord of Dorset goe from the Table'. However, do not be put off by this, as the bitter piquancy of capers does enhance some dishes and is traditional in many robust Mediterranean recipes. Common substitutes for capers are the 'bean caper', *Zygophyllum fabago*, and especially nasturtium seeds. Other common species are *C. sodala* (Timbuktu caper), *C. corymbifera* (South African caper), *C. herbacea* (Russian caper), *C. inermis* (spineless caper) and *C. rupestris*.

Capper, Prickly Caper
French: câpre, tapéno (Provençal)
German: Kaper
Italian: càppero
Spanish: alcaparra, tápana, tápara
Greek: káparis
Arabic: azaf

Tartare Sauce

There are many versions of this famous sauce but the one given is easy to make and can be modified with olives, chives and white wine to appeal to all tastes. Serve with fried fish or scampi, fill the halved egg whites with some of the tartare sauce for use as a garnish. Serves 6

Imp	Metric	US
1tsp lemon juice	5ml	1tsp
½tsp French mustard	½tsp	½tsp
2 egg yolks, hard boiled and sieved	2	2
2tsp capers, finely chopped	2tsp	2tsp
2tsp gherkins, finely chopped	2tsp	2tsp
1tsp onion, finely chopped	1tsp	1tsp
2tsp parsley, fresh, finely chopped	2tsp	2tsp
½pt mayonnaise, home-made or a good commercial brand	285ml	1¼ cups
salt		
pepper		

1 Blend lemon juice, French mustard and egg yolks.
2 Add finely chopped capers, gherkins, onion and parsley, mixing well.
3 Blend these into the mayonnaise, adding salt and pepper to taste.

Liptauer Cheese

Originally from Hungary, a colourful, spicy spread for biscuits or dip for *crudités* to serve with drinks. Make several hours in advance to allow flavour to develop, or freeze if desired. Serves 6–8

Imp	Metric	US
5oz butter	140g	5oz
8oz medium fat cream cheese	225g	8oz
½tsp Dijon mustard	½tsp	½tsp

Imp	Metric	US
1tsp sweet paprika	1tsp	1tsp
1tsp salt	1tsp	1tsp
½tsp black pepper, freshly ground	½tsp	½tsp
1tsp caraway seeds	1tsp	1tsp
1tsp chives, very finely chopped	1tsp	1tsp
1tsp capers, finely chopped	1tsp	1tsp
3–4 anchovy fillets – optional, if added reduce salt	3–4	3–4

1 Cream the butter well.
2 Add mustard, paprika, salt and pepper and blend thoroughly.
3 Add remaining ingredients and mix together.
4 Transfer to a half-pint pot and chill.

Caraway

Carum carvi
Fam Umbelliferae

SPICE DESCRIPTION
The ripe fruit divides into two seeds, 3–6mm (⅛–¼in) long, boat-shaped, light to dark brown with five paler ribs. It is available whole.
Bouquet Sweet, warm, aromatic and slightly peppery.
Flavour Like the bouquet but sharper and reminiscent of both aniseed and fennel.
H Scale: 1

PREPARATION AND STORAGE
Caraway is usually used whole but should the ground spice be required, pound immediately before use. Store in airtight containers away from the light.

USES
Caraway seed is possibly the world's most ancient spice, having been in use since the Neolithic age. It was used in Elizabethan times to flavour bread, cakes and fruit, especially apples, and was at the height of its popularity in England during the eighteenth and early nineteenth centuries. However, it is now characteristic of German and Austrian cookery, as well as

figuring largely in eastern European and Scandinavian dishes. In Scandinavia, caraway-flavoured spirits and liqueurs are often used in cooking instead of the spice itself. Caraway seed is sprinkled on to cabbage soups; in the Balkans these are often taken as a cure for hangovers. It is added to salads and vegetable dishes, especially red cabbage, *Sauerkraut*, coleslaw, beetroot and potatoes. Hungarian goulash and other highly seasoned meat stews are enhanced by the spice, which also seems to counteract the fattiness in dishes of pork, duck and goose. Dumplings and sausages often contain the seeds, as do rye breads throughout the world. Numerous smoked and skimmed-milk cheeses from such countries as Austria, Germany, Hungary, Holland and Scandinavia contain whole caraway. It is not only savoury food that is associated with caraway, but also sweet things such as biscuits and cakes, especially English seed cake. Many liqueurs are flavoured with caraway, the best known being *Kümmel*. Caraway is the principal flavouring agent of *akvavit* and is also used to flavour gins and schnapps.

CHEMICAL COMPOSITION

Caraway seeds contain protein, cellulose, minerals, a fixed oil (oleic and linoleic) and 3–8 per cent essential oil which itself contains 50–70 per cent carvone. This oil also contains terpene, limonene and many other organic compounds, including furfural (a constituent of cinnamon), eucalyptol, eugenol and pinene.

ATTRIBUTED PROPERTIES

Caraway water, like dill water, which has a similar amount of carvone, is well known for its carminative effect, particularly for babies. This property of the seeds has been known and used from ancient times until today. In 1579, Langham, the Elizabethan gardening authority, noted 'caraway breaketh winde'. Caraway is also used as a flavouring for children's medicines. It is a good digestive and stomachic. Other properties it is believed to have are: antispasmodic, aphrodisiac, appetitive, emmenagogic, expectorant and galactagogic. A once favoured remedy for earache was a mixture of crushed seeds, breadcrumbs and spirit. There was an old superstition that caraway seeds kept witches away from children. Dioscorides is quoted as recommending pallid girls to take a tonic of caraway oil.

PLANT DESCRIPTION

An annual, sometimes treated as a biennial, herb of the Umbelliferae family, 30–80cm (1–2½ft) in height, growing in temperate regions. The root is thick and tuberous, parsnip-like, pale coloured with several offshoots. The hollow fluted stems, compound-sheathed feathery leaves and very small white, yellow or green flowers in umbels are typical of the Umbelliferae. To distinguish from fennel and dill remember:
'Fennel and dill have yellow blooms
Caraway has green
Fennel is twice as high as dill
Caraway and dill are e'en.'   (Anon)

CULTIVATION

An easily grown plant, free from pests and diseases.
Sow: Either autumn (September) or spring (March) in drills 30cm (12in) apart; thin to 15–20cm (6–8in) when established.
Soil: Any well drained soil.
Aspect: Sunny.

Cultivation: No dressings or fertilisation required. Weed occasionally.

Harvest: Seeds ready from June to August. Either cut stems, dry in sun, then thresh out seeds; or hang stems upside down in dry place and collect seeds on paper.

After the plants have been established they will be self-seeding.

REMARKS

Caraway is one of the oldest known spices. It is mentioned in classical literature and the seeds have been found in excavations of ruins dating from 3000BC. Originating in the region where Asia meets Europe, it is now grown worldwide in suitable conditions. Today caraway is grown commercially all over Europe, especially in Holland, Germany, and Russia, as well as in Turkey, India and North Africa. Holland is considered to produce the best. It also grows wild in these areas and is naturalised in similar climatic conditions in the United States and Canada. In India, a weed known as 'Black Caraway' (*Carum bulbocastanum*) is extensively harvested for its seeds. Some authorities believe the name caraway comes from the Arabic *karawya*, whilst others say it is from Caria in Asia Minor. The carminative properties of caraway seeds are, like dill and fennel, excellent; the seeds are chewed to relieve flatulence and sweeten the breath. Other parts of the plant are used. For instance, the leaves can be cut up and added to salads or used to garnish soups. The roots resemble parsnips in flavour and may be cooked in similar ways. As aniseed attracts dogs, so caraway attracts fowl, and will keep chickens from straying.

OTHER NAMES

Caraway Fruit, Caraway Seed, Carvies (Scot), Wild Cumin

French: carvi, graines de carvi (seeds)
German: Cumich (southern Germany), Kümmel, Kümmelkörner (seeds)
Italian: caro, carvi
Spanish: alcaravea
Arabic: karawya

Coleslaw (colour page 190)

A simple summer coleslaw. Serves 6-8

Imp	Metric	US
2 apples, peeled and diced	2	2
1 medium cabbage, hard white, finely sliced	1	1
1tsp caraway seeds	1tsp	1tsp
4 carrots coarsely grated	4	4
2 stalks celery, finely sliced	2	2
2 medium onions, finely chopped	2	2
salt and pepper		
1tbsp parsley, chopped	1tbsp	1⅓tbsp
¼pt mayonnaise	140ml	9½tbsp
¼pt vinaigrette	140ml	9½tbsp

1 Mix all ingredients together.
2 Keep in refrigerator 1-2 hours. Toss well before serving.

Caraway Bread

'Easy blend' yeast allows a very simple method for making rye bread. This bread improves with keeping for a day or two.

Makes 3 loaves

Imp	Metric	US
12oz rye flour	340g	12oz
12oz wholemeal flour	340g	12oz
1tbsp salt	1tbsp	1tbsp
2oz sugar, dark brown	2oz	2oz
2tbsp caraway seeds	2tbsp	2tbsp
1pkt yeast (easy blend)	1	1
3tbsp oil	60ml	4tbsp
½pt sour cream	285ml	1¼ cups
¾pt water, luke warm	425ml	1¾ cups
wholemeal flour for kneading		

1 Mix all dry ingredients together except for the extra wholemeal flour. Add oil, sour cream and water and knead well.

2 Cover and put in a warm place to prove for about 1 hour.
3 Knock back the dough and prove again, about another hour.
4 Knead the dough, shape into 3 round loaves, brush with milk, place on a greased baking sheet and bake in the oven Gas mark 5, 375°F, 190°C for about 45 minutes.

Cardamom

Elettaria cardamomum
syn *Amomum cardamomum*
Fam Zingiberaceae

SPICE DESCRIPTION

Cardamom comes from the seeds of a ginger-like plant. The small, brown-black sticky seeds are contained in a pod in three double rows with about six seeds in each row. The pods are between 6–20mm (¼–¾in) long, the larger variety, known as 'black', being brown, and the smaller being green. In the Middle East the green variety enjoys the best price. White-bleached pods are also available and expensive. The pods are roughly triangular in cross section and oval or oblate. Their dried surface is rough and furrowed, the large 'blacks' having deep wrinkles. The texture of the pod is that of tough paper. Pods are available whole or split and the seeds are sold loose or ground. It is best to buy the whole pods ground cardamom quickly becoming neutral.

Cheaper substitutes known as '*beda elachi*' are the seeds of *Afromomum aromaticum* (Bengal cardamom), *Amomum xanthoides* and *A. subulatum* (Nepal cardamom). Other varieties that enter into trade are Java cardamom (*A. kepulaga*), Cambodian cardamom (*A. krervanh*) and Chinese cardamom (*Alpinia globosa*).

Bouquet Pungent, warm and aromatic.
Flavour Warm and eucalyptine with camphorous and lemony undertones. Black cardamom is blunter, the eucalyptus and camphor suggestions very pronounced.

H Scale: 2

PREPARATION AND STORAGE

The pods can be used whole or split when cooked in Indian substantial dishes – such as pulses. Otherwise, the seeds can be bruised and fried before adding main ingredients to the pan, or pounded with other spices as required. Keep the pods whole until use. The pod itself is neutral in flavour and not generally used.

USES

Cardamom is used mainly in the Near and Far East. Its commonest Western manifestation is in Dutch 'windmill' biscuits and Scandinavian-style cakes and pastries, and in *akvavit*. It features in curries, is essential in *pilaus* (rice dishes) and gives character to pulse dishes. Cardamom is often included in Indian sweet dishes and drinks. At least partially because of its high price, it is seen as a 'festive' spice. Other uses are: in pickles, especially pickled herring; in punches and mulled wines; occasionally with meat, poultry and shellfish. It flavours custards, and some Russian liqueurs. Cardamom is also chewed habitually (like nuts) where freely available, as in the East Indies, and in the Indian masticory, *betel pan*. It is a flavouring for Arab and Turkish coffee.

43

CHEMICAL COMPOSITION

Cardamom yields about 2–10 per cent of essential oil, which is mainly composed of cineol, limonene and terpineoles. Fixed oil, some resin, starch, sugar, protein, cellulose and mineral elements are also present. The volatility of the essential oil has been demonstrated in the United States. After six weeks of exposure to air whole seeds lose half the oil; ground cardamom loses half in one week and the rest in thirteen weeks. This illustrates the importance of using fresh cardamoms.

ATTRIBUTED PROPERTIES

A stimulant and carminative, cardamom is not used in Western medicine for its own properties, but forms a flavouring and basis for medicinal preparations for indigestion and flatulence using other substances, entering into a synergetic relationship with them. The Arabs attributed aphrodisiac qualities to it (it features regularly in the *Arabian Nights*) and the ancient Indians regarded it as a cure for obesity. It has been used as a digestive since ancient times. A medicinal (perhaps aphrodisiac) cordial can be made by macerating seeds in hot water.

PLANT DESCRIPTION

A perennial bush of the ginger family, with sheathed stems reaching 2–5m (6–16ft) in height. It has a large tuberous rhizome and long, dark green leaves 30–60cm (1–2ft) long, 5–15cm (2–6in) wide. It grows in the tropics, wild and in plantations. Trailing leafy stalks grow from the plant base at ground level. These bear the seed pods. The flowers are green with a white purple-veined tip.

CULTIVATION

Cardamoms are traditionally grown in partially cleared tropical rain forests, leaving some shade. Similarly, in plantation cultivation, forest undergrowth is cleared and trees thinned to give just enough shade and the rhizomes or seeds planted at 3m (10ft) intervals. The plants flower in April–June and the fruits are gathered in October–December, before they ripen, to avoid the capsules splitting during drying. They are dried in the sun or bleached with sulphur fumes.

REMARKS

Cardamom is one of the world's very ancient spices. It is native to the East, originating in the forests of the western *ghats* in southern India, where it grows wild. Today it also grows in Sri Lanka, Guatemala, Indo-China and Tanzania. The ancient Egyptians chewed cardamom seeds as a tooth cleaner; the Greeks and Romans used it as a perfume. It was known in Europe from early times, but in old English and French writings it is often confused with Grains of Paradise. Cardamom is an expensive spice, second only to saffron. As observed under Spice Description, it is often adulterated and there are many inferior substitutes from cardamom-related plants, such as Siam cardamom, Nepal cardamom, winged Java cardamom and bastard cardamom. However, it is only *Elettaria cardamomum* which is the true cardamom. Indian cardamom is known in two main varieties: Malabar cardamom and Mysore cardamom. The Mysore variety contains higher levels of cineol and limonene and hence is more aromatic.

OTHER NAMES

Cardamon, Lesser Cardomom
French: cardamome
German: Kardamom
Italian: cardamomo, cardamone
Spanish: cardamomo
Burmese: phalazee
Chinese: ts'ao-k'ou
Indian: chhoti elachi, e(e)lachie, ela(i)chi, illaichi
Indonesian: kapulaga
Malay: buah pelaga
Sinhalese: enasal
Tamil: elam
Thai: grawahn, kravan

Festive Pilau (colour page 103)

A simple, colourful and aromatic *pilau*. There are many variations on the *pilau* theme, some with uncoloured rice and some with meat. More elaborate *pilaus* are called *birianis*. These have more *ghee* and the meat is double the quantity of rice, and they are usually coloured with saffron or turmeric as is festive *pilau*.   Serves 4–6

Imp	Metric	US
1lb *patna* rice	455g	1lb
5tbsp *ghee*	5tbsp	6⅔tbsp
2 onions, medium, finely chopped	2	2
6 cardamoms, whole	6	6
2in cinnamon, stick, splintered	5cm	2in
4 cloves, whole	4	4
½tsp *garam masala* (see Spice Mixtures)	½tsp	½tsp
2 garlic cloves, chopped	2	2
⅛tsp saffron, powdered	⅛tsp	⅛tsp
or 1tsp turmeric, ground	1tsp	1tsp
or ⅛tsp colouring powder, yellow	⅛tsp	⅛tsp
2pts *yakhni* stock (see Spice Mixtures)	1140ml	5 cups
salt to taste		
2oz sultanas	55g	2oz
1oz almonds, split, flaked, fried	55g	2oz
silver or gold leaf (*vark*)		

1 Wash rice and soak for 1 hour, drain thoroughly.
2 Melt *ghee* in pan.
3 Fry onions and spices until onions are golden.
4 Fry rice for 5 minutes, stirring well.
5 Add *yakhni* stock, sultanas and salt to taste, lightly cover and cook for about 20 minutes over low heat. Do not disturb during this time. The rice should absorb all the stock.
6 Remove from heat, uncover and stand for a few minutes.
7 Optional. Mix in meat pieces from the *yakhni* preparation.
8 Transfer to a brass or silver server and garnish with almonds and *vark*.

Sheek Kebabs (colour page 103)

Mild but aromatic, these *kebabs* can be served as a starter with lemon wedges or as a main course with rice and chutneys. Beef may be substituted for the lamb.   Serves 6

Imp	Metric	US
1lb lamb, minced two or three times	455g	1lb
1 small onion	1	1
1tsp fresh grated ginger	1tsp	1tsp
1tbsp flour, preferably *besan* (chick pea)	1tbsp	1⅓tbsp
2 garlic cloves, crushed	2	2
2tsp lemon juice	2tsp	2tsp
3 cardamom pods	3	3
¼tsp chilli powder	¼tsp	¼tsp
¼tsp ground cloves	¼tsp	¼tsp
½tsp cinnamon	½tsp	½tsp
1tsp ground coriander	1tsp	1tsp
¼tsp grated nutmeg	¼tsp	¼tsp
1tsp salt	1tsp	1tsp

1 Grate the onion and ginger into the meat; add garlic, lemon juice and flour and mix thoroughly.
2 Grind the cardamom seeds and mix well with the remaining ingredients and add to the meat.
3 Knead the mixture and spices for several minutes.
4 Form round skewers in a sausage shape about 150mm × 25mm (6in × 1in) and refrigerate for at least two hours to firm up.
5 Brush with oil and cook under a hot grill, turning carefully until evenly browned.

Carob

Ceratonia siliqua
Fam Leguminosae

SPICE DESCRIPTION
The carob is a flattened pod up to 13–30cm (5–12in) long, about 25mm (1in) broad, and 6mm (¼in) thick, shiny and dark brown to black in colour, with very fine wrinkles; it is curved or sometimes twisted, with a leathery appearance. The row of seed compartments is visible along the depressed centre of the pod. The seeds are ovoid, red brown, very hard and identical in size, 10mm (⅜in) long. They are removed before the pods are ground to make carob flour or powder. Pods and powder are available at health food stores.

Bouquet The pods are sweet but rather fetid when broken. The powder has a warm chocolate-like aroma.

Flavour The pods and powder are sweet with a mild chocolate flavour.   H Scale: 0

PREPARATION AND STORAGE
Although it is quicker to use commercially made carob powder, good results can be obtained by the following method, which is much cheaper. For 28g (1oz) powder, allow one pod. Break open the pods and remove the seeds. Reduce the pods to smaller pieces and grind to a coarse powder in a liquidiser or coffee grinder. Gently roast the powder until it is perfectly dry and then grind again. After sifting, the resulting powder will be as fine as the commercial product.

USES
Carob can be used as a substitute for chocolate and cocoa, taking their place in beverages, baking, desserts, ice-creams and confectionery. As carob is sweet in itself, correspondingly less sugar need be used in carob dishes. It is particularly useful where chocolate has been proved to produce allergic reactions. Carob has an affinity with honey, vanilla and cinnamon. Some Middle Eastern *shabats* contain carob.

CHEMICAL COMPOSITION
Carob powder is made from the pods which have had the seeds removed. Carob gum is made from the endosperm of the seeds. Carob powder contains nearly 8 per cent protein, 2 per cent fat, 73 per cent carbohydrates including 38 per cent sucrose (total sugar 47 per cent) and 6 per cent starch, and minerals (¼ per cent calcium, 1 per cent magnesium, ¼ per cent potassium and traces of eleven others). The

pigment carotene is present with vitamins A, B_1, B_2 and B_5 in appreciable amounts plus pectin and lignin. The calorific value is 180 per 100g or 51 per ounce, according to one source, and nearly double that according to another analysis. Carob gum contains protein 5 per cent, cellulose 4 per cent, pentosans 3 per cent, mannan 58 per cent, galactan 29 per cent and an enzyme ceratoniase.

ATTRIBUTED PROPERTIES
Carob benefits the digestive organs and arrests vomiting in infants. Its pectin and lignin content is held to be useful for diarrhoea. It has no other specific medical properties, but is a well balanced nutritive and a healthy substitute for chocolate and sugar. Carob gum is used as a substitute for gum tragacanth.

PLANT DESCRIPTION
A small tree up to 10m (35ft) in height or sometimes a smaller shrub. The leaves, 30cm (12in) long, are compound, with tough shiny leaflets, dark green on the upper surface, paler underneath. The flowers are tiny, dioecious, on racemes, without petals, greenish with five yellow stamens. Like the pods they have an unpleasant odour, usually at night.

CULTIVATION
Not normally cultivated but can be propagated by seed. A Mediterranean-type climate is essential.

REMARKS
The carob grows around the Mediterranean, in the Middle East and India. It has been known and used since antiquity, especially during scarcity: it is the 'locust' food of John the Baptist. The seeds, with a fairly constant mass of 0.21g, provided the Arabs with a small-scale weight, known as a *carat* – the jewellers' term of today. Carob gum (the separated endosperms of the seeds) is used as a thickening agent in the food industry and as a size for yarns, fabrics and paper. The pods are a good animal feed, particularly

for equines, and are so used especially in Spain and Portugal. Alcohol is produced from the pods and the wood is valued for marquetry. Carob should not be confused with caroba (*Jacaranda procera*), honey locust (*Gleditsia triacanthos*) or the locust tree (*Robinia pseudacacia*).

OTHER NAMES
Algar(r)oba (Bean), Carouba, Caroube, Honey Locust, John's Bread, Karoub, Locust Bean or Seed, St John's Bread, Sugar Pod, Swine's Bread (St Luke 15. 16: 'And he would fain have filled his belly with the husks that the swine did eat . . .')
French: caroube
German: Johannisbrot
Italian: carruba
Spanish: algarroba
Arabic: bharout, kharub
Indian: kharnub

Carob Cake

A dark chocolate-coloured cake with a characteristic flavour.

Makes a 7in (18cm) cake

Imp	Metric	US
5oz butter	140g	5oz
4oz sugar	115g	4oz
2tbsp carob powder	2tbsp	2⅔tbsp
3tbsp water, boiling	60ml	4tbsp
3 eggs	3	3
½tsp vanilla essence	2½ml	½tsp
8oz flour, self raising, sieved	225g	8oz

1 Cream butter and sugar until light and white.
2 In a separate basin sieve the carob powder, and add boiling water, stir well and beat into the creamed mixture.
3 Mix the eggs together with the vanilla and beat them into the creamed mixture little by little.
4 Beat a little flour into the mixture and then fold in the rest.
5 Turn into a greased 7in (18cm) cake tin and bake in the oven 50 minutes at Gas Mark 4, 350°F, 180°C.

Cassia

Cinnamomum cassia
Fam Lauraceae

SPICE DESCRIPTION
Cassia is an aromatic bark, similar in its nature to cinnamon, but differing in strength and quality. Cassia bark is somewhat thicker and coarser, and the corky outer bark is often left on. In the United Kingdom, cassia is usually sold in pieces or chips up to 75mm (3in) long and 6mm (¼in) thick. The outer surface is rough and greyish-brown, the inner smoother and dark reddish-brown. Cassia is less costly than cinnamon. Other varieties come in quill form like cinnamon, but are coarser and thicker. Straightness and uniformity in each piece is a sign of quality. Cassia is also available ground to a yellow-brown powder, usually being blended. Cassia buds, sometimes available, are the dried unripe fruits, about 14mm (⁹⁄₁₆in) long, and half as wide. They resemble cloves. The brown pericarp is visible at the opening of the ashen-coloured calyx.

Bouquet The buds have a slight aroma. Chinese cassia is slightly aromatic, the other varieties more so. The aroma is sweet-spicy like cinnamon, but more pungent.
Flavour The bark and the buds have similar flavours – warm, sweet, aromatic and pungent. The Saigon variety is

believed the best. The flavour is stronger but cruder than that of cinnamon.

H Scale: 3

PREPARATION AND STORAGE

The pieces are hard and tough, so they are very difficult to grind. They can be used whole in stews and casseroles. The bark will flatten during cooking. The buds are also used whole. If required in powdered form, it is best to buy it ready ground. Store in airtight containers.

USES

Where cinnamon and cassia are differentiated, cinnamon is. used for sweet dishes, or ones requiring a subtle flavour, and cassia for strong, spicy main dishes. However, the two spices are treated similarly in many countries, and thus we find cassia being used in sweets, pies, buns, cakes, biscuits and breads. In Germany and South European countries, cassia is preferred to cinnamon to flavour chocolate, and in the United States the more robust cassia is generally preferred. Another popular use for cassia is in stewed fruits, especially apples. It is also a constituent of mixed spices, featuring in pudding spice, pastry spice and mincemeat spice. Pickling spice contains the cracked quills. More appropriate uses for this piquant spice are in curries, *pilaus* and spicy meat dishes. The whole buds are also good as a flavour in these preparations. Dried cassia leaves are the Indian herb *tejpat*, sometimes erroneously called 'bay leaves'. Cassia is an ingredient of Chinese Five Spices.

CHEMICAL COMPOSITION

The bark contains 1–2 per cent of a volatile oil. This contains 80–95 per cent cinnamic aldehyde – a yellow, pungent sweet liquid with a strong cinnamon odour. This is the active ingredient, also found in cinnamon. Also present in the oil are cinnamyl acetate and small amounts of seven other chemicals. The bark also contains a fixed oil, resin, starch, minerals, proteins, cellulose, tannic acid and other substances. The buds yield up to 3 per cent of the volatile oil, much fixed oil and substances similar to those in the bark.

ATTRIBUTED PROPERTIES

The properties of cassia and cassia oil are similar to those of cinnamon. Cassia is a tonic, carminative and stimulant. It is used in diarrhoea, nausea and flatulence, and supposedly decreases lactation. It is the basis for some inhalant preparations. It has been found to be inhibitory to certain organisms. Over-used, it can be a strong internal irritant. Oil of cassia is identical with oil of cinnamon in the US Pharmacopoeia.

PLANT DESCRIPTION

Small, evergreen laurel-like tree, with tough elliptical leaves up to about 18cm (7in) in length, and bunches of small yellow flowers hanging from long stalks. Shoots, 3m (10ft), grow from the base of the trunk. The bark is ashen and cracked. All cassia species are largely similar.

CULTIVATION

Cassia requires a hot, wet tropical climate but will grow in indifferent soil. It is grown from seed and cultivation is easier than that of cinnamon. Care is taken in transplanting seedlings as the roots are fragile. The tree stems are cut down when the bark is mature, the wood being cut into portable lengths. The bark is removed by careful incisions and scraped or not as desired. The short lengths of bark dry and curve, some varieties contracting into quills.

REMARKS

Cassia is native to Burma and grown in China, Indo-China, the East and West Indies and Central America. Cassia was known to the Chinese in the third millennium BC and in Egypt in the second. It is mentioned in the Psalms. The buds were known in the West in the Middle Ages. Cinnamon itself was discovered later, in Sri Lanka, by the Renaissance Dutch. Because cassia is so hard, the powdered form is produced commercially by a series of grinding and sieving processes. The powder is usually a blend, with some adulterant included. Some countries, especially the United States, do not distinguish between cinnamon and cassia, whether as quills or powder, in their pharmacopoeias. But in the United Kingdom they must be distinguished by law. This seems reasonable enough, for they are quite different. Cassia buds are used in the production of chocolate and liqueurs, occasionally in gin.

There are many varieties of cassia, the most important being:

Chinese cassia (*Cinnamomum cassia*) or cassia. From Burma and South China. Also source of cassia buds. Quills or rolled.

Indian cassia (*C. tamala*). Native of India. The leaves (*tejpat*) are used as a herb.

Indonesian cassia (*C. burmanni*) or Padang cassia or Batavia cassia. Smoother bark in double quills. Also much used in the East Indies and exported to the United States.

Saigon cassia (*C. loureirii*). Native to Indo-China and formerly exported to the United States. Also grown in Japan and Korea. Single and double quills, roughish surface.

Oliver's Bark (*C. oliveri*). Australian substitute for cassia and cinnamon.

Mossoia Bark (*C. mossoia*). Papua New Guinea. Inferior substitute for cassia and cinnamon.

It would be unwise to confuse cassia (*Cinnamomum*) with *Cassia fistula*, a leguminous plant grown in Egypt and the Indies, East and West, which is a strong purgative used like senna.

OTHER NAMES
Bastard Cinnamon, Canel, Canton Cassia, Casia Bark, Cassia Lignea, Chinese Cinnamon, Tramboon Cassia
French: canéfice, casse
German: Kaneel, Kassia, Kassiarinde
Italian: cassia
Spanish: casia
Indian: dal(-)chini, dhall cheene (cinnamon), nagkesar, nagkeser (buds), tejpat(tar) (leaves)

Chinese Drumsticks

Chicken marinaded in aromatic spices and then grilled. Ideal for barbecues and picnics. Serves 4–6

Imp	Metric	US
12 chicken legs	12	12
6tbsp soy sauce	120ml	8tbsp
2tbsp oil	40ml	2⅔tbsp
2 garlic cloves, crushed	2	2
1tsp ginger, grated	1tsp	1tsp
1tsp 5 spice powder	1tsp	1tsp
1tsp cassia, ground	1tsp	1tsp

1 Lay chicken legs in a dish.
2 Mix remaining ingredients together and pour over chicken. Leave for at least two hours or refrigerate overnight.
3 Grill chicken until cooked and brown, turning and basting frequently.

Cayenne

Capsicum frutescens
Fam Solanaceae

SPICE DESCRIPTION
Cayenne pepper is a finely ground powder prepared from the seeds and pods of various types of chilli. The cayenne variety is commonly called 'Bird Chilli', and the botanical name variously given as *C. minimum* or *C. baccatum*. As most powders are blends, the names of the varieties used are not very important. The capsicums used are the small-fruited varieties: thinnish tapered seed pods up to 12cm (5in) long and 2.5cm (1in) in diameter. Cayenne is made from the ripened fruit, varying from red to yellow. The powder is red or red-brown in colour. Some cayennes include the ground seeds and are hotter than those which exclude them. Cayenne pepper is well known and easily available in the West. It should not be confused with the vine peppers which yield common black pepper. Chilli derivatives are summarised under Chilli – Remarks.
Bouquet Dusty but slightly aromatic.
Flavour Hot, pungent and biting, although not as powerful as the hotter chillies. H Scale: 5–8

PREPARATION AND STORAGE

Cayenne should not be used to the same degree as paprika, which it resembles, for it is much stronger. When used as a condiment it should be sprinkled sparingly (it tends to clog the small holes of the pepper pot). It should be kept in a dark container as it is affected by sunlight, and bought in small quantities as it deteriorates rapidly, losing its pungency.

USES

Cayenne pepper can be used as a spice in cooking; or as a condiment at table, generally with seafoods, such as oysters, sardines, smoked salmon and trout, scallops, fried mussels, crab, lobster and crayfish. It may be sprinkled over soups and hors d'oeuvres. It can be eaten with eggs cooked in any way, and egg dishes such as omelettes and soufflés. It is good with kedgeree and meat roasted, grilled, fried or stewed. It can be sprinkled on bacon prior to frying and used in the dusting flour for fried chicken, fish and vegetables. Potted shrimps always contain cayenne and it is often included in savouries and devilled dishes. It adds piquancy to stews, casseroles and sauces, especially cheese, barbecue and shellfish sauces. It can be used in the making of cheese straws and biscuits, marinades, pickles, ketchups, chutneys and smoked foods. It is an ingredient of Worcestershire sauce. 'Hideous crimes, which, like cayenne in cookery, do give a pungency and flavour to the dull detail of history' (W. Irving, 1809).

CHEMICAL COMPOSITION

Deriving from varieties of chilli, cayenne has a similar chemical structure to the other capsicums. It has a high vitamin C content, and also contains vitamins A, B and E. The pungency is due to the active ingredient, capsaicin, and the red pigment is capsanthin. Also present are other pigments, proteins, carbohydrates, fibre, moisture and a fixed oil. See also under Chilli.

ATTRIBUTED PROPERTIES

Cayenne pepper is not used medicinally, although chilli peppers, from which it is made, are. Chilli is a digestive aid, and intestinal and gastric tonic. It normalises dilated blood vessels, and is used externally in rheumatism and neuralgia as a counter-irritant. It was once used in gout and scarlet fever. In large doses it becomes an irritant poison.
See also under Chilli.

PLANT DESCRIPTION

The capsicums are a vast collection of highly crossbred varieties of perennial and annual shrubs of the potato and tomato family. Cayenne pepper comes from the fruits of small berried species of *C. frutescens*, the perennial types. Charac-

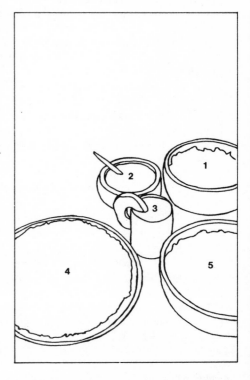

1. Chile con Carne (page 81); 2. Papaya Vinaigrette (page 145); 3. Piña Colada Cocktail (page 74); 4. Annatto Chicken and Pork (page 28); 5. Groundnut Chop (page 59)

teristic features of these species are densely branching stems, sometimes purple-tinged, alternate leaves, dark green above, lighter on the underside, and white flowers borne singly, or in pairs or threes, in axils. The plant averages 60cm (2ft) in height, some African varieties being smaller. The pod-like berries appear in countless different sizes, shapes and colours, but those used for cayenne are generally small, slender, and red to yellow when ripe.
See also under Chilli.

CULTIVATION

Chilli is propagated from seed in nurseries. The plants are transplanted outside some six to eight weeks later. They thrive in hot temperatures. Peppers for cayenne are allowed to ripen, green chilli being picked three months after planting. Although *C.*

frutescens can live up to three years, it is grown as an annual because its yield is poor after the first year.
See also under Paprika.

REMARKS

Cayenne pepper takes its name from its supposed centre of origin – the Cayenne region of French Guiana, Cayenne deriving from a Tupi Indian name. It is now grown largely in Africa, Mexico and the United States, in fact most tropical and sub-tropical regions. Chillies originated in South America, where they have been under cultivation since prehistoric times. The seed's long viability facilitated the rapid spread of the plant throughout the tropics and sub-tropics by the Spanish and Portuguese, the spice becoming as popular there as vine pepper. Chilli was long known as 'Indian' pepper – meaning 'of the New World' rather than 'of India'. Despite its specific name, and the supposed use of special chillies for it, there is little to distinguish cayenne from ordinary pure chilli powder, except that commercial 'chilli powder' usually contains other spices such as garlic or cumin, and is rougher in texture. Home-made chilli powder (see Chilli), finely powdered, will equal or surpass most commercial cayenne. Nepal pepper is a brown or yellow cayenne-type powder, produced in the Himalayas. It is said to be milder and, some say, better than ordinary cayenne.

OTHER NAMES

Bird's Beak, Chilliepin, Guinea Pepper, Mad Pepper (see also under Chilli)
French: piment enragé, poivre de Cayenne, poivre rouge
German: Cayennepfeffer
Italian: pepe di Caienna
Spanish: guindilla, pimentón picante, pimienta de cayena
Japanese: togarashi

1. Lions' Heads (page 105); 2. Marbled Eggs (page 179); 3. Prawn Sesame Fingers (page 174); 4. Chicken in Rice Paper (page 177)

Seafood Cocktail (colour page 155)

An appetising but simple starter. The piquancy can be increased with extra cayenne pepper.   Serves 6

Imp	Metric	US
½pt mayonnaise, home-made or a good commercial brand	285ml	1¼ cups
3tbsp tomato purée	3tbsp	4tbsp
2tbsp lemon juice	2tbsp	2⅔tbsp
1tbsp brandy (optional)	1tbsp	1⅓tbsp
½–1tsp cayenne pepper	½–1tsp	½–1tsp
salt to taste		
12oz shelled prawns and/or crab claws	340g	12oz

1 Mix the mayonnaise with the tomato purée.
2 Add lemon juice, brandy, cayenne and salt to taste.
3 Fold in the fish and serve in individual bowls on a bed of shredded lettuce. Alternatively, the fish and sauce may be spooned into halved avocado pears.

Cheese Straws

A favourite snack to have with drinks.

Makes about 50 straws

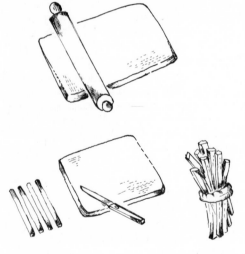

Imp	Metric	US
4oz plain flour	115g	4oz
1 pinch salt	1	1
¼tsp cayenne pepper	¼tsp	¼tsp
2oz butter or margarine	55g	2oz
2½oz mature cheddar cheese, grated	70g	2½oz
½oz parmesan cheese	15g	½oz
½–1tbsp water	10–20ml	½–1⅓ tbsp
1 egg yolk	1	1

1 Sift flour, salt and cayenne.
2 Rub the butter into the flour until the mixture resembles fine breadcrumbs.
3 Mix in the grated cheese and bind together with the egg yolk and sufficient water to make a firm dough.
4 Roll out thinly and cut into strips about 10cm (4in) long and 1cm (⅜in) wide. Also cut out a few rings.
5 Place on a greased baking tray and cook for about 8–10 minutes on the top shelf of a fairly hot oven, Gas Mark 6, 400°F, 200°C.
6 Cool and make into neat bundles with the rings.

Celery Seed

Apium graveolens dulce
Fam Umbelliferae

SPICE DESCRIPTION
This is properly the seed of a wild celery plant, but now of the cultivated garden variety, *A.g. dulce*. The seeds are commonly under 1mm (1/25in) long. They are oval, and green to brown with light ridges running along them. They grow in pairs, in sets of fused carpels. Dried celery seed is available whole or ground, or in the mixture 'celery salt'.
Bouquet Pungent and aromatic, reminiscent of the cooked stalks.
Flavour Warm and bitter, pungent and lingering; like a very pronounced version of the fresh stalks. H Scale: 2–3

PREPARATION AND STORAGE
It is preferable to buy the whole seeds, which can be added to dishes without further preparation, but are otherwise easy to crush in a pestle and mortar. Store in airtight containers.

USES
Celery seed is an occidental spice and can be used in all dishes which demand celery, either as a substitute or to accentuate the flavour of the vegetable. It is used in soups and sauces, pickles and chutneys, and to

put bite into grilled meats and casseroles. It is commonly available ground with salt or pepper as the condiments 'celery salt' and 'celery pepper' and is an ingredient of barbecue spice. Having a particular affinity with tomatoes, celery seed can be included in tomato-based sauces for pasta and rice dishes. It is frequently sprinkled on tomato juice before drinking, and adds zest to a 'Bloody Mary'. It is sometimes an ingredient of processed cheeses and used to flavour cheese pastries and biscuits. It also flavours breads, rolls and cocktail savouries, as well as fish, fish marinades, vegetable juices, eggs, salads and salad dressings. It is particularly good sprinkled into coleslaw, adding bite and contrast of texture.

CHEMICAL COMPOSITION

Celery seed yields 2–3 per cent of essential oil, mainly limonene and selinene, and sedanolide and sedanic acid anhydride, which are the main contributors to the aroma. There is about 16 per cent fixed oil. Some minerals and fatty acids are also present, plus protein, cellulose and resin.

ATTRIBUTED PROPERTIES

The seed has tonic properties. It is also diuretic, carminative and stimulant. It is good for nervous disorders and rheumatism, and enjoys aphrodisiac qualities. It has been used as an emmenagogue, but its sedative properties are dubious.

PLANT DESCRIPTION

A wild Mediterranean plant of the parsley family, unlike garden celery. It thrives in marshy places and has a vile smell. The cultivated varieties are biennial and grow to 0.5m (18in) with umbelliform white flower clusters and jagged leaves. The familiar flowering leaf stalks are bunched,

grooved and curved around each other. Cultivated varieties are blanched or self-blanching. These have been developed over the ages from the wild form.

CULTIVATION

Celery is a hardy biennial. It is best grown in rich sandy loam and needs a lot of moisture, its forebears being marsh plants. For its stalks, it is grown as an annual in trenches so that they can be blanched by earthing up as the plant grows. For the seeds, allow the plants to continue into the second year and harvest them in autumn. As with other Umbelliferae – dill, fennel, caraway – dry the umbels and thresh out the seeds.

REMARKS

Native to southern Europe, celery is now grown throughout Europe, and in the Near East and the United States. Its wild form (*A.g.* var *sylvestris*) was known to the Ancients and features in ancient Chinese medical writings. The Romans used the leaves as wreaths, the plant being symbolic of death probably because of its malodour and toxicity. The stalks of this wild form, also called 'smallage', are poisonous when raw and very bitter. Modern white-stalked celery was developed in Italy around the beginning of the eighteenth century. The bulbous root of the variety *A.g rapaceum*, celeriac, is also edible and rich in many minerals and vitamins.

OTHER NAMES

Smallage
French: céleri
German: Sellerie
Italian: apio, sedano
Spanish: apio
Indian: ajmoda
Indonesian: sel(e)dri
Japanese: cereri
Malay: daun seladri (leaves)
Thai: pak chi farang

Bloody Mary Cocktail
(colour page 155)

A new recipe for the world-famous cocktail.   Serves 1

Imp	Metric	US
1½fl. oz vodka	40ml	1½fl oz
1fl. oz dry sherry	30ml	1fl oz
3fl. oz tomato juice	85ml	3fl oz
¼tsp Tabasco sauce	1ml	¼tsp
1tsp Worcestershire sauce	5ml	1tsp
½fl. oz lemon juice (½ lemon)	15ml	½fl oz
pinch celery salt	pinch	pinch
salt and pepper		
slice of lemon and cucumber		

1 Mix all ingredients except slice of lemon and cucumber. Add ice.
2 Pour into Old-Fashioned glass. Decorate with a slice of lemon and cucumber.

Pomodoro (Tomato) Sauce
(colour page 34)

The traditional Italian tomato sauce to go with *pastas* such as *spaghetti*, *macaroni*, shells, *ravioli* etc. It is easy to make and this particular recipe contains no meat.

Serves 4-6

Imp	Metric	US
3tbsp olive oil	60ml	4tbsp
1 onion, medium, finely chopped	1	1
2 garlic cloves, finely chopped	2	2
1 carrot, very finely chopped	1	1
1 celery stick, very finely chopped	1	1
1tsp celery seeds	1tsp	1tsp
2×15oz tomatoes, canned, roughly chopped, with liquid	2×425g	2×15oz
1tsp basil leaves, dried, crushed	1tsp	1tsp
or 1tbsp basil leaves, fresh	1tbsp	1⅓tbsp
1tbsp tomato purée	1tbsp	1⅓tbsp
1 bay leaf	1	1
1tsp sugar	1tsp	1tsp
½tsp salt	½tsp	½tsp
pepper		

1 Heat oil, add onions and garlic, cooking gently until soft.

2 Add rest of the ingredients, bring to the boil and simmer gently, uncovered, for 1 hour.
3 Remove bay leaf and serve or sieve first if a smoother sauce is preferred.

Chilli

Capsicum frutescens spp
Fam Solanaceae

SPICE DESCRIPTION
Chilli is the common name given to a variety of species of capsicum, the number and range of which is astonishing and defies any exhaustive description. Common characteristics of the pod-like berries are a thin, shiny outer skin, covering a pithy layer of flesh, the fruit being hollow, often with a central core stuffed with small, white disc-shaped seeds. The fruits generally contain between two and four long interior ridges, often dividing the berry into chambers. Chillies vary enormously in size, shape and colour – see Chilli Guide – the distinctions between the various types often becoming blurred. They are usually associated with hotness and pungency, although some relatively mild varieties exist. Perhaps best known in the West are the hot slender varieties 5–10cm (2–4in) long. Chillies are available whole – either fresh or dried. Fresh chillies are green until they ripen, when they turn red, yellow, brown, purple or black. They should be firm. Dried, they can be dark red, brown or black. Ground and crushed chilli is also available, as is chilli powder and pickled chilli.
Bouquet Hot, acrid, pungent. Can cause sneezing and weeping.
Flavour Sharp and fiery, with a characteristic capsicum undertone. The seeds are generally the hottest part. The strength varies from fairly mild to nuclear fission.   H Scale: 7–10
'"Try a chili with it . . ."
"A chili", said Rebecca, gasping; "oh yes!" She thought a chili was something cool, as its name imported.' (*Vanity Fair*).

Chillies can literally burn. While it is not necessary to wear gloves to handle the fresh chillies commonly sold in the West, it is advisable to be circumspect in tasting the raw article. For mouth burns, take cold milk, yoghurt, ice cream or bread and butter. Chillies should be used sparingly. It is best to discard the seeds. Wash hands after touching and do not touch eyes or other sensitive areas. Dried chillies can be whole or ground, or pre-soaked and ground to a paste in a pestle and mortar. To make chilli powder: roast the dried pods till dark, grind and sieve. Other spices such as garlic, cumin, oregano or (in Mexico) chocolate can be added to the powder. Chilli extract can be made by macerating the fresh or dried fruits in alcohol – sherry is excellent – obtaining a liquid handy for flavouring soups. Should a dish be overseasoned with chilli, the addition of a little sugar may alleviate the hotness. Always store in airtight containers away from sunlight.

USES

Whether fresh or dried, chilli is primarily associated with Asian and Mexican cookery, *chile con carne* perhaps being the best known example of the latter. Chilli's hot pungency features in other Mexican dishes such as *tamale, tacos, guacamole* and turkey *mole*. It is widely used in South America, the Caribbean and West Africa, where many of the regional recipes require a massive measure of the hotter chillies. It is essential in Indian and South East Asian cookery where the fieriness of the food depends mainly on the quantity of chilli included. Many curry pastes and powders are based on chilli. In Indonesia, *sambal* implies something fried with numerous chillies; these are either condiments and similar accompaniments or the main dishes themselves. In China too, chilli is a popular seasoning and particularly important in the Szechwan region. It is an ingredient of *hoisin* sauce. A favourite flavouring in Tunisia, chilli provides the base of the searingly hot *harissa* sauce, served with *couscous* and many other meat dishes. It is not such an important spice in European cookery but appears in recipes from Spain and Portugal, and in French *rouille* adds a finishing touch to *bouillabaisse* and fish soups. Chilli is generally used to flavour sauces, pickles, chutneys and ketchups – Tabasco sauce being the most famous. Dried chillies are an ingredient of pickling spice.

CHEMICAL COMPOSITION

Raw (and dried) chilli contains up to 2.3 (9.1) per cent fixed oil, 3.7 (12.9) per cent protein, 9 (26.2) per cent fibre, 9 (33.6) per cent sugar and starch, 0.1 (1.0) per cent pungent principle, resin, colouring matter, minerals, vitamins and 74 (13) per cent moisture. The fixed oil contains oleic, palmitic and stearic acids. The pungent principle is capsaicin, a decylenic acid derivative of vanillylamine. It is highest in hot chillies, reducing to nil in mild or sweet capsicums. The main colouring substance is the carotenoid pigment capsanthin; other contained pigments are capsorubin, carotene, cryptoxanthin, lutein and zeaxanthin. *Capsicum annuum* is a rich source of vitamin C and *C. frutescens* is high in vitamin A, the dried varieties having proportionately more of A and less of C. Other vitamins present are B (thiamine), B_2 (riboflavin), B_5 (niacin) and possibly E. Dried chilli is rich in potassium and also has calcium, phosphorus, iron and sodium. The calorific value of dried chilli pods is 321/100g, and 93/100g for fresh pods including the seeds. Chillies yield 11–16 per cent oleoresin, with the capsaicin content varying between 0.1 and 1.0 per cent.

ATTRIBUTED PROPERTIES

Chilli is healthful in small amounts, being a high vitamin digestive aid. Large doses can cause stomach troubles and internal burns. Medically it is used as a carminative in atonic dyspepsia, and is an external counter-irritant in rheumatism and nervous pains, also a local stimulant and rubefacient. However, excessive use can cause skin burns and blisters. Capsicum oleoresin, used medicinally, contains some 0.8 per cent capsaicin and is highly pungent and irritant. An antiseptic sticking-plaster coating is produced from capsicum and belladonna. Chilli was once used against gout and scarlet fever.

PLANT DESCRIPTION

A large number of related shrub-like perennials of the potato family, now bred largely as annuals. Average height is 60cm (2ft), although the African varieties are smaller. Branching stems bear alternate leaves and flowers borne in axils, in ones, twos or threes. The fruits are pod-like berries, varying in size and in shape from spherical to conical to square.

CULTIVATION

Chillies are grown from seed in nurseries, and the seedlings transplanted outside. Green capsicums are picked three months after planting. The period of harvest extends over three months. Chillies may be dried artificially or in the sun. They are cultivated as annuals because the yield reduces sharply after the first year.

REMARKS

Native to South America, chillies are now grown extensively throughout the tropics and sub-tropics, and even in some tem-perate regions. Main areas of production are Mexico, India (the world's largest producer), the United States, the West Indies and East and West Africa. The capsicums are ancient vegetables, found in prehistoric Peruvian remains. They have been widely in cultivation for so long that their botany is a mystery, defying neat classifications (see Chilli Guide). The seeds remain viable for two to three years, an asset that facilitated the distribution of the plants by the Spanish in the sixteenth century. Chillies are widely consumed in India, South America and Africa in quantities that would be dangerous for the delicate Western palate. Some of the hottest chillies are fierce enough to cause acid-like burns if gloves are not used to handle them. The fruits are used in herbal medicines and in commercial products – bottled sauces such as Tabasco, ketchups, chewing tobacco, ginger beer and rum. A fungicidal agent is prepared from capsaicin. Research in the United States is being conducted into the anti-cancer properties of capsaicin. In Japan, capsaicin is used in an oyster-proof paint for ships' keels. The 'roqueto pepper' (C. baccatum), known only in South America, is often used for chile con carne. It is more pulpy than the usual chilli and contains black seeds. The following is a summary of chilli derivatives:

Chilli powder: Either the ground powder from chillies of no specific type, mild to extremely hot depending on the chilli used, or as above but with oregano, cumin and/or garlic added, peculiar to the Americas and used for dishes of that region, eg chile con carne. Not so hot as the above.

Chilli seasoning: Chilli powder with salt and other spices such as cumin and garlic added. A modern variation of the second chilli powder. Mild to hot.

Red pepper: The ground powder from chillies of no specific type; synonym for chilli powder. Hot to extremely hot.

Paprika: Hungarian chilli powder made from C. annuum varieties with the seeds pre-treated to reduce capsaicin (hotness) content. Mild to hot depending on treatment, also sweet and used as a colouring (red).

Cayenne: The ground powder from chillies of the *C. frutescens* varieties. Hot to very hot. Originally from the Cayenne region of French Guiana.

Pimentón: The Spanish form of paprika.

Pepper: Term for chilli in Africa, Caribbean and the Americas.

OTHER NAMES

Africa(n) Pepper, Agi, Aji, American Pepper, Aztec Pepper, Bell Pepper, Bird Chilli, Bird Pepper, Bird's Eye Pepper, Bonnet Pepper Blume, Capsicum, Cherry Pepper, Chilli Pepper, Chilly, Cockspur Pepper, Cone Pepper, Congo Pepper, Devil Pepper, Goat's Pepper, Guinea Pepper, Indian Pepper, Long Pepper, Louisiana Sport Chilli, Mombassa Chilli, Nepal Pepper, Nigerian Chilli, Pod Pepper, Red Cluster Pepper, Red Pepper, Roqueto Pepper, Scotch Bonnet Pepper, Spanish Pepper, Spur Pepper, Tabasco, Wrinkled Pepper, Zanzibar Pepper. 'Pepper' and 'chilli' are interchangeable.

French: piment, piment fort, piment-oiseau, piment rouge

German: Roter Pfeffer, Spanischer Pfeffer

Italian: diavoletto peperonicino, peperoncini peperone

Spanish: chile, guindilla (cayenne), pimentón

Mexican: chile

Arabic: uran filfil

Burmese: nil thee (fresh red)

Chinese: fan chiew

Hindi: degi mirich (mild red from Kashmir), hari mirich (green), sabz mirich (green), lal mirich (fresh red), mirchi, sooka mirchi (dried red)

Japanese: kosho (capsicums), piman (green capsicum), togarashi

Indonesian: lombok (fresh red), lombok hijan (green), tjabé

Lao: mak phet kunsi (fresh red)

Malay: cabai hijan (green), chilli

Sinhalese: amu miris (green), malu miris (mild, long, fresh), rathu miris (fresh red)

Tamil: kochikai (fresh red), mo(o)lo-(o)ga(h)

Thai: nil thee sein (green), prik chee pha (fresh red), prik ki fah, prik ki nu

Satay Sauce (colour page 85)

A hot peanut sauce to serve with small cubes of beef steak threaded on wooden skewers, basted with coconut milk and grilled.   For 1lb beef 4–6 servings

Imp	Metric	US
6oz peanuts, roasted and coarsely ground or crunchy peanut butter	170g	6oz
1 onion, medium, grated	1	1
2 garlic cloves, crushed	2	2
1tsp chilli powder	1tsp	1tsp
2tsp brown sugar	2tsp	2tsp
1tbsp oil	20ml	1⅓tbsp
1tbsp tamarind water or lemon juice	20ml	1⅓tbsp
½pt coconut milk	285ml	1¼ cups
2tsp salt	2tsp	2tsp

1 Pound together the peanuts, onion, garlic, chillies and sugar.
2 Fry this mixture in oil for a minute, stirring.
3 Add remaining ingredients, bring to the boil and simmer until a thick pouring consistency is obtained.
4 Refrigerate until required (it will keep for at least a week) and reheat.

Groundnut Chop (colour page 51)

A traditional West African meal popular with European expatriates as an alternative for Sunday curry lunches. Served with side dishes it resembles the Dutch *rijsttafel*. 'Groundnut' is the West African term for peanut. This hot and nutty stew will serve 4–6.

Imp	Metric	US
Groundnut Chop		
2 cups peanuts	400g	2½ cups
3lb chicken pieces	1.4kg	3lb
2tbsp oil – groundnut or palm if possible	2tbsp	2⅔tbsp
1 onion, chopped	1	1
1–1½pt chicken stock	570–855ml	2½–3½ cups
1tbsp chilli powder	1tbsp	1⅓tbsp

Imp	Metric	US
1tbsp tomato purée	20ml	1⅓tbsp
½tsp allspice, ground	½tsp	½tsp
salt		
4–6 hard-boiled eggs, optional	4–6	4–6

Side Dishes
List 1
1 aubergine, sliced and salted
2 bananas, sliced
2 tomatoes, sliced
2 onions, sliced
1 coconut, grated
a little oil
List 2
1 can pineapple cubes
1 pawpaw, small, seeded, skinned and cubed
½ cup sultanas
½ cup peanuts
½tbsp chilli powder

Groundnut Chop

1 Roast peanuts until brown, remove skins, grind into a paste, adding a little oil if necessary.
2 Heat oil in large enamel casserole. Fry onions and chicken pieces until onions golden and chicken pieces sealed.
3 Pour in stock with chilli powder, tomato purée, allspice and salt to taste.
4 Simmer for 30 minutes. Add peanut paste. Stir well and simmer for 45 minutes. Add, towards end of cooking, hard-boiled eggs (optional).
5 Serve with rice and side dishes.

Side dishes

1 From List 1 fry half the bananas, tomatoes and onion slices and all the aubergine. Brown half the coconut.
2 Place all items from both lists in individual dishes.

Cinnamon

Cinnamomum zeylanicum
Fam Lauraceae

SPICE DESCRIPTION

Cinnamon is the dried inner bark from the shoots of a small laurel-like tree. The spice is in the form of cylinders, known as 'quills', consisting of strips of bark rolled one in another. The pale-brown bark strips may be only 1½mm (1/16in) thick, the spongy outer bark having been scraped off. Scrolled together, the length and diameter of the cylinders vary, but on average are 75mm (3in) and 8mm (5/16in) respectively. The dried bark is hard and brittle, the best varieties being pale and parchment-like in appearance. Cinnamon is readily available in the West, as in the East, and is also sold in powdered form. Cinnamon is similar to cassia. These spices are differentiated by law in Britain and some other countries, although others, including the United States, do not make this distinction.
Bouquet Sweet and fragrant, the powdered form yielding more aroma.
Flavour Warm and aromatic.

H Scale: 3

PREPARATION AND STORAGE

Like other powdered spices, powdered cinnamon tends to deteriorate, and should be kept dry, airtight and out of sunlight. This is the more common form, however, as the quills are difficult to grind in a pestle and mortar. At its best cinnamon is quite potent: large amounts will overpower. A mixture of sugar and cinnamon for sprinkling over desserts is best in a ratio of between 15:1 and 20:1. In cooking liquids, a whole quill can be steeped and removed when it has imparted its flavour. Cracked sticks may be used in sweet-and-sour pickling mixtures. Whole quills will uncurl during cooking.

USES

Cinnamon and cassia have similar uses, but since the former is less biting, it is generally advisable to use it in delicate or dessert dishes. Cinnamon is used in bakery for flavouring cakes and biscuits and is popular in numerous countries sprinkled on doughnuts and sweet fritters. Cinnamon toast is a traditional English tea-time snack. Milk and rice puddings feature in so many different cuisines – English, Scandinavian, Mexican and Indian, to name but a few – where cinnamon is the common spice. It goes well with desserts composed of chocolate or fruit, particularly apples and pears. In Greek and Middle Eastern cookery, stuffings for aubergines and sweet peppers often require cinnamon. Also it may flavour *avgolemono* soup and *moussaka* as well as casserole of lamb and lemon. It is used in curries and *pilaus* and in spicing Arab meat dishes. Cinnamon may be used to spice mulled wines, creams and syrups, and is an ingredient of *garam masala*, Chinese Five Spices and sometimes of pickling spice mixtures.

CHEMICAL COMPOSITION

Cinnamon bark yields ½–1 per cent essential oil, the main aromatic of which is cinnamic aldehyde, 60–75 per cent. The oil also has up to 10 per cent eugenol plus eleven other organic compounds. Besides the volatile oil, cinnamon bark contains tannins, protein, starch, cellulose, mucilage, mineral elements and other substances. The leaf also yields ½–1 per cent of essential oil but its main constituent, up to 95 per cent, is eugenol. Cinnamon leaf oil is thus used as a clove oil substitute and is sometimes known as 'clove oil'. The bark oil is very expensive and used in European perfumery.

ATTRIBUTED PROPERTIES

Cinnamon, one of nature's most aromatic spices, strangely does not have many properties attributed to it and its uses are minimal. Even in India and Africa, where most aromatics are ascribed powers bordering on the phenomenal, it was used only superficially; otherwise it was used violently, as in gonorrhoea when oil was injected into the infected parts. Perhaps, being so powerfully aromatic, healers were wary and only prescribed it when the very source of life was in peril. However, more mildly, cinnamon is carminative, stimulant, astringent and aromatic. It has been used in diarrhoea and stomach upsets, in nausea and occasionally as an inhalation. In various pregnancy problems efficacy is attributed to it. In modern times, oil of cinnamon has been found to be bactericidal against some organisms and ground cinnamon is antifungal.

PLANT DESCRIPTION

A tropical evergreen tree of the laurel family, reaching 5–7m (16–56ft) in the wild state. The deeply-veined leaves are dark green on the top and paler underneath. The smooth bark varies from grey to yellowish. Both bark and leaves are strongly aromatic. There are small white flowers which have an offensive smell, and purplish-black acorn-like berries.

CULTIVATION

Cinnamon grows in virtually any soil but prefers poor, sandy or lateritic soils. A hot, wet tropical climate at low altitude is essential. Commercially grown trees appear as small bushes up to 3m (10ft) high, for the stems have to be continually cut back to yield bark. The stems are cut during the monsoon, when they are easier to peel. After fermenting for one day, the outer bark, cork and the pithy inner lining are scraped off. These parts either adulterate or alter the composition. The bark is then left to dry completely, when it curls and forms into quills. Several are rolled together to make compound quills up to 1m (3ft) in length. Further drying and daily hand-rolling produce the compact final product with its characteristic pale brown colour. The quills are graded according to thickness, aroma and appearance, 0–00000, the latter being the highest grade. Other forms are: 'quillings' – broken quills, 'featherings' – inner bark of twigs, and 'chips' – coarse bark remnants.

REMARKS

Believed to be native to Sri Lanka, cinnamon grows now also in India, Brazil, the islands of the Indian Ocean and the East and West Indies. It was known to the ancient Chinese and Egyptian civilisations. It is quoted in the Bible in the book of Exodus as an ingredient of anointing oil and in Proverbs: 'I have perfumed my bed with myrrh, aloes and cinnamon. Come, let us take our fill of love until the morning: let

61

us solace ourselves with loves'. In Egypt, it was used medicinally and as a flavouring for beverages. It was also used in embalming, as part of the most expensive method, filling the body cavities with spiced preservatives. In the ancient world, cinnamon is supposed to have been more precious than gold. This is not surprising in Egypt, where the abundance of gold made it a fairly common ornamental metal. Cinnamon was known in medieval Europe, where it was still very expensive. As well as a spice, it was used for incense in religious (and irreligious) rites. The trees were not actively cultivated by Westerners until 1770 in Sri Lanka, because Dutch traders, who had then the monopoly, preferred to use the wild trees. Cinnamon leaf oil, distilled from the leaves of the tree, is used as a substitute for clove oil in India. Commercially, cinnamon is used in perfumery. Some toothpastes used to contain cinnamon oil, but these were withdrawn after reports of allergic reactions.

OTHER NAMES
Ceylon Cinnamon, True Cinnamon
French: cannelle
German: Ceylonzimt, Kaneel, Zimt
Italian: cannella
Spanish: canela
Burmese: thit-ja-boh-gauk
Chinese: yook gway
Indian: dal(-)chini, darchini, dhall cheene, kulmie darchini (cf Cassia)
Indonesian: kaju manis, kayu manis, manis djangan
Malay: kayu manis
Sinhalese: kurundu
Tamil: karuvappadai
Thai: op chery

Cinnamon Toast
Traditional English tea toast. Serves 2–4

Imp	Metric	US
6 slices any bread	6	6
1tsp cinnamon	1tsp	1tsp
caster sugar		
butter		

1 Toast bread on one side.
2 Butter untoasted side.
3 Sprinkle with mixture of cinnamon and caster sugar.
4 Place under slow grill until evenly brown.
5 Cut into generous fingers and serve hot.

Lemon Lamb (colour page 138)
A really delicious but very simple dish. Serve with plain rice or bread and a green salad. Serves 4–6

Imp	Metric	US
1oz butter	30g	1oz
1tbsp olive oil	20ml	1⅓tbsp
2lb lamb fillet or boned leg, cubed	905g	2lb
½–1tsp cinnamon, ground	½–1tsp	½–1tsp
salt		
pepper, freshly ground		
¼tsp saffron strands in ½pt chicken stock, freshly made	¼tsp 285ml	¼tsp 1¼ cups
1 lemon, very thinly sliced	1	1
2tsp parsley, chopped	2tsp	2tsp

1 Heat the butter and oil in a shallow pan and brown the lamb evenly.
2 Sprinkle with cinnamon, salt and pepper.
3 Pour on the saffron-flavoured stock and stir well.
4 Cover with the lemon slices.
5 Put a lid on the pan and simmer very gently for ¾ to 1 hour until the meat is tender.
6 Transfer to a heated dish, sprinkle with parsley and serve.

Citus

Citrus spp
Fam Rutaceae

SPICE DESCRIPTION

The citrus family includes the lemon (*Citrus limonia*), the bitter orange (*C. aurantium*), the sweet orange (*C. sinensis*), the grapefruit (*C. paradisi*) and tangerines and mandarins (*C. reticulata*). The fruits are available fresh or canned in syrup or natural juice. The juice is also sold, and the peel is candied or dried. The lime (*C. aurantifolia* or *C. acita*) is now quite widely available in the West. The citron (*C. medica*) is a lemon-shaped fruit up to 20cm (8in) long with a thick green to yellow rind and bitter flesh. It is generally used for its peel, which is candied. The leaves are used either fresh or dried. Only dried are available in the United Kingdom. They are usually a pale olive green, crisp and curled. A variety from the wild tree *C. hystrix* (Kaffir Lime) is imported from Thailand. These are similar in colour and average 7cm (2¾in) in length.

Bouquet Fruits have a mild flowery aroma. The juice, and the oil in the rind, produce a sharper scent. The bouquet of the leaves is sweetly aromatic and faintly like tobacco.

Flavour Fruits all have some degree of sharpness, owing to their citric acid content. Sharpest are the bitter oranges, inedible raw, and the lemon and lime, too strong for many. The sweet orange and mandarin have a tang offset by sweetness; the grapefruit stands in between the two extremes. The flavour of the leaves is pleasantly aromatic, sweet and lemony with a little bitterness.

H Scale: Variable 0–2

PREPARATION AND STORAGE

The oily peel, or zest, is aromatic and full of flavour. When peeling, avoid including the white pith (which is merely bitter) under the rind. Use a potato peeler for large pieces and, if necessary, dry in the oven for two hours at 200°F (93°C).

Special citrus fruit peelers, or 'zesters' are available: when drawn over the rind, the small circular blades flay off thin strips of peel. Canelling knives can produce larger strips of peel for decoration. An ordinary grater is quite adequate when grated peel is required and it is advisable to wash and dry the fruit before use. Hand presses are available to extract the juice: it is best to quarter the fruit before pressing the pieces. The seeds are edible but bitter. Expressed juice should be made as necessary; it does not keep well. Citrus fruits may be kept for several weeks in a refrigerator or may be deep frozen. Warm the fruit before extracting the juice. When buying candied peel, the large pieces are superior to the diced peel and can quite easily be chopped.

Canelling knife

USES

As flavourings, all the citrus fruits can be used in a multiplicity of ways. Whole lemons and limes are salted or pickled for chutneys, curry accompaniments or as souring agents. Sharp lemon pickle and hot lime pickle are popular in India. In the Middle East, whole dried limes are sometimes added to meat stews. Citrus rind and juice is used in soups, sauces, stuffings, marinades, salads and salad dressings, pâtés, cakes and pastries. An important feature of lemon juice is that it retards the oxidisation or discolouration of vegetable matter; sprinkled over sliced aubergines or apples, for instance, it prolongs their natural colour. It also whitens and tenderises the flesh of fish and pale meats. A major use for bitter or Seville oranges is in marmalade. Other jams and preserves often require lemon juice for its high pectin content to aid setting. Grated lemon peel may be added to poultry stuffings and grated orange to orange butter, a delicious accompaniment to grilled fish. Cumberland sauce, served with game, contains both orange and lemon peel. *Gremolata*, traditionally sprinkled on to *osso buco* before serving, is a mixture of chopped parsley, garlic and grated lemon rind. Dried orange peel may be added to *bouquets garnis* and dried tangerine peel features subtly in many savoury Chinese recipes. Crystallised or candied peel is an addition to Italian *agrodolce* (sweet-sour) sauces. In English cookery citrus peel is characteristic of fruit cakes, buns, mincemeat and Christmas pudding, and a curl of citron peel traditionally decorates Madeira cake. Citrus leaves are used in Indonesian cookery in *satay* sauces, seafood soups and curries, and leaves from the lime are particularly popular in Thai cookery.

CHEMICAL COMPOSITION

Proportions of the following substances, water (up to 90 per cent), protein, fat, carbohydrates, fibre, ash, calcium, phosphorus, iron, sodium, potassium, vitamins A, B, B_2, B_5 and C, are more or less the same for each type of citrus fruit. The calorific value of sweet oranges and grapefruit is about 40 per 100g (4oz) which is twice that of lemons and limes. The colouring of the peel is due to xanthophyll and the terpene, carotene. The essential oil from the peel contains other terpenes, principally limonene, and glucosides. The oil also contains the aldehyde, citral. The albedo or mesocarp (white portion of the

peel) has pectin, sugar, glucosides and vitamin C. The juice contains citric and other acids which are replaced by the aromatics as ripening takes place.

ATTRIBUTED PROPERTIES

Citrus fruits supply a large proportion of essential vitamins, A, B, B_2, B_5 and C which is antiscorbutic. Tonic, refrigerant, stomachic and carminative, the fruit or juice reduces fever, nausea and thirst and is good in rheumatism and narcosis. Citrus fruit oils are astringent and rubefacient, and are used to flavour bitter medicinal preparations. The dried rind of bitter oranges has been helpful in indigestion. Vitamin C is a popular remedy for colds and has recognised properties in the prevention of haemorrhaging and healing wounds. Lemon juice has been used for tumours of the skin such as warts and corns. Modern remedies for lessening freckles and elbow roughness incorporate lemons or lemon juice.

PLANT DESCRIPTION

Trees vary in height from the lime, 5m (15ft), to the grapefruit, 15m (50ft). All species bear white flowers, those of the lemon having purple bases. The leaves are generally dark green and ovate, while the lemon has serrated leaves and the grapefruit lighter ones. Branches are spiny or thorny, although smooth in the grapefruit.

CULTIVATION

Citrus grows between latitudes 45°N and 45°S, the greatest proportion being in the sub-tropics. Cool nights are necessary for good colour, thus tropical citrus tend to be greener than others. The cultivation of citrus is now a vast, worldwide commercial industry, with the United States and Brazil producing over half the world crop.

REMARKS

Citrus fruits are very ancient, all being native to the Middle or Far East. The lemon is probably native to the region where India, Burma and China meet and was introduced into Europe by the Arabs in the twelfth century. It now grows also in Africa and the Mediterranean, especially Italy and Sicily. The bitter or Seville orange, probably native to Indo-China, is grown now in the West Indies, Spain and North Africa, and its oil is used in perfumery and in digestive liqueurs. The sweet orange is probably Chinese. It is now the most widely used citrus and grown worldwide. The grapefruit probably developed in the West Indies. Limes, originally East Indian, grow mainly in the West Indies, India, Egypt and Florida. Their oil is used in cordials and mineral water. Mandarins and tangerines were discovered by Westerners in China in the eighteenth century, reaching Europe in 1805. They are now cultivated also in southern Europe, Africa and the United States. Bergamot oil, made from a variety of bitter orange, is used in perfumery, eau-de-cologne and hair lotions. Orange flower water, made from the blossoms, is used to scent confectionery such as Turkish delight. Other varieties of citrus, which the Westerner rarely sees at home, are the sweet lime (*C. limetta*) and the pomelo or shaddock, (*C. grandis*), both eaten as fruits in the tropics. Many liqueurs and cordials are based on or contain citrus.

OTHER NAMES

Grapefruit
French: pamplemousse
German: Pampelmuse
Italian: pompelmo
Spanish: pomelo, toronja

Lemon
French: citron limon, jaune citron
German: Zitrone
Italian: limone
Spanish: limon
Indian: burra, nimboo, u
Indonesian: djeruk nipis
Malay: liman nipis
Tamil: yellumshikai
Thai: makrut
Japanese: remon, yuzu(citron)

Lime
French: limette (sweet), citron (sour), limon
German: Limonelle
Italian: cedro
Spanish: lima
Indian: nimboo, u
Indonesian: djeruk nipis
Malay: liman kestum, liman nipis
Tamil: yellumshikai
Thai: makrut, ma now

Mandarin/Tangerine
French: mandarine
German: Mandarine
Italian: mandarino
Spanish: mandarina
Chinese: gom pei (peel)
Japanese: mikan, tachibana (clementine)

Seville Orange
French: bigarade, orange amère
German: Pomeranze
Italian: arancio amara
Spanish: bigarada, naranja agria, naranja amarga, naramja cajel

Sweet Orange
French: orange (douce)
German: Apfelsine, (Susse) Orange
Italian: arancio (dolce)
Spanish: naranja
Indian: narrangee
Indonesian: djeruk perut (cit leaves)
Malay: limau purut (cit leaves)
Tamil: kitchelly pullum
Thai: makrut bai (cit leaves)
Japanese: hanay(uzu) (evergreen), mikan, orenji

Osso Buco (colour page 34)

Sawn pieces of shin of veal with marrowbone, braised in tomatoes and white wine. An Italian dish traditionally accompanied by *risotto Milanese* (p. 163).

Serves 4

Imp	Metric	US
2oz butter	55g	2oz
2½–3lb shin of veal, sawn into 2in pieces (5cm)	1.1–1.4kg	2½–3lb
1 onion, chopped	1	1
1 carrot, diced	1	1
1 celery stick, diced	1	1
¼pt dry white wine	140ml	9½tbsp
1lb tomatoes, skinned and chopped	455g	1lb
¼pt white stock	140ml	9½tbsp
1 bouquet garni	1	1
salt		
pepper		
1tbsp parsley, finely chopped	1tbsp	1⅓tbsp
1 garlic clove, finely chopped	1	1
1tbsp lemon peel, grated	1tbsp	1⅓tbsp

1 Melt butter in a frying pan and brown meat. Remove meat and place upright in a cast iron casserole or heavy pot. (The marrow should not escape during cooking).
2 Now fry onions, carrots and celery to soften them and then add to the meat.
3 Add the wine to the casserole and cook for five minutes.
4 Add the tomatoes, cook for a few moments then add the stock, bouquet garni, and season to taste.
5 Put on the lid and simmer for 1½–2 hours.
6 Transfer the meat carefully on to a serving dish and strain the sauce over the meat.
7 Mix together the parsley, garlic and lemon peel (*gremolata*), sprinkle over and serve.

Lemon Trout

A simple method to give trout some zest.

Serves 4

Imp	Metric	US
4 fresh trout	4	4
2 lemons, squeezed and grated	2	2
salt and pepper		
4oz clarified butter	115g	4oz
1tbsp flour, sifted	1tbsp	1⅓tbsp
1tbsp parsley, finely chopped	1tbsp	1⅓tbsp

1 Marinade the trout in the lemon juice, salt and pepper in a refrigerator for 2–3 hours. Dry with kitchen towel.
2 Lightly sprinkle the fish with flour and fry in the clarified butter.
3 When nearly done coat each side with some of the grated lemon peel and continue cooking.
4 Remove when ready. Add the remaining grated lemon peel and parsley to the pan and cook quickly for a few minutes.
5 Pour sauce over fish and serve at once.

Clove

Eugenia caryophyllus
syn *E. caryophyllata, E. aromatica, Caryophyllus aromaticus, Syzygium aromaticum*
Fam Myrtaceae

SPICE DESCRIPTION

Cloves are the immature unopened flower buds of a tropical tree. When fresh, they are pink, but they are always sold at least partially dried – some overdried – finally turning to a red-brown or rust-brown colour. In shape they resemble small nails, with a tapering stem of rounded cross section whose larger end is topped with an open four-pointed crown containing the flower bud. The whole clove measures 12–16mm (½–⅝in) in length. The stem is quite tough, but the head should be more fragile and easily crumbled between the fingers. Most cloves are highly flavoured and therefore even the inferior ones are acceptable, but the best retain their natural oils even after drying and are plump and not brittle or withered. Cloves are sold whole or ground and are freely available at a reasonable cost.

Bouquet Warm, pungent and aromatic.
Flavour Sweetly pungent, astringent and strongly aromatic. H scale: 5

PREPARATION AND STORAGE

Cloves are best bought whole – the powder quickly deteriorates. They are difficult to pulverise in a pestle and mortar so it is best to use an electric grinder. Another quick way to obtain the powder is by crumbling the heads between the fingers, saving the stalks for future use. Store the spice in airtight containers.

USES

Cloves are used both in main courses and desserts. They can be used whole in soups, casseroles and *courts-bouillons*. Only a few need be used – otherwise they will overpower the dish. Their most picturesque use is in studding hams and pork. After partial cooking, the meat is scored through the fat into a patchwork of diamond shapes and a clove pushed into the middle of each section like a nail. The meat is then basted with honey, fruit juice or cider and baked until well glazed. The result is a traditional and typically English and American substantial delicacy. An onion studded with cloves is frequently used to impart an elusive character to *courts-bouillons*, stocks and occasionally soups. Baked apples are also greatly improved by studding with a few cloves; this addition is considered essential by some. The use of a single clove will add fullness to the aroma of a meat dish without intruding into the flavour. Casseroles of game, especially venison and hare, are often spiced with cloves, as are slow beef braises and traditional English spiced beef. Cloves are common in gravies, pickles, preserves and spiced sweets. They should always be included in the preparation of bread sauce. They flavour marinades, mulled wines and liqueurs. Many varieties of cakes and puddings require them and they are an ingredient of mixed spice preparations, including curry powders. Cloves are used in the production of smoked meats and cheeses. The ripe

fruit of the clove tree is also dried, or preserved in sugar.

CHEMICAL COMPOSITION

Cloves contain 14–20 per cent essential oil, 70–90 per cent of which is eugenol. The oil also includes traces of carvone, eucalyptol, limonene, pinene, caryophyllene, furfural, vanillin and several other substances. Whole cloves consist of cellulose, protein, resin, volatile and fixed oils, tannins and various minerals.

ATTRIBUTED PROPERTIES

Eugenol is a very strong antiseptic – hence the effectiveness of cloves in preserving preparations such as pickling liquids. Clove oil is a powerful stimulant and carminative. It is used to treat flatulent colic, nausea, indigestion and dyspepsia. Cotton wool soaked in clove oil is applied directly to an aching tooth, bringing immediate relief. Compounded with zinc oxide, it is employed in dentistry as a temporary tooth filling. Externally applied, clove oil is irritant, rubefacient and mildly analgesic. It is used in liniments with a base of olive oil. Cloves themselves are astringent, owing to the large percentage of tannins present.

PLANT DESCRIPTION

A tropical, evergreen myrtaceous tree, reaching up to 14m (45ft) and conical in shape. The bark is grey, the elliptical leaves a shiny dark green. Small crimson flowers grow in triple clusters at the ends of the branches. The fruit is a purple drupe

2.5cm (1in) long. The leaves bear fragrant oil glands and the whole plant is aromatic. Plantations can be smelt from miles away.

CULTIVATION

Cloves grow in the tropics and best near the sea. A dry season is essential for harvesting and curing. Rainfall needs to be over sixty inches per year. Lateritic soils appear the most suitable and must be well drained. The clove clusters are picked by hand before the buds open and then are dried on palm mats. Clove trees live to eighty years or more but cropping is variable, big crops occurring only once in four years.

REMARKS

The clove tree is native to the Moluccas – the Spice Islands. It began to be spread by traders and colonists in the 1700s and is now also cultivated in Brazil, the East and West Indies, Mauritius, Madagascar, India, Sri Lanka, Zanzibar and Pemba, which latter two are traditional sources. Cloves thrive close to the sea and islands are naturally a good habitat for them. The spice is recorded by the Chinese around 400BC. Two centuries later there is a reference to courtiers keeping cloves in their mouths to avoid offending the Emperor while addressing him. The Romans discovered the spice when they encountered the oriental trade routes, but it remained something exotic to them. However, cloves became established in Europe shortly after the fall of Rome and have been popular since the Middle Ages. Pomanders have been in common use since the sixteenth century – 'They used to be carried by men of dignity in the presence of malodourous persons' (Briggs, *A Pinch of Spices*, 1978). *Pot-pourris* usually contain the powdered spice. Cloves are nowadays too cheap to be worth adulterating; the adulterants would cost more than the spice, except in the case of Mother of Cloves (the dried fruit), though it was otherwise in earlier times when clove production was limited. Commercial products of clove oil are found in dentistry, medicine and

perfumery. Shredded cloves are mixed with tobacco for cigarettes in Indonesia. The name derives from the Latinate word for 'nail' – *clou, clavo* etc. 'Cloves ben calde Gariophili and ben perfyte frute with sharpe savoure' (Trevisa, 1398).

OTHER NAMES

French: clou de girofle
German: Gewürzenelke
Italian: chiodo di garofano
Spanish: clavo de especia
Burmese: ley-nyin-bwint
Chinese: ding heung
Indian: lao(o)ng, laung, lavang, lavungam
Indonesia: cengkeh, tjengkeh
Malay: bunga c(h)ingkeh, bunga chingkek, bunga cingkeh
Sinhalese: karabu
Tamil: lavungam
Thai: gahn plu

Baked Apples

A tasty version of this simple dish.

Serves 4–6

Imp	Metric	US
4–6 cooking apples	4–6	4–6
2oz dried apricots	55g	2oz
16–24 cloves, whole	16–24	16–24
2oz sultanas	55g	2oz
2oz butter	55g	2oz
2oz soft brown sugar	55g	2oz
water		

1 Wash and core apples.
2 Peel off the top quarter of each apple and stud the exposed part with 4 cloves.

3 Soak dried apricots in boiling water for 5–10 minutes and chop.
4 Mix the chopped dried apricots, sultanas, butter and sugar and fill the centres with this mixture. Add a knob of butter on the top and place apples in a roasting pan.
5 Add water to the pan, about ⅛in (3mm) deep, and bake in a moderate oven, Gas Mark 4, 350°F, 180°C, for about ¾–1 hour, until the apples are soft.
6 Serve with the juices from the pan and a spoonful of cream.

Forester's Venison (colour page 137)
A simple recipe that can be used also for hare, rabbit or pigeon. Serves 6

Imp	Metric	US
2lb venison	905g	2lb
4tbsp flour	4tbsp	5⅓tbsp
2oz butter	55g	2oz
2 onions, finely chopped	2	2
3 allspice, whole	3	3
3 bay leaves	3	3
6 cloves, whole	6	6
rind of one lemon, grated		
½tsp mixed herbs	½tsp	½tsp
½tsp pepper	½tsp	½tsp
1tsp salt	1tsp	1tsp
½pt red wine	285ml	1¼ cups
½pt stock	285ml	1¼ cups
2 carrots, diced	2	2
2 potatoes, diced	2	2
1 turnip, diced	1	1

1 Trim and cut meat into 1½in (4cm) cubes.
2 In enamel casserole fry onion until golden, remove and keep.
3 Coat meat in flour and fry until brown.
4 Add remaining ingredients, cover and cook in oven for 2 hours at Gas Mark 2, 300°F, 150°C.

Cocoa

Theobroma cacao
Fam Sterculiaceae

SPICE DESCRIPTION
Cocoa powder and chocolate are produced from the seeds of the fruit of the cocoa tree. These seeds are fermented, dried, roasted and ground to produce what is known as 'cocoa mass'. Processed cocoa comes in the following most familiar forms.

1 **Cocoa powder** – a fine, rich brown powder made from the cocoa mass from which a proportion of the cocoa butter has been removed. It is usually sweetened and is insoluble in cold water.
Bouquet Warm with characteristic chocolate aroma.
Flavour Dry and bitter.   H Scale: ½
2 **Drinking chocolate** – made from pre-cooked cocoa powder with added sugar, salt and flavourings. It is paler and less fine than cocoa powder.
Bouquet Warm and sweet.
Flavour Sweet.   H Scale: ½
3 **Cooking chocolate or bitter chocolate** (United States) – made from the cocoa mass with added cocoa butter. (In the United States it is unsweetened but in Europe a little sugar is usually added). Coating, covering chocolate or '*couverture*' has a larger cocoa butter content. It is available in chips, bars or large blocks and varies in colour from very dark brown to brown.
Bouquet Variable.
Flavour Bitter to semi-sweet. H Scale: ½
4 **Eating chocolate, both plain and milk** – comes in a large assortment of flavours and forms, often with the addition of dried fruit, nuts, fillings and liqueurs. Milk chocolate has full cream, dried or powdered milk added. Diabetic chocolate contains sorbitol instead of sugar.

PREPARATION AND STORAGE
Cocoa powder and drinking chocolate should be kept in cool moisture-free conditions. Cocoa must be mixed to a paste with a little milk or water before adding hot milk, but this is not necessary with drinking chocolate. Chocolate should not be kept for long as it will go stale and discolour. Care should be taken not to overheat chocolate when melting it; the safest method is in a basin over simmering water. The Mexicans use a special long beaker with a swizzle stick, called a

'*molinillo*', for beating hot chocolate drinks to a good froth.

Surprisingly enough, chocolate is used in many savoury dishes. These come from Mexico in particular, but also from Spain and Italy. The Mexican national dish, *mole*, is turkey cooked in a complicated sauce using chocolate as well as many other ingredients including several varieties of chilli. Chocolate is also an ingredient of the hot *enchillada* sauces, and is sometimes added to chilli powders. In Spain, chocolate and cocoa is used in beef and game stews, and in Italy it can form part of *agrodolce*, the sweet-sour sauce accompanying game, especially hare. Chocolate is an ingredient in some recipes for *pumpernickel*, the dark rye bread. More familiarly, chocolate and cocoa are used in cakes and pastries, in icings and cake fillings, in ice-cream, in sauces, especially laced with rum or brandy, in sweet mousses and soufflés and in home-made confectionery. Chocolate has a special affinity with oranges, vanilla and cinnamon. Cocoa appears in many liqueurs, the most famous being *Crème de Cacao*.

CHEMICAL COMPOSITION
Cocoa bean kernels contain 40–60 per cent solid fat, known as 'cocoa butter', 2.5 per cent sugar, 1–3 per cent of the xanthine theobromine, 0.1 per cent caffeine, acetic acid, minerals, polyphenols (5 per cent), proteins etc. The characteristic flavour of cocoa results during the curing processes from enzymatic reactions and changes in the chemistry of the beans. The shells contain theobromine (0.5–2 per cent), vitamin D and fat but are, with the embryos, removed during processing. To make cocoa powder the fat is reduced by over half, but added back to make chocolate.

ATTRIBUTED PROPERTIES
The theobromine in cocoa has similar stimulative and diuretic properties to caffeine. Isolated, it is used as a diuretic, heart muscle stimulant and arterial dilator. Theobroma, on the other hand, is a pharmacopoeic form of cocoa powder which is used as a medium, particularly to mask disagreeable flavours. It is well known as a medium for the laxative phenolphthalein. Cocoa butter is used for salves and suppositories and in cosmetics, lipstick being a typical example. Theobromine is poisonous to most farmyard animals and it follows that chocolate should not be given to domestic pets.

PLANT DESCRIPTION
Theobroma cacao is a small, secondary, evergreen tree reaching to 8m (26ft) and occasionally nearly double that height. The pods ripen from green to yellow or orange, some varieties to red or purple, after five months. They are 10–30cm (4–12in) long, oval, melon-shaped, with lateral ridges of varying prominence, smooth or rough. The seeds, known as 'beans', arranged in rows, average about forty per pod and are enclosed in a whitish sticky pulp.

PRODUCTION
Cocoa is only grown in the rain forests of the tropics, either on small holdings or in large plantations. It is usually propagated by seed. As the trees grow, the forest is cleared around them, until finally only a few large shade trees remain. The trees crop twice a year. The pods are harvested, cut open and the seeds placed in heaps to

ferment for about a week. The fermented beans are dried, bagged and exported.

REMARKS
Cocoa, or *Theobroma cacao*, is native to tropical America. It was first brought to Europe by the Spaniards in the sixteenth century. Cortés had found Montezuma drinking *xocolatl*, a preparation of cocoa, vanilla, spices and honey. Sometimes the Aztecs mixed chilli and maize flour with roasted, crushed cocoa beans for their beverage. The Spaniards created a sweet beverage by adding sugar, and once their secret had been discovered its popularity spread through Europe, but it was very expensive. Fashionable chocolate houses similar to coffee houses sprang up in the European cities. The name *Theobroma* means 'food of the Gods', since the Aztecs ascribed divine origin to the cocoa tree. Today, West Africa is the biggest producer of cocoa, and Brazil is the largest grower in the Americas. Two landmarks in the development of the use of cocoa were the treatment invented by the Dutchman, C. J. van Houten, in 1828, which neutralised the acidity of cocoa by alkali additions, at the same time improving its solubility, and in 1876, the development of 'milk chocolate' for eating, by M. D. Peter of Vevey, Switzerland, by adding cocoa butter, sugar and milk to the cocoa mass. Cocoa and chocolate in England have been associated with the celebrated Quaker families of Cadbury, Fry and Rowntree since the early nineteenth century.

OTHER NAMES
Cacao, Chocolate
French: cacao, chocolat
German: Kakao, Schokolade
Italian: cacao, cioccolata
Spanish: cacao, chocolate
Mexican: cacauatl

Mexican Turkey
A cooler version of turkey *mole*, which traditionally is incredibly hot using large quantities of pungent chillies. Accompany with rice and tortillas. Serves 4–6

Imp	Metric	US
3lb turkey joints	1.4kg	3lb
water		
1 bay leaf	1	1
1tsp salt	1tsp	1tsp
2tbsp oil	40ml	2⅔tbsp
2oz almonds	55g	2oz
1oz peanuts, raw	30g	1oz
2tbsp sesame seeds	2tbsp	2⅔tbsp
½ slice bread	½	½
3 chillies, fresh, seeded	3	3
2 garlic cloves	2	2
2 green peppers	2	2
2oz raisins	55g	2oz
1lb tomatoes	455g	1lb
1½tsp chilli powder	1½tsp	1½tsp
1tsp cinnamon, ground	1tsp	1tsp
¼tsp cloves, ground	¼tsp	¼tsp
½tsp marjoram, dried	½tsp	½tsp
1oz chocolate, plain, grated	30g	1oz
1tsp sugar, brown	1tsp	1tsp

1 Skin and bone the meat and cut into serving pieces, cover with water, add bay leaf and salt and simmer until tender. Reserve stock.
2 Meanwhile, heat oil and fry almonds, peanuts and sesame seeds until lightly browned. Remove and grind them together.
3 Now fry the bread, chillies, garlic, peppers, tomatoes and raisins until soft.
4 Add chilli powder, cinnamon, cloves and marjoram and cook for a minute.
5 Pound the mixture with the nuts or use an electric blender.
6 Return to the pan, add sugar, chocolate, 1 pint (570ml) turkey stock and cook, stirring until thick.
7 Arrange the turkey pieces in a serving dish and pour on the sauce.

Chocolate Leaves
Perfectly veined leaves to make a delightful decoration for cold puddings, desserts and cakes. Makes about 4 dozen leaves

Imp	Metric	US
8oz plain cooking chocolate	225g	8oz
rose leaves, washed and dried		

1 Melt chocolate over boiling water.
2 Carefully draw each leaf face down over the surface of the chocolate, one side

only. Place on wire rack to set.

3 As soon as the chocolate has solidified, gently peel off the leaf from the chocolate.

4 Store the leaves in an airtight tin until required.

Coconut

Cocos nucifera
Fam Palmae

SPICE DESCRIPTION
The coconut is the seed of one of the largest fruits in the vegetable kingdom. The oval fruit, yellow brown when ripe, measures around 30cm (12in) long. The nut, also oval, with three small 'eyes' at the base, is 15cm (6in) or more in length, surrounded by a fibrous mass, 'coir', most of which is removed before export. The shell of the nut is thickish, hard and tough. Inside is a white layer of hard moist flesh, and the hollow interior is partly filled with a clear liquid, known as 'coconut water'. Coconuts are widely available in the West. Heavy coconuts are freshest. For culinary purposes coconut is available in the following forms:

Desiccated – small dried flakes of the white flesh.

Canned – thick coconut milk that can be diluted (US).

Frozen – frozen coconut cream in cartons (Australia).

Creamed – compressed coconut cream which is partly soluble in hot water.

Dried – large pieces known as copra.

Bouquet The aroma of the fresh meat is not as strong as coconut cream, which is sweet and rather cloying.

Flavour Fairly sweet and nutty with a crunchy fibrous texture.   H Scale: 0

PREPARATION AND STORAGE
To extract the flesh from a fresh coconut, pierce the softest 'eye' and one other, then pour off the water which can make a refreshing drink or be used to prepare coconut milk. Break open the nut by

hitting it hard across the middle with a hammer. The flesh may then be prised out with a knife (warming the nut in the oven for ten minutes facilitates this), and then peeled and finely grated. There is a special device which will perform extraction and grating simultaneously. An average

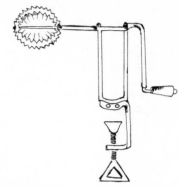

Coconut grater

coconut will yield about three cups of grated meat which in turn should produce three cups of 'milk'. Thick milk is obtained by adding 2½ cups of hot water to 2 cups of grated or desiccated coconut. Knead, allow to cool and then strain through a sieve or muslin, squeezing out as much liquid as possible. Alternatively, use an electric blender and then strain. If the process is repeated with more water and the same coconut, 'thin' milk is obtained. Coconut 'cream' is obtained by leaving the first extract overnight, when the cream will rise to the top. To prevent curdling when cooking with thick coconut milk, stir as it comes to the boil and do not cover the pan. Freshly grated coconut will keep for two days under refrigeration and may be deep frozen for a month. 30g (1oz) of creamed coconut mixed with 280ml (½pt) hot water will yield thin milk and 85g (3oz) with the same amount of water will yield thick milk.

USES
In the West, coconut is best known in desserts, bakery and confectionery. In India and South East Asia, the 'milk' is used as a thickening and flavouring agent

in curries, and appears in *birianis* and *pilaus*, especially those including chicken. Coconut is an important ingredient in a variety of fish and shellfish dishes. It is a base for sweet-sour chutneys and is common in certain Indonesian *sambals*. Among sweet dishes, coconut appears in Indian rice puddings, *halva* and in desserts based on *khoa* – a semi-solid dairy milk reduced by boiling. In South America and the Caribbean, coconut is popular in soups, sweet breads, desserts and ice cream. It is an essential ingredient of the cocktail *piña colada*, which became fashionable in the 1970s. Coconut milk or cream may be used in any dessert calling for ordinary milk or cream – rice pudding for instance. The flesh can be used in home-made confectionery.

CHEMICAL COMPOSITION

Coconut meat contains 35–50 per cent water, 3–4.5 per cent protein, 35–40 per cent fat, 9–13 per cent carbohydrate, 4 per cent fibre and 0.5–1 per cent minerals. Also present are small amounts of vitamins B_1, B_2, B_5 and C. Vitamin A is absent. Copra – the dried kernels – contains 65 per cent oil with high levels of lauric and myristic acids. The toddy (flower sap) averages 15 per cent sugar and is rich in vitamin B complex. There are 346 calories per 100 grammes of fresh coconut meat.

ATTRIBUTED PROPERTIES

Coconut oil is a substitute for cod liver oil, and used in disorders of the lungs. The fermented sap juice is mildly laxative. The meat is a vermifuge. The water from ripe nuts is diuretic, and the ash of coconut palm bark is locally used as an antiseptic and dentifrice.

PLANT DESCRIPTION

Has the characteristics of the Palm family. The noded, upright unbranched stem, up to 60cm (24in) in diameter, rises 5–30m (16–100ft), ending in an impressive crown of pinnate leaves which may be 6m (20ft) in length. There is a mass of roots at the base, above and breaking through the soil. Male and female flowers occur in spadixes. The fruit, a drupe, is up to 30cm (12in) in diameter and weighs up to 2kg (4.4lb).

CULTIVATION

Coconut requires a low altitude, a humid atmosphere, and a minimum of 1,000mm (40in) of rain annually. It thrives on tropical coastal plains, but can be grown inland. The fruit is produced after about seven years, taking a year to mature, but once started, fruit will yield monthly. The trees are propagated only by seed. Coconuts are grown on small holdings and commercial plantations. A single palm can yield up to sixty fruit.

REMARKS

The palm has been in existence throughout the tropics too long for there to be a definite answer as to its origins. The coconut palm is one of nature's most useful plants: every single part of the tree is used in some way, providing a complete life-support system. It is important commercially for copra and oil, the leading exporters of which are the Philippines, Sri Lanka, Indonesia and Papua New Guinea. Coconut is a valuable food crop and a staple in the Caribbean and the Indo-Pacific region. The buds are often eaten as a salad. A strong liquor, *arrack*, is distilled from the fermented toddy or sap of the unopened flower spathes. Palm sugar or 'jaggery' is boiled down from the fresh toddy. The coir, or husk fibre, goes to make ships' ropes, carpets, upholstery filling and mats for cricket pitches and gold recovery. Copra yields an oil used in soaps, cosmetics, candles and margarine. The wood, called 'porcupine wood', makes ornamental carvings, and the leaves and trunks are essential building materials. Coconut is used in liqueurs and commercial confectionery.

OTHER NAMES

French: noix de coco
German: Kokosnuss
Italian: Cocco
Spanish: Coco

Indian: nareul, narikel nariyel, nar(r)ul, thainga
Malay: kelapa, nyiur, santan kental (milk)
Thai: hang kathi (thin milk), hua kathi (thick milk)

Coconut Sambal (colour page 86)

Sambals accompany curries in Indonesia as chutneys do in India, and there is a huge variety of them. This one is quite hot but can be tempered to taste. Try it as an accompaniment to barbecued meats. Serves about 4.

Imp	Metric	US
4oz fresh or desiccated coconut	115g	1 cup
6tbsp water or milk	120ml	8tbsp
2tsp chilli sauce	2tsp	2tsp
½ lemon, juice of	½	½
1 onion, medium, finely chopped	1	1
1tsp shrimp paste (*blachan*) or powder (optional)	1tsp	1tsp

1 Grate fresh coconut or moisten desiccated with hot milk or water.
2 Mix all ingredients together and serve with curries.
3 If desired, a little shrimp paste or powder may be included to give the flavour a seafood undertone.

Molee (colour page 104)

A delicious yellow sauce from southern India for prawns, cooked chicken or hard-boiled eggs. Ideal for left-overs. Serve with *chapatis*, rice or potatoes. Serves 4

Imp	Metric	US
1½–2lb king prawns, cooked	680–905g	1½–2lb
2oz *ghee* or clarified butter	55g	2oz
1 onion, finely sliced	1	1
2 garlic cloves, crushed	2	2
1tsp ginger, grated	1tsp	1tsp
2 chillies, fresh, seed and chopped	2	2
1tsp turmeric	1tsp	1tsp
½pt coconut milk, thick	285ml	1¼ cups
1tsp salt	1tsp	1tsp

1 Shell prawns or just remove head and legs if preferred.

2 Heat the *ghee* in a pan and fry the onions, garlic and ginger until soft.
3 Add the turmeric and fry, stirring for a minute.
4 Gradually add the coconut milk, stirring all the time, then add the chillies and salt.
5 Simmer uncovered for 10 minutes, add prawns and simmer for a further two minutes.

Piña Colada (colour page 51)

A cocktail now very popular with young people. Serves 1

Imp	Metric	US
3fl oz golden rum	85ml	3fl oz
2fl oz coconut cream, tinned	55ml	2fl oz
4fl oz pineapple juice or crushed pineapple	115ml	4fl oz
½ cup ice, crushed	½ cup	½ cup
1 pineapple stick	1	1
1 maraschino cherry	1	1

1 Shake or blend the rum, coconut, pineapple juice and ice.
2 Pour into tall glass containing crushed ice.
3 Decorate with pineapple stick and cherry.

Coriander

Coriandrum sativum
Fam Umbelliferae

SPICE DESCRIPTION

Coriander is the seed of a small plant. The seeds are almost spherical, one end being slightly pointed, the other slightly flattened. There are many longitudinal ridges. The length of the seed is 3–5mm (⅛–³⁄₁₆in) and the colour, when dried, is usually brown, but may be green or off-white. The seed is generally sold dried and in this state is apt to split into halves to reveal two partially hollow hemispheres and occasionally some internal powdery matter. Bought batches of dried coriander seed may contain a portion of broken seeds, which may lose their aroma more quickly. Coriander is available both whole and ground. Not much used in the West, but very common elsewhere, is 'green coriander' – the fresh leaves of the plant. This is used as a herb, especially in curries, and may be found in shops specialising in Asian and Middle Eastern food and in some supermarkets.

Bouquet Seeds are sweet and aromatic when ripe. Unripe seeds are said to have an offensive smell. The leaves, called 'fetid' by Western writers, are 'delicate and fresh' according to Eastern cooks.

Flavour The seeds are warm, mild and sweetish. There is a citrus undertone remarkably similar to orange peel. The flavour improves with keeping. The flavour of the leaves has also invited similar disagreement to that of the bouquet, but, although strange to the unaccustomed palate, it combines well in certain pungent dishes. H Scale: 1

PREPARATION AND STORAGE

Coriander seed is generally used coarsely ground or more finely powdered, depending on the texture desired. It is best bought whole as, being brittle, it is easy to mill or to pound in a mortar. Ground coriander is apt to lose its flavour and aroma quickly and should be stored in an opaque airtight container. Whole seeds keep indefinitely. Their flavour may be enhanced by a light roasting before use. As coriander is mild, it is a spice to be used by the handful rather than the pinch. The leaves can be chopped or minced before use. They do not respond to drying, but may be frozen either blanched or chopped and frozen in ice cubes.

USES

The commonest use of coriander seed is in curry powders, where it is the bulkiest constituent, often rough ground in India to give a crunchy texture. The seeds can be likewise used in stews and soups. They blend well with smoked meats and game and feature in traditional English black pudding recipes and Italian *mortadella* sausage. Coriander is an ingredient of *garam masala*, pickling spices and pudding spices and is used in cakes, breads and other baked foods. Sugared comfits made from the seeds are a traditional sweetmeat and breath sweetener. Coriander is a characteristic of Arab cookery, being common with lamb, kid and meat stuffings. *Taklia*, a popular Arab spice mixture, is coriander and garlic crushed and fried. Coriander with cumin is a common combination and features in *falafel* and in the Egyptian appetiser *dukka*, which consists of those spices plus sesame seeds, hazelnuts, salt and pepper, roasted and crushed. It is often distinctive in dishes *à la Grecque*. Coriander goes well with ham and pork, especially when orange is included. It enhances fish dishes and, with other spices, may form a delicious coating for spiced fish or chicken, rubbed into the scored flesh and grilled. Try frying a few seeds with sausages to add an unusual flavour. Coriander complements chilli and is included in many chilli recipes, such as *harissa*, the hot North African red pepper sauce. It may be added to cream or cottage cheese. The leaves are always used fresh. They feature in Spanish, Middle Eastern, Indian, Oriental and South American cookery. They are sprinkled like parsley on cooked dishes, minced or puréed in sauces, soups and curries, especially *bhuna*. Both seeds and leaves can be used in salads. In Thailand, the root of the coriander plant is used to flavour meats and curries.

CHEMICAL COMPOSITION
Coriander seeds yield up to 2 per cent essential oil, the major part, 45–65 per cent, of which is linalool (coriandrol). The oil also contains pinenes, terpinenes, borneol, cymene, decylaldehyde and geraniol. The seeds also contain a fixed oil, malic acid, tannin, mucilage, cellulose, protein and minerals.

ATTRIBUTED PROPERTIES
Coriander seed oil is strongly antibacterial against several organisms. The seed is an aromatic stimulant, a carminative (remedial in flatulence), an appetiser and a digestant stimulating the stomach and intestines. It is generally beneficial to the nervous system. Its main use is in masking foul medicines, especially purgatives, where it has anti-griping qualities. Coriander cakes were once taken against 'St Anthony's fire', or 'Rose', a severe streptococcal skin infection called 'erysipelas', which caused many deaths (including that of Charles Lamb), before the advent of antibiotics. The *Ananga Ranga* recommends a mixture of ground orris root, elk horn and coriander seed for youthful acne. It continues with another recipe for lightening the skin which includes coriander seed, '. . . if this be

applied to the body for seven days, it will make the aspect clean and brilliant as the moon'. In Asia the herb is used in piles, headache and swellings; the fruit in colic, piles and conjunctivitis; the essential oil in colic, rheumatism and neuralgia; the seeds as a paste for mouth ulceration and a poultice for other ulcers.

PLANT DESCRIPTION
A herbaceous hardy annual, of the parsley family, occasionally surviving into a second year. Its height averages 60cm (2ft). Its erect slender stems are branching and bright green. The small pink, pale blue or white flowers are borne in compound umbels. The upper leaves are wispy and finely divided, the lower ones broad, undivided and trilobate. The fruits are achenes, crowned with a minute calyx. The plant has an unpleasant odour – see Spice Description.

CULTIVATION
Coriander is grown from seed. It prefers warm dry conditions. For seed, it is sown in the spring, in drills 13mm (½in) deep, 25cm (10in) apart. It needs little maintenance. Harvest in about ninety days as soon as seeds are ripe and before they drop. Cut, dry and thresh as with the other Umbelliferae. An indication of ripeness is that the seeds' aroma turns pleasant. For leaf, the seeds are sown during the summer. Coriander grows easily in boxes.

REMARKS
Coriander is probably native to the Middle East and southern Europe, but has also been known in Asia and the Orient for millennia. It is found wild in Egypt and the Sudan, and sometimes in English fields. It is referred to in the Bible in the books of Exodus and Numbers, where the colour of 'manna' is compared to coriander. The seed is now produced in Russia, India, South America, North Africa – especially Morocco – and Holland. It was introduced to Britain by the Romans, who used it in cookery and medicine, and was widely used in English cookery until the Renaissance,

when the new exotic spices appeared. Among ancient doctors, coriander was known to Hippocrates, and to Pliny, who called it *coriandrum* for its 'buggy' smell, *coris* being a bug; or perhaps because the young seed has an uncanny resemblance to *Cimex lectularius*, the European bed-bug. As a herb, 'green coriander' has been largely ignored in the West, but is widely used practically everywhere else – in the Far East, Asia, and Central and South America. As a seasoning it is also used in Russia, Spain and the Middle East. The steam-distilled essential oil is used commercially in liqueurs, gin and bakery, and medicinally in horse and cattle drugs.

OTHER NAMES
Chinese Parsley, Cilantro, Dizzycorn, Japanese Parsley
French: coriandre
German: Koriander
Italian: coriandolo
Spanish: cilantro, culantro
Arabic: kizbara
Burmese: nannambin (leaves), nannam-zee (seed)
Chinese: hs(i)ang tsai, yen-sui, yuen sai, yuin si tsoi (leaves)
Indian: dhan(y)ia, dhuniah, kothimbir, kotimear, kotimli (seed)
dhania patta(r), dhania sabz, hara dhania (leaf)
Indonesian: ketumbar
Lao: phak hom pom
Malay: daun ketumba(r) (leaves), ketumba(r) (seed)
Sinhalese: kottamalli (seed), kottamalli kolle (leaves)
Tagalog: kinchay
Tamil: kothamilee
Thai: pak chee (met)

Falafel (colour page 33)
This Middle Eastern snack, also known as *ta'amia*, is served with drinks.

Serves 10–12

Imp	Metric	US
8oz chick peas or skinned *fava* beans, dried	225g	8oz
1 onion, very finely chopped	1	1
1 garlic clove, crushed	1	1
1 slice of white bread, soaked in a little water	1	1
¼tsp cayenne	¼tsp	¼tsp
1tsp coriander, ground	1tsp	1tsp
1tsp cumin, ground	1tsp	1tsp
2tbsp parsley, finely chopped	2tbsp	2⅔tbsp
salt, to taste		
oil for frying		

1 Soak the chick peas or beans overnight.
2 Cover with plenty of fresh water and cook for 1–1½ hours until tender.
3 Pound or blend the chick peas or beans to a purée.
4 Squeeze out the bread and add to the chick peas together with the rest of the ingredients. Knead well for a few minutes.
5 Let the mixture rest for 1–2 hours, then roll between the palms into firm 1in (25mm) balls. (Wetted hands make this easier).
6 Heat oil (at least 1in (25mm) deep) in a pan to about 360°F, 180°C, and fry the balls, a few at a time, until nicely brown all over – about 2–3 minutes.
7 Drain and serve hot with lemon wedges.

Pork with Coriander
A version of a traditional Greek dish.

Serves 4–6

Imp	Metric	US
½pt dry cider	285ml	1¼ cups
2tbsp lemon juice	2tbsp	2⅔tbsp
8tbsp olive oil	160ml	10⅔tbsp
1tbsp coriander, crushed	1tbsp	1⅓tbsp
½tsp pepper, freshly ground	½tsp	½tsp

Imp	Metric	US
½tsp salt	½tsp	½tsp
2lb pork fillet, cut into ½in (10cm) slices	1.4kg	2lb
2tbsp cream	40ml	2⅔tbsp

1 Mix together the cider, lemon juice, three quarters of the oil, coriander, pepper and salt.
2 Lay the meat in a dish and pour over the marinade. Leave overnight.
3 Remove the meat from the marinade and pat dry.
4 Heat the remaining oil in a large frying pan and brown the meat on both sides.
5 Add the marinade, bring to the boil, cover and simmer gently until the meat is tender (about 20 minutes).
6 Place the meat in a serving dish and keep warm.
7 Add cream to the juices in the pan and heat through. Pour over the meat and serve.

Cubeb

Piper cubeba
Fam Piperaceae

SPICE DESCRIPTION
This spice is the dried unripe fruits from a type of vine pepper (see Pepper). The corns, or berries, are dark brown with a wrinkled leathery skin. They are similar in shape and size to black peppercorns, except for an elongated 'tail', and grow in clusters rather like blackcurrants. Cubeb is available in health food shops, usually in ground form.
Bouquet Pungent, slightly camphorous with a touch of nutmeg.
Flavour Peppery, aromatic and rather bitter. H Scale: 3

PREPARATION AND STORAGE
As with other pepper, grind as necessary: ground pepper rapidly loses its aroma. Buy ground cubeb in small quantities and store in airtight containers.

USES
Cubeb is used in local Indonesian cookery, especially in Javanese *gulés* (curries). It was once popular in Arab cooking. Although there are no specific uses for cubeb in modern Western cookery, it was popular in the Middle Ages and in moderation may still be used to effect both as a spice and a pepper substitute. Because of its aromatic qualities, cubeb would go well with meat, cheese and vegetable dishes. It may be substituted for pepper in spice mixtures such as *quatre-épices* for flavouring pâtés, sausages, gingerbreads and spiced biscuits. Another use for cubeb is in place of allspice, where it will give a more peppery flavour.

CHEMICAL COMPOSITION
Cubeb contains alkaloids, carbohydrate, cellulose, protein, essential oil, fat, minerals and resin. Unlike black pepper, cubeb contains no piperine, its pungent principle being cubebine. Again, it yields up to five times as much essential oil as black pepper. The essential oil contains cineol, camphene, pinene and terpineol, plus other organic substances. There is up to 18 per cent essential oil, 6 per cent resin and 1 per cent cubebic acid.

ATTRIBUTED PROPERTIES
Cubeb and its oil are carminative, diuretic, stimulant and antiseptic and were employed as genito-urinary antiseptics and especially for clearing up gonorrhoea. Extract of cubeb is also expectorant, being helpful in pulmonary infections such as bronchitis. The powder from dried and crushed cubebs is added to cigarettes for the relief of asthma.

PLANT DESCRIPTION
A tropical, climbing perennial vine with a round grey stem. The leaves are smooth and ovate with a pointed tip. The small white flowers are arranged in spikes that later develop into an aggregate of berries along the central axis. The fruits are brown. See Spice Description.

Cubeb is found wild in the forests of Indonesia. It is also cultivated, usually in plantations.

REMARKS
Native to Indonesia, particularly Java, cubeb came to Europe via India through Venetian trade with the Arabs. Javanese growers protected their monopoly of the trade by sterilising the berries by scalding, thus ensuring that the vines were unable to be cultivated elsewhere. Its main use appears to have been in medicine, although its similarity to pepper made it a handy substitute. Today it has local use in the tropical East and there is renewed interest in cubeb in the West.

OTHER NAMES
Java Pepper, Tailed Cubebs, Tailed Pepper
French: cubèbe
German: Kubebe
Italian: cubebe
Spanish: cubebe
Indonesian: tjabé djawa

Lamb Gulé (colour page 86)

Gulés are Indonesian curries of Indian origin. They vary from island to island; this one uses cubeb which is peculiar to Java and where mutton is the meat usually used.   Serves 4

Imp/Metric/US	Imp/Metric/US
1 onion, large, chopped	½tsp cumin, ground
1 lemon – juice	2 curry leaves, optional
2 garlic cloves	1tsp galangal, ground – optional
1tsp almonds, ground	
2tsp ginger, fresh, grated	½tsp lemon rind, grated or lemon grass stalk
4 chillies, red, whole	
1in/25mm cinnamon stick	½tsp turmeric, ground
2tbsp desiccated coconut, browned five minutes	2–4tbsp oil (half to blend, half to fry)
	1lb/455g lamb, cubed 1in (25mm)
1tsp coriander, ground	1 tomato, pulped
1tsp cubeb, ground	1 cup coconut milk
	salt

1 In a blender mix onion, lemon juice and garlic.
2 Gradually add all the ingredients from almonds through to turmeric, introducing a little oil periodically to circulate the mixture until a smooth paste is formed. NB Do not include the lemon grass stalk if available.
3 Heat the rest of the oil in a pan and fry the spice and onion paste for a few minutes.
4 Add the meat and fry until light brown, then add the tomato and coconut milk, stirring well. Add the lemon grass stalk if available.
5 Simmer for about 1½ hours or until the meat is tender. Serve with rice.

Cumin

Cuminum cyminum
Fam Umbelliferae

SPICE DESCRIPTION
Cumin is the seed of a small umbelliferous plant. The seeds come as paired or separate carpels, and are 3–6mm (⅛–¼in) long. They have a striped pattern of nine ridges and oil canals, and are hairy, brownish in colour, boat-shaped, tapering at each extremity, with tiny stalks attached. They resemble caraway seeds, but are lighter in colour and, unlike caraway, have minute bristles hardly visible to the naked eye. They are available dried, or ground to a brownish-green powder. Cumin is freely available in the West, although it is not a traditional European spice.
Bouquet Strong, heavy and warm. A spicy-sweet aroma.
Flavour Pungent, powerful, sharp and slightly bitter.   H Scale: 3

PREPARATION AND STORAGE
The seeds should be lightly roasted before being used whole or ground to bring out the aroma. Cumin may also be pounded with other spices in mixtures such as curry powder. Ground cumin must be kept airtight, to retain its pungency. This spice

should be used with restraint – it can exclude all the other flavours in a dish. Less than a teaspoon of it will flavour a meal for four.

USES

Cumin is used mainly where highly spiced foods are preferred. It features in Indian, Eastern, Middle Eastern, Mexican. Portuguese and Spanish cookery. It is an ingredient of most curry powders and many savoury spice mixtures, and is used in stews, grills – especially lamb – and chicken dishes. It gives bite to plain rice, and to breads and cakes. Small amounts can be usefully used in aubergine and kidney bean dishes. Cumin is essential in spicy Mexican foods such as *chile con carne*, casseroled pork and *enchiladas* with chilli sauce. In Europe, cumin flavours certain Portuguese sausages, and is used to spice cheeses, especially Dutch Leyden and German Münster, and burned with woods to smoke cheeses and meats. It is a pickling ingredient for cabbage and *Sauerkraut*, and is used in chutneys. In the Middle East, it is a familiar spice for fish dishes, grills and stews and flavours *couscous* – semolina steamed over meat and vegetables, the national dish of Morocco. *Zeera pani* is a refreshing and appetising Indian drink made from cumin and tamarind water. Cumin together with caraway flavours *Kümmel*, the famous German liqueur.

CHEMICAL COMPOSITION

Cumin yields 2.5–4.5 per cent of volatile oil and about 10 per cent of a fatty fixed oil.

The light yellow volatile oil is composed mainly of cumaldehyde, known as cyminol, and includes other organic compounds such as cymene and pinene etc. Also present in the seeds are proteins, cellulose, sugars, pentosans, tannins and minerals. The seed coat contains a high proportion of tannin and some ash.

ATTRIBUTED PROPERTIES

Cumin is stomachic, diuretic, carminative, stimulant, astringent, emmenagogic and antispasmodic. It is valuable in dyspepsia, diarrhoea and hoarseness, and may relieve flatulence and colic. In the West, it is now used mainly in veterinary medicine, as a carminative, but it remains a traditional herbal remedy in the East. It is supposed to increase lactation and reduce nausea in pregnancy. Used in a poultice, it relieves swelling of the breast or the testicles. Smoked in a pipe with *ghee*, it is taken to relieve the hiccups. Cumin stimulates the appetite.

PLANT DESCRIPTION

A small, slender, glabrous herbaceous annual, of the parsley family. It usually reaches 25cm (10in) (some varieties can be double this height), and tends to droop under its own weight. The blue-green linear leaves are finely divided, and the white or pink flowers are borne in small compound umbels. The fruits are schizocarpic and are the 'seeds' of culinary use.

CULTIVATION

Cumin is grown from seed. A hot climate is preferred, but it can be grown in cooler regions if started under glass in spring. A sandy soil is best; when the seedlings have hardened, transplant carefully to a sunny aspect, planting out 15cm (6in) apart. Weed regularly. The plants bloom in June and July. The seeds are normally ready four months after planting. Cut the plants when the seeds turn to brown, thresh and dry like the other Umbelliferae.

Cumin is native to the Levant and Upper Egypt. It now grows in most hot countries, especially India, North Africa, China and the Americas. The spice is especially associated with Morocco, where it is often smelt in the abundant street cookery of the *medinas*. Cumin was known to the Egyptians five millennia ago; the seeds have been found in the Old Kingdom Pyramids. The Romans and the Greeks used it medicinally and cosmetically to induce a pallid complexion. In Indian recipes, cumin is frequently confused with caraway, which it resembles in appearance, though not in taste, cumin being far more powerful. This is due to a misunderstanding of the Indian word *jeera*. The term usually means cumin, but can occasionally mean caraway, so in doubtful cases, cumin is generally to be understood. The use of the terms 'black cumin' for nigella, and 'sweet cumin' for aniseed or fennel, further confounds this confusion. As a general rule interpret *jeera* or *zeera* (*jira*, *zira*) as cumin and *kalonji* as nigella. When the seeds themselves are in doubt, cumin is easily distinguished from the other Umbelliferae by its flavour, and in shape and colour is quite different from nigella. Classically, cumin symbolised greed; thus the avaricious Roman Emperor, Marcus Aurelius, came to be known privately as '*Cuminus*'.

OTHER NAMES

Anise Acre, Cumin Acre, Cummin, Sweet Cumin
French: cumin
German: Kreuzkümmel, Römische Kümmel
Italian: cumino
Spanish: comino
Arabic: kammun, kemoun
Indian: jeera, jeeraka, jira, zeera, zira sufaid . . ., safed . . . (white), kala . . . (black), kalonji (cf Nigella)
Indonesian: (d)jinten
Malay: jintan puteh
Sinhalese: cheeregum, jeera, su(du)duru
Tamil: cheeregum

Chile Con Carne (colour page 51)

The ubiquitous Texan-Mexican dish, easy to make and popular with the family.

Serves 4–6

Imp	*Metric*	*US*
4oz red kidney beans	115g	4oz
2tbsp oil	40ml	2⅔tbsp
1 onion, chopped	1	1
1 garlic clove, crushed	1	1
1lb beef, minced	455g	1lb
½lb tomatoes, chopped, fresh or tinned	225g	½lb
1 green capsicum, seeded and sliced	1	1
½pt water or liquid from tin and water	285ml	1¼ cups
1tsp chilli powder	1tsp	1tsp
1tsp cumin, ground	1tsp	1tsp
1tsp oregano, dried	1tsp	1tsp
2 bay leaves	2	2
salt to taste		
1tbsp parsley or fresh coriander, chopped	1tbsp	1⅓tbsp

One tablespoon of chilli seasoning (see Spice Mixtures) can be substituted for the garlic, chilli, cumin and oregano.

1 Soak beans overnight, then cook in plenty of water for 1 hour or until tender. BUT NOT LESS THAN 30 MINUTES BOILING.
2 Heat oil in a heavy saucepan, fry onion and garlic until soft.
3 Add mince and brown evenly.
4 Add tomatoes, capsicum, water, chilli powder, cumin, oregano, bay leaves and salt to taste.
5 Stir well and simmer uncovered for 1 hour, stirring occasionally. Twenty minutes before serving add the beans.
6 Garnish with parsley or fresh coriander and serve with plain rice and a salad.

Samosas (colour page 103)

Savoury snacks to serve with drinks or at any time.

Imp	*Metric*	*US*
Pastry		
14oz flour, plain	395g	3 cups
½tsp salt	½tsp	½tsp
2tbsp *ghee*, melted	40ml	2⅔tbsp
water, warm		

Imp	Metric	US
Filling		
2 onions, finely chopped	2	2
1 garlic clove, crushed	1	1
2tbsp oil	40ml	2⅔tbsp
¼–½tsp chilli powder	¼–½tsp	¼–½tsp
⅛tsp cloves, ground	⅛tsp	⅛tsp
1tsp coriander, ground	1tsp	1tsp
1tsp cumin, ground	1tsp	1tsp
½tsp ginger, freshly grated	½tsp	½tsp
pepper to taste		
salt to taste		
2oz peas, cooked	55g	2oz
1lb potato, cooked and diced	455g	1lb
oil for deep frying		

1 Sieve flour and salt into a basin, add *ghee* and sufficient warm water to make a stiff dough. Knead well, cover and leave to rest.
2 Fry onion and garlic until soft, add the spices and cook for one minute, stirring well.
3 Add peas and potato and cook, turning until well coated. Allow to cool.
4 Roll out dough very thinly. Cut out rectangles 9½in (25cm) by 3in (7.5cm).
5 Place 2 to 3 teaspoons of filling near the end of each pastry strip, fold over to form a triangle, as shown in the diagram. Moisten final fold with water or beaten egg to seal.
6 Heat oil and deep fry until golden brown, drain on absorbent paper and serve.

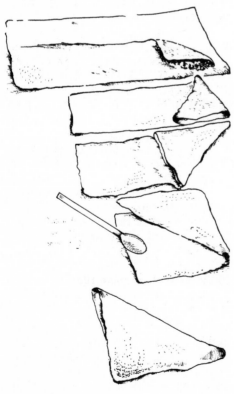

Folding of a Samosa

Curry Leaf

Murraya koenigii
syn *Chalcas k., Bergara k.*
Fam Rutaceae

SPICE DESCRIPTION
These are the leaflets of a tree that is common in southern India. They resemble bay leaves in shape but are smaller, much thinner and not at all leathery. Their colour is olive green with a paler underside and they have a delicate appearance. They vary considerably in size: 1–4cm (½–1½in) in length. When fresh they are very shiny. Curry leaves are available fresh or dried from specialist Indian shops.
Bouquet An intriguing warm fragrance with more than a hint of sweet green pepper.
Flavour Aromatic and more pronounced when the leaves are fresh.   H Scale: 1

PREPARATION AND STORAGE
Curry leaves are used whole or they can be macerated or minced before adding to stews, curries and marinades. They can be fried, and the spiced butter or fat drained off for further use. Store the leaves in airtight containers.

USES
Curry leaves are used extensively in Asian cookery rather as bay leaves are used in the West, although they do not, of course, resemble them in flavour. The leaves are added, sometimes several at a time, to

The seeds are used to make a medicinal oil called 'zimbolee oil'.

curries, especially to mildly spiced lamb dishes. They are also added to vegetables, *pilaus*, thick soups and sea food. A dish of curried crab from Sri Lanka is particularly delicious and decorative. As part of a marinade for *kebabs* they impart a most subtle flavour to the meat. Chutneys, pickles and relishes often contain the leaves. They can be finely minced or powdered and added to omelettes. They are an ingredient of curry powders and pastes particularly for Madras-style dishes. *Daun salam* (*Eugenia polyantha*), a larger but similarly flavoured leaf, features widely in the hot, spicy dishes of Indonesia. If *daun salam* is not available, substitute three or four curry leaves.

CHEMICAL COMPOSITION
The leaves contain an essential oil (0.5–0.8 per cent), fixed oil, protein, sugar, starch, cellulose, pigment and the mineral elements sodium, potassium and phosphorus. The volatile oil contains alpha and beta pinene and caryophyllene, the latter also being a constituent of allspice, clove and cinnamon. There is a decrease in the volatile oil as the leaves mature.

ATTRIBUTED PROPERTIES
Said to be tonic and stomachic. In India, the young leaves are taken for dysentery and diarrhoea. An infusion of the toasted leaves is anti-emetic. A paste of the bark and roots is applied to bruises and poisonous bites.

PLANT DESCRIPTION
A small tropical tree of the citrus family with reddish-brown wood. The leaflets are slightly serrated, arranged alternately on the stalks. The plant bears small clusters of ovoid berries which turn purplish-black when ripe. The flowers are white and fragrant.

CULTIVATION
The curry leaf tree is only grown in the tropics and sub-tropics. It is not cultivated commercially but is either in the wild state or grown in domestic gardens like an orange tree. It can be used as rootstock for citrus.

REMARKS
The curry leaf tree is native to Sri Lanka and India and is widely cultivated in domestic gardens in southern India. Sometimes it is confused with *Murraya paniculata*, otherwise known as the orange jasmine, mock orange, chinese boxwood or satinwood. Again it is often mistaken for *daun salam* (*Eugenia polyantha*), which is used in a similar way in Indonesia and the islands. Contrary to popular belief, curry leaf is not a regular ingredient of curry powders except Madras. The vacuum drying process produces the greenest curry leaf.

OTHER NAMES
Curry Pak, Nim, Nim Leaf, Sweet Nim Leaves
French: feuille de cari
German: Curryblatt
Italian: foglia di curry
Spanish: hoja de cari
Burmese: pyi-naw-thein
Indian: kadhinim(b), karipatta, kari phulia, katnim, kitha neem, meetha nim, misht nim, mitha neem, patta(r)
Indonesian: daun sala(a)m
Malay: daun kari, karupillay
Sinhalese: karapincha
Tamil: karuvepila

Crab Curry

An impressively presented crab curry from Sri Lanka, and equally as tasty.

Serves 4–6

Imp	Metric	US
2 crabs, medium sized, cooked	2	2
1½tsp chilli powder	1½tsp	1½tsp
2in cassia bark	5cm	2in
2pt coconut milk, thin	1140ml	4¾ cups
8·curry leaves	8	8
6 garlic cloves, finely chopped	6	6
1tsp ginger, fresh, grated	1tsp	1tsp
2 onions, large, finely chopped	2	2
2tsp salt	2tsp	2tsp
1tsp turmeric, ground	1tsp	1tsp
1tbsp coconut, desiccated, dry-fried to golden	1tbsp	1tbsp
1tbsp rice, ground, dry-fried to golden	1tbsp	1⅓tbsp
1pt coconut milk, thick	570ml	2½ cups
1tbsp tamarind, dry	1tbsp	1⅓tbsp
3tbsp water, hot	3tbsp	4tbsp

1 Remove large shells, 'dead men's fingers' and inedible parts from crabs. Detach legs but leave claws attached. Quarter body in the Chinese style by cleaving across twice, at right angles.
2 Put all ingredients from chilli to turmeric into a saucepan and simmer for ½ hour.
3 Add the crab pieces and simmer for 5 minutes.
4 Infuse the tamarind with the hot water for 5 minutes, then blend the water with the desiccated coconut, ground rice, thick coconut milk. Add to the pan.
5 Simmer for 15 minutes. Remove crab pieces and arrange on a bed of rice with the claws and legs in a wheel formation. Garnish with the curry leaves from the pan.

Dill

Anethum graveolens
syn *Peucedanum graveolens*
Fam Umbelliferae

SPICE DESCRIPTION

The part used is the 'seed' – actually a tiny fruit dividing into two carpels. The seed is dried after ripening. It is hard, light brown, winged and oval, with one side flat, the other convex. There are three ridges on the convex side and three vittae, or oil channels; the flat side bears two ridges. The seed is about 3.5mm (0.15in) long. Although dill is not greatly used in traditional English cooking it is available in most shops where spices are sold. The aromatic leafy plant tops and stalks are also used.

Bouquet Fresh, rather sweet and aromatic.

Flavour Aromatic and slightly bitter. Reminiscent of caraway.   H Scale: 1

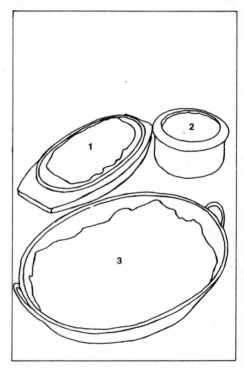

1. *Japanese Steak (page 26)*; 2. *Satay Sauce (page 59)*; 3. *Ma Ho (page 99)*

PREPARATION AND STORAGE

The seeds can be used whole or crushed. They can be ground if desired in a mill. A coffee grinder especially for spices is a good idea in a kitchen where spices are widely used. The dried seeds should keep indefinitely with airtight storage out of sunlight.

USES

The major use of dill is in pickling, when often practically the whole plant is used. American pickled cucumbers are known as 'Dill pickles' because dill is the dominant flavour. *Sauerkraut* and cauliflower pickle also contain the spice. 'Dill vinegar' contains only the seeds. It is very popular in Russia and Scandinavia and may feature there in *courts-bouillons* and sauces for fish, in pickled salmon, in chicken or lamb casseroles, certain soups where herbs are dominant and with braised cucumber. The French use a sprinkling on cakes and breads, but dill is particularly delicious in rye bread used in the same way as caraway. It is occasionally included in fennel and gooseberry sauce and goes well with yoghurt and sour cream. Sometimes it occurs in American apple pie. Both seeds and leaves are used in Sri Lankan cookery, mostly in fish and minced meat dishes. The immature flower heads are eaten in salads. Dill may be used as a substitute for fennel although its flavour is more delicate.

CHEMICAL COMPOSITION

Dill seeds contain about 3.5 per cent essential oil, of which 40–60 per cent is carvone, the active principle. Some limonene is also present. *Sowa*, or Indian dill, yields an oil containing about 20 per cent carvone, and apiol.

ATTRIBUTED PROPERTIES

Carminative, stimulant, stomachic. Dill water is given as a digestive to children. It eases stomach upsets and is said to be a cure for hiccups. 'The wonder-working Dill . . . Which curious women use in many a nice disease' (Drayton, *Polyolbion*, 1612).

PLANT DESCRIPTION

An erect hardy annual of the parsley family. The leaves are thin, wispy and fern like. The glossy stem is usually single,

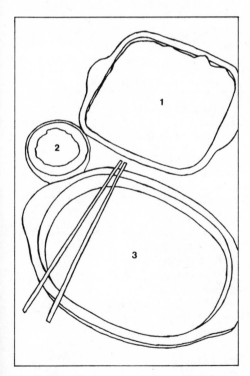

1. Lamb Gulé (page 79); 2. Coconut Sambal (page 74); 3. Fish in Soy Sauce (page 97)

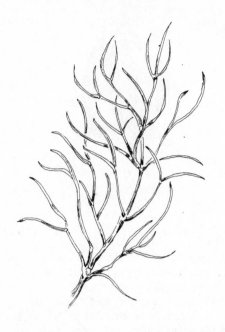

Anethum sowa is the botanical name of Indian dill (Japanese dill). The plant is thinner and paler than the European variety. Sowa oil is used to perfume soaps. 'Dill Pickles' is the name of a classic ragtime composition by Scott Joplin.

OTHER NAMES
Dill Fruit, Dill Seed, Dilly, Garden Dill
French: aneth
German: Dill
Italian: aneto
Spanish: éneldo
Indian: surva (Indian Dill)
Lao: phak si
Sinhalese: enduru

Dill Pickle (colour page 190)
Another arrangement for the spices is given under Pickling Spice – see Spice Mixtures.

Makes 3 1lb (½kg) jars

Imp	Metric	US
2lb ridge cucumbers	1kg	2lb
salt		
1pt water	570ml	2½ cups
½pt white vinegar	285ml	1¼ cups
1tbsp salt	1tbsp	1⅓tbsp
1tbsp sugar	1tbsp	1⅓tbsp
3 dillweed, fresh sprigs	3	3
1tsp dill seeds	1tsp	1tsp
3 chillies, small, whole	3	3
3 cloves	3	3
1tsp mustard seeds	1tsp	1tsp

1 Wash cucumbers well. Layer in bowl and sprinkle with salt. They may be quartered longitudinally if preferred before salting. Cover and keep overnight.
2 Dry cucumbers well and pack in three 1lb (½kg) jars.
3 Add 1 sprig dillweed, 1 chilli, 1 clove, ⅓ teaspoon dill seeds and ⅓ teaspoon mustard seeds to each jar.
4 Boil vinegar, water and salt. Pour into jars to cover cucumbers.
5 Allow to cool then seal.

Sauerkraut
Fermented cabbage greatly regarded in Germany, especially as an accompaniment to smoked meats and pork dishes. It takes

reaching up to 1m (3ft). Yellow flowers are borne in umbels.

CULTIVATION
Dill is not always easy to grow and it prefers a sunny aspect. Any soil will do, but transplanting is not advisable. Sow in spring, in drills 25cm (10in) apart. Thin out and weed often. Harvest two months later. Thresh and dry seeds. The plant flowers in July to August. Do not grow dill near fennel as it may be difficult to distinguish between them.

REMARKS
Possibly native to southern Europe or Asia, dill grows wild in the warmer parts of the northern hemisphere. It was known as a medicinal herb to the Greeks and Romans and mentioned by the voluminous Pliny. Medieval Europe used it as a magic herb, both for and against witchcraft. 'Therewith her Veruayne and her Dill, That hindreth Witches of their will' (Drayton, *Nymphidia*, 1627). It was common in seventeenth century England in sauces and pickles but is not now so widely used in Britain as it is in Germany, Scandinavia, Russia and Turkey.

over 3 weeks in preparation and you will need about 1oz (30g) salt to every 1lb (455g) cabbage.

Imp/Metric/US
cabbages, large white
rock salt
dill seeds or whole dill heads
juniper berries

Preparation
1 Wash cabbage, discarding outer leaves. Quarter, cut out heavy stalk. Reserve a few outer leaves.
2 Finely shred cabbage.
3 Line a crock with a few leaves and then fill with layers of shredded cabbage, sprinkling salt and a few dill seeds and juniper berries as you go.
4 Cover with a layer of cabbage leaves and press down. Sprinkle surface with salt.
5 Spread a damp cloth over the top, cover with a lid or board (slightly smaller than the crock) and weight down.
6 Keep in a warm place until fermentation starts – water and bubbles will rise to the top of the cabbage. Remove to a cooler place and agitate with a wooden spoon every few days, draining off any water above lid.
7 Replace cloth and top layer of cabbage leaves after 2 weeks.
8 *Sauerkraut* will be ready in 3 to 4 weeks.
9 Drain and it will now keep for up to a year.

Cooking
1 Drain, transfer to pan of boiling water and cook slowly for 1–2 hours.
2 Add a little salt and pepper and a few caraway seeds.
3 Serve with Frankfurters, bacon, ham, pork knuckle etc.

Fennel

Foeniculum vulgare
Fam Umbelliferae

SPICE DESCRIPTION
Fennel yields both a herb and a spice. The spice comes from the dried seeds. The seeds split into two, one sometimes retaining the stalk. They are 4–8mm (⅛–⁵⁄₁₆in) long, thin and curved. The colour varies from light green to brown, the green being regarded as superior. There are five longitudinal ridges with deepish furrows, giving the appearance of stripes. Fennel is available ground, but best bought whole. It is common and readily found in the West.
Bouquet Warm, sweet and aromatic.
Flavour Resembles a mild anise, although less sweet.   H Scale: 1

PREPARATION AND STORAGE
Grind seeds in a spice mill or pestle and mortar and store in airtight containers away from light.

USES
As a herb, fennel leaves are used in French and Italian cookery, most commonly in sauces for fish, stuffings, and in mayonnaises. Fennel has a special affinity with fish and the dried stalks can be used as a bed for grilled fish or the seeds scattered sparingly on to bass, red mullet or sardines while barbecuing; it also adds a subtle flavour to creamed fish soup. Fennel is a popular flavouring with pork in Italy. The seed is not so widely used, but like many other seeds, it flavours breads and cakes, puddings, pastries and confectionery. It is an ingredient of Chinese Five Spices, sweet pickling spice and of certain curry powders, especially those of Sri Lanka. In India it is an ingredient of *mukhwas*, a 'chew' to aid digestion and sweeten the breath. Spicy Italian sausages, both sweet and sharp, contain the seed, especially the Florentine salami *finocchiona*. It can be

used in meat loaves, in pickled shrimps, and with mushrooms. In Italy it is used to impart a special flavour to dried figs. Several alcoholic drinks are flavoured with fennel, such as *fenouillette*, gin, *akvavit* and, formerly, *absinthe*. A fennel tea – one teaspoon seeds to half pint of water infused – is a warming and refreshing drink.

CHEMICAL COMPOSITION

Fennel contains 2–4 per cent essential oil, the main ingredients of which are anethole, 50–60 per cent (the active ingredient of anise), and fenchone, 10 per cent. Also present are pinene and six other organic compounds. Fennel also contains 10 per cent of a fixed oil plus protein, starch, cellulose and mineral elements.

ATTRIBUTED PROPERTIES

Stimulative, stomachic and carminative. It is used in 'gripe water' given to flatulent children, and is an ingredient of 'Compound Liquorice Powder'. It appears to help in chronic coughs. In India many properties are attributed to it, including aphrodisiac, digestive, emmenagogic and galactagogic. The oil is used against hookworms. Anethole, the main constituent of the oil, has demonstrated antimicrobial activity. Fennel should not be used in high doses as it causes muscular spasms and hallucinations.

PLANT DESCRIPTION

A hardy, aromatic perennial related to parsley, reaching 1.5–2.5m (5–8ft). It has small yellow flowers in umbels and a mass of green thread-like leaves. Florence fennel, *finnochio*, (*F.v. dulce*) has a bulbous stem which is used as a vegetable, otherwise the plant is similar to common fennel.

CULTIVATION

Aspect: Sunny
Soil: Any well drained, but prefers rich and chalky
Sow in April in drills 40cm (15in) apart, then thin out. Flowers in July and August. Harvesting is carried out in September or

October before the seeds are ripe. Collect the flower heads and lay out on paper, indoors, to dry. Turn them over often as a mould may develop. When completely dry thresh out the seeds. The plant is long lasting if it is kept out of flower.

REMARKS

Fennel is native to the Mediterranean. It is an ancient and common plant, known to the ancient Greeks and spread by Imperial Rome throughout Europe, where it is still widespread. It is also grown in India (a big exporter of the seed), the Orient, and has become naturalised in the United States, especially California, Australasia and South America. Roman and medieval medical writers believed fennel to promote or restore good vision. Renaissance Europe thought it a cure for obesity. Eastern Europe and Russia prefer the bitter variety which is wild or 'escaped', while sweet fennel is more commonly grown in the West. Fennel is also used to scent soaps and perfumes, to flavour candies, and as a cattle condiment, whence the name from *foenum*, Latin for 'hay'. Common varieties are *F.v. dulce*, *F.v. sativum*, *F.v. piperitum* and *F.v. azoricum*.

Common Fennel, Large Fennel (US),
Sweet Fennel (US), Wild Fennel, (US),
King Cumin, Large Cumin, Sweet Cumin
French: anet douce (Florence fennel),
fenouil
German: Fenchel
Greek: márathon
Italian: finocchio
Spanish: hinojo
Burmese: samouk-saba
Chinese: wooi heung
Indian: barisaunf, madhurika, sonf
Indonesian: adas
Malaysian: jintan manis
Sinhalese: maduru
Thai: yira (or cumin)

Grilled Bass (colour page 156)
The fish should ideally be grilled over a
charcoal fire but it is quite satisfactory
under an ordinary grill.   Serves 1 each

Imp/Metric/US
sea bass or red mullet
oil
pepper
salt
fennel stalks, dried
fennel seeds

1 Scale and clean bass but leave the mullet
  uncleaned.
2 Score the fish diagonally two or three
  times on each side, brush with oil and
  season with salt and pepper.
3 Brush double sided grill or grill pan
  with oil and lay on a few fennel stalks.
4 Place the fish on top and grill quite
  gently until cooked, turning once and
  brushing with a little oil from time to
  time.
5 Serve immediately with bread and
  butter and wedges of lemon.

Fish Soup
A subtly flavoured white fish soup.

Serves 4

Imp	*Metric*	*US*
1lb fish heads and bones from your fishmonger	455g	1lb
1 bay leaf	1	1
½tsp fennel seeds, well bruised	½tsp	½tsp
½ onion, sliced	½	½
2–3 parsley stalks	2–3	2–3
6 peppercorns	6	6
½tsp salt	½tsp	½tsp
1lb cod or haddock fillets	455g	1lb
¾pt milk	425ml	1¾ cups
¼pt cream, single	140ml	9½tbsp
2 egg yolks	2	2
fresh fennel or chives		

1 Put the fish trimmings in a saucepan,
  add bay leaf, fennel seeds, onion,
  parsley stalks, peppercorns and salt.
2 Cover with water and simmer with the
  lid on for 30 minutes. Strain and reserve
  liquid.
3 Poach the fish in the milk and ½pt of
  fish stock for 10 minutes.
4 Pass all through a sieve or use an electric
  blender then return to the pan.
5 Beat egg yolks and cream together and
  gradually add to the hot soup stirring
  constantly. Do not allow to boil.
6 Serve sprinkled with chopped fennel or
  chives.

Fenugreek

Trigonella foenum-graecum
Fam Leguminosae

SPICE DESCRIPTION
Fenugreek is the small stony seeds from the pod of a bean-like plant. The seeds are hard, yellowish brown and angular. Some are oblong, some rhombic, others virtually cubic, with a side of about 3mm (⅛in). A deep furrow all but splits them in two. They are available whole and dried, or as a dull yellow powder, ground from roasted seeds. This powder is a common household spice and easily available.

Bouquet Warm and penetrating, becoming more pronounced when the seeds are roasted. Ground, they give off a 'spicy' smell, pungent, like an inferior curry powder which would probably contain too much fenugreek.

Flavour Powerful, aromatic and bittersweet, like burnt sugar. There is a bitter aftertaste, similar to celery or lovage.

H Scale: 2

Fenugreek leaves are also available fresh or dried. The dried variety is a mass of

crushed grey-green leaves and thin stalks.
Bouquet Similar to the ground seed.
Flavour Milder than the seeds.

H Scale: 1

PREPARATION AND STORAGE
Dried seeds should be lightly roasted because, if this is overdone, they will be merely bitter, so do not let them darken to more than a golden brown. After roasting, they are quite easy to grind. A small amount will complement other spices and flavours; too much will overpower the dish. If the seeds are required as part of curry paste, soak them overnight when they will swell, become gelatinous and be easy to incorporate with the other ingredients.

USES
The major use of fenugreek is in curry powders, figuring in many mixtures, especially *vindaloo* and the hot curries of Sri Lanka. It is an ingredient of *Panch Phora* – see Spice Mixtures. In home-made powders, the amount used can be controlled, but in cheap bought powders it often overpowers. When fish is curried, particularly strong-tasting fish such as tuna and mackerel, more often than not fenugreek is included in the spice mixture. Many chutneys and pickles incorporate it, and it gives a tangy aroma to vegetables. The leaves, both fresh and dried, are used in meat curries, *dhal* and vegetable dishes and chutneys. The young sprouts make a good home-grown salad similar to bean sprouts. The seeds are an ingredient of the Middle Eastern confection *halva*. Flour mixed with ground fenugreek makes a spicy bread. In India the roasted ground seeds are infused for a coffee substitute or adulterant. A tea can be made by infusing a teaspoon of seeds in a pint of boiling water for five minutes.

CHEMICAL COMPOSITION
Fenugreek is a complex substance which has not yet been fully analysed. It is believed to contain about 30 per cent mucilage, up to 7 per cent fixed oil with some bitter constituents, a minute

quantity, 0.02 per cent, of a brown volatile oil that has a very strong odour, the alkaloids trigonelline and choline, lecithin, saponins, flavones, phytosterols, plus resin, protein, carbohydrates, cellulose, minerals and a yellow colouring substance. Modern researchers have named fenugreek as a possible source of diosgenin, a substance used in the manufacture of oral contraceptives.

ATTRIBUTED PROPERTIES

Fenugreek is a digestive aid. As an emollient it is used in poultices for boils, cysts and similar complaints. It is also a febrifuge, diuretic and galactagogue. Reducing the sugar level of the blood, it is used in diabetes in conjunction with insulin. As early as 1030, the great Arabian philosopher and physician, Abu Ali al-Husam ibn Abdullah ibn Sina (Avicenna), was prescribing fenugreek for diabetes. It also lowers the blood pressure. In the East, beverages are made from the seed to ease stomach trouble. The chemical make-up is curiously similar to that of cod liver oil, for which a decoction of the seed is sometimes used as a substitute. It is used as a hypoglycaemic aromatic in veterinary medicine. Many other properties are ascribed to it in India and the East and not surprisingly include aphrodisiac.

PLANT DESCRIPTION

An erect hairy annual of the bean family, reaching 30–60cm (1–2ft). The long slender stems bear tripartite, toothed, grey-green obovate leaves, 20–25mm (¾–1in) long. The sessile axillary flowers are white or pale yellow. The root is a mass of fingery structures. The thin, sword-shaped indehiscent pods, 10–15cm (4–6in), with a curved beak-like tip, each carry 10–20 seeds. The plant radiates a spicy odour which persists on the hands after touching. Wild and cultivated varieties exist.

CULTIVATION

Mild Mediterranean climates are most suitable. Sow in spring in light, limey well drained soils in shallow drills, 25cm (10in) apart. After thinning the seedlings, the plants mature in about four months. The whole plants are then uprooted and allowed to dry. The seeds are threshed out and further dried.

REMARKS

Fenugreek is native to India and southern Europe. For centuries it has grown wild in India, the Mediterranean and North Africa, where it is mainly cultivated. A limited crop grows in France. It was used by the ancient Egyptians to combat fever, and grown in classical times as cattle fodder. Commercially, it is used in the preparation of mango chutneys and as a base for imitation maple syrup. In India it is used medicinally, and provides by extraction a yellow dyestuff. It is also an oriental cattle fodder and is planted as a soil renovator. The seeds are enjoyed by cattle, and make a good cattle condiment. Because of its high protein content it figures in proprietary, and quack, horse conditioners. In the West, fenugreek's therapeutic use is now largely confined to the treatment of animals, though historically it featured in human medicine. The name derives from the Latin 'Greek hay', illustrating its classical use as fodder.

OTHER NAMES

Bird's Foot, Foenugreek, Goat's Horn, Helbeh (Egypt), Methi (leaves)
French: fenugrec Sénegré, trigonelle
German: Bockshornklee, Griechisches Heu
Italian: fieno greco
Spanish: alholva, fenogreco
Indian: mayti, methe(e), methi
Tamil: venthium
Malay: alba
Sinhalese: uluhaal

Vindaloo (colour page 189)

The king of curries, *vindaloo*, of Portuguese origin, is very hot and well worth making.   Serves 10–12

Imp	Metric	US
1tsp cardamom seeds	1tsp	1tsp
1tbsp chilli powder or 4 whole chillies, medium, dried	1tbsp	1⅓tbsp
4 cinnamon sticks, 3in (75mm)	4	4
12 cloves, whole	12	12
1tbsp coriander seeds	1tbsp	1⅓tbsp
2tsp cumin seeds	2tsp	2tsp
2tsp fenugreek seeds	2tsp	2tsp
2tsp ginger, fresh, finely chopped	2tsp	2tsp
1tsp peppercorns, black, whole	1tsp	1tsp
2tsp salt	2tsp	2tsp
2tsp garlic cloves, finely chopped	2tsp	2tsp
2tsp mustard powder	2tsp	2tsp
2tsp turmeric powder	2tsp	2tsp
½pt vinegar, malt or wine	285ml	1¼ cups
4lb beef (or pork, lamb, chicken) cubed	1.8kg	4lb
4–6tbsp mustard oil or *ghee* (no substitutes)	80–120ml	5⅓–8tbsp
2 onions, medium, chopped	2	2
4 bay leaves, broken	4	4

1 Gently dry roast the spices from cardamom through to peppercorns for about 5 minutes on top of the stove.
2 Put in blender together with salt, garlic, mustard and turmeric and add the vinegar to form a liquid. Add water if necessary.
3 Place the meat in non-metallic bowl(s) and add the vinegar mixture. Mix well and leave to marinade for 24 hours, turning occasionally.
4 Heat *ghee* and fry onion, cumin, garlic onions until soft. Remove and keep. Now fry the meat for a few minutes, adding more oil if necessary.
5 Add the remnants of the vinegar mixture and onions and simmer until the meat is tender. Taste and add salt or more chilli if necessary.
6 Keep the curry another day, then reheat and serve with rice, side dishes, *dhal*, *chapatis*, etc.

Dhal

A spicy and nutritious accompaniment to curries.　　　　　　　　　　Serves 4–6

Imp	Metric	US
8oz lentils	455g	8oz
1½–2pt water or stock	855–1140ml	3½–4¾ cups
½tsp chilli powder	½tsp	½tsp
½tsp fenugreek leaves, dried	½tsp	½tsp
½tsp fenugreek, ground	½tsp	½tsp
½tsp salt	½tsp	½tsp
1tsp turmeric, ground	1tsp	1tsp
2–3tbsp *ghee* (clarified butter)	40–60ml	2⅔–4tbsp
1 onion	1	1
½tsp cumin, ground	½tsp	½tsp
1 garlic clove	1	1
1tsp ginger, grated	1tsp	1tsp
lemon wedges		

1 Wash lentils thoroughly, picking out foreign matter.
2 Drain and boil in 2 cups of water or stock, removing any scum.
3 Add chilli, fenugreek powder and leaves, salt and turmeric. Stir and simmer for 30–45 minutes until lentils are cooked and mushy, adding water or stock as necessary to obtain desired consistency.
4 Heat *ghee* and fry onion, cumin, garlic and ginger for a few minutes.
5 Pour oil and spices on to *dhal* on serving. Alternatively, cook the *dhal* in this for 5 minutes.
6 Serve with lemon wedges.

Galangal

Greater: *Languas galanga*
　　　　　syn *Alpinia galanga*
Lesser: *Languas officinarum*
　　　　　syn *Alpinia officinarum*
Kaempferia: *Kaempferia galanga*,
　　　　　Kaempferia pandurata,
　　　　　Kaempferia rotunda
　　　　　Fam Zingiberaceae

SPICE DESCRIPTION
The galangals are fascinating ginger-like spices used in South East Asia. It is not

always clear which is which and we can go back to Gerard (1597) for the clearest delineation between the 'Lesser' and the 'Greater'.

Greater galangal (*laos*): Used as a flavouring throughout Indonesia, Malaysia and parts of India. Orangey-brown skin with pale yellow or white interior. The rhizomes are longer than lesser galangal. Available as slices, 3mm (⅛in) thick or powder.
Bouquet   Gingery and camphorous.
Flavour   Pungent but less so than lesser galangal.   H Scale: 5

Lesser galangal (*kencur*): Used as a flavouring in Indo-China and Indonesia but not in Chinese cooking. The 8 × 2cm (3 × ¾in) rhizome has a reddish-brown skin and a red-brown interior. The texture is fibrous. Available as slices or powder.
Bouquet   Aromatic and gingery.
Flavour   Aromatic and pungent, peppery and gingerlike.   H Scale: 6

Kaempferia galangal: Used as a flavouring in South East Asia. Often identified as greater galangal. Red skin and white interior.
Bouquet   Sweet and sickly with pungent undertones.
Flavour   Like bouquet but much stronger.
                                          H Scale: 5

PREPARATION AND STORAGE
Use like ginger, powdered, bruised or crushed. One slice of the root is equivalent to half a teaspoon of powder. Generally, small quantities are specified in recipes, *laos* being used in larger amounts than *kencur*. The powders should be stored in airtight containers and used within a short space of time.

USES
The use of greater galangal is confined to local Indonesian dishes such as curries. Although known in Europe since the Middle Ages, galangal is now used only in Far Eastern cookery from Indonesia, Indo-China, Malaya, Singapore and Thailand. Like ginger, galangal is a 'de-fisher' and so appears frequently in fish and shellfish recipes often with garlic, ginger, chilli and lemon or tamarind. *Laos* powder is more important than *kencur* and, as well as with fish, is used in a wide variety of dishes such as sauces, soups, *satays* and *sambals*, chicken, meat and vegetable curries. Although used in the often searingly hot Indonesian cookery, *laos* powder enhances dishes such as chicken delicately spiced with fennel and lemon grass and gently cooked in coconut milk. However, these mild dishes are usually accompanied by vegetable or fish *sambals* fiery with chilli.
'A Cook they hadde with hem for the nones
To boille the chiknes with the Marybones
And poudre Marchant tart and galyngale',
                              Chaucer, 1386.

CHEMICAL COMPOSITION
Lesser galangal yields from 0.5–5 per cent volatile oil. A bitter resin, galangol, is the other ingredient responsible for flavour and aroma. Also present in the essential oil are the dioxyflavanol, galangin, plus traces of cadinene (an ingredient of peppermint oil), cineol, eugenol, methyl cinnamate, pinene and a sesquiterpene similar to zingiberene (the chief constituent of ginger oil). Greater galangal has a similar chemical make-up but contains a lesser proportion of the active ingredients.

ATTRIBUTED PROPERTIES
Resembling ginger in its effects, galangal is an aromatic stimulant, carminative and stomachic. It is used in nausea, flatulence, dyspepsia, rheumatism, catarrh and enteritis. It also possesses tonic and anti-bacterial qualities and is used for these properties in veterinary and homeopathic medicine. In India it is used as a body deodoriser and halitosis remedy. Both galangals have been used in Europe and Asia as an aphrodisiac for centuries. Gerard (1597) says: '. . . they conduce to venery, and heate the too cold reines [loins]'.

Greater galangal: a tropical herbaceous plant of the ginger family reaching to about 2m (6½ft). The blade-like leaves are long and wide, 50 × 9cm (18 × 3½in); the flowers are greenish white with a dark-red veined tip. The fruits are red berries. The rhizomes are orange to brown and ringed at intervals by the yellowish remnants of atrophied leaf bases.

Lesser galangal: smaller than the greater as the name implies. The leaves are long and slender, roughly half the dimensions of the greater. The whole plant, rarely more than 1m (3¼ft) high, vaguely resembles an iris. The flowers are small, white with red streaks. The rhizomes are reddish brown, about 2cm (¾in) in diameter. They are more pungent than the greater and are similarly ringed.

Kaempferia galangal: The rhizomes are reddish with a white interior. The plant is similar in appearance to lesser galangal.

CULTIVATION

Galangal is widely cultivated in South East Asia in a similar manner to ginger.

REMARKS

Greater galangal is native to Java. It is widely used in Indonesia and Malaysia as a food flavouring and spice. Lesser galangal is native to China, growing mainly on the south-east coast. It is also grown in India and the rest of South East Asia. Although little used in Europe today, both galangals were formerly imported in great quantity, as medicine and spice. Galangal was known to the ancient Indians, and has been in the West since the Middle Ages. Its stimulant and tonic properties are recognised by the Arabs, who ginger up their horses with it, and by the Tartars, who take it in tea. In the East, it is taken powdered as a snuff, and is used in perfumery and in brewing. The seeds of the galangals are used as cardamom substitutes in these regions. The old term 'galingale' may mean galangal, or 'sedge'.

OTHER NAMES

Galanga, Galengale, Galingale, Garingal
Greater: Big Galangal, Galangal Major, Java Galangal, Kaempferia, Siames Ginger
Lesser: Aromatic Ginger, China Root, Chinese Ginger, Colic Root, East India Catarrh Root, East Indian Root, Gargaut India Root, Siamese Ginger

Greater
French: grand galanga
German: Galanga
Italian: galanga
Spanish: galanga
Arabic: khalanjan
Chinese: kaoliang-chiang, ko-liang-kiang
Indian: barakalinjan, kulanjan
Indonesian: laos
Lao: kha
Malay: languas, lenguas
Thai: kha

Lesser
French: galanga de la Chine, galanga vrai petit galanga
Chinese: sa leung geung, sha geung fun
Indonesian: kencur, kentjur
Malay: kunchor, zedoary
Sinhalese: ingurupiyati
Thai: krachai

Java Chicken

A delicately flavoured Indonesian curry The coconut milks can be prepared whil the chicken is marinading.　　Serves 4–6

Imp	Metric	US
3lb chicken	1.4kg	3lb
4 brazil nuts, ground	4	4
½tsp chilli powder	½tsp	½tsp
2tsp coriander, ground	2tsp	2tsp
1tsp galangal (*laos* powder)	1tsp	1tsp
1 garlic clove, crushed	1	1
½tsp turmeric, ground	½tsp	½tsp
3tbsp oil	60ml	4tbsp
2 onions, chopped	2	2
1pt coconut milk, thin	570ml	2½ cups
2in cassia bark	50mm	2in
1 lemon grass stalk or 2 pieces lemon rind	1	1
¼pt coconut milk, thick	140ml	9½tbsp
2tbsp lemon juice	40ml	2⅔tbsp
salt		

1 Joint chicken and cut across bone into serving pieces.
2 Mix nuts, chilli, coriander, galangal, garlic and turmeric to a paste with a little oil and rub over the chicken. Leave for a few hours.
3 Heat remaining oil in a *wok* or pan and fry onions until golden. Add chicken pieces and fry until golden.
4 Gradually add thin coconut milk, stirring while bringing to the boil to prevent curdling. Add lemon grass and cassia and simmer uncovered for about 30 minutes.
5 Now add thick coconut milk, stirring well and cook for about 10 minutes or until the sauce is thick.
6 Stir in lemon juice and add salt to taste.
7 Serve with plain rice and *sambals*.

Fish in Soy Sauce (colour page 86)

Indonesian sweet and sour fish. Plain rice and a cucumber salad make a good accompaniment.   Serves 4

Imp	Metric	US
3tbsp oil	60ml	4tbsp
2 garlic cloves, chopped	2	2
1 onion, small, chopped	1	1
½tsp chilli powder	½tsp	½tsp
1tsp galangal powder	1tsp	1tsp
1½lb cod fillets cut into serving portions	680g	1½lb
2 tomatoes, skinned and chopped	2	2
3tbsp tamarind water or lemon juice	60ml	4tbsp
2tbsp soy sauce	40ml	2⅔tbsp
1tbsp sugar, dark brown	1tbsp	1⅓tbsp

1 Heat oil, fry garlic and onions until soft and golden.
2 Add chilli and galangal, stirring for a minute.
3 Now add fish and brown on both sides.
4 Add tomatoes, tamarind, soy sauce and sugar. Cover and simmer gently until the fish is cooked but still firm.
5 Place fish on serving dish and cover with the sauce.

Garlic

Allium sativum
Fam Alliaceae

SPICE DESCRIPTION
Garlic is a bulb of a lily-like plant. It is similar in shape to an onion, but ridged. The bulb is compound, consisting of anything up to twenty segments, called 'cloves'. Usually there are about ten cloves to a bulb, packed side by side around a thin central core, separated by scaly membranes and enclosed by a brittle parchment-like skin. The flesh of the clove is ivory-coloured, and should be hard and firm though easily cut with a finger nail. The cloves should be tightly packed – loose cloves are a sign of deteriorating or inferior garlic. The skin is usually white, but may have a pale pink or purplish tinge. The peeled clove should be unblemished. Garlic is widely variable in size, some Continental bulbs are minute. Garlic is best bought whole, but also available in the form of granules (minced), powder or garlic salt.
Bouquet Harsh, penetrating and lasting. The whole clove has no aroma.
Flavour Sharp and acrid. The powerful oniony flavour can easily become overpowering if used to excess.

H Scale (Raw): 5–6

PREPARATION AND STORAGE
Separate a clove from the bulb as necessary. Either peel like an onion, first slicing off the ends, or crush the clove with the flat of a knife when the skin will be much easier to remove. The garlic can then be chopped or mashed with the addition of a little salt – this will absorb the juice which would otherwise be lost and also prevent the pieces from slipping about. Although it is usually advised to use the point of a knife to mash garlic, a fork is even better. Wooden surfaces and utensils are best avoided – a stale garlic odour will cling to them. If using a garlic press, there is no need to peel the clove as the skin will remain in the press and is easily removed

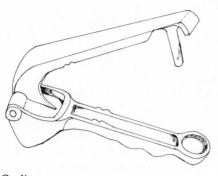

Garlic press

after use. When several cloves are to be crushed, use a pestle and mortar with a little salt. Keep heads of garlic in a cool dry atmosphere. Processed garlic must be kept in airtight containers.

USES
The uses of garlic are infinite and it is an important ingredient in the cuisine of most nations. A small amount will 'lift' dishes of meat, fish and vegetables and be virtually undetectable. *Bouquets garnis* sometimes include it. Garlic is essential in the robust cookery of the Mediterranean region. Garlic butters accompany snails, mussels and grills of fish or meat. Pasta dishes often call for sauces flavoured with garlic. French and Spanish *aïoli* and Greek *skordalia* are powerful garlic sauces. Garlic appears frequently in soups, salad dressings, pâtés, terrines, salamis and smoked spiced sausages. It is usual to include garlic in dishes of game. Joints of lamb benefit greatly by spiking the skin with slivers of garlic before roasting, few or many, according to taste. For just a hint of garlic, rub the salad bowl or cooking pot with a cut clove. A bruised garlic clove can be used to effect in a bottle of vinegar or salad dressing. Garlic is indispensable to Indian cookery and is widely used in China and South East Asia.

CHEMICAL COMPOSITION
Garlic has similar constituents to onion – protein, sugar, cellulose, minerals (phosphorus, potassium), a fixed oil, an essential oil and over 60 per cent water. The essential oil content is small, 0.1 per cent, and is made up mainly of sulphides. This sulphur element is responsible for the penetrating quality of garlic aroma and its antimicrobial properties. The chemistry of garlic is extremely complex and has only been fully developed since 1941. Like onion, the odour and pungent principles of garlic are released by the enzymatic reaction of alliinase on alliin to produce allicin only on rupture of the tissues by cutting or bruising. 'The peculiar penetrating odour of Garlic . . . is so diffusive that when the bulb is applied to the soles of the feet, its odour is exhaled by the lungs' (M. Grieve, *A Modern Herbal*, 1931). The calorific value of garlic is 137 calories per 100g.

ATTRIBUTED PROPERTIES
Garlic has been used since ancient times for innumerable complaints and amongst the properties attributed to it are: diaphoretic, diuretic, expectorant and intestinally antispasmodic. It is a good digestive aid, and used in flatulence. It stimulates blood flow and lowers blood pressure. Garlic juice in a syrup of honey and sugar is used in colds, coughs, influenza and helps to relieve asthma. Today garlic oil is often administered in gelatine capsules to obviate the unpleasantness of the odour to those susceptible to it. Formerly, garlic was used as a vampirifuge. In modern times the constituents of garlic have been shown to be bacteriostatic – in World War I the juice was extensively used on wounds; a glycoside compound has been proved to be lethal to certain organisms. In Russia allicin is so much esteemed that it is known as 'Russian penicillin'. The Japanese also favour garlic as a cure-all, and one researcher has patented a garlic spray machine that is claimed to provide beneficial therapy for a multitude of ailments. The aphrodisiac properties of garlic have been much praised; however, it is advisable that both partners take the recommended prescription.

A perennial of the lily family, grown from a bulb. The leaves are flat and lance-shaped. They are green, sometimes with a blue tinge. Flowers and bulbils are borne in umbels enclosed in long beaked leafy membranes that split on one side. The bulbils, similar in colour to the peeled cloves, are about 1cm (⅜in) in diameter; the flowers, on slim stalks, are small, white or pink but often never seen as they wither in the bud.

CULTIVATION

Garlic is common as a kitchen-garden plant. It is propagated by planting the cloves.
Soil: rich, light, well drained and manured. Plant 5cm (2in) deep, 15cm (6in) apart in autumn (or spring in cooler climes); cloves must be upright.
Aspect: Sunny. Turn soil regularly. Pick bulbs and dry in August or September, when the tops turn yellow. Dry before tying up in bundles and store in a cool dry place.

REMARKS

Garlic has been in cultivation for so long that it is impossible to determine precisely its place of origin. Possibly it is native to Asia. It is now grown in most warm lands, especially in Italy and southern France, and throughout the Mediterranean. Garlic is recorded in Egypt from the earliest times and was eaten by the builders of the Pyramids. In the Bible (Numbers 11.5) the Israelites remember the garlic eaten in Egypt. Known in Europe as 'the noblest onion', garlic was used as a medicine and a charm in classical and medieval times. According to Gerard, 'with Figge leaves and cumin it is laid on against the bitings of the Mouse'. Roman legionaries chewed it before vanquishing their barbarian foes in close combat; local opposition withered away, but the Imperial army was not popular. Garlic has grown in popularity in the United States since World War II when the American forces overseas acquired a taste for (and a resistance to) it. It is known as 'Poor Man's Treacle' – 'treacle' being an old word for an all-round nostrum. According to an Arab legend, garlic grew from the Devil's footprint as he left Eden. Culpeper, the herbalist, advises that stale garlic breath is freshened by chewing some cumin or green beans. The name derives from Old English *gar* 'spear' and *leac* 'leek'. It is said that several glasses of red wine sweeten garlicky breath. Many varieties of garlic exist. In South East Asia a small variety with only four to six cloves grows and is similar to rocambole (Spanish garlic, *Allium sativum ophioscorodon*). A giant variety is grown in California.

OTHER NAMES

Clown's Treacle, Poor Man's Treacle
French: ail, gousse d'ail (clove)
German: Knoblauch
Italian: aglio, capo d'aglio (clove)
Spanish: ajo
Arabic: toom
Burmese: chyet-thon-phew
Chinese: suen tau
Indian: lashuna, las(s)an, lassoon, lus(s)on
Indonesian: bawang puteh, b. putih
Japanese: ninniku
Malay: bawang puteh, putih
Sinhalese: sudulunu
Tamil: vellaypoondoo
Thai: krathiem

Ma Ho (colour page 85)

This colourful Thai snack is also called Galloping Horses. About 50 pieces

Imp	Metric	US
2tbsp oil	40ml	2⅔tbsp
4 garlic cloves, minced	4	4
8oz pork, minced	225g	8oz
3tbsp peanuts, coarsely ground	3tbsp	4tbsp
2tbsp sugar, dark brown	2tbsp	2⅔tbsp
2tsp oyster sauce	10ml	2tsp
½tsp black pepper	½tsp	½tsp
½tsp salt	½tsp	½tsp
6 tangerines (or equivalent kiwi, lychees or pineapple)	6	6
1tbsp coriander leaves or parsley, chopped	1tbsp	1⅓tbsp
1–2 chillies, fresh, seeded and finely sliced	1–2	1–2

1 Heat oil, fry garlic for a minute, add pork and stir until evenly brown.
2 Now add peanuts, sugar, oyster sauce, pepper and salt and cook for about 10 minutes stirring constantly. Put aside.
3 Open out the tangerine segments by cutting them down the outside and place them skin side down.
4 Put a little of the mixture on each segment and top with coriander and a slice of chilli.
5 If using kiwi fruit, skin and slice them. If lychees fill the centres, and if pineapple, cut into pieces about the size of a kiwi fruit cross-section.

Snails with Garlic Butter
(colour page 156)

Not only for snails *à la bourguignonne*, this butter is lovely with mussels, shellfish and grilled meat.   Serves 4–6

Imp	Metric	US
6oz butter, unsalted	170g	6oz
2 garlic cloves, mashed with a little salt	2	2
3tbsp parsley, finely chopped	3tbsp	4tbsp
1tbsp shallots or spring onions, finely chopped	1tbsp	1⅓tbsp
pepper		
salt		
4doz snails with shells	4doz	4doz

1 Cream butter.
2 Add garlic, parsley and shallots and mix well.
3 Season to taste and chill until required.

4 Put a knob of butter into each shell, follow with a snail and fill the shell with more butter.
5 Place the snails upright in special dishes or in a baking tray on a bed of salt. Cover with foil and bake for about 10 minutes in the oven Gas Mark 5, 375°F, 190°C.

Ginger

Zingiber officinale
syn *Amomum zingiber*
Fam Zingiberaceae

SPICE DESCRIPTION

Ginger is available in various forms, the most common of which are as follows:

Fresh or 'green' ginger: ginger is a bulbous, tuberous, irregularly shaped root. It is sold as whole rootstocks or pieces of these in various shapes and sizes, usually 5–20cm (2–8in) long. The larger pieces resemble a hand with knobbly arthritic fingers. It has a pale yellow interior and a skin varying in colour from brown to off-white. Jamaican ginger, which is pale buff, is reckoned the best variety. African and Indian ginger is darker skinned and generally inferior, with the exception of Kenya ginger.

Dried ginger: dried ginger root is sold either 'black' with the cork or root skin attached, or 'white' with the cork peeled off (an unpleasant task for those involved), and is sometimes bleached or limed to improve the colour. The dried root is available whole or sliced and is usually tough and fibrous.

Ground ginger: formerly the most common manifestation of ginger, the ground spice is a slightly fibrous buff-coloured powder made from dried ginger.

Preserved or 'stem' ginger: tender immature rhizomes are preserved by several boilings in ginger solution. The final product, in its familiar Chinese jar, consists of the ginger pieces in syrup, usually yellow-brown in colour. They are soft and pulpy like fruit, but extremely hot and spicy. A spectacular Chinese variety is bright red in a similarly coloured syrup, the ginger being thinly sliced.

Crystallised or candied ginger: this is a confection and baking ingredient. Young ginger is skinned, blanched and steeped in a sugar syrup for several days, then dried and coated in sugar. Exceedingly sweet with the characteristic ginger flavour.

Bouquet A warm, sweetish pungent aroma, Asian ginger being the most highly aromatic. When a piece of green ginger is broken, it has a lemony freshness and a strong resemblance to rosemary, whose essential oil has many of ginger's constituents.

Flavour Fiery and pungent but pleasant in moderation. Jamaican ginger is renowned as the best flavoured, Indian ginger is harsher and African even harsher still. However, Kenya ginger is of top quality.

H Scale: 7

PREPARATION AND STORAGE

In Asian cooking ginger is almost always used fresh. In this form it may be minced, crushed or sliced and is superior to ginger bought as a powder, both in flavour and in aroma. Fresh ginger can be peeled and preserved in dry sherry, or kept for about a month in the salad drawer of a refrigerator. As with many other spices it is best to buy it whole and use pieces of it as required. Ginger bought dried can be 'bruised' before use – that is, beaten strenuously to open the fibres. It can then be infused in cooking or making ginger beer and removed when the flavour has been extracted. Drying the root is best accomplished by hanging it in a dry place –

a garage or larder, for example. It should be kept dry or it will resume its growth and spoil. Store all forms of dried ginger in airtight containers.

USES

Ginger is so familiar to us as a ground spice that it is not usually realised how important it is in the East in its raw form. Fresh ginger is essential to Asian and oriental cookery but the ground dried spice is rarely used, except in curry powders. It is not exaggerating to say that fresh ginger appears in nearly every savoury dish from India to Indonesia. It is also widely used in Chinese and Japanese cookery. One of its main roles is in seafood dishes, acting as a 'de-fisher'. Again, it has a particular affinity with chicken and beef. It is also used in pickles, chutneys and curry pastes and the ground dried root is a constituent of several curry powders. When young and tender, the fresh sliced root may be eaten as a salad in the Indian style. Sometimes the roots will produce green shoots which should not be discarded: finely chopped, they are a delectable addition to a green salad. Chinese red pickled ginger is a delicious accompaniment to *satays* and a colourful garnish to many Chinese dishes. In the West, dried ginger is mainly used in cakes and biscuits, especially ginger snaps, brandy snaps and gingerbread, of which Edinburgh gingerbread is one of the best examples. Equally famous are the French *pain d'épice* and German *Pfefferkuchen*. Ginger is used also in puddings, jams and preserves, and drinks such as ginger beer, dry ginger, cordials and ginger wine. It is one of the ingredients in mixed and pickling spices. Powdered ginger is often served as an accompaniment to melon. Preserved ginger is eaten as a confection, chopped up for cakes and puddings, and sometimes is an ice cream ingredient.

CHEMICAL COMPOSITION

Ginger contains proteins, cellulose, starch, minerals, a fixed oil with gingerol, a bitter resin and 1-3 per cent volatile oil. Nineteen substances have been isolated from the essential oil including phellandrene, camphene, borneol, cineol, linalool, citral, cumene, pinene and cymene. Fresh ginger contains 80 per cent water, whilst dry ginger has up to 10 per cent moisture. The pungent principles of ginger are now recognised as being gingerols, shogaols and zingerone, in that order of pungency. Three gingerols have been identified and these on dehydration become the less pungent shogaols. The oleoresin has gingerols, shogaols plus other components of the essential oil and various polyphenolic substances and sometimes zingerone.

ATTRIBUTED PROPERTIES

Stimulant, carminative, stomachic, expectorant, rubefacient, counter-irritant. Ginger is used in diarrhoea, piles, rheumatism and lung troubles. As an infusion it is taken in coughs and nausea and apparently helps amenorrhea due to cold. It has long been ascribed aphrodisiac powers – taken either externally or internally. It is mentioned in the *Kama Sutra*, and in Melanesia it is employed 'to gain the affection of a woman'. Conversely, in the Philippines it is chewed to expel evil spirits. It opens the pores and induces perspiration.

PLANT DESCRIPTION

An erect, tropical herbaceous perennial, reed-like and closely related to the banana family, Musaceae. It reaches 30–100cm (1–3ft). The leaves are bright green, 15–20cm (6–8in) long, lance-shaped, with a prominent longitudinal rib, enclosing small yellow flowers in conical clusters. Each flower has a purple speckled lip.

CULTIVATION

Ginger is grown only in the tropics. It is propagated by dividing the rhizomes. The best soil is old forest loam, well tilled to produce good shaped rhizomes, and it should be well drained. Ginger rapidly depletes the soil so it must be well fertilised, usually with manure. The most suitable climate for ginger has about 1500mm (60in) of rainfall, a mean temperature of 21°C (70°F) and a hot dry season. Plants shoot in ten days and are harvested after nine to ten months. For preserved ginger the rhizomes are dug up earlier, when they are less fibrous.

REMARKS

Not known as a wild plant, common ginger is probably native to South East Asia and has long been cultivated in northwest India and Pakistan. It was introduced to Jamaica by the Spanish and is now also grown in Central and South America, China, Japan, Africa and Australia. It has been known since antiquity in Greece and Rome, and in India and China where it was used medicinally. It was also one of the earliest spices known in Western Europe, used since the ninth century. A common article of medieval and Renaissance trade, it was

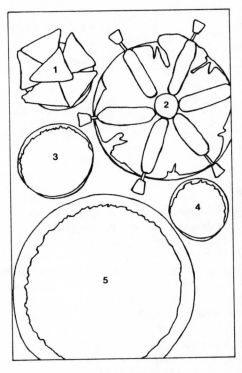

1. Samosas (page 81); 2. Sheek Kebabs (page 45); 3. Sev (page 17); 4. Tamarind Chutney (page 185); 5. Festive Pilau (page 44)

one of the spices used against the plague. In order to 'gee-up' a lazy horse, it is a time-honoured practice of Sussex farmers to apply a pinch of ginger to the animal's rear end. Ginger is usually grown on small-holdings rather than on vast estates. The root is known as a 'hand' or a 'race', Old English for root or rhizome. *Z. officinale* is the 'red' or 'common' ginger known as Jamaica Pepper or East Indian Pepper. The Japanese wild ginger, *Z. mioga*, whose rhizome is inedible, is grown for the shoots of the plant which are blanched and used in soups, *tempura*, pickles and for spicing bean curd. *Z. cassumunar*, 'Bengal root', and *Z. zerumbet* are related but different South East Asian varieties, grown as village plants and used as condiments and medicines. Wormwood is sometimes known as 'green ginger'.

OTHER NAMES
Cochin Ginger, East Indian Pepper, Jamaica Ginger, Jamaica Pepper
French: gingembre
German: Ingwer
Italian: zenzero
Spanish: jengibre
Burmese: gin
Chinese: cheung, chiang, jeung, sang keong (green)
Indian: adruk (green), ard(r)ak(h) (green), sont(h) (dried), udruk (green)
Indonesian: aliah (green), djahe, jahe
Japanese: beni(-)shoga/u (red pickled), mioga, myoga, shoga
Malay: halia (green)
Sinhalese: inguru
Tamil: ingee
Thai: k(h)ing (green)

Lions' Heads – Chinese Meatballs (colour page 52)

These delicately spiced meatballs with Chinese cabbage are said to resemble a lion's head with mane.   Serves 4–6

Imp	Metric	US
1½lb pork, minced	680g	1½lb
3tsp ginger, fresh, minced	3tsp	3tsp
3 spring onions, finely chopped	3	3
1 garlic clove, minced	1	1
6 water chestnuts (tinned), finely chopped	6	6
1tbsp sherry, dry	20ml	1⅓tbsp
2tbsp soy sauce	40ml	2⅔tbsp
1tsp sugar	1tsp	1tsp
2tsp cornflour	2tsp	2tsp
4tbsp oil	80ml	5⅓tbsp
1lb Chinese cabbage, cut into 1in slices	455g	1lb
½pt chicken stock, hot	285ml	1¼ cups

1 Mix meat well with garlic, ginger, onion and water chestnuts.
2 Then blend in sherry, soy sauce, sugar and cornflour.
3 Divide the mixture into ten and shape into balls.
4 Heat 2 tablespoons of oil in a pan, brown the meatballs all over and put them aside.
5 Heat the rest of the oil in a casserole,

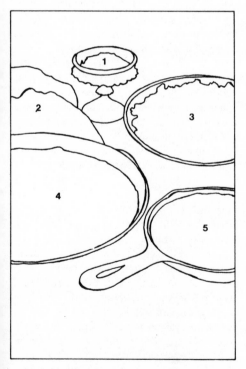

1. Pan (page 214); 2. Naan Bread (page 134); 3. Lobhia (page 134); 4. Prawn Molee (page 74); 5. Yoghurt with Coriander (page 75)

add the cabbage and cook for a minute, stirring constantly.

6 Place the meatballs on top of the cabbage, add stock, cover and simmer for 15–20 minutes.
7 Serve with noodles.

Gingerbread (colour page 137)

A traditional gingerbread using both ground and stem ginger. Makes 2 loaves.

Imp	Metric	US
8oz flour, plain	225g	8oz
⅛tsp salt	⅛tsp	⅛tsp
1tsp bicarbonate of soda	1tsp	1tsp
1tsp cinnamon, ground	1tsp	1tsp
2tsp ginger, ground	2tsp	2tsp
3oz fat, white cooking	85g	3oz
4oz sugar, soft brown	115g	4oz
8oz treacle, black	225g	8oz
2 eggs	2	2
2–3tbsp milk	40–60ml	2⅔–4tbsp
4oz ginger, stem, chopped	115g	4oz
3oz walnuts, chopped	85g	3oz
2 standard loaf tins, buttered and lined with greaseproof paper	2	2

1 Sift flour, salt, bicarbonate of soda, cinnamon and ground ginger together into a mixing basin.
2 Put fat, sugar and treacle in a saucepan and melt over low heat. Stir until blended and remove pan from heat. Cool until hand can be held comfortably against the side of the pan.
3 Now add eggs and enough milk to form a dropping consistency. Mix well together and pour into the middle of sifted ingredients. Beat until smooth.
4 Stir in stem ginger and 2oz (55g) of walnuts and pour into tins. Sprinkle with remaining nuts and bake in the centre of the oven Gas Mark 4, 350°F, 180°C, for 30 minutes until the gingerbread is risen and firm. Cool in the tins.

Horseradish

Armoracia rusticana
syn *Cochlearia armoracia, Armoracia lapathifolia*
Fam Cruciferae

SPICE DESCRIPTION
Horseradish is a cylindrical white root with a yellowish brown skin, on average 30cm (1ft) long and 2cm (¾in) in diameter. It is slightly gnarled or ringed, often with small fibrous roots growing from the main root, especially in semi-wild horseradish; in cultivated varieties the root is unbranched and fairly straight. Horseradish is sold fresh, but is more often available grated. Dried, flaked and powdered horseradish is also sold and this retains its pungency more fully than the grated form which is stored in vinegar. The best fresh roots are thick and well grown; thin and insubstantial roots, apart from being hard to use, are inferior in pungency. Japanese horseradish, or *wasabi*, is a pale green powder, similar in flavour to horseradish but made from the tuber of a herb, *Wasabia japonica*.
Bouquet When intact, the root has little aroma. On being scraped or broken, it exudes a penetrating smell, similar to watercress, and is apt to irritate the nostrils, making the eyes stream even more than onions do.
Flavour Similar to watercress, but hotter and sharper, with a sweetish undertone.
H Scale: 5–7

PREPARATION AND STORAGE
Fresh horseradish can be grated at home quite easily but the root should first be trimmed and scrubbed or scraped under running water to remove any traces of soil. Not much flavour lies in the central core, which is difficult to grate, and should be discarded. The whole root can be kept in the salad drawer of a refrigerator for a few weeks. Grated horseradish may be kept in white vinegar or successfully frozen in a sealed container and used as required. Powdered horseradish is reconstituted by mixing with water but, like powdered

mustard, remember to allow time for the full flavour to develop.

USES

The main use is in horseradish sauce. This is made most simply by mixing the grated root with sugar and vinegar to the desired consistency. However, cream, sour cream or wine is also a common base for this traditional English sauce to accompany roast beef; sometimes spices such as garlic, mustard and pepper are added. 'His prejudices as a gentleman and a scholar were offended by the absence of horse-radish' (Besant and Rice, *The Chaplain of the Fleet*, 1881).

Albert sauce is a classic accompaniment to boiled or braised beef and is served hot. As a sauce, horseradish also complements tongue, sausages, cold egg dishes, cheese, chicken and hot ham. It is good with fish and nowadays is always served with smoked trout. Mixed with yoghurt it is a piquant topping to baked potatoes. Horse-radish's popularity is evident in recipes from Eastern Europe, Germany, Austria and Scandinavia, for sauces, soups and cream cheeses. It has a particular affinity with apple, beetroot and dill. Horseradish butter is excellent with grilled fish and meat. In America, horseradish is a favourite flavouring in party dips. With grated apple it makes a sharp dressing for fish, and in tomato-based sauces it flavours seafood such as prawns. When served hot, horseradish loses its pungency and is quite mild. *Wasabi* is used in Japanese cookery in the fillings for *sushi* and as a dipping sauce to accompany raw fish. It is mixed to a paste in the same way as mustard and used similarly as a condiment.

CHEMICAL COMPOSITION

Similar to the chemistry of black mustard, horseradish root contains the glucoside sinigrin and the enzyme myrosin, which react with water to form a volatile oil containing allyl-isothiocyanate and two other isothiocyanates. Also present in raw horseradish are protein 3 per cent, fat 0.3 per cent, carbohydrate 20 per cent, calcium, phosphorus, potassium, other sulphurous compounds and vitamin C (ascorbic acid). There are 87 calories per 100g.

ATTRIBUTED PROPERTIES

Stimulant, diuretic, diaphoretic, rubefacient and antiseptic. Being a gastric stimulant, it is good with rich or fatty indigestible foods. In dropsy, it benefits the system by correcting imbalances in the digestive organs. Bruised horseradish was once used to soothe rheumatism, gout, swellings and chilblains. Infused in wine it becomes a general stimulant and causes perspiration. It is believed to be a good vermifuge for children. It is also expectorant, and emetic if taken to excess. It is richer in vitamin C than orange or lemon. The volatiles in horseradish have been shown to be antimicrobial against some organisms.

PLANT DESCRIPTION

A hardy perennial of the mustard family, reaching 60cm (2ft) in height. Large, docklike green leaves grow at ground level and its light green stalks bear small sessile leaves. Small white flowers are borne in racemes, and small angular pods develop when the plant is ready to reproduce. The plant rarely flowers; when it does, it does so in July.

CULTIVATION

A hardy perennial with a notorious propensity for revival and multiplication – so keep isolated.
Soil: rich, manured.
Aspect: Sunny.
Propagate in March from 20cm (8in) or more root sections ('thongs') planted erect under the soil, 30cm (1ft) apart. Remove all the side shoots from the root and rub it to prevent multiple crowning and branching. Repeat operation after six weeks. Harvest in October. The tubers can be stored in sand for the winter. Replant after two seasons, cleaning out all traces of root.

Horseradish probably originated somewhere in south-eastern Europe. It now grows also in northern Europe, Britain and the United States. It thrives in temperate rather than warm zones. It was reported growing wild in England in the sixteenth century, and has long been wild in the United States. Because of its hardy and prolific nature, it thrives beyond cultivation, growing if the minutest root particle is left in the soil, and has become a horticultural pest. The root and leaves were formerly used only medicinally, but soon after the Middle Ages it began to be used as a spice and condiment in Scandinavia and the Germanic states. Contemporary English reports viewed this with restrained alarm, in much the same way as the consumption of raw garlic is viewed today. However, during the seventeenth century, its use started to spread throughout northern Europe, though it is still largely absent from southern European cuisines. Horseradish only becomes pungent when broken or bruised because the active ingredients myrosin and sinigrin, inert until mixed, are locked apart in separate cells in the intact root. Each year several tons of horseradish are imported to Britain where the enzyme is extracted and exported to the United States for medical research. There is some confusion over the taxonomic classification of horseradish. Some authorities call it *Armoracia rusticana*, others *Cochlearia armoracia* or *Armoracia lapathifolia*. The first now appears to be the accepted form. In India grows the horseradish tree, *Moringa oleifera*, whose roots are said to be used similarly to horseradish; the rest of the plant is used extensively in herbal remedies and the seed oil, known as 'Ben oil', in perfumery and cosmetics and as a lighting fuel. Japanese horseradish, *wasabi* (*Wasabia japonica matsumura*, syn. *Eutrema wasabi*), is ubiquitous in that country despite the complex methods of cultivation required. It is usually grown on rockery beds in running water out of reach of direct sunlight.

Great Raifort, Horse Plant, Mountain Radish, Red cole
French: moutarde des Allemands, raifort
German: Meerrettich
Italian: rafano
Spanish: rábano picante

Horseradish Sauces

A miscellany of uses for horseradish.

Cold horseradish sauce

Imp	Metric	US
2tsp caster sugar	2tsp	2tsp
2tbsp horseradish, grated	2tbsp	2⅔tbsp
½tsp mustard powder	½tsp	½tsp
squeeze lemon juice	squeeze	squeeze
salt and pepper to taste		
2tsp vinegar	2tsp	2tsp
¼pt double cream	140ml	9½tbsp

1 Mix all ingredients except cream.
2 Whip the cream and fold in the mixture. Serve with fish, smoked trout especially, and cold tongue.

Hot horseradish sauce

1 Make ½pt (285ml) of *béchamel* sauce and add the cold horseradish sauce made with only one eighth the quantity of cream.
2 Serve hot with boiled beef.

Horseradish butter

1 Mix 3 parts grated fresh horseradish with 8 parts creamed butter.
2 Chill, shape and use to garnish steaks, grills etc.

Horseradish dip (colour page 155)

Imp	Metric	US
2tsp horseradish powder	2tsp	2tsp
¼pt yoghurt	140ml	9½tbsp
optional chives, finely chopped		

1 Mix horseradish powder and yoghurt; sprinkle with chives if desired.
2 Serve as a dip with *crudités* or as a topping for baked potatoes.

Horseradish relish

1 Mix horseradish powder with water to a mustard-like paste.
2 Serve with beef.

Juniper

Juniperus communis
Fam Cupressaceae

SPICE DESCRIPTION

Juniper berries are the fruit of a small tree widespread throughout Europe. The berries are fleshy and globular, measuring 7–10mm (¼–⅓in) in diameter. They contain three sticky, brown irregular-shaped seeds. The fruits should be used when ripe, that is, after the skin has turned blue. On drying and storing, the smooth shiny skin darkens to a purple black and becomes slightly wrinkled or indented. The unripe fruit is green. The interior flesh of the mature berry is brown-yellow and the brown seeds are crunchy but not hard. Juniper grows wild in Great Britain and the United States. In the country it can be freely picked, although caution is advisable due to the hostile spikes on the plant. 'Sweet is the Iunipere, but sharpe his bough' (Spenser, *Amoretti* 1594). Most commercial supplies are imported from southern Europe.

Bouquet Fragrant and flowery, combining the aromas of gin and turpentine.

Flavour Aromatic, bittersweet and piny. Eaten raw, they may make the breath redolent of gin.   H Scale: 1

PREPARATION AND STORAGE

It is possible to make a purée from these berries or to extract the flavour and aroma by macerating them in hot water, but as all parts are edible and the texture is agreeable, it is usually just as well to use the entire fruit, split or crushed. The berries are quite powerful, one heaped teaspoon of crushed fruits serving for a dish for four people.

USES

The strong hearty flavour of juniper goes well with strong meats, such as game. It will flavour a stuffing suitable for small birds such as the wild birds eaten in Europe, wood pigeon, or small chickens. Venison, rabbit and wild boar profit from a suggestion of it. Other meats may be enlivened – such as pork chops, joints of bacon, roast leg of lamb and veal. It can effectively be added to wine marinades for meats, and with coriander is used in smoking meat. It seasons pâtés and sauces and in Sweden is used in a preserve. Goulash and *Sauerkraut* often feature a juniper taste, as do some home-pickled meats like salt beef, salt pork and ham. The cure for the famous 'York ham' includes juniper and there is a kosher salami made from beef flavoured with garlic, mustard and juniper. Generally juniper can well be used in any dish requiring alcohol. Fruit dishes, such as apple tart and pickled peaches, also harmonise with this flavour. In Norway the traditional cheese from Viking times, *Gammelost* ('old cheese') is matured in straw soaked with juniper berry juice.

CHEMICAL COMPOSITION

Juniper berries yield 0.5–2.0 per cent of a volatile essential oil. This yellow-green substance includes terpenes. Some 10 per cent of resins are present. There is also about 30 per cent of invert sugars, some salts, wax, gum and phytonicides. The bitter principle is juniperin.

ATTRIBUTED PROPERTIES

Medicinal preparations involving juniper use the green unripe berries, whose properties are more pronounced than those of the ripe fruits. Juniper is diuretic, stimulant, stomachic and carminative and is used in flatulence and colic. It was once believed to promote a healthy circulation of the blood and help combat rheumatism; in effect a grand panacea. Juniper oil is to be avoided in complaints of the genito-urinary tract as it is an irritant and may cause contraction of the uterus. It should not be given in pregnancy. Large doses of juniper cause the urine to smell of violets. Being disinfectant and insectifugal, the berries are used in veterinary medicine to treat open wounds.

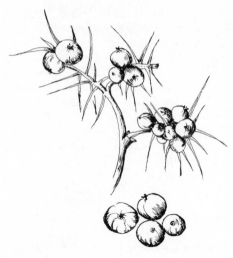

PLANT DESCRIPTION

An evergreen, dioecious coniferous tree of the cypress family. The plant grows wild throughout the northern hemisphere. In Britain, juniper generally reaches about 2m (6ft) in height and is more like a shrub, but in Scandinavia it can reach 10m (33ft). The leaves are dull green needles, very sharp, arranged in groups of three. The male flowers are yellow and conical, the female green and rounded.

CULTIVATION

Aspect: Sunny.
Soil: Lime, chalk or flint.
The fruits are green throughout the first two years. Thereafter they ripen every two years, and at different times. Harvest from September to October and the berries must be dried below 35°C (95°F) to retain the essential oil.

REMARKS

Juniper is widely distributed throughout the northern hemisphere and its birthplace is obscure. It is found in Europe, North Africa, the United States and northern Asia. The main producers are Hungary and southern Europe, especially Italy. The berries were known to Greek, Roman and early Arab physicians as a medicinal fruit and are mentioned in the Bible. In the Renaissance, they were recommended against snake bite, and plague and pestilence. The fruit becomes more potent the further south it grows: Scandinavian juniper is weak compared with the Italian varieties. When picking the berries, gloves should be worn against the sharp spikes which protect the plant. The fruit is found in many different stages of maturity on each tree. Only the blue berries should be taken. The oil from the fruit is most famous in the manufacture of gin, also certain liqueurs and bitters. A Swedish beer is flavoured with the same extract. Cade oil, or juniper tar oil, comes from a related species, *J. oxycedrus*, growing in southern France and the United States. It is used in veterinary medicine. *J. virginiana*, the red cedar or US juniper, provides furniture wood and oil used in insecticides and perfumery. The word 'gin' comes from *geneva*, the Dutch for juniper.

OTHER NAMES

Juniper Berry, Juniper Fruit
French: genièvre
German: Wacholder
Italian: ginepro
Spanish: enebro, junípero, nebrina
Indian: dhup, shur (Indian Juniper)

Juniper Pork Chops

Pork braised in cider with a creamy and aromatic sauce.   Serves 6

Imp	Metric	US
1oz butter	30g	1oz
2tbsp oil	40ml	2⅔tbsp
1 onion, medium, chopped	1	1
6 pork spare-rib or boneless chops	6	6
2 bay leaves	2	2
6 peppercorns	6	6
½pt cider, dry	285ml	1¼ cups
Sauce:		
1oz butter	30g	1oz
1 garlic clove, crushed	1	1
2tsp juniper berries, crushed	2tsp	2tsp
1oz flour	30g	1oz
½pt stock (reserved cooking liquid)	285ml	1¼ cups
4tbsp sour cream	80ml	5⅓tbsp
salt		
pepper		

1 Heat butter and oil in a large frying pan and cook onions until golden. Remove onions and reserve.
2 Add chops and brown on both sides.
3 Transfer meat to a casserole and add onions, bay leaves, peppercorns and cider. Cover and cook in the oven Gas Mark 4, 350°F, 180°C for 45 minutes or until tender.
4 Remove chops and set aside in a serving dish to keep warm while making sauce.
5 Melt butter in a saucepan and gently cook garlic and juniper for 5 minutes.
6 Add flour, stir for a few minutes, then gradually add the stock, stirring until smooth.
7 Now add sour cream, season to taste and reheat very gently.
8 Pour sauce over chops and serve.

Country Pâté (colour page 156)

A coarse pâté, simple to make and ideal for picnics or as a starter with French bread or toast. It is even better if refrigerated for a few days.   Serves 8

Imp	Metric	US
12oz pork belly, boned, skinned and minced	340g	12oz
8oz rabbit meat, boned and chopped	225g	8oz
8oz chicken livers, minced	225g	8oz
¼tsp allspice, ground	¼tsp	¼tsp
5 juniper berries, crushed	5	5
½tsp pepper	½tsp	½tsp
1tsp salt	1tsp	1tsp
¼tsp thyme	¼tsp	¼tsp
3tbsp vermouth, dry	60ml	4tbsp
2oz lard or butter	55g	2oz
2 garlic cloves, crushed	2	2
1 onion, chopped	1	1
1 egg	1	1
8oz streaky bacon	225g	8oz

1 Mix together the meat, allspice, juniper, pepper, salt, thyme and vermouth. Leave for a few hours.
2 Melt lard and cook onion and garlic until soft but not brown.
3 Add onion and garlic to the meat mixture and then mix in the egg.
4 Cut the rinds off the bacon and stretch each rasher with the back of a knife.

Line a terrine or a 2lb loaf tin by laying the bacon across the bottom and sides of the terrine.
5 Spoon in the meat mixture and fold any overlapping bacon back across the mixture.
6 Cover tightly with a double layer of foil, stand in a baking tin half filled with water and bake for 1¼ hours in a moderate oven, Gas Mark 4, 350°F, 180°C.
7 Allow to cool weighting the top and chill.

Kokum

Garcinia indica
Fam Guttiferae

SPICE DESCRIPTION
This is the dried rind of the fruit of an Indian coastal tree. Resembling a thick plum skin, the flattened rind is 4cm (1½in) in length. Dark brown to black in colour, it is soft and smooth in texture with the calyx intact. Kokum is available from Asian food shops.
Bouquet Sweet and sour.
Flavour Astringent and sour. It may also be salty owing to preservation.

H Scale: 1

PREPARATION AND STORAGE
A vinegar-like infusion, similar to tamarind, is made by steeping a few skins in half a pint of hot water. Kokums should be kept airtight or they will dry out.

USES
Kokum has the same souring qualities as tamarind. The skins are not usually chopped but are added whole to the cooking pot. Seasoning should be checked as they are quite salty. Kokum is particularly associated with fish curries – three or four skins being sufficient for an average dish. Other curries may be garnished with kokum, and it is included in chutneys and pickles. Beware of biting on a stone as a few of these sometimes remain in the skins.

The fruit contains carbohydrate, protein, fixed oil, gum, resin, tannins, cellulose, acids and minerals. The seeds yield 26 per cent of a non-drying oil, rich in stearic and oleic acids, the famous kokum butter or mangosteen oil of Indian commerce. At normal temperatures this is a greyish-white odourless fat.

ATTRIBUTED PROPERTIES

The fruit is febrifuge, coolant, astringent and demulcent. It is useful as an infusion, or by direct application, in skin ailments such as rashes and eruptions caused by allergy. Kokum butter is an emollient helpful for burns, scalds and cracked skin. In Western medicine the butter is used as a base for suppositories. A hot infusion of the fruit rinds is emetic. The juice of the fruit is a dyeing mordant.

PLANT DESCRIPTION

A slim, tropical evergreen tree, related to the pearl of tropical fruits, the mangosteen, reaching to 15m (50ft). The thin bark is lined, the leaves ovate or broad lanceolate. The round, dark purple fruit is about 4cm (1½in) in diameter with up to eight beanlike seeds.

CULTIVATION

The trees are usually solitary forest trees and difficult to cultivate.

REMARKS

Native to the western coastal region of southern India, *Garcinia indica* is not known elsewhere. The fruit are eaten and were familiar to the Portuguese in Goa. Kokum butter is a valuable commodity in local Indian trade, at times extending its 'usefulness' to the adulteration of *ghee* and dairy butter. The family Guttiferae, to which kokum belongs, is interesting in that another member, *Mesua ferrea*, known in India as '*nagkeser*', is the source of a spice. *Nagkeser* appears among the ingredients of a famous Anglo-Indian curry powder dating from 1883. It may be a coincidence that, ten years earlier, Burton's translation of the *Ananga Ranga* frequently mentions *nagkeser* in potions for impotence, virility and sexual stimulus. Little information exists about which part of this tree is actually used in the recipe, if it is this tree and not cassia buds as some authorities translate it. Nevertheless, in 1896 the Governor of Bombay gave the curry powder his seal of approval, aware perhaps that the continuity of the Raj depended on better public relations.

OTHER NAMES

Black Kokam, Black Kokum, Cocum, Kokam, Kokum Butter Tree, Mangosteen Oil Tree
French: cocum
German: Kokam
Italian: cocum
Spanish: cocum
Indian: kokam, kokum, raktapurka

Fish Curry

A curry method suitable for any firm fish, easy to make and having a unique tang.

Serves 2–4

Imp	Metric	US
3tbsp *ghee* or butter	60ml	4tbsp
2 onions, medium, finely chopped	2	2
2 garlic cloves, finely chopped	2	2
1tbsp ginger, fresh, grated	1tbsp	1⅓tbsp
½tsp chilli powder	½tsp	½tsp
2tsp coriander, ground	2tsp	2tsp
½tsp cumin, ground	½tsp	½tsp
½tsp fenugreek, ground	½tsp	½tsp
½tsp pepper, black, ground	½tsp	½tsp
1+cup coconut milk, thick	1+cup	1+cup
2 kokum pieces, whole	2	2
1lb fish fillets	455g	1lb

1 Heat *ghee* and fry the onion, garlic and ginger until golden.
2 Add all the dry ground spices from chilli to pepper. Stir and fry briefly.
3 Add the coconut milk, stir well. Add the kokum pieces and bring to the boil. Simmer a few minutes.
4 Add the fish fillets and simmer until cooked – about 10 minutes.
5 Serve with rice.

Lemon Grass

Cymbopogon citratus and spp
syn *Andropogon schoenanthus*
Fam Gramineae

SPICE DESCRIPTION

This flavouring is hardly known in the West. It consists of the base and the white fleshy leaf-stalks and green leaves of a tall tropical grass – see Plant Description. The tops of the leaves are usually cut off about 15cm (6in) from the base. It is normally used fresh, but is also sold in dried form. The dried spice comes in three forms: the whole stem; longitudinally sliced; or horizontally chopped. The chopped pieces may have been treated with salt, so check when seasoning a dish. A powder made from lemon grass, *sereh* powder, is also available, and an oil expressed from the plant is sold for culinary purposes.
Bouquet Sweet scented and lemony.
Flavour Lemon, faintly gingery and reminiscent of sherbet. The plant contains the substance that characterises lemon zest, citral. H Scale: 1

PREPARATION AND STORAGE

The lower part of the plant, 10–15cm (4–6in), is used, the upper blades being discarded. If using dried lemon grass, twelve strips are equal in potency to one fresh stem. The stem can be bruised and used whole or cut across in slices. Store separately as the flavour is imparted to other foods. Lemon peel works very well as a substitute, being virtually identical in flavour. Dried lemon grass should be soaked in water for two hours before use.

USES

Lemon grass features in Indonesian, Sri Lankan, Malaysian and Indian cooking and is widely used in savoury dishes and meat, poultry, seafood, offal and vegetable curries. When an ingredient of fish dishes, it is important as a detractor of any unpleasant 'fishy' odour. Its delicate flavour harmonises particularly well with coconut and there are countless Sri Lankan recipes exploiting this agreeable combination. Chicken with lemon grass is a popular Vietnamese dish. A bunch of stems is used as a *bouquet garni*. The bulbous bases are curried as a vegetable or used in pickles and in flavouring marinades. The plant is used commercially in artificial lemon flavourings.

CHEMICAL COMPOSITION

Fresh lemon grass contains 0.2–0.4 per cent essential oil. The distilled oil contains over 70 per cent aldehydes – mainly citral – and is also called 'Indian verbena' or 'Melissa oil'. It has a strong violet perfume, and is used in the manufacture of ionones, vitamin A and flavourings. Citronella oil, from the variety *C. nardus*, and palmarosa oil, from the tops of the variety *C. martini* (*Motia*), contain large amounts of citronellal and geraniol.

ATTRIBUTED PROPERTIES

Lemon grass has sedative properties and was formerly used as a carminative. It features in British, Indian and Brazilian pharmacopoeias. It is a mild insect

repellent, diaphoretic and stimulant; as an external liniment it is used in rheumatism, lumbago, sprains and similar complaints. A preparation of lemon grass with pepper is said to be efficacious in menstrual troubles and nausea. Lemon grass tea, to which Queen Victoria was partial, is an effective stomachic for children, also a refrigerant and diuretic. In the form of paste it is applied on ringworm.

PLANT DESCRIPTION

A tropical and subtropical perennial tufted grass. The tall, 50–100cm (1½–3ft), sharp-edged blades grow in dense clumps. It rarely flowers. The plant has a tuberous rootstock and a whitish slightly bulbous base at ground level. There are four main species of *Cymbopogon*: *C. citratus* and *C. flexuosus* grow to 2m (6ft); *C. martini* is somewhat taller, while *C. nardus* rarely exceeds 1m (3ft).

CULTIVATION

A hot, sunny climate with adequate rainfall is suitable for lemon grass cultivation. Sandy loams are preferred, as heavy fertile soils produce more leafage with low citral content. It is usually propagated by root division, as it rarely flowers. The plants last three to four years, being harvested every three to four months.

REMARKS

Lemon grass grows throughout tropical Asia. 'These sunny expanses . . . are covered with tall lemon-grass' (Tennant on Ceylon, 1860). It is also cultivated in Brazil, Guatemala, Central Africa, and the West Indies and is a village industry on the Malabar Coast. It is also grown in Florida for the production of citral. As well as a crop, it is planted for soil conservation and as a mulch. The oil, extracted by steam distillation, is used in the preparation of soaps and in industry. Palmarosa oil, from *C. martini* (*Motia*), is used to adulterate attar of roses and to flavour tobacco. It exudes a sweet geranium odour. The *martini* variety *Sofia* yields gingergrass oil, which goes to make cheap perfumes sold around the Red Sea. It has a woody roseate aroma. Lemon grass was used by the Romans, Greeks and Egyptians as a medicine and cosmetic.

OTHER NAMES
Camel's Hay, Citronella, Geranium Grass, Oil Plant, Sereh Powder
Malabar or Cochin Grass (*C. flexuosus*)
Rosha Grass (*C. martini*)
Citronella Grass (*C. nardus*)
French: herbe de citron
German: Zitronengras
Italian: erba di limone
Spanish: hierba de limon
Indian: bhustrina, ghandhtrina, sera
Indonesian: sere, sereh
Lao: bai mak nao
Malay: serai
Sinhalese: sera
Thai: takrai

Hot and Spicy Grilled Chicken (colour page 189)

This Indonesian version of barbecued chicken makes an interesting and delicious change.　　　　　　　　　　Serves 4–6

Imp	Metric	US
3lb chicken	1.4kg	3lb
2–3 chillies, fresh, seeded and chopped	2–3	2–3
2 garlic cloves, chopped	2	2
1 onion, chopped	1	1
1 lemon grass stalk, fresh, chopped	1	1
3tbsp oil	60ml	4tbsp
1tsp salt	1tsp	1tsp
2tsp sugar, brown	2tsp	2tsp
3tbsp tamarind water or lemon juice	60ml	4tbsp
½tsp turmeric, ground or substitute 1tsp of dried lemon grass or grated lemon peel	½tsp	½tsp

1 Divide chicken into 8 pieces and score several times through skin and flesh.
2 Put chillies, garlic and onion into a blender or mortar, add all remaining ingredients and blend or pound to a paste.
3 Coat the chicken with the paste and

leave to marinade for several hours or overnight.

4 Barbecue or grill under high heat, basting with the marinade until chicken is cooked.

Liquorice

Glycyrrhiza glabra
Fam Leguminosae

SPICE DESCRIPTION
Known best as a candy, liquorice is the rhizome of a bean plant, both the vertical main tap root and horizontal subsidiary stolons being used. The dried root sections are available in various lengths and diameters, on average 1cm (⅜in) in diameter and 10cm (4in) in length. They are brown skinned with a yellow interior, fibrous, woody and brittle. Diagonal, dried pieces come from the thicker part of the root. The ground spice is also obtainable. More commonly, liquorice comes as black, brittle cylindrical sticks, approximately 8mm (⅓in) in diameter and 12cm (5in) in length, manufactured from the boiled and solidified root extract.
Bouquet Slightly aromatic, 'sweet-shop' fragrance.
Flavour Bitter-sweet, sometimes slightly salty.   H Scale: 0 (root)

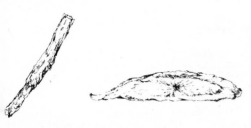

PREPARATION AND STORAGE
No special storage of the dried root is required but the powder should be stored in an airtight container and the sticks should be kept free of moisture. The dried root can be sliced or ground before use.

USES
Liquorice is mainly encountered in confectionery, especially 'Pontefract cakes'. The sticks may be dissolved in hot water and drunk as a *tisane* and the roots may flavour fruit juices, syrups and dried-fruit salad. Liquorice flavours drinks (*anesone, raki, sambuca*, sometimes gin), and is used in brewing.

CHEMICAL COMPOSITION
Liquorice contains about 0.03 per cent volatile oil, but this is not an important constituent, being odourless and tasteless. The root yields, however, 25 per cent of a water-soluble substance, known as 'Extract of Liquorice.' While the root contains about 7 per cent of the active ingredient glycyrrhizin (glycyrrhizic acid salts), the extract contains up to 25 per cent glycyrrhizin and is powerful in aroma and flavour. Liquorice also contains 30 per cent starch, resin, sugar, gum, protein, under 1 per cent of fat and some asparagine and potassium. Glycosides are also present.

ATTRIBUTED PROPERTIES
Demulcent and expectorant, liquorice has been for centuries much used in cough medicines and lozenges, for sore throats and for hoarseness and chest conditions such as bronchitis ('Carry him this sticke of Licoras . . . 'twill open his pipes the better', Beaumont and Fletcher, *Knight of the Burning Pestle*). An alterative, emollient and anti-inflammatory, it has been used to treat peptic ulcers and bowel and urinary problems. Liquorice extract is widely utilised to conceal the nauseous taste of otherwise orally inadministrable drugs. It relieves the persistent thirst characteristic in dropsy, and its sugar component is safe in diabetes. Continual large doses can cause metabolic disorders including sodium retention and potassium loss – leading to acute hypertension. It has been used in place of cortisone in the treatment of Addison's disease. Liquorice has an ancient reputation as an aphrodisiac; the *Kama Sutra* and *Ananga Ranga* contain numerous recipes for increasing sexual vigour which include liquorice.

A small perennial legume reaching to 1.5m (5ft) with loose racemes of purple-blue flowers in spiked clusters. It is a bean-like plant, with small pods. The root descends vertically for about 1m (3ft), sending forth long underground rhizomes, or stolons, horizontally. Both root and rhizome are harvested.

CULTIVATION

Climate: Mediterranean.
Aspect: Sunny.
Soil: Clay or sandy.
Propagate from root cuttings in early spring. Manure or fertilise. The plant flowers from June to July. Harvest in spring or autumn, when three to four years old, carefully removing soil from whole roots. These are washed and cut into convenient lengths. Sometimes they are scraped.

REMARKS

Liquorice is native to south-eastern Europe and the Middle East, where it grows wild. It is cultivated nowadays in Russia, Spain, other Mediterranean lands, the Near East, Asia and Africa. It was known to the Greeks, mentioned in the Hippocratic texts, and to the Romans, who made liquorice extract as we do today. The raw roots have been enjoyed for millennia as a wild (and free) sweetmeat. Its cultivation has been widespread in Europe since the Middle Ages when it was used as a cough remedy. There is a small agricultural industry in England devoted to producing liquorice root for the manufacture of extract. Unlike the swarthy, brittle foreign varieties, British liquorice root is pale, tough and supple. Liquorice is used in beers and chewing tobacco to add darkness and body. In India, another plant whose roots contain glycyrrhizin, 'Indian liquorice' (*Abrus precatorius*), has been used as a liquorice substitute in herbal medicine. However, the roots and the famous red seeds are poisonous, and are used only in small doses.

OTHER NAMES

Black Sugar, Licorice (US), Liquorice Root, Spanish Juice, Sweetroot, Sweetwood
French: réglisse
German: Lakritze, Süssholz
Italian: liquirizia
Spanish: regaliz
Indian: jethi madh, madhuka, mithi lakdi

Dried Fruit Salad (colour page 137)

A colourful winter fruit salad with a gentle hint of liquorice.

Imp	Metric	US
4oz dried pears	115g	4oz
4oz dried apricots	115g	4oz
8oz prunes, pitted	225g	8oz
2oz sultanas	55g	2oz
¾pt water	425ml	1¾ cups
3 liquorice roots, 4in (10cm) each, bruised	3	3
1tbsp *sambuca* or brandy	1tbsp	1⅓tbsp
1tbsp flaked almonds	1tbsp	1⅓tbsp

1 Rinse the fruit in cold water and place in a bowl starting with the pears.
2 Bring the water to the boil with the liquorice root and pour over the fruit. Bury the root in the fruit.
3 When the fruit is cool, add the *sambuca* or brandy, cover and refrigerate for 48 hours, turning it two or three times.
4 Transfer to a serving bowl, scatter with the almonds and serve with cream.

Mace

Myristica fragrans
Fam Myristicaceae

SPICE DESCRIPTION

Mace is the aril of the nutmeg, an aril being a fleshy appendage attached to certain seeds. In its natural state, mace is a bright crimson network up to 35mm (1½in) long, encaging the brown nutmeg in irregular, fleshy tentacle-like lobes. The mace of commerce is dried to a dull yellow-brown, becoming horny and brittle, although superior mace, if not overkept, should retain some degree of pliability and exude a little oil when pressed. It is flattened and sometimes roughly broken, appearing in solid, branched or segmented pieces. Mace is sold also in powdered form, or, more decoratively, still enclosing the nutmeg. It is commonly available, though more expensive than nutmeg.

Bouquet Similar to nutmeg, but stronger: sweetly pungent and fragrant.

Flavour Warm, sharp and aromatic with a bitter undertone.   H Scale: 1–2

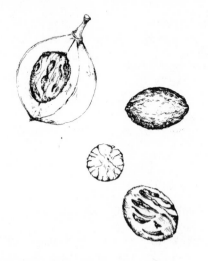

PREPARATION AND STORAGE
Dried mace pieces are impracticable to grind at home. Ready powdered mace is acceptable, but tends to deteriorate even when kept airtight, so it is advisable to buy little and renew often. Whole mace pieces can be steeped in liquids during cooking and removed after use. Being quite powerful, one 'blade' or its equivalent will suffice to flavour a family-sized dish.

USES
Like nutmeg, mace can be used in both sweet and savoury dishes, but more often in savoury. A small amount will enhance many recipes, adding fragrance without intruding on the flavour. Mace combines especially well with milk desserts, such as custard, and will aromatise warm cream sauces nicely. It is used in creamed soups, casseroles (especially Middle Eastern meat dishes), poultry stuffings and sauces. Add a little to mashed potatoes and root veg-

etables. The spice also contributes to cakes and pastries, particularly doughnuts, as well as fruit jellies. It goes well with jellied veal and fish, and is traditionally used in British potted cheese and potted meats such as tongue, but perhaps its best known English association is with potted shrimps. It combines well with cherries, is good in bread pudding, and is an ingredient in spice mixtures used for pickling and preserving. Some beverages will improve with a hint of mace, especially chocolate drinks, and it is one of the flavourings used to spice alcoholic drinks and punches. It is also used in meat and fish curries in India and Sri Lanka.

CHEMICAL COMPOSITION
The chemical composition is similar to that of nutmeg.

ATTRIBUTED PROPERTIES
Carminative, stimulant, and tonic, mace aids the digestion, is beneficial to the circulation and is used to mollify febrile upsets and in Asia to relieve nausea. Mace butter is employed as a mild counter-irritant and used in hair lotions and plasters. As with nutmeg, large doses of mace can lead to hallucination and epileptiform fits, myristin being poisonous, but dangerous doses are unlikely to be taken in the course of everyday use.

PLANT DESCRIPTION
A large, tropical, dioecious evergreen tree reaching up to 20m (66ft) in the wild, while in cultivation it grows to 13m (43ft). The thick, densely branched trunk is grey-green. The oval leaves are around 10cm (4in) long, dark green above, lighter underneath and deeply veined. The bell-shaped flowers are pale yellow, the female flowers larger and more elongated. The fruit, also pale yellow, is grooved like an apricot some 6cm (2½in) long. Some trees are hermaphroditic but they yield inferior spices.

CULTIVATION
See Nutmeg.

Myristica fragrans is native to the Moluccas and New Guinea, and is now cultivated also in the West Indies and Sri Lanka. The tree grows best in deep loam in humid and hot climates. It is best cultivated near the sea, islands being naturally favoured for plantation. A ratio of one male to ten female trees is maintained as the optimum for fertilisation and production. The fruit splits on ripening to reveal the seed, to which the enclosing mace is cemented at one end. The seeds are harvested as they fall, or as the fruit splits, and the mace is removed, flattened and sun dried for ten to fourteen days. Nutmeg was known to Chaucer, and mace has been used in Europe since medieval times. Regarded as somewhat luxurious, it has been traditionally used in England in potted meats for centuries. Taken in a toddy, it was a cure for insomnia, but prolonged over-indulgence is now avoided as addictive. Like nutmeg, mace may be used to spice (or spike) alcohols.

OTHER NAMES
French: macis
German: Muskatblüte, Samenmantel
Italian: mace, macis
Spanish: macía
Indian: jaffatry, javatri, jawatrie, tavitri
Sinhalese: wasa-vasi
Tamil: japatri

Potted Shrimps (colour page 138)
Home-made potted shrimps are very economical and worth the time taken.

Serves 6

Imp	Metric	US
1½pt (12oz) shrimps (6oz picked)	340g	3½ cups (12oz)
4oz butter	115g	4oz
⅛tsp cayenne	⅛tsp	⅛tsp
¼tsp mace, ground	¼tsp	¼tsp
⅛tsp pepper, white, freshly ground	⅛tsp	⅛tsp

1 Melt 1½oz (40g) butter, remove from heat, add shrimps and spices and turn until well coated.

2 Divide shrimps into six small ramekin dishes.
3 Clarify remaining butter and pour over shrimps and refrigerate.
4 Serve at room temperature with hot toast and lemon wedges.

Meat Loaf
A simple tasty loaf which can be served hot or cold. Serves 6

Imp	Metric	US
1lb beef, minced	455g	1lb
1lb sausage meat	455g	1lb
1 onion, large, minced	1	1
½tsp garlic powder	½tsp	½tsp
½tsp mace	½tsp	½tsp
2tsp parsley, chopped	2tsp	2tsp
salt		
pepper		
2 eggs, hard-boiled	2	2
breadcrumbs		

1 In a bowl, combine meat, onion, spices and seasonings.
2 Cover the bottom of a 1lb (½kg) loaf tin with some of the mixture and lay the two eggs on top.
3 Pack the rest of the mixture tightly around the eggs and shape into a neat loaf. Sprinkle with breadcrumbs.
4 Bake in a moderate oven, Gas Mark 4, 350°F, 180°C, for 45 minutes. Half way through baking, remove from oven and pour off liquid.
5 At end of cooking time pour off any more liquid and serve with tomato sauce – see page 56. Alternatively, cool and serve cold, sliced thinly, with pickles and salad.

Mahlebi

Prunus mahaleb
Fam Rosaceae

SPICE DESCRIPTION
Mahlebi is the dried kernel of a small cherry stone. It is ovoid, about 5mm (³⁄₁₆in) long, buff-coloured with a finely wrinkled skin and a cream-coloured interior. The powdered spice is yellowish, similar in

colour to mace. Mahlebi is not easily available outside the Middle East.

Bouquet Quite sweet with notes of cherry and almond.

Flavour Nutty and faintly bitter.

H Scale: 1

PREPARATION AND STORAGE

Mahlebi is available whole or ground but, as it quickly deteriorates once ground, it is preferable to pulverise the kernels when needed. Use a pestle and mortar; a coffee grinder is ideal. Generally only small quantities of ground mahlebi are specified in recipes. Store in airtight containers.

USES

Mahlebi is an ancient spice and is used widely in Mediterranean countries and the Middle East, especially Turkey, in breads, biscuits and less sweet cakes and pastries. It is a feature of Easter buns and those spectacular brioche wreaths decorated with brightly coloured eggs. It is well worth experimenting with this unfamiliar but intriguing flavouring. One or two spoonfuls added to a rich pastry for fresh fruit flans gives them a subtle note. Simple milk puddings can be transformed with a few pinches of mahlebi, an example of which is Turkish rice. Glazed mahlebi biscuits are quick and easy to make and look attractive with their finger or crescent shapes.

CHEMICAL COMPOSITION

Mahlebi contains protein, carbohydrate, a fixed oil and minerals. Little is known of its chemistry but it can be assumed that it has some constituents common to the kernels of *Prunus* fruit stones. A bitter principle, possibly amygdalin, may occur in small quantities. Macerated mahlebi has an odour reminiscent of tonka bean, suggesting the presence of coumarin.

ATTRIBUTED PROPERTIES

Diuretic and lithontriptic.

PLANT DESCRIPTION

A deciduous tree, 1–12m (3–40ft), with many spreading branches. The bark is smooth and mahogany red. The leaves, up to 6cm (2½in) long, are bright green, shiny, oval and finely toothed. The flowers are white, single, on long stalks in clusters. The fruit is small, 5-10mm (¼–⅜in), slightly oval, green at first then black.

CULTIVATION

This early flowering tree grows wild in southern Europe, Mediterranean areas, Turkey and the Levant. It is grown as an ornamental tree in other parts of Europe, including Britain. It can be propagated by seed and is used as a root stock for the sweet cherries.

REMARKS

The major use of mahlebi is confined to the Middle East and Turkey. Many kernels of the *Prunus* family (peach, apricot, bitter almond) produce prussic acid. Bitter almond is well known for this, as when the great detective smells almonds and concludes the victim has been murdered by prussic acid poisoning. However, mahlebi is not at all dangerous; together with the almond it is the only form of *Prunus* kernel that is used separately. It is interesting to note that Gerard (1597) referred to bastard privet as 'macaleb' or 'mahaleb' and described the use of its fruit kernels. Presumably this was a confusion arising from the plants' similarity in many respects such as form, leaves and especially fruit. The leaves of the plant are sometimes used in the manufacture of Dalmatian *maraschino* to improve its flavour. Beads are made from the kernels: '. . . the fragrant kernels of Prunus Mahaleb . . . strung as necklaces, which are much valued by the women of Sinde . . .' (Simmonds, *Dictionary of Trade*, 1858).

Mahalabi, Mahaleb(i), Mahlab, Mahlepi, Marlev, St Lucie's Cherry
French: mahaleb
German: Mahaleb
Italian: mahaleb
Spanish: mahaleb
Greek: mahlepi
Arabic: mahlab, mahleb

Mahlebi Biscuits

These light textured biscuits have a delicious and distinctive flavour. Ground almonds may be substituted for the mahlebi.   Makes about 24 biscuits

Imp	Metric	US
3oz butter	85g	3oz
3oz lard	85g	3oz
1 egg	1	1
4tbsp water, warm	80ml	5⅓tbsp
1tbsp mahlebi, freshly ground	1tbsp	1⅓tbsp
12oz flour, self-raising	340g	12oz
4oz sugar	115g	4oz
pinch salt	pinch	pinch

1 Cream butter and lard together.
2 Beat the egg and water together and mix half with the creamed mixture.
3 Sift the mahlebi with the flour, sugar and salt, add to the mixture, knead well and form into a ball. Allow to rest in a cool place for 30 minutes.
4 Roll out dough to ¼in (6mm) and shape into fingers or crescents.
5 Lay the biscuits on a greased baking sheet, brush with the remaining egg and water and bake in the oven for about 30 minutes at Gas Mark 4, 350°F, 180°C. Transfer to a rack and allow to cool.

Mastic

Pistacia lentiscus
Fam Anacardiaceae

SPICE DESCRIPTION
Mastic is a resin, the hardened sap from a tree. It appears as pea-sized globules, known as tears. They are rounded, pear-shaped, sometimes oblong. Mastic may also be sold in small congealed chunks. The resin is semi-translucent, ageing to a horny opacity, pastel yellow or faint green at its best, white mastic being inferior. Sometimes the resin is frosted with a whitish powder. Although well known in the Balkans and the Middle East, mastic is not widely available elsewhere.

Bouquet Slightly piny. Mastic does not have a powerful bouquet, but purifies the breath.

Flavour: A cedar taste. Mastic has a pleasant texture, forming on mastication a firmish, malleable mass.   H Scale: 0–½

PREPARATION AND STORAGE
Mastic is pulverised before use so that it may be evenly distributed in the dish under preparation. Pounding it becomes easier with the addition of a little sugar or salt. Only small amounts are necessary, under a teaspoon sufficing for a dish for four people. Store in airtight containers.

USES
In Greece the best mastic comes from the island of Chios. It is used in the baking of bread and pastries, and also for one of the traditional 'spoon sweets', *gliko tou koutaliou*. A spoonful of this gooey sweet followed by a glass of ice-cold water is marvellous in hot weather. In Cyprus, small rings of mastic-flavoured bread are topped with sesame seeds. Mastic pounded with sugar and rose or orange blossom water is a popular flavouring in the Middle East, used in desserts, sweetmeats, ice cream, syrups and cordials. A favourite flavoured thus is rice pudding topped with pistachio nuts and almonds. It is essential in *rahat locum*, the authentic Turkish delight. The famous *shawirmah* from Damascus, similar to the Turkish *döner kebab*, is a large vertical spit holding tightly packed slices of lamb or veal previously marinaded in a mixture of oil, lemon juice, spices and mastic, the mastic acting as a binding agent. As the meat cooks, thin slivers are sliced off and served in *pitta* bread.

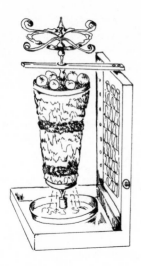

'weeps' in tears. At its prime, a tree will yield 4.5kg (10lb) of mastic in one season.

REMARKS
The mastic tree grows in the Greek archipelago, Cyprus, Portugal, North Africa, even England. The main commercial producer is the island of Chios, with a special mastic (*Pistacia lentiscus chia*); it was so important during the Turkish occupation that the island was granted its own parliament. Mastic is used in dentistry as a filling for carious teeth and in industry in varnishes for metal and for paintings. A Greek grape spirit, *mastiha*, is flavoured with the resin, as is the Turkish liqueur, *raki*. In Arabia, water jars were perfumed with mastic smoke and in ancient Egypt mastic was used as an embalming agent. It is related to the pistachio tree, which is often grafted on to the mastic shrub in the course of commercial propagation.

CHEMICAL COMPOSITION
There is a small proportion, 2 per cent, of volatile oil, masticinic and masticonic acids and masticoresene. The main ingredients are a soluble and an insoluble resin. Mastic contains about 10 per cent of each of these.

ATTRIBUTED PROPERTIES
Stimulant and diuretic, mastic was widely used medicinally in the past. 'The Masticke is also good against spitting of bloud' (Langham, 1579). It is given for diarrhoea in children and chewed to neutralise foul breath. Compound mastic paint is a plastic substance painted as a sealant over wounds. It has been used as a temporary tooth filling either by itself or as a cotton wool plug soaked with a mastic solution in alcohol.

PLANT DESCRIPTION
A Mediterranean shrub with dense twisted branches, 1–4m (3–13ft) in height. The leaves are paripinnate with four to ten elliptical, glossy and leathery leaflets. It bears red berries in tightly packed clusters, which turn black on ripening.

PRODUCTION
The resin occurs in the bark of the shrub. Harvesting is from June to September. Incisions are made in the stem and main branches, and the resin collected as it

OTHER NAMES
Lentisk
French: mastic
German: Mastix
Greek: masti(k)ha
Italian: lentischio, mastice
Spanish: lentisco, mastique
Arabic: aza

Mastiha Gliko
A traditional Greek speciality offered to guests on arrival. Other spoon sweets are made of fruit preserves. Serves 4

Imp	Metric	US
¾pt water	425ml	1¾ cups
1lb sugar, granulated	455g	1lb
2tsp lemon juice	2tsp	2tsp
3tsp mastic, finely pounded with a little sugar	3tsp	3tsp

1 Put the water and sugar in a saucepan, bring to the boil stirring until the sugar is dissolved.
2 Add one teaspoon of lemon juice and boil until the syrup is at the firm ball stage, 115°C–120°C (240°F–250°F). Remove from the heat and cool.

3 When the syrup is cold beat briskly and add another teaspoon of lemon juice and the mastic.
4 Continue beating until it is clear shiny white. Add a little water if the mixture is too thick – it should be gooey and gluey in substance.
5 Turn into a bowl and serve on a tray with a teaspoon and a glass of iced water.

Melegueta Pepper

Aframomum melegueta
syn *Amomum melegueta*
Fam Zingiberaceae

SPICE DESCRIPTION
This is the small, red-brown irregular seeds of a cardamom-like plant. The seeds are 3–4mm (⅛in) in diameter and are numerously contained in a brown, wrinkled, fig-shaped dried capsule about 30mm (1¼in) in length; they have a white kernel. They will hardly be found in the West.
Bouquet Aromatic, spicy.
Flavour Pungent and peppery, tasting strongly of ginger and cardamom.

H Scale: 5

PREPARATION AND STORAGE
The seeds can be ground in a mill like peppercorns or may be used in the same way as cardamom, either by frying whole or pounding with other spices. Store in airtight containers.

USES
Melegueta pepper may be used for culinary purposes and as a substitute for pepper in centres of local production. Its use is generally confined to West African cookery. Some ancient European recipes may call for it, but pepper mixed with a little ginger may be substituted. Today in Scandinavia, the seeds are used to flavour *akvavit*. They may be chewed to sweeten the breath.

CHEMICAL COMPOSITION
The seeds yield an inactive, aromatic essential oil and a viscid, brown pungent resin. Also present are carbohydrates, protein and minerals.

ATTRIBUTED PROPERTIES
Stimulant, carminative and diuretic, the seeds are mainly used in some veterinary medicines. They appear in old pharmacopoeias. Gerard (1597) says: 'The graines chewed in the mouth draw forth from the head and stomacke waterish pituitous humors . . . They also comfort and warme the weake, cold, and feeble stomacke, helpe the ague, and rid the shaking fits, being drunke with Sacke'. The seeds and rhizomes are used in West African herbal medicines.

PLANT DESCRIPTION
A tropical reed-like plant of the ginger family, related to the cardamom. Growing from a rhizome, it reaches 1m (3ft). The leaves are narrow, bamboo-like, 25 × 2.5cm (10 × 1in); the flowers are single pink lilies at the base of the plant. These are followed by reddish-brown ovoid capsules, almost 30mm (1¼in) long, enclosed in leafy bracts. The capsules contain many red to brown angular seeds, 3–4mm (⅛in) in diameter, in a jelly-like pulp. The flowers and rhizomes have a gingery smell.

CULTIVATION
A plant of the moist forest regions of West Africa, it is sometimes cultivated for the

spicy seeds. The methods used are similar to those for cardamom and ginger.

REMARKS
Melegueta pepper is native to tropical West Africa and grows mainly in Ghana. The spice is practically unknown in the modern Western cuisine, although it was used in Europe in the Middle Ages and Renaissance. It was a flavouring for the old wine 'Hippocras' and is still used for the production of beer, wine and spirits, and the flavouring of vinegar. Melegueta pepper was generally known as 'Grains of Paradise'. In fact there are two spices, melegueta pepper and the true Grains of Paradise, *Aframomum granum paradisi*, referred to by this name. The Grain Coast of West Africa is named for the spice in the same way as the other 'Coasts' are called Ivory, Gold and Slave. Originally transported across the Sahara by caravan, the spices were popular in Europe from the time of Elizabeth I, who personally had a predilection for them, until the time of George III who proscribed them, amongst other things. Trade dwindled and only the Scandinavians, who had a West African foothold, continued to use them.

OTHER NAMES
Alligator Pepper, Ginny Grains, Ginny Pepper, Graines, Greater Cardamom, Grenes, Guinea Grains, Guinea Pepper, Guinea Seeds, Maniguetta, Maniguette, Melaguata, Meligetta Pepper, Paradise Grains, Paradise Nuts
French: poivre de Guinée, malaguette, maniguette
German: Malagettapfeffer, Paradieskörner
Italian: grani de Meleguetta, grani de paradiso
Spanish: malagueta

Jollof Rice
This dish has the authentic aroma of the cooking fires of West Africa.   Serves 4

Imp	Metric	US
1lb chicken, lamb or beef, cubed	455g	1lb
1pt water	570ml	2½ cups
3tbsp oil	3tbsp	4tbsp
1lb tomatoes, sliced	455g	1lb
2 onions, large, sliced	2	2
½tsp chilli powder	½tsp	½tsp
1tsp melegueta pepper or	1tsp	1tsp
½tsp ginger, ground and	½tsp	½tsp
½tsp cardamom, ground	½tsp	½tsp
salt and pepper		

1 Boil meat in water until tender. Remove the meat and reserve water.
2 Heat oil and fry meat until brown. Remove and keep.
3 Fry tomatoes, onions and spices. Add the meat, water and seasoning. Simmer for 10 minutes.
4 Add the rice, stir a couple of times, and cook covered for 45 minutes, Gas Mark 4, 350°F, 180°C. Add water if too dry.
5 Serve with chutney, pickles, aubergines, okra, fried bananas or any green vegetable.

Mint

Mentha spp
Fam Labiatae

SPICE DESCRIPTION
The leaves of several species of the plant *Mentha*, the commonest in culinary use being spearmint (*M. spicata* or *crispa*) and applemint (*M. rotundifolia*). Pennyroyal (*M. pulegium*) is also used in the kitchen and peppermint (*M. piperita*) is cultivated for its oil. There are many other varieties of mint in cultivation, each with a distinctive bouquet and flavour, but we describe below only the main varieties in culinary use. Spearmint leaves are deep green, long, pointed and crinkled. Applemint is lighter in colour with round downy leaves and a more delicate flavour. Pennyroyal has small oval leaves, greyish in colour. Peppermint is similar in appearance to spearmint but one variety is tinged reddish brown. Dried rubbed mint is available under the name of 'mint' or pennyroyal.

Bouquet Spearmint – aromatic, fresh and appetising.

Applemint – stronger than spearmint with a hint of apple.

Pennyroyal – highly aromatic, pungent and acrid.

Peppermint – very aromatic.

Flavour Spearmint – a sweet flavour.

H Scale: 0

Applemint – as spearmint but more delicate. H Scale: 0

Pennyroyal – strong and rather medicinal. H Scale: 0–1

Peppermint – a strong menthol taste, imparting a cool sensation to the mouth. H Scale: 1–4

PREPARATION AND STORAGE

Mint can be used fresh or dried. Fresh mint may be chopped by hand or milled in a device specially designed for the purpose. Fresh mint may be preserved in vinegar. A concentrated mint sauce keeps well under refrigeration and may be thinned out as required. Store dried mint in airtight containers away from sunlight and it will retain its flavour for quite some time.

USES

In England, mint is an important flavouring, mint sauce or jelly being traditionally served with roast lamb or mutton. For most culinary purposes spearmint and applemint are the best varieties. Mint combines well with many vegetables such as new potatoes, tomatoes, carrots, aubergines and peas. It is a good complement to some soups – pea soup, iced cucumber soup and soups based on pulses. A few finely chopped leaves give refreshment to green salads and salad dressings. It is sometimes added to apple sauce and cream cheese. Pennyroyal spices haggis and black puddings, while peppermint is more commonly used in desserts, combining well with fruits such as apples and pineapple, and with ices and sherbets. Oil of peppermint is used in confectionery such as humbugs and peppermint creams. Spearmint is popular in the Balkans and the Middle East, where it is used both fresh and dried with grilled meats, stuffed vegetables and rice, and is an essential ingredient of *dolmas*, stuffed vine leaves. Dried mint is sprinkled over *hummus* and other pulse and grain dishes. Yoghurt dressings, dips and soups often include mint. In India fresh mint chutney is served particularly with *birianis*. Here too, mint is very often included in dishes with yoghurt and cucumber. American mint julep is well known and a glass of English Pimms No. 1 can never be without its sprig of mint. Mint tea is enjoyed in many countries throughout the world. Although mints combine well with a wide variety of foods, they are not often mixed with other herbs and spices in Western cookery.

CHEMICAL COMPOSITION

Mint contains around 2.5 per cent essential oil, some 5 per cent tannin, resin, pigment, cellulose and minerals. Spearmint oil contains mostly carvone while the major ingredient of peppermint oil is menthol. Some limonene and several esters are common to both species.

ATTRIBUTED PROPERTIES

The mints are carminative, stimulant, stomachic, diaphoretic, emmenagogic and antispasmodic. Peppermint is the strongest, while preparations of spearmint are often given to children. Mint is used in intestinal and gastric complaints such as colic, dyspepsia and bile, and in gall bladder disorders. In Tudor times, mint provided a bath for skin diseases and a wash for scabious heads and aching ears. A glass of *crème de menthe* is excellent for motion sickness taken before or after travelling. Mint is a general pick-me-up, good in colds, flu and fevers.

PLANT DESCRIPTION

Mints show such variations that they are hard to typify except in very general terms. Spearmint is a herbaceous perennial, around 1m (3ft) at maximum height, with grey-green leaves and tiered clusters of small pale blue or purple flowers in spikes. Peppermint is thought to be a hybrid of spearmint and a wild species, water mint. It has spikes of pale mauve flowers, bears red-tinged leaves and forms underground shoots. Applemint, or round-leaved mint, has paler and rounder leaves and the whole plant is hairy. Pennyroyal is a small plant with square stems and pink flowers. All parts of plants have the characteristic mint odour.

CULTIVATION

Most mints thrive in cool and moist places, but will grow in most soils (peppermint prefers a warmer environment) and in window boxes. Propagate by division or transplanting underground shoots in a humid shady aspect. Harvest at any time. For drying, the best time is at the young leafy stage. Either hang sprigs in bunches in a warm airy place or lay flat in suitable containers in similar conditions. First cut off all disfigured leaves. Continue drying process until all leaves and stalks are dry and brittle. Artificial drying hastens the process but loss of flavour and bouquet results.

REMARKS

Native to the Mediterranean, mint is now virtually worldwide in the more temperate climates, an escape in most of these places, and a weed in the United States. There are many species, mostly wild (about fifteen in Britain alone), and many varieties among cultivated species. It has been in use for centuries and was known to the ancients as a perfume and a flavouring. The name drives from the nymph Menthe, of Greek legend, who was metamorphosed into the plant by the jealous Proserpine. The Romans brought mint and mint sauce to Britain, where it became widely used as a cheap (or free) and plentiful seasoning, especially popular in the Middle Ages. Mint probably reached the United States on the *Mayflower*. The Japanese have distilled peppermint oil for several centuries, and this product is now used in toothpaste, chewing gum and liqueurs such as *crème de menthe*. Peppermint oil is further treated to produce menthol. Mice will avoid the smell of mint, and pennyroyal, as its botanical name *M. pulegium* (from Latin *pulex*, a flea) suggests, was found to be an effective insecticide against fleas. Pennyroyal is also regarded as insecticidal against aphids.

OTHER NAMES

Spearmint: Fish Mint, Garden Mint, Green Mint, Lamb Mint, Mackerel Mint, Mint, Our Lady's Mint, Peamint, Sage of Bethlehem, Spire Mint
French: menthe verte
German: Grüne Minze
Italian: menta verde
Spanish: menta verde
Greek: dhiózmos, ménda
Indian: podina, pudeena, pudina
Japanese: hakka (field mint)
Lao: pak hom ho
Malay: daun kes(s)om, d. pudina
Sinhalese: meenchi
Tamil: pootheena, puthina
Indonesian: daun kes(s)om
Peppermint: Balm Mint, Brandy Mint, Curled Mint, Lamb Mint
French: menthe anglaise, menthe poivrée
German: Pfefferminze
Italian: menta peperina
Spanish: menta, piperita

Dolmades (colour page 33)

This famous Greek *mezze* is an accompaniment to summer drinks. Serves 12

Imp	Metric	US
6tbsp olive oil	120ml	8tbsp
2 onions, finely chopped	2	2
4oz rice, long grain	115g	4oz
4tbsp water, hot	80ml	5⅓tbsp
2oz currants	55g	2oz
2tbsp mint, dried	2tbsp	2⅔tbsp
2tbsp parsley	2tbsp	2⅔tbsp
2oz pine nuts	55g	2oz
½tsp mixed spice	½tsp	½tsp
pepper and salt		
6 doz vine leaves, fresh or	6 doz	6 doz
canned or vacuum packed		
lemon juice		

1 Heat the oil and cook the onions gently until soft.
2 Add the rice and stir until transparent.
3 Now add the water, currants, mint, parsley, mixed spice and pine nuts and simmer until the water is absorbed.
4 Let the mixture cool and season to taste.
5 Blanch the fresh vine leaves for 3 minutes, rinse and drain. Canned leaves should be rinsed and well drained.
6 Lay each vine leaf shiny side down and place a heaped teaspoonful of the rice in the centre and roll up like a parcel as illustrated. Do not roll too tightly as the rice will continue to swell.
7 Oil the bottom of a shallow saucepan and pack the vine leaves quite tightly together in layers.
8 Add the lemon juice and just enough water to cover the Dolmades, place a saucer on the top, cover and simmer for about an hour. Check occasionally if a little more water is required.
9 Allow to cool in the pan, chill and serve with lemon wedges.

Tabbouleh (colour page 33)
A refreshing but substantial salad from the Lebanon. Traditionally *tabbouleh* is eaten by scooping it up with lettuce leaves. (*Pourgouri* is the Greek for *burghul*).
Serves 6–8

Imp	Metric	US
8oz *burghul* (precooked cracked wheat)	225g	8oz
1 onion, finely chopped	1	1
3 tomatoes, peeled, seeded and chopped	3	3
3tbsp mint, dried or fresh, finely chopped	3tbsp	4tbsp
6tbsp parsley, finely chopped	6tbsp	8tbsp
¼pt lemon juice	140ml	9½tbsp
¼pt olive oil	140ml	9½tbsp
pepper to taste		
salt to taste		
black olives to garnish (optional)		
1 cos lettuce	1	1

1 Soak *burghul* in plenty of warm water for ½ hour.
2 Drain and squeeze well with your hands and place in a mixing bowl.
3 Add all remaining ingredients, mix thoroughly and garnish with black olives.
4 Serve from a large salad bowl with cos lettuce.

Mustard

Brassica alba, B. juncea, B. nigra
syn *Sinapsis alba*
Fam Cruciferae

SPICE DESCRIPTION
Three varieties of mustard exist, deriving from the seeds of three related plants:
White mustard is a round hard seed about 2mm (0.08in) in diameter, varying in colour from yellow brown to white. Its light outer skin is removed before sale.
Black mustard is a round hard seed about 1.5mm (0.06in) in diameter, varying in colour from dark brown to black.
Brown or Indian mustard is similar in size to the black variety and varies in colour from light to dark brown. The seeds are available whole.
Bouquet The seed itself has no aroma.
Flavour Sharp and fiery. White mustard is less powerful, Indian mustard is cruder.
H Scale: 6–8

English mustard is a fine, bright yellow powder made from a blend of the white and black seeds with a little added wheat flour and turmeric. A blend of the seeds alone is also obtainable.

Bouquet When mixed, mustard has a fiery and pungent aroma, powerfully aromatic, irritating and acrid.

Flavour Sharp and fiery. Bitter, turning to pungent. For other made-up mustards see under Uses.   H Scale: 7–8

PREPARATION AND STORAGE

Mustard develops its pungent qualities only after mixing with liquid, which should always be cool. Powdered mustard is made up by adding water, milk, grape juice, verjuice, lemon or lime juice, vinegar, beer, cider or wine. For traditional English mustard, two parts of powder to one of liquid are used. Leave to stand for fifteen minutes to allow the pungency to develop. When using powdered mustard in sauces, make it up with liquid first to avoid lumps.

Country mustard can be made by pulverising or crushing the seeds and mixing with herbs, spices and a chosen liquid. Sugar and honey are sometimes added. Stored in an airtight tin, mustard powder should keep almost indefinitely but ready-made mustards should be stored in a cool place and used within six months.

USES

Whole white mustard seed is used in pickling spice and in spice mixtures for cooking meats and seafood. It can give added piquancy to *Sauerkraut* and braised cabbage and is sometimes used in marinades. The brown seed is pounded with other spices in the preparation of curry powders and pastes. Fried in *ghee*, the seeds make an Indian garnish. Prepared thus, they are quite mild, for the pungency is diminished in the cooking. Mustard acts as an emulsifier in the preparation of mayonnaises and salad dressings. There are numerous made-up mustards from mild and sweet to very sharp and strong. They

may be smooth or coarse and flavoured with a wide variety of herbs, spices and liquids, but basically they can be described as follows:

English mustard is used as a condiment, traditionally with roast beef but is also very good with roast pork, ham, gammon, sausages and pork pies. It is added to Welsh rarebit and macaroni cheese and is an ingredient in the mustard sauce to accompany grilled herrings. It is essential in piccalilli (see Turmeric).

Dijon mustard is made from the husked black seeds blended with wine or verjuice, salt and spices. It is pale yellow and varies in strength from quite mild to very hot. This is the mustard generally used in classic French mustard sauces, and in salad dressings, mayonnaise, and other sauces such as *rémoulade*, devil and Cumberland. The Scandinavians are particularly fond of mustard sauces to go with fish and shellfish.

Bordeaux mustard is made from black seeds blended with unfermented wine. Because the seeds are not husked the mustard is dark brown. It is quite strong and aromatic and often flavoured with tarragon. It accompanies steaks as well as cold meats and spicy food. It is spread on slices of French bread and added to *carbonnade à la flamande*, beef stewed in beer.

Meaux mustard is the partly crushed, partly ground black seed mixed with vinegar and spices. The texture is crunchy and the flavour quite hot. It goes well with bland foods and a green peppercorn variety is especially good.

German mustard is usually a smooth blend of vinegar and black mustard, varying greatly in strength and eaten in liberal quantities with all sorts of German sausages. *Weisswurstsenf* is a coarse-grained, pale mild mustard made to accompany white veal sausages such as *Bratwurst*.

American mustard is made from the white seeds only, blended with sugar and wine or vinegar. It is pale yellow, very mild and sweet and is thinner than other mustards. It is the traditional accompaniment to the ubiquitous hot dog and hamburger as well as flavouring American mayonnaises.

Mustard oil obtained from *B. juncea* or *B. campestris* has a piquant flavour and is widely used in India in the same way as *ghee*. This oil is also used in commercial salad creams and in Italian *mostarda di frutta*, mixed fruits preserved in syrup.

CHEMICAL COMPOSITION
All mustards contain protein, cellulose, mucilage, a fixed oil and mineral elements. The most important constituents are, however, glucosides and the enzyme myrosin. In separate cells and neutral when dry, the glucosides and enzymes of mustard react in the presence of water to form an acrid essential oil.

White mustard: The fixed oil is 22–30 per cent and mucilage 25 per cent. The glucoside is sinalbin, which with myrosin and water yields sinalbin mustard oil, parahydroxybenzyl isothiocyanate (acrinyl isothiocyanate), glucose and choline.

Black mustard: The fixed oil is 24–40 per cent, and differs from that of white mustard in not having the glyceride of stearic acid. The glucoside is sinigrin, which reacts with myrosin and water to produce volatile mustard oil, allyl isothiocyanate, which is more pungent than sinalbin mustard oil.

Brown mustard: 35 per cent fixed oil; the glucoside is sinigrin. Only 0.6–2 per cent of volatile oil is yielded by distillation after the fixed oil has been expressed and the residue steeped in water to effect the enzymatic reaction.

ATTRIBUTED PROPERTIES
Mustard is a strong emetic, a counter-irritant and rubefacient. Black and brown mustard are much stronger than white mustard. Although the volatile oil of mustard is a powerful irritant, blistering tender skins, in dilution as a liniment or poultice it soothes, causing a sensation of warmth and redness. Mustard papers or plasters, 'sinapisms', are made by applying

mustard flour to paper coated with rubber solution; these are applied as counter-irritants. In bath water or as a footbath mustard relieves muscular aches. 'It helpeth the Sciatica, or ache in the hip or huckle bone . . .' (Gerard, 1597). (Bath mustard is a coarse powder of black and white mustards). Mustard is used to treat respiratory troubles, rheumatism and colic. The mucilage in the seeds absorbs moisture, so seeds are used in laboratories to make test tubes 'chemically' dry.

PLANT DESCRIPTION
An erect herbaceous annual (though botanists believe the original form was biennial), related to the cabbage. The white form is hardy, thriving like a weed. Mustards belong to the family Cruciferae, the name coming from the cross-like figure formed by the four petals. White and black mustards are distinguished by their leaves, pods and seeds.

White mustard (*B. alba*) is a hairy plant growing to 80cm (30in). The leaves are pinnatifid, the flowers bright yellow with four petals 1cm (⅜in) long. The fruit pods, 2.5–5cm (1–2in) long, are hairy with a pronounced beak; they grow horizontally and contain about half a dozen seeds – see Spice Description.

Black mustard (*B. nigra*) is a slightly larger plant than white mustard, reaching to 1m (39in). Some varieties achieve double this height. The upper leaves are smooth and lanceolate, the lower ones lyrate-pinnate, toothed and bristly. The bright yellow flowers are smaller than those of white mustard. The fruit pods, 2cm (¾in) long, are smooth and bulging, growing vertically close to the stem. These erect pods contain about a dozen seeds.

Brown mustard (*B. juncea*) is similar to black mustard in size. It is the *rai* of India. The leaves have a large ovate end-segment. The flowers are pale yellow and the pods are 3–5cm (1¼–2in) long.

Field mustard (*B. campestris*) is widely grown in India as an oilseed crop. Two varieties, *sarson* (Indian colza) and *toria* (Indian rape), are the best known. The plant is similar to the other mustards.

CULTIVATION

The mustards are cultivated as annuals; white is usually grown as a salad plant and black for its seeds.

Sow: Early spring, (black a week before white), although white will grow anytime under glass, except in frost. Allow 30–40cm (12–15in) between plants.

Soil: Black prefers a light soil, white a heavy one.

Aspect: Sunny.

Cultivation: Very wet conditions are unsuitable; otherwise it is a trouble-free crop. Salad mustard is easy to grow at home using a damp soil-free medium such as sacking, cottonwool etc. Cover this with seeds and moisten. The seeds will quickly germinate and be ready in about ten days. If grown side by side with cress, sow the cress three days earlier.

Harvest: Mustard pods must be harvested before they burst – that is, when they are nearly fully developed but not ripe. Stack in sheaves to dry out completely, then thresh and collect the seeds. Cut salad growths at the seedling stage.

REMARKS

Mustard is one of the oldest spices and one of the widest used. It has been known and harvested for millennia. Black and white mustards are probably native to the Mediterranean, while *juncea* possibly originated in Africa and spread thence to Asia and the Orient. It grows now mainly in China and India, while the other forms are cultivated in Europe and not used in Eastern cooking. The first medical mention is in the Hippocratic writings, since when mustard has been in constant use as a general muscular relief. The Romans used it as a condiment and pickling spice. Today, *juncea* largely replaces *nigra* in commerce because the plant is easier to harvest by machine – it is less apt to scatter its seeds, cutting down wastage. The 3 per cent of relatively bland fixed oil yielded by mustard is used as a cooking oil, and in soaps, lubricants and lighting fuels. Mustard is also eaten as a vegetable in salads and in mustard and cress. It is a good animal fodder.

OTHER NAMES

White

Yellow Mustard (US)
Charlock Salad Mustard
French: moutarde blanche
German: Senf, Weisser Senf
Italian: senape bianca, mostarda
Spanish: mostaza silvestre

Black

Brown Mustard (UK)
Grocer's Mustard
French: moutarde noire
German: Schwarzer Senf
Italian: senape nera
Spanish: mostaza negra
Chinese: gai lat, gai mo
Indian: Banarsi rai, kurva teil (oil), rai
Japanese: karashi
Malay: biji sawi
Sinhalese: abba
Tamil: kudoo

Brown

Indian Mustard
Black Mustard
French: moutarde de Chine
German: Indischer Senf
Italian: senape Indiana
Spanish: mostaza India
Indian: kimcea, Phari rai, rai
Tamil: kaduhennai (oil)

Carbonnade of Beef

A Belgian stew cooked with beer or ale.

Serves 4

Imp	Metric	US
2lb chuck steak	1kg	2lb
2oz butter	55g	2oz
1 onion, sliced	1	1
1 garlic clove, finely chopped	1	1
1tsp sugar	1tsp	1tsp
1 bay leaf	1	1
1 thyme, sprig	1	1
1tsp mustard, Bordeaux	1tsp	1tsp
1tbsp flour, plain	1tbsp	1⅓tbsp
salt, to taste		
pepper, to taste		
¼pt stock, beef	140ml	9½tbsp
½pt brown ale	285ml	1¼ cups
4 bread pieces spread with Bordeaux mustard	4	4

1 Trim and cut steak into 1in (25mm) cubes.
2 Melt butter in a casserole and fry onions and garlic until soft. Add meat and brown evenly.
3 Reduce heat. Add sugar, bay leaf, thyme and mustard. Stir.
4 Sprinkle with flour, salt and pepper to taste. Add stock and ale, stir well and bring to the boil.
5 Cover and cook gently in oven for 1½–2 hours at Gas Mark 3, 325°F, 160°C.
6 Fifteen minutes before serving remove thyme stalk and bay leaf and add the bread spread with Bordeaux mustard. Return to oven without cover and serve when the bread is brown.

Country Mustard (colour page 137)

A coarse mustard the ingredients of which can be varied to taste.

Makes about ½ cup

Imp	Metric	US
1oz black mustard seeds	30g	1oz
1oz white mustard seeds	30g	1oz
1tsp green peppercorns	1tsp	1tsp
¼tsp ajowan seeds, bruised or ½tsp dried thyme	¼tsp	¼tsp
2tsp honey	10ml	2tsp
1tsp sugar, brown	1tsp	1tsp
4tbsp wine vinegar	80ml	5⅓tbsp

1 Pound the mustard seeds coarsely with a pestle and mortar or use a coffee grinder.
2 Mash the peppercorns and add to the mustard.
3 Add remaining ingredients and leave overnight for the flavour to develop. Store in a cool place.

Nasturtium

Tropaeolum majus, T. minus
syn *Nasturtium indicum*
Fam Tropaeolaceae

SPICE DESCRIPTION

This neglected spice is the seed of a common decorative garden plant, whose leaves sometimes contribute to salads. The seeds are small, oval and wrinkled when dried, measuring 6mm (¼in) on average. They vary from cream to dark brown in colour and are exceptionally tough. The flowers and flower buds are also used, being pickled in vinegar and used as a caper substitute.
Bouquet Pungent, increasing on being pickled, and releasing the characteristic smell of capers.
Flavour When pickled, reminiscent of capers – pungent and peppery. The dried seeds are powerful, hot and mustardy, the buds weaker. The dried seeds resemble watercress in flavour.   H Scale: 6–7

PREPARATION AND STORAGE

Like all aromatics, nasturtium seeds must be kept airtight and preferably out of sunlight. In vinegar they should be well preserved and any suitable container will be satisfactory. Leaves, flowers and buds should be used as soon as plucked; wash if necessary.

USES

The most common use of nasturtium seed is pickled as a caper substitute. Indeed, all the flower parts can be pickled, the buds and fruit being used as seasoning in the Americas. The seeds should be left in the vinegar pickle-base for one month to mature to full flavour. Nasturtium vinegar consists of the whole opened flowers in a solution of vinegar, garlic and spices. Dried nasturtium seed is also ground as an inferior pepper substitute. The leaves, and especially the flowers, are an exotic addition to salads. The flavour is deliciously sharp and pungent, but use with discretion. The leaves make an unusual sandwich and can be nibbled on their own. Try them with cheese in place of celery or radishes. Grind a few seeds into cooked cheese dishes such as Welsh rarebit, cauliflower and macaroni to add a different piquancy. Give zest to a lettuce soup by adding a handful of leaves to the soup base and a few pickled seeds to each bowl on serving.

CHEMICAL COMPOSITION

The seeds contain carbohydrate, minerals, bitter principle, fixed and essential oils, cellulose and ash. The sulphurous oil antecedes the glycoside sinigrin, which together with the bitter principle contribute to the character of this spice.

ATTRIBUTED PROPERTIES

Nasturtium is said to be purgative in quantity. It is used as an urinary antiseptic and is useful for clearing congestion of the respiratory system. A derivative of the seeds is said to be an unstable germicide and is an irritant, the latter property probably owing to the conversion of sinigrin to allyl isothiocyanate as in mustard oil. Nasturtium appears to be neglected in the pharmaceutical field as well as the culinary.

PLANT DESCRIPTION

A trailing garden annual, reaching 2.5–3.5m (8–12ft). Nasturtium originated in the Andes but now grows anywhere with a sunny aspect. The tubiform flowers vary from orange to yellow, with red spots or stripes; the leaves are a colourful bright green. A dwarf variety Tom Thumb (*T. minus*) has been developed which is only 25cm (10in) high. Other varieties for the garden range between this and *T. majus*.

CULTIVATION

An easily grown annual that conveniently prefers poor soils. A sunny aspect will produce best results. Plant in early spring. Pick seed-buds when green – before fully mature. Wash and dry. Store in strong salty vinegar one month before use or dry seeds for grinding later. Because the plant flowers over a long period, harvesting is not easy and must be done intermittently when seeds are available.

REMARKS

Nasturtium is native to the Peruvian Andes. It is now widely cultivated as a decorative garden plant in many other countries, its introduction to Europe dating from 1646, and grows well in sunny temperate zones. The plant travelled round the world from Peru via the Philippines, Zanzibar and the Middle East. The peppery-flavoured leaves are used to brighten up salads, although nasturtium is grown more for its visual than its culinary impact. In America, the plant symbolises patriotism. Inca warriors chewed the seed to inspire courage and offend their enemies.

Another plant exists, of the same name. This is *Rorippa nasturtium-aquaticum* (formerly *Nasturtium officinale*), the common watercress, which has some similarities, especially in pungency and flavour. The name of this South American plant derives from its similarity in so many ways to European watercress, which is also known as nasturtium.

OTHER NAMES
Canary Creeper, Capuchin, Capucin, English Caper, Indian Cress
French: câpre, capucine (seeds)
German: Kapuzinerkresse, (Brunnenkresse – watercress)
Italian: nasturzio
Spanish: capuchina

Lettuce Soup (colour page 137)
A delicately coloured soup with a gentle nip.   Serves 4

Imp	Metric	US
1lb lettuce leaves	455g	1lb
1oz nasturtium leaves	30g	1oz
1oz butter	30g	1oz
1 onion, medium, finely chopped	1	1
8oz potatoes, sliced and chopped	225g	8oz
1pt chicken stock	570ml	2½ cups
salt and pepper		
½–1pt milk	285–570ml	1¼–2½ cups

sugar to taste
croûtons
nasturtium seeds, pickled
If nasturtium is not available use watercress leaves and capers

1 Wash and shred lettuce and nasturtium leaves.
2 Melt butter in a pan and gently fry onions and potatoes for 5 minutes.
3 Add lettuce, nasturtium, salt, pepper and stock. Bring to the boil and simmer until potatoes are tender.
4 Rub through a sieve or blend. Return to pan, add milk and simmer for a few minutes. Add sugar to taste.
5 Serve with croûtons and a few pickled nasturtium seeds to each bowl.

Nigella

Nigella sativa
Fam Ranunculaceae

SPICE DESCRIPTION
Nigella seeds are small, matt-black grains with a rough surface and an oily white interior. They are roughly triangulate, two sides being flat, 1½–3mm ($\frac{1}{16}$–$\frac{1}{8}$in) long, one rounded, 1½mm ($\frac{1}{16}$in) wide. They are similar to onion seeds. The dried seeds are available in the West, though not always correctly identified.
Bouquet The seeds have little bouquet unless rubbed, when they produce a dry aroma, curiously similar to carrots.
Flavour Bitter, pungent and peppery with a crunchy texture.   H Scale: 3

PREPARATION AND STORAGE
The seeds may be used whole or ground, often after a preliminary frying or roasting. They are easily crushed with a rolling pin or pestle and mortar. Store in airtight containers.

USES
Nigella is used in India and the Middle East as a spice and condiment and occasionally in Europe as both a pepper substitute and a spice. It is widely used in Indian cookery, particularly in mildly spiced braised lamb dishes such as *korma*. It also occurs in vegetable and *dhal* recipes as well as in pickles and chutneys. Occasionally spicing fish, nigella can be added to frying batters. The seeds are sprinkled on to *naan* bread before baking to accompany *tandoori* chicken and lamb *kebabs*. Nigella is an ingredient of some *garam masalas* and is one of the five spices in *panch phora* – see Spice Mixtures. In the Middle East, especially Egypt, the seeds are sprinkled on to cakes and added to bread doughs.

CHEMICAL COMPOSITION
Nigella seed yields about 1.5 per cent volatile oil and 35 per cent non-volatile oil. Also present are melanthin (a saponin),

nigellin(e), damascene (alkaloids) and tannin. Melanthin is toxic in large doses. Nigelline is paralytic, so this spice must be used in moderation.

ATTRIBUTED PROPERTIES

Nigella is used in Indian medicine as a carminative and stimulant. It has diuretic, diaphoretic, emmenagogic, antispasmodic, abortifacient and anthelmintic powers. Without irritating visceral linings, it stimulates intestinal and bilious activity and is used in indigestion and bowel complaints. In India a decoction is used to induce post-natal uterine contractions and promote lactation.

PLANT DESCRIPTION

An erect herbaceous annual of the buttercup family, reaching up to 60cm (2ft) in height. The grey-green leaves are wispy and threadlike. The flowers are small, five petalled, about 25mm (1in) across, and distinguished by blue veins. They are blue or white and appear between June and September. They are followed by five-compartmented capsules which are crowned by five prominent spikes. The pods are sometimes described as being surrounded by many spindly tendrils. This is the more ornate N. damascena. The compartments eventually explode to disperse the seeds.

CULTIVATION

Sow seeds in the open in the late spring in drills 50cm (18in) apart. Thin out the young plants to 30cm (12in). The plants flower from summer to spring and the seed capsules are collected as they ripen. These are further dried and broken to yield the seeds.

REMARKS

Nigella is native to western Asia and southern Europe, where it grows both wild and in cultivation. Today India is a large producer; nigella also occurs in Egypt and the Middle East. It was used for culinary purposes by the Romans, and has been known since antiquity by Asian herbalists

and pharmacists. The melathin content is deadly to cold-blooded creatures. The seeds are offensive to insects and are used like moth balls. An ornamental relative, *N. damascena*, is grown in temperate gardens of southern Europe; this is 'Love-in-a-mist'. The name nigella derives from the Latin *nigellus*, the diminutive of *niger*, black. In French cookery nigella seed is known as *quatre épices* or *tout-épice. Nigella (sativa) indica*, the Indian variety, is known as *kalonji* or *kala jeera*; as a general rule interpret *jeera (jira)* and *zeera (zira)* as cumin and *kalonji* as nigella; the latter is also sometimes referred to as 'wild onion seed' in certain cookery books. The 'fitches' of the Bible are *N. sativa* (F. N. Hepper, *Bible Plants at Kew*) '. . . but the fitches are beaten out with a staff, and cumin with a rod.' (Isaiah 28. 25, 27).

OTHER NAMES

Black Caraway, Black Cumin, Damascena, Devil-in-the-bush, Fennel Flower, Gith, Love-in-a-mist, Melanthion, Nutmeg Flower, Roman Coriander, Wild Onion Seed
French: cheveux de Vénus, nigelle (de Damas), poivrette
German: Schwarzkümmel (black caraway)
Italian: nigella
Spanish: neguilla
Indian: kala zeera (lit, 'black cumin', also kalajira), kalonji, krishnajiraka

Naan Bread (colour page 104)

The soft puffy bread so familiar with *tandoori* chicken.   Serves 6

Imp	Metric	US
ltsp sugar	ltsp	ltsp
¾ cup water, warm	210ml	⅞ cup
loz dried yeast	30g	loz
llb strong white flour	455g	llb
ltsp nigella seeds (or caraway)	ltsp	ltsp
ltsp salt	ltsp	ltsp
6tbsp yoghurt	120ml	8tbsp
2tbsp *ghee* or butter, melted	40ml	2⅔tbsp
oil to coat		

1 Dissolve sugar in the warm water and sprinkle yeast on it. Leave for 15 minutes. Make sure it froths, otherwise use new batch.
2 Sift flour and salt into bowl and mix in nigella seeds.
3 Make a depression in the flour and pour in yoghurt, *ghee* and the yeast mixture. Mix well and knead into a dough for about 10 minutes. Form a ball.
4 Put a little oil in another bowl and turn the ball of dough in it until it is covered by the oil. Discard excess oil. Cover with a damp cloth and allow to double in size – about 2 hours.
5 Knead the ball down again and divide it into 6 portions.
6 Flatten these in turn and mould into pear shapes.
7 Place on a greased tray and bake for 10–15 minutes at Gas Mark 8, 450°F, 230°C. Finish under grill if necessary.
8 Serve at once or freeze, which actually improves flavour.

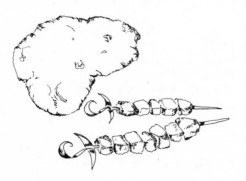

Lobhia (colour page 104)

An Indian dish of black-eyed beans served on their own with yoghurt and fresh coriander or as a side dish for curries.

Serves 4–6

Imp	Metric	US
8oz black-eyed beans, washed and soaked overnight	225g	8oz
1 *yakhni* spice bag (see Spice Mixtures)	1	1
ltsp salt	ltsp	ltsp
2tbsp oil	40ml	2⅔tbsp
½ onion, chopped	½	½
½tsp cumin, ground	½tsp	½tsp
½tsp *garam masala*	½tsp	½tsp
½tsp nigella, ground	½tsp	½tsp
½tsp turmeric, ground	½tsp	½tsp
¼pt yoghurt	140ml	9½tbsp
ltbsp lemon juice	20ml	1⅓tbsp
ltbsp coriander leaves, chopped	ltbsp	1⅓tbsp

1 Drain the beans, place in a saucepan, cover with plenty of fresh water and add *yakhni* spices.
2 Bring to the boil, cover and simmer until tender. Remove spices and drain.
3 Heat oil, add onion and fry until cooked and brown.
4 Add spices and fry together for a minute and then add beans, stirring until well coated with the mixture.
5 Serve accompanied by yoghurt mixed with a litle lemon juice and chopped coriander leaves.

Nutmeg

Myristica fragrans
Fam Myristicaceae

SPICE DESCRIPTION

The nut-like seed found in the fruit of a large tree, the fresh nutmeg is enclosed in a hard brown shell, enclosed in turn in a crimson cage-like aril. The aril dries to a yellow-brown colour, and is the mace of culinary use. Nutmegs are commonly sold without the mace and the hard shell. They are oval, measuring about 25mm (1in) in length, with a diameter around 2cm (¾in). The dark brown surface is lightly wrinkled; the inner substance is hard and lighter brown. When the nutmeg is cut or grated, the exposed surface develops a waxy sheen. Nutmeg is sold whole or ground to a powder. Sometimes the whole nuts have a thin coating of lime, against worms and fungus, otherwise they are fumigated before reaching the shops. Nutmegs are freely and constantly available.

Bouquet Sweet, aromatic and nutty.
Flavour Nutty and woody. Warm and gently bitter, both sweetish and slightly camphorous.   H Scale: 1

PREPARATION AND STORAGE

As powdered nutmeg deteriorates quickly, it is best to keep whole nuts, which last indefinitely, and grate as required. Special nutmeg graters are sold for this purpose. Nutmeg is slightly poisonous, and should therefore be used in moderation – a pinch will harm no-one. It should be noted that nutmeg increases the potency of alcohols. Store both nuts and powder in airtight containers.

USES

Nutmeg has a great variety of uses, seeming to be more or less habitually added to English puddings, a tradition centuries old, and widely used in Italy. Most pies, puddings, custards and cakes may benefit from its inclusion. It also combines well with cheese, and is frequently added to soufflés and cheese sauces. Other sauces which require it are onion sauce and bread sauce. It complements egg dishes, and vegetables such as sprouts, broad beans, broccoli and – especially in Italy – spinach, used in *ripiena* (stuffed pastas). Sweet-sour pickling mixtures often call for a pinch of it. Nutmeg flavours German *Extrawurst* and Italian *mortadella* sausages, haggis, and Middle Eastern meat dishes – especially mutton. As part of a spice mixture, it contributes to mincemeat spice, pudding spice, pastry spice, poultry dressing and Indian *garam masala*. Indian sweet dishes are spiced with nutmeg, as are a wide variety of Caribbean puddings, breads and cakes. Use it in eggnog and sprinkle it on mulled wines and punches. With other herbs and spices, it flavours French vermouth. See Mulling Spice, page 214, for mulled wine recipes.

CHEMICAL COMPOSITION

Nutmeg yields about 5 per cent volatile oil, oil of myristica, which gives it its odour and flavour. This oil contains mainly camphene (72 per cent) and pinene (8 per cent), and about 4 per cent myristicin, a poisonous narcotic. Proteins, starch, cellulose and minerals are also present. There is 25–35 per cent fixed oil ('nutmeg butter'), an orange-red to brown buttery solid, containing trimyristin (60–75 per cent) and oleic and linoleic glycerides. Ground nutmeg has little or no antimicrobial effect. The volatile oils are rapidly lost when nutmeg is ground. Grenadine nutmegs are the sweetest as they do not contain eugenol and safrole, like those of the East Indies.

ATTRIBUTED PROPERTIES

In small doses nutmeg is a gastric stimulant, a mild external stimulant, a counter-irritant and anti-nauseant. It is used in flatulence and rheumatism. However, myristicin is a toxic narcotic, and may be the factor causing euphoria and hallucination when nutmeg is taken in excess. Too much nutmeg may also cause epileptic symptoms. Nutmeg extract can be addictive. These effects will not be induced with a culinary-sized dose of the spice. At most, combined with a nightcap, it will act as a mild soporific.

PLANT DESCRIPTION

A large, tropical, evergreen dioecious tree reaching to 13m (43ft), occasionally 20m (66ft). The bark is a dark grey-green, yielding a yellow juice which oxidises to red. The tree is thickly branched, with dense foliage, the tough, dark-green oval leaves about 10cm (4in) long. The flowers are small, light yellow and bell-shaped. The fruit, a drupe, is grooved like an apricot. It is also pale yellow, some 6cm (2½in) long, and splits when ripe, eventually casting the seed. The spice is the kernel. Some trees are hermaphroditic but they yield inferior spices.

CULTIVATION

The nutmeg grows best on islands in the tropics. It prefers hot and humid conditions and a high rainfall, over 215mm (85in). Rich volcanic soils, that do not get water logged or dry out too much, are the most suitable. Nutmegs are propagated by seeds in nursery beds: other methods have not been very successful. After six months the seedlings are transplanted to the plantation at 7.6m (25ft) intervals. However, because of the almost perfect dioeciousness of the tree it is necessary to cut out the surplus males, which can only be done after five years when the trees first flower. A ratio of one male to four female trees is considered best. Full bearing occurs after 15 years and the trees continue to bear up to fifty years. A single tree produces 1,500–2,000 nutmegs a year. The fruit drop, the seed is removed, then the mace from the seed. The mace is flattened and the seeds dried until they rattle, when they are shelled.

REMARKS

Native to the Moluccas (the Spice Islands), nutmeg is now cultivated mainly in Indonesia, Sri Lanka, the West Indies, Malaysia and some other tropical and sub-tropical regions. Today's main commercial sources are Grenada and Indonesia. Nutmeg was known in England in Chaucer's time, and was used as a fumigant against the plague, among other evils. In the Renaissance, when Western spice trading snowballed, nutmeg became one of the subjects of feud and intrigue among the Portuguese, Dutch, French and English; it has remained in great demand since the fifteenth century. Up until 1512 the Arabs, the only importers of the spice to Europe, had concealed their source, but in that year the Portuguese discovered the Spice Islands. To preserve their new monopoly

the Portuguese and then the Dutch restricted the trees to the islands of Banda and Amboina. However, they were thwarted by fruit pigeons who carried the seeds to neighbouring islands. The final blow to the Dutch monopoly came in the early 1800s when Christopher Smith, the English botanist, collected thousands of plants from the islands for Malaya, India and Kew. In eighteenth century England elaborate silver travelling pocket graters were popular amongst the gentry, and are now fairly common as antiques. Nutmeg butter is made by heating and pressing inferior nutmegs and left-over bits, and one of its uses is in soaps. The oil from the leaves is used in weedkillers. The fresh husks go to make nutmeg jelly, and are preserved in syrup or vinegar. Locally they

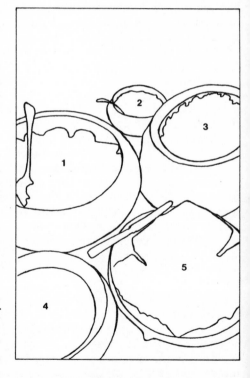

1. Dried Fruit Salad (page 116); 2. Country Mustard (page 130); 3. Forester's Venison (page 69); 4. Lettuce Soup (page 132); 5. Gingerbread (page 106)

are eaten raw. Commercially they are employed in the production of perfumes, confections and liqueurs. Cultivated nutmeg is sometimes adulterated with inferior wild varieties, deriving from the *Myristica argentea* of New Guinea or *M. malabarica* (Bombay nutmeg, mace). Connecticut is called the 'Nutmeg State' because the early inhabitants sold wooden nutmegs as real. In 1711, Addison in *The Spectator* reports the Emperor of Persia styling himself 'The sun of glory and the nutmeg of delight'.

OTHER NAMES

French: noix muscade
German: Muskatnuss
Italian: noce moscata
Spanish: nuez moscada
Chinese: taukau
Indian: jaiphal(l), jaiphul, jauphull, taiphal, taipmal

1. Peach Melba (page 197); 2. Lemon Lamb (page 62); 3. Potted Shrimps (page 118)

Indonesian: pala
Malay: buah pala
Sinhalese: sadikka
Tamil: jathikkai
Thai: jathikkai, look jun

Swiss Spinach Pancakes (colour page 190)

A light luncheon or supper dish.

Serves 6

Imp	Metric	US
1lb spinach, fresh or 12oz (340g) frozen	455g	1lb
8oz cottage cheese, sieved	225g	8oz
½tsp nutmeg, grated	½tsp	½tsp
pepper		
salt		
6oz ham	170g	6oz
6 pancakes 7in (18cm) in diameter	6	6
2oz butter	55g	2oz
2oz flour	55g	2oz
¾pt milk	425ml	1¾ cups
1oz Gruyère cheese, grated	30g	1oz

1 Cook the spinach in very little water, drain, and finely chop. Reserve water.
2 Mix the spinach with the cottage cheese and season with nutmeg, pepper and salt.
3 Cut the ham into 6 rectangles, 7 × 2in (18 × 5cm) and lay a piece in the centre of each pancake.
4 Spread some spinach filling over the ham, roll up the pancakes and lay them side by side in a buttered, oven-proof dish.
5 Make a sauce with the butter, flour, milk and ¼pt (140ml, 9½tbsp US) reserved spinach water. Season, pour over the pancakes and top with cheese.
6 Reheat in a moderate oven Gas Mark 4, 350°F, 180°C. Brown under grill and serve.

MULLED WINE
See Mulling Spice, page 214.

Onion

Allium cepa
Fam Alliaceae

The onion is an edible bulb. While it is a vegetable at heart, it also acts as a spice inasmuch as it can provide an aromatic undertone to various meat and vegetable dishes, without being a major ingredient. The characteristic appearance of the onion is well known, but there are many variations of colour, shape and size. The colour varies from white to red to purple, the shape from spherical to almost conical, and the diameter at the largest point from 10mm (⅜in) to 8cm (3in) or more. Onions should be firm, though not rock hard. The papery skin should be tight over the surface of the bulb. Spring onions, or scallions, are immature plants where the bulb has not completely formed. They may be cylindrical, the green stem shading into the white bulblet, which may be almost spherical. Onions are also available in processed form, as dried flakes and powder, or liquid.

Bouquet Sharp. Raw onions when cut or bruised may irritate the eyes and nose.

Flavour Generally pungent and bitter with a sweet note. Onions actually cover the whole gamut of aroma and pungency from mild to intolerable.   H Scale: 3–7

PREPARATION AND STORAGE
Onions may be used whole, sliced, chopped, diced or liquidised. It is important to observe the cooking instructions carefully, as the flavour of onions is greatly influenced by their treatment. A recipe where onions are to be 'fried till golden' will suffer if the onions are browned. Small onions and picklers are easier to peel if they are first immersed in boiling water for ten seconds and then rinsed in cold water before removing the skins. To prevent the eyes from watering, peel onions under cold water or put them in the freezer for ten minutes before chopping. Should onions be excessively strong, boil them whole for five minutes before proceeding with the recipe. An easy method for dicing an onion is illustrated below. Firm unblemished onions should keep for several weeks if stored in a cool airy place. Too much warmth will encourage sprouting. Home-grown onions must be quite dry before stringing. Dried onion flakes and powder should be stored in airtight containers.

USES
Onion is a basic flavouring in the kitchen. It is used as a vegetable, or as a spice to bring out the flavour of other dishes without overpowering them. It often accompanies meat – especially mince and meat dishes such as shepherds pie and meat loaf which would be insipid without it. Onion is also widely used in soups, pickles and cooked vegetable dishes, sauces, hearty casseroles, and bean and lentil dishes. It is a common ingredient in marinades, and an onion studded with cloves is often a main flavouring in stocks and *courts-bouillons*. There are many classic recipes featuring onion including such familiar dishes as tripe and onions, steak and onions, French onion soup, *coq au vin, sauce soubise*, to name but a few. Equally famous in India is *do pyaza*, a dish of meat cooked with as much as double its weight of onions. The

shallot is frequently used in Mediterranean and American cookery, the rocambole in country recipes. Spring onions are common in fresh summer salads and in Chinese and Japanese cookery.

CHEMICAL COMPOSITION

Onion contains protein, sugars, cellulose, minerals, a fixed oil, an essential oil and over 80 per cent water. The amount of essential oil is very small but it contains the aromatic and tear-producing properties associated with onion. These are caused by sulphides which are produced by the reaction of the enzyme alliinase on an amino acid. These substances are normally in separate cells in the tissues, but when the onion is cut and bruised, rupturing the cells, the reaction takes place. Cooking has the opposite effect, preventing the enzymatic action and thus milder and less pungent flavours are produced. The chemistry of the Alliaceae family, including garlic, shallots etc, is very similar. The calorific value of raw onion is 38 calories per 100g, or roughly 20 calories for a 3oz onion.

ATTRIBUTED PROPERTIES

Antiseptic, diuretic, expectorant and rubefacient. Onion's antiseptic properties as a juice or paste have been used for wound healing, skin complaints (acne), insect bites, haemorrhoids, boils, toothache, ('as moch for that purpose as to lay an unyon to my lytel fynger for the tothe ache', Brinklow, 1545), earache and respiratory complaints. The raw juice is diuretic and the whole onion is an appetite stimulant and digestant. It has been used as a vermifuge. It is believed to stimulate the liver and is beneficial to the heart and nervous system.

PLANT DESCRIPTION

A hardy biennial but cultivated as an annual. Although the bulbous plant with its long-bladed leaves has many varieties of shape and colour, it is so familiar that it is not necessary to add to what has already been said under Spice Description.

Formerly the genus *Allium* was included in the family Liliaceae and then removed to the Amaryllidaceae. However, the simplest solution has been to place onions in a family of their own, the Alliaceae, which is between the other two.

CULTIVATION

Onion is a common kitchen-garden plant. It is propagated by seeds or sets.
Soil: Well drained, light loam that has been manured.
Sow: Mid-February through March in shallow drills 30cm (12in) apart. Thin seedlings to 5–10cm (2–4in) apart.
Plant: March–April 15cm (6in) apart in rows 30cm (12in) apart.
Aspect: Very sunny.
Harvest: Salad onions when ready and other onions when leaves turn yellow. Lift and leave along rows to dry; then store in a cool dry place.

REMARKS

The onion is among the oldest recorded cultivated plants. Its pre-history is obscure, but it is probably native to Asia and the Mediterranean. It is cultivated in temperate and warm areas of the northern hemisphere. The pyramids are said to have contained records mentioning the onion as a staple food of the builders. In the Bible (Numbers 11. 5) the Israelites lament the loss of their Egyptian food, onions included. The rocambole and the shallot are onion varieties growing wild in Europe. Both are compound bulbs (like garlic). Shallots are deemed superior to common onions, while rocamboles are rougher. Also related are chives, garlic, leeks, the Welsh onion or cibol (*A. fistulosum*) native to the Orient, the tree onion (*A. cepa* var *proliferum*) growing two feet above the ground on stems, and the potato onion, a large-bulbed Irish variety.

OTHER NAMES
French: oignon
German: Zwiebel
Italian: cipolla
Spanish: cebolla

Arabic: basal
Chinese: choong
Indian: palandu, pe(e)az, piaz, pyaz
Indonesian: bawang merah, daun bawang (spring onion)
Japanese: naganegi (spring onion), negi, nira (chive), rakkyo (Chinese onion), tamanegi
Malay: bawang merah, daun bawang (spring onion)
Tamil: vungium, vunguim
Thai: hua horm, ton horm (spring onion)

Shabu-Shabu (Mongolian Fire Pot or Steam Boat)

This is fun. *Shabu-shabu* is the Japanese equivalent of the Western *fondue*, its name deriving onomatopoeically from the sound of cooking as meat and vegetables are held by chopsticks in a boiling stock on the table. Cooked pieces are then dipped in sauces and eaten immediately. Westerners may find it easier to cook their morsels on the end of a *fondue* fork.   Serves 4–6

Imp	*Metric*	US
Sesame Sauce		
5tbsp sesame seeds	5tbsp	6⅔tbsp
½pt chicken stock	285ml	1¼ cups
½tsp chilli sauce	½tsp	½tsp
2tsp ginger, fresh, finely chopped	2tsp	2tsp
1tsp onion juice	1tsp	1tsp
2tbsp *shoyu* (Japanese soy sauce)	40ml	2⅔tbsp
sesame oil		
Tofu Sauce		
8oz *tofu* (soya bean curd)	225g	8oz
½tsp garlic powder or 1 clove minced	½tsp	½tsp
1½tbsp lemon juice	30ml	2tbsp
3tbsp mustard oil	60ml	4tbsp
1tsp *shoyu*	1tsp	1tsp
salt to taste		
cayenne to garnish		
Shabu-Shabu		
2lb lean steak	905g	2lb
8oz bamboo shoots	225g	8oz
2 carrots, young, parboiled	2	2
1 Chinese leaves (cabbage)	1	1
1 *daikon* (Japanese radish)	1	1
8oz mushrooms, button	225g	8oz
12 spring onions	12	12

1 Dry fry the sesame seeds until they jump. Cool.
2 Blend them with the rest of the sesame sauce ingredients in an electric blender, adding enough sesame oil to obtain a creamy texture. Serve in individual dishes.
3 Mix all the *tofu* sauce ingredients in a blender. Garnish with cayenne and serve in individual dishes.
4 Slice the steak into thin strips. Partially freezing it first makes this easier.
5 Cut the vegetables into pieces suitable for holding with chopsticks or *fondue* forks.
6 Serving. Boil the stock and transfer to a special *shabu-shabu* cooker or use a *fondue* pan or other table-top cooking device. Keeping the stock piping hot; meat and vegetables are held in it to cook and then dipped in the sauce and eaten. Replenish stock as necessary. Serve *wasabi* as a condiment. When all the meat and vegetables have been eaten the stock is poured into bowls and served as soup.

French Onion Soup (colour page 190)

A simple recipe for this popular soup.
          Serves 4–6

Imp	*Metric*	US
1–2oz butter	30–55g	1–2oz
8oz onions, thinly sliced	225g	8oz
¼tsp salt	¼tsp	¼tsp
pinch sugar	pinch	pinch
1½pt beef stock	855ml	3½ cups
1–2tbsp white vermouth (optional)	1–2tbsp	1⅓–2⅔tbsp
4–6 slices French bread	4–6	4–6
4–6oz cheese – Gruyère preferred	115–170g	4–6oz

1 Melt butter and fry onions gently until they are soft and yellow.
2 Add salt and sugar and continue cooking at a slightly higher heat until onions are cooked and golden brown.
3 Add the stock and vermouth (optional) and simmer for 30 minutes. Skim if necessary.
4 Dry the bread in the oven, cover with grated cheese and place one slice in each

soup bowl (earthenware). Pour on the soup and add a bit more cheese to the bread when it floats to the top. Put bowls in oven (Gas Mark 3, 160°C, 325°F) and brown the tops – about 15 minutes. Serve at once.

Papaya

Carica papaya
syn *Papaya carica*
Fam Caricaceae

SPICE DESCRIPTION

These are the seeds of a tropical fruit. Although the fruit is widely eaten where it grows, and is known in the West, the use of the seeds is more or less confined to areas of local production. The ripe seeds resemble large caviar and are dark grey or brown-black in colour. Numerously contained in a hollow cavity in the fruit, they are jelly-like in appearance and texture, covered in a juicy, bittersweet gelatinous coating. When the coating is removed, it leaves hard black seeds similar to peppercorns but with wrinkled ridges. Whole fresh papayas are seasonally available.
Bouquet Mildly aromatic when fresh, diminishing as the seed dries.
Flavour: Slightly pungent when fresh, resembling cress. When dried, the flavour is greatly reduced.   H Scale: 3–4

PREPARATION AND STORAGE

Cut the ripe fruit in half lengthways and scoop out the seeds. Use immediately or refrigerate and use within two days. Alternatively, spread out the seeds to dry on a windowsill and then store in an airtight container. These dried seeds will not have the pungency of the fresh papaya seeds.

USES

Although papaya seed is used as a spice in the tropics but is as yet hardly known in the West, papain, extracted from the papaya tree, is familiar to us in powdered form as a meat tenderiser. Fresh seeds may be used similarly, however. Rub the seeds and fruit skin on to steak and leave for several hours. Remove before cooking. Include some crushed seeds in marinades for kebabs and barbecued meats; the meat will be tender with a piquant flavour. Papaya seed dressing is delicious and different; it goes with both green and fruit salads. A Haitian recipe for papaya ice cream includes the addition of a few of the crushed seeds for a tangy flavour. The dried seeds may be ground and used like pepper. The fruit itself is wonderfully versatile and may be used when unripe in all sorts of vegetable dishes – baked, boiled or stuffed with meat, in pickles and chutneys, and as a substitute for cooking apple. When ripe, it may be used in puddings, fruit salads, ice cream, preserves and drinks.

CHEMICAL COMPOSITION

The plant latex is rich in the enzymes papain and chymopapain. The fruit is nearly 90 per cent water with sugar 10 per cent (half glucose and half fructose), protein 0.5 per cent, plus fat, acids, fibre and ash. It is also a good source of vitamin A with some C. The seeds contain some papain and the bitter alkaloid caricin or carpain(e), which gives them their characteristic bitter taste.

ATTRIBUTED PROPERTIES

In India the seeds are used as a vermifuge, emmenagogue, counter-irritant and carminative. Juice from the seeds is prescribed for haemorrhaging piles and with the seeds is made into abortifacient pessaries. In Australia the seeds are much valued by the Aborigines as an aphrodisiac. The latex from the unripe fruit, being rich in papain, is an excellent digestive. Again, this is used as a vermifuge and can be applied for the removal of horny matter such as warts as well as freckles. Present British medical research finds that papain may be useful in back pains as a chaemonucleolysitic agent, the meat tenderising properties dissolving the nuclear tissue in prolapsed vertebrae. The fruit and leaves have powerful meat tenderising and milk-clotting properties, in the latter case as a substitute for rennet.

PLANT DESCRIPTION
A palm-like, tropical, herbaceous perennial tree. The single, tapering stem reaches up to 10m (33ft). It is grey-brown and scarred, being of a fleshy woody substance, soft and hollow. There is a crown of large maple-like leaves, seven-lobed. The melon-like fruits, which are berries, are 10–30cm (4–12in) long and can weigh up to 10kg (22lb). The skin is thin and green, turning yellow or orange when ripe, and the flesh is orange to red. The internal cavity contains the seeds which are white, turning to black when the fruit is ripe. The plant is dioecious, the male flowers small and trumpet-shaped, the female ones large and fleshy. Old male trees become hermaphroditic. Do not use fruit that is borne by trees growing in insanitary areas, as bacteria can be carried through the tree's sap system into the fruit.

CULTIVATION
Papaya thrives in the tropics up to 1,500m (5,000ft), best in well drained soil. It is grown from seed but cannot stand frost. It

matures in one year and lasts five or six. It is cultivated on a commercial scale on plantations for its papain for the meat-packing industry, the unripe fruit being tapped for their latex rather like rubber trees. The tree is ubiquitous in the tropics, being seen in city back-lots, villages and abandoned farms.

REMARKS
Native to tropical America, papaya is now widespread in the tropics, especially in South East Asia, the Pacific and Africa. It is common as a garden plant. The fruit, which contains much vitamins A and C, is available fresh or candied, and is used commercially in soft drinks and ice cream. The unripe fruit yields a latex which is used in the manufacture of chewing gum, meat tenderisers and medicines. It is used in chill-proof beer, preventing it clouding with chilling, and figures in the processing of wool to make it shrink-resistant. Papaya has strong tenderising powers; meat wrapped in the leaves will soften, and animals fed on it will yield tender flesh. In the tropics the seeds are chewed like betel. Papaw is also a name for the wild American fruit *Asimina triloba*. In Kenya the Mountain Pawpaw, *Carica canda marcensis*, whose fruit is small, acidic and perfumed, grows well above 1700m (5,600ft).

OTHER NAMES
Papaw, Pawpaw, Mamaeiro, Melon Tree, Tree Melon
French: papaye
German: Melonenbaum, Papaia
Italian: papaia
Spanish: papaya
Chinese: shu-kua
Indian: papaya, papeeta, papita
West Indies: fruta de bomba, lechosa

Papaya Marinade
A meat-tenderising marinade particularly good for preparing steaks for barbecues.
Enough for 6–8 steaks

Imp	Metric	US
¼pt red wine or lemon juice	140ml	9½tbsp
¼pt olive oil	140ml	9½tbsp
1 carrot, finely chopped	1	1
½tsp chilli powder	½tsp	½tsp
2 garlic cloves, finely chopped	2	2
1tsp mustard powder	1tsp	1tsp
2oz papaya flesh, mashed	55g	2oz
1tbsp papaya seeds, fresh or dried	1tbsp	1⅓tbsp
1 onion, finely chopped	1	1
1tbsp sugar	1tbsp	1⅓tbsp
½tsp salt	½tsp	½tsp

1 Mix all the ingredients in a blender.
2 Coat barbecue steaks with the marinade and leave for 4 hours before cooking.

Papaya Vinaigrette (colour page 51)

A salad dressing with a pleasantly 'cressy' undertone.

Imp	Metric	US
½tsp mustard powder	½tsp	½tsp
1tsp pawpaw seeds, fresh	1tsp	1tsp
¼pt olive oil	140ml	9½tbsp
¼tsp salt	¼tsp	¼tsp
1tbsp sugar	1tbsp	1⅓tbsp
4tbsp vinegar, any	80ml	5⅓tbsp

Mix all ingredients together in a blender, but only cracking the papaya seeds. Shake well, bottle and keep.

Paprika

Capiscum annuum
Fam Solanaceae

SPICE DESCRIPTION
Paprika, or paprika pepper, is a fine powder ground from certain varieties of *Capsicum annuum*. It is not to be confused with the vine peppers which yield the common table pepper. The peppers which yield paprika are various in shape and size, but are generally pointed or cone-shaped. They are larger and milder than chilli peppers, the flesh being without the extreme fiery pungency of the chilli. The species is variously named as *C.a.microcarpum*, *C.a.tetragonum* or *C.a.grossum*, but the botany of the entire capsicum family is confused. Paprika is produced from peppers ripened to redness, sometimes called 'pimento' (as used to stuff cocktail olives). The powder varies in colour from bright red to a rusty brown. Several grades of flavour are manufactured, though the choice is fairly limited outside Hungary and Spain. Sweet, semi-sweet and pungent varieties are available, depending on the proportion of the hot seeds used, and on whether the seeds are first macerated to remove their pungency. Hungarian paprika is reckoned the best, followed by that of Spain. Chilli derivatives are summarised under Chilli and Remarks.

Bouquet Very slightly warm and sweetish.
Flavour Mild paprika is sweet, adding more colour than flavour to cookery. Hot paprika can be pungent and fiery. Most Western paprikas are mild or semi-sweet.

H Scale: 2–6

PREPARATION AND STORAGE
Except for the most pungent varieties, paprika can generally be used in generous quantities. If it is fried, care should be taken that the sweeter varieties do not burn or caramelise, so cook gently. Paprika must be stored in a dark container as it reacts to sunlight. Being a spice that tends to deteriorate rapidly, it should be bought in small amounts, as necessary.

USES
Paprika has a wide variety of uses, blending well with most savoury flavours. It can be used as a table condiment, like salt and pepper, for sprinkling over many dishes, adding colour and flavour to soups, meats and vegetables. Its most extensive use is in Eastern Europe, especially Hungary, where it is traditional in the meat stews which foreigners call 'goulash'. In fact, there are four types of goulash: *gulyás*, a cross between a soup and a beef stew served with potatoes and tiny dumplings; *pörkölt*, cubes of beef, pork or game with a thick onion sauce; *tokány*, strips of meat with just a little paprika and often with

mushrooms and sour cream; and *paprikás*, white meat or fish dishes served with a fresh or sour cream sauce. Many spiced sausages incorporate it, the Spanish *chorizos* being one of the better known. Also there is *paprikaspeck*, fat bacon coated with paprika and eaten with other cold meats. Other meats that marry well with it are pork chops, bacon, and casseroled veal and chicken. Paprika is sprinkled on boiled, poached and fried eggs, on salads, hors d'oeuvres, lobsters, shrimps and other seafood. It can colour and flavour butter and sauces made with cream or mayonnaise. Among vegetables, its closest friends are cabbage, mushrooms, potatoes and cucumber. Paprika spices cheese and cheese spreads, and is used in marinades and smoked foods. It can be incorporated in the flour dusting for fried chicken and other meats. Many Spanish, Portuguese and Turkish recipes use paprika to flavour soups, fish, stews, casseroles and vegetables. A few Indian recipes, *tandoori* chicken for example, sometimes use paprika to give the characteristic red colour.

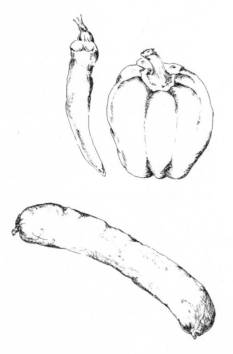

CHEMICAL COMPOSITION
Paprika is chemically similar to chilli, although lower in capsaicin, the pungent principle. It is rich in vitamin C (ascorbic acid), and contains a high amount of vitamins A and B complex. Also present are the red pigment capsanthin, other pigments and various proteins, sugars, fibre, moisture and a fixed oil. The sweeter the paprika, the less capsaicin it contains. See also under Chilli.

ATTRIBUTED PROPERTIES
Being a rich source of vitamins, paprika is generally healthful. However, it has no specific medicinal uses, its stronger relative, chilli, being used instead. It is said to improve night vision.

PLANT DESCRIPTION
Paprika is produced from the berries of *Capsicum annuum*, related to the chilli, of the potato family. This is an annual herbaceous sub-shrub, not found in the wild, erect, densely branched, reaching between 0.5 and 1.5m (20–60in) high. The lower portion of the plant is often woody. The leaves are placed alternately, and are dark green above, light green on the undersides. The white flowers are generally borne singly, as is the fruit, which is green when unripe, but ripens to red, brown, white or purple. The whitish, disc-shaped seeds are up to 5mm ($^3/_{16}$in) in diameter. Only red-ripening fruits are used for paprika. The varieties used in Spain are called *Ramilette, Tres Cascos, Bola* and *Albar*. See also under Chilli.

CULTIVATION
Some varieties of *C. annuum* are hardier than *C. frutescens*, and can grow further north in the northern hemisphere. However, very young plants are kept warm in nurseries, to be planted out after six to eight weeks. Harvest is usually in the autumn. Capsicum cannot stand frost and is best grown under glass.
Sow: Seeds in pots in March under glass.
Plant: Plant out in May to June, 40cm (15in) apart.

Soil: Any well drained and enriched.
Aspect: South, sunny and sheltered – best against a wall.
Harvest: August to September, pick as required.

REMARKS
Like all capsicums, the paprika varieties are native to South America. They have been under cultivation so long that their earliest botany is unknown. Originally a tropical plant, *C. annuum* can now grow in cooler climates, and in fact was first grown for paprika in Europe, the original producer being Spain. These European varieties have evolved into much milder forms than their tropical ancestors. Today paprika is intimately associated with the Hungarian cuisine, although it is also produced and used in Turkey, Yugoslavia and the United States. In Spain and Hungary paprika is produced in a series of grades. The Spanish grades of *pimentón* are *dolce* (sweet), *agridulce* (semi sweet) and *picante* (hot). The spice is also graded as to quality, depending on the proportion of seeds and placenta (the white internal ridges) to flesh. Second quality is known as *arena*, sand. In Hungary there are six classes:

Különleges (exquisite delicate): very mild; suitable for light diets.
Delicatessen (delicate): very red; less mild than the above.
Édesnemes (noble-sweet): red and sweetish, made from the flesh of the peppers with the stalks, calyxes and placenta removed and the seeds washed and macerated in water to remove some of the capsaicin. The most common variety.
Félédes (semi-sweet): similar to noble-sweet but some placenta included, thus slightly stronger.
Rosza (rose or first quality): slightly less red than the above two, made from the whole pepper less stalks and calyxes.
Erös (hot or pungent, second quality): like rose; made from second quality peppers, browny red in colour. As hot as cayenne.
Uncommon today is a third quality,

Commercial or Mercantile, made from the remnants of the peppers used for the above paprikas. Colour varies from yellowy brown to brown-red. Paprika is milled, ground, sifted, blended, homogenised and graded in factories using a compound series of roller mills. For the milder paprikas of inferior quality, the seeds are macerated before being ground to remove their bitterness. The spice is used in commercial food production, for example in salamis and cheese spreads. It was known to Mrs Beeton and the Edwardians as 'krona pepper'.

OTHER NAMES
Hungarian Pepper, Pimento Pepper, Sweet Pepper
French: piment
German: Paprika
Italian: paprica
Spanish: pimentón, pimiento colorado (Andalucia)
Hungarian: paprika (see above)

Hungarian Goulash (colour page 190)
A delicious, simple beef goulash. Serve with a green salad and rye bread and butter.   Serves 4–6

Imp	Metric	US
2lb lean stewing steak	1kg	2lb
1oz lard	30g	1oz
1lb onions, sliced	455g	1lb
1 small green pepper, seeded and chopped	1	1
1 small red pepper, seeded and chopped	1	1
2 garlic cloves, crushed	2	2
1lb ripe tomatoes, peeled and chopped	455g	1lb
½pt water	285ml	1¼ cups
½–1tsp caraway seeds	½–1tsp	½–1tsp
2tsp sweet paprika	2tsp	2tsp
1tsp hot paprika	1tsp	1tsp
1tsp salt, or to taste	1tsp	1tsp
1lb potatoes, peeled and cut into ½in (12mm) cubes just before needed	455g	1lb
¼pt sour cream (optional)	140ml	9½tbsp
chives		

1 Trim meat and cut into 1in (25mm) cubes.

147

2 Melt fat in a saucepan or large frying pan and fry onions, peppers and garlic until the onions are golden.
3 Add meat, sprinkle with salt and turn for about five minutes until sealed on all sides.
4 Stir in paprika and caraway, then add tomatoes and water. Stir well.
5 Transfer to a casserole, cover and cook in a slow oven Gas Mark 2, 300°F, 150°C, for 2 hours.
6 Add potatoes and cook for a further hour.
7 Top each serving with a spoonful of sour cream if desired.

Habas à la Asturiana

A substantial Spanish casserole of broad beans (*fava*) cooked with wine and paprika.
Serves 4

Imp	Metric	US
2tbsp olive oil	40ml	2⅔tbsp
8oz onions, chopped	225g	8oz
2 garlic cloves, crushed	2	2
1 *chorizos* sausage, sliced	1	1
2oz ham, chopped	55g	2oz
1tsp paprika	1tsp	1tsp
1½lb broad beans (*fava*), shelled	680g	1½lb
4oz carrots, diced	115g	4oz
½pt stock	285ml	1¼ cups
¼pt white wine	140ml	9½tbsp
pepper		
salt		
12oz potatoes, in chunks	340g	12oz

1 Heat oil and fry onions and garlic until golden brown.
2 Take the pan off the heat, add sausage and ham and stir in paprika.
3 Return pan to the heat and add beans, carrots, stock and wine. Season to taste, cover and simmer gently for 30 minutes.
4 Add potatoes and cook for a further 30 minutes until the potatoes are done.

Pepper

Piper nigrum Black, White, Green
Piper longum Long Pepper
Fam Piperaceae
Schinus terebinthifolius Pink Pepper
Fam Anacardiaceae

SPICE DESCRIPTION
Pepper, the 'King of Spices', derives from several species of vinous plant, the spice being the whole fruit, called 'peppercorns'. *Piper nigrum* provides the black and the white pepper commonly used in the West. **Black Pepper** is the dried unripe fruit. The corns are spherical and wrinkled, measuring about 5mm (⅕in) in diameter. **White Pepper** is from fruit picked when almost ripe, with the dark outer skin removed by retting in water. These corns are slightly smaller than the black, both varieties containing a grey horny seed with a tiny cavity. **Long Pepper**, rarely used in the West, consists of a fused mass of minute fruits in the form of a conical spike, 1–3cm (⅓–1¼in) long. **Mignonette Pepper** or **Shot Pepper**, widely used in France, is a rough-ground mixture of black and white corns. Pepper is available whole, partially ground – as steak pepper for example – or in powder form. **Green Pepper** is a recently marketed flavouring. This is the unripe fresh corns, bottled or canned in brine or vinegar or, more recently, freeze-dried. Also recently marketed from Réunion is **Pink Pepper**, the almost-ripe berries of the tree *Schinus terebinthifolius* – a native of South America – which is not a vinous pepper. It is available usually in vinegar or as dried

berries. The latter have a brittle, papery pink skin enclosing a hard irregular seed, much smaller than the whole fruit. The pickled variety is soft and easily mashed. Although attractive in appearance, they are a poor substitute for real pepper. They are used in Mediterranean areas, especially with fish, and by the Indians of South America for making alcoholic beverages. After a brief spell as a chic new gourmet spice its reputation has been damaged by reports of ill effects. If used, do not add more than fifteen 'peppercorns' to a dish.

Bouquet Aromatic, pungent.

Flavour Black pepper is very pungent, fiery and aromatic. H Scale: 8

White pepper is less pungent. H Scale: 7

Long pepper is slightly sweeter. H Scale: 7

Green pepper tastes clean and fresh and is milder. H Scale: 6½

Pink pepper is bitter, resinous and aromatic. H Scale: 3

PREPARATION AND STORAGE

Pepper is best bought whole, as freshly ground pepper is vastly superior to the ready bought powder. Ground pepper quickly loses its aroma and is easily adulterated. Peppercorns are quite hard but are ground easily in a peppermill.

Their aroma is preserved in hot food if they are added well towards the end of the cooking process. Some dishes demand crushed or cracked pepper – that is, partially broken. This is achieved with moderate effort using a mortar and pestle, but if there is much pepper to crush, simply place the corns in a polythene bag and crush them with a rolling pin. Whole corns keep indefinitely when stored in airtight containers. Pink or green pepper can easily be mashed to a paste. These, being fresh fruit, do not keep well, but will survive some weeks in a refrigerator. Dried green peppercorns can be reconstituted in minutes by soaking them in a little water.

USES

It would be otiose to list the uses of pepper as it occurs in practically all main courses, soups, savoury sauces, salads and entrées. As a condiment it is present on every table. In cookery it is better ground directly on to food than used in its pre-powdered form. Whole peppercorns may be used in *courts-bouillons* and pickling mixtures. They are characteristic of many German smoked sausages and French and Italian salamis. A traditional German Christmas is never without its *Pfefferkuchen*, a kind of ginger-bread spiced with ground pepper. Mixed sweet spices for cakes and buns may contain pepper instead of the more usual allspice. Certain French soft cheeses (such as *Boursin*) are coated with crushed pepper. A layer of mignonette pepper or ordinary crushed pepper pressed on to steak provides the fiery crunch in *steak au poivre*. White pepper is used in white sauces rather than black pepper, which would give the sauce a speckled appearance. Green pepper can be used to effect in spiced butters, mashed with other ingredients such as garlic or cinnamon. With heated cream it makes a fresh and attractive sauce for fish.

CHEMICAL COMPOSITION

Pepper yields 1–3 per cent of a volatile oil which is aromatic though not pungent. The pungency derives from the alkaloids – piperine, piperidine, piperethine and chavian. Cubeb pepper (*P. cubeba*) contains cubebin in place of piperine. Betel (*P. betle*) contains a mild narcotic.

ATTRIBUTED PROPERTIES

Carminative, stimulant, diuretic, diaphoretic, pepper has long been known to improve the digestion. It was used to treat gastro-intestinal upsets, flatulence, fevers and congestive chills. It is supposed to be of help in anal, rectal and urinary troubles. Pepper calms nausea and has been used against vertigo. Cubeb pepper has been used in Asia for gonorrhoea in its secondary stages. It is little used in modern medicine. A paste of ground white pepper and butter, licked at intervals, is a surprisingly effective cure for sore throats and loss of voice.

PLANT DESCRIPTION

A tropical, perennial climbing vine with aerial roots. The plant may grow as high as 10m (33ft) but is commercially maintained around 4m (12ft). It bears alternate, glossy, green wide leaves and dense spikes of white flowers containing around 50 blossoms each. Flowers bloom triennially. The berries are green when unripe, turning red as they mature. Long pepper (*P. longum, P. retrofractum* and *P. chaba*) is similar in appearance except that the berries are fused into catkins. Cubeb pepper bears longer narrower leaves. The corns are slightly larger, forming elongated clusters (see Cubeb).

CULTIVATION

Pepper needs a hot, wet tropical climate and a well-drained humus-rich soil. It is propagated from stem cuttings and grown in partial shade with trees or poles for support. The plants may yield for up to forty years. Black pepper is produced by plunging the green berries in boiling water and then drying them for three to four days. White pepper is obtained by washing and rubbing off the skin of the almost mature fruit.

REMARKS

P. nigrum is native to south and east India and Cambodia. It is also cultivated in the East and West Indies and in other tropical Asian countries, one of the more famous producers being the Malabar coast. Long pepper, wild in India (Himalayas) and Java, and cubeb pepper (also Java) are nowadays used virtually only where they grow, although they were popular in Europe in the Middle Ages. The Romans preferred long pepper to *P. nigrum*. Since early historic times, pepper has been cultivated as a spice and condiment. It has long been an important article of trade and an exchange medium like money. In classical times 'tributes' were often paid in pepper, like salt, and both Attila the Hun and Alaric I the Visigoth are said to have demanded pepper as a substantial part of Rome's ransom. From the Middle Ages, pepper was the backbone of the European spice trade, Genoa and Venice dominating the market. The Italian monopoly of overland trade routes was a major factor in the search for an eastern sea route. It can be said with justification that the modern European empires and today's Western technological civilisations resulted from the old spice trade, of which pepper was the most important product. Some species of pepper are not condiments. Betel (*P.*

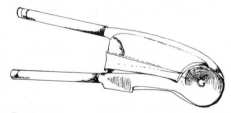

Betel cutter

betle) chewed with areca nuts (wrongly called 'betel nuts') is the Indian *pan*, a tooth-rotting and red-staining narcotic 'chew'. *Piper methysticum* is the basis of the infamous *kava*, a somniferous South Sea Island beverage. The word 'pepper' derives from the Sanskrit *pippeli* (long pepper). It is widely used in a number of unrelated spices such as Jamaica pepper, Chinese pepper, anise pepper, melegueta pepper, cayenne pepper, paprika pepper and chilli pepper. Finally, capsicums and chillies are often called 'pepper' or 'peppers'. They are distinguished from vine peppers by the epithets 'red', 'green' or 'sweet'.

OTHER NAMES

Black
French: poivre
German: Pfeffer
Italian: pepe nero
Spanish: pimienta negra
Arabic: filfil
Burmese: nga-youk-kaun
Indian: gol/kala,i, mir(i)ch(i)
Indonesian: merica hitam, meritja, lada
Lao: phik noi
Malay: lada hitam
Sinhalese: gammiris
Tamil: moloo
Thai: prik ki tai

White
French: poivre blanc
German: Weisser Pfeffer
Italian: pepe bianco
Spanish: pimienta blanca

Green
French: poivre vert
German: Grüner Pfeffer
Italian: pepe verde
Spanish: pimienta verde

Pink
French: poivre rose
German: Blassroter Pfeffer
Italian: pepe rosa
Spanish: pimienta rosa

Long
French: poivre long
German: Langer Pfeffer
Italian: pepe lungo
Spanish: pimienta largo
Indian: Krishna, pip(p)al, pipar, pippli

Steak au Poivre

The classic piquant steak.   Serves 6

Imp	Metric	US
2tsp peppercorns, black	2tsp	2tsp
1tsp peppercorns, white	1tsp	1tsp
6 steaks, 8oz (225g) each	6	6
2tbsp butter	2tbsp	2⅔tbsp
1tbsp olive oil	20ml	1⅓tbsp
salt		
2tbsp brandy	40ml	2⅔tbsp
¼pt stock	140ml	9½tbsp
watercress		

1 Coarsely crush peppercorns in a pestle and mortar.
2 Wipe steaks and rub the peppercorns on to both sides pressing them firmly with the hands. Cover and set aside for one or two hours to allow the flavour to penetrate.
3 Heat the butter and oil in a frying pan and sauté the steaks according to taste. Remove, sprinkle with a little salt and keep warm.
4 Add brandy to the pan and cook for a minute scraping up the residue.
5 Now add the stock and boil rapidly, reducing it to half its original quantity.
6 Pour the sauce over the meat, garnish with watercress and serve.

Green Peppercorn Sauce

An agreeable, fresh sauce for various fish dishes.   Serves 4

Imp	Metric	US
2tsp green peppercorns, mashed	2tsp	2tsp
¼pt cream	140ml	9½tbsp
salt to taste		

1 Mix the peppercorns with the cream and salt to taste.
2 Warm through gently, then serve with poached or grilled fish.

Green Peppercorn Butter

A spiced butter for steaks and grills.
Serves 4–6

Imp	Metric	US
4oz butter	115g	4oz
1tbsp green peppercorns, mashed	1tbsp	1⅓tbsp
1 garlic clove, finely chopped	1	1

1 Cream the butter and mix well with the peppercorns and garlic. Spread thickly on to a board and refrigerate.
2 When cold, cut the butter into squares and serve on top of steaks, grills etc.

Pomegranate

Punica granatum
Fam Punicaceae

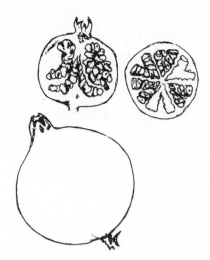

SPICE DESCRIPTION

This spice is the dried or fresh seed of the pomegranate fruit, which is a little larger than an orange, with a tough smooth skin varying in colour from brown-yellow to red. The dried seeds are hard and reddish-brown, angular and elongated, measuring about 8mm (⅓in) in length. They are slightly sticky. Fresh, they are enclosed in a case of jelly-like translucent red pulp, packed into compartments surrounded by a bitter whitish aril, or pith. The seeds are sold dried, sometimes with the aril in pieces, the fleshy pulp being removed. However, it is easy to dry fresh seeds removed from the whole fruit when in season.

Bouquet The dried seeds have only a mild scent, described as fruity or flowery.

Flavour An agreeable *mélange* of sweet and bitter. The aril itself is quite bitter.

H Scale: 1

PREPARATION AND STORAGE

Fresh seeds are easily dried in a slow oven after removing the red pulp (this can be used separately). Use a pestle and mortar to grind the seeds. Do not use a mill as the seeds are too sticky. Sometimes pomegranate is used in the same way as tamarind or lemon juice, in which case cover 2oz (55g) of seeds with hot water, steep for one hour and strain. The dried seeds should be stored in an airtight container.

USES

The dried seeds and aril, from the bitter eastern pomegranate, constitute the widely used Indian condiment *anardana*. This can be used as a souring agent in much the same way as tamarind or lemon juice, or it can be finely ground and sprinkled directly on to food to add piquancy. The seeds are an ingredient of *parathas* and *pakoras* (savoury vegetable fritters). The dried seeds are used as a garnish for Eastern and Middle Eastern sweet dishes and fruit salads and occasionally are scattered over *hummus bi tahini*, a chick pea and sesame seed purée. In the West, the seeds may be used to impart an exotic flavour to casseroles and stews and they can be found in recipes from countries as far apart as Russia and Mexico. The juice or puréed flesh is used in fruit drinks and meat dishes, but perhaps the best known use for the juice is in grenadine, the French non-alcoholic cordial.

CHEMICAL COMPOSITION

The bark contains tannin and nearly 1 per cent of four pelletierine alkaloids; the rind contains tannin, sugar and gum mucilage. A yellow colouring body is also present, which is used in North Africa as a leather dye. The fruit pulp is mostly water with 16 per cent carbohydrate, some potassium and minute traces of other elements.

ATTRIBUTED PROPERTIES

The seeds and bark, especially the root bark, are anthelmintic – a taenifuge, getting rid of tapeworm. However, it is

152

highly toxic and not now used. The rind and fruit are astringent and demulcent. They are used in gargles and douches against fevers and diarrhoea. Excessive doses produce nausea, cramp and other nasty effects. The juice is used as a styptic in India.

PLANT DESCRIPTION
A deciduous sub-tropical bush or small tree, reaching 4–7m (13–23ft). The deep green foliage is luxuriant, the leaves about 8cm (3in) long. The flowers are a striking vermilion and the plant is grown decoratively in warm regions. It has no botanic next of kin, and is therefore classified in a taxonomic group of its own. White and yellow flowered and thorned varieties exist, as do seedless ones in India.

CULTIVATION
The most suitable climate for pomegranate features hot dry summers and cool winters. In more humid regions it does not fruit well. A deep loam, well drained, is the best soil. The tree flowers in June and the fruit ripens in September. Pomegranate is usually propagated from hardwood cuttings.

REMARKS
Native to Iran, pomegranate is cultivated in the Mediterranean, Africa, the southern United States and California. Man's earliest encounter with the fruit may have been in the Garden of Eden: it is arguably the Tree of Life in Genesis. It was known in ancient Egyptian medicine as an astringent and vermifuge, and later to the Romans, via Carthage, as the Latin name *Punicum malum granatum* suggests. It is often mentioned in the Bible, the most vivid references occurring in the Song of Solomon, and it is still used in certain Jewish ceremonies. Muhammed refers to it in the *Koran*, suggesting that it suppresses envious thoughts. It is a Turkish custom for a newly-wed bride to cast a pomegranate on the ground, the number of seeds falling out indicating the number of children she will bear. The roots and rind go to make tanners' dye, and jet black ink in India; the puréed fruit to make grenadine and flavourings for wines. The leaves are infused for a 'tea'. Very sour varieties exist, but are not sold fresh in the West. Sir Richard Burton describes three varieties in his *Pilgrimage to Mecca: Shami* (Syrian), red and sweet; *Turki*, large and white, and *Misri*, greenish and acid. He continues, 'I never saw in the East, except at Meccah, finer fruits than the Shami: almost stoneless like those of Maskat, they are delicately perfumed, and as large as an infant's head'.

OTHER NAMES
Grenadier
French: grenade
German: Granatapfel (fruit)
Italian: melagrana
Spanish: granada (fruit), granado (tree)
Indian: a(r)nar, anardana (seed), dalim
Japanese: zakuro
Tamil: mathulam param

Pakoras (colour page 189)
Deep fried vegetable fritters served as a snack with tamarind chutney.   Serves 4

Imp	Metric	US
4oz *besan* (chick pea flour)	115g	4oz
¼tsp chilli, ground	¼tsp	¼tsp
½tsp cumin, ground	½tsp	½tsp
½tsp turmeric, ground	½tsp	½tsp
1tsp salt	1tsp	1tsp
water		
2tsp pomegranate seeds, crushed	2tsp	2tsp
Selection of vegetables such as cauliflower, courgettes, aubergine, capsicum, cut into bite-sized pieces (about 20)		
oil for deep frying		

1 Sift flour with chilli, cumin, turmeric and salt.
2 Add water gradually to make a fairly stiff batter.
3 Now stir in the pomegranate and rest the mixture for ½ hour.
4 Dip the vegetable pieces in the batter and deep fry a few at a time for 5–10

minutes until light golden. Remove.

5 When all are fried, raise temperature of oil and return *pakoras* to the pan for about half a minute until golden brown and crisp. Drain and serve immediately.

Poppy

Papaver somniferum
fam Papaveraceae

SPICE DESCRIPTION
The seeds of the poppy flower are like tiny hard grains. Two kinds of seeds occur. The Western type is slate blue; the Indian type, off-white. Both are kidney-shaped. The blue seeds average 1mm (.04in) in length, while the white seeds are somewhat smaller. They are similar in flavour and texture and their uses are interchangeable. The seeds mature in a capsule left after the flower fades. They are widely available in a dried form.

Bouquet A mild sweetish aroma which is brought out by roasting or baking.

Flavour Mild until heated, then it becomes nutty, with sweet-spicy undertones.   H Scale: 0

PREPARATION AND STORAGE
Poppy seed is very hard to grind. If you do not have a special poppy seed grinder, first lightly roast the seeds and use a pestle and mortar. They can be used either whole or crushed in cooking and bakery. When using them with uncooked food, such as salads, it is as well to roast them lightly first, as this strengthens their flavour and aroma. When poppy seeds are used for pastries, they are covered with boiling water and allowed to stand for one to three hours before grinding.

USES
In the West, the blue poppy seeds are used principally in confectionery and in baking. Like several other spicy seeds, they are sprinkled on breads and buns and used in a variety of Western cakes and pastries, for example in 'poppy cake' and in a sweet forcemeat for strudels and Danish pastries.

Poppy seed complements honey spread on bread, giving a nice contrast of texture. Fried in butter, poppy seed can be added to noodles (as the Americans like it) or to pasta. It flavours vegetables and their accompanying sauces, especially asparagus and root vegetables. Sprinkled into coleslaw, the seeds give a contrast of both colour and texture. They are used to top creamed potatoes and *au gratin* dishes, and sometimes appear in fish dishes. In Middle Eastern and Jewish cookery, poppy seeds go on breads and in cakes and candies and are often seen studding *pretzels*. In the East the white poppy seed is generally used. *Chappatis* (Indian whole-wheat griddle breads) may contain it, and certain

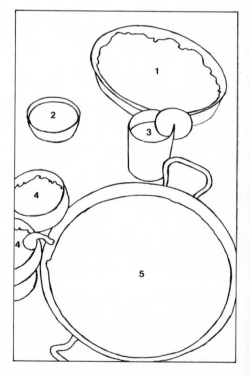

1. American Noodles (page 158); 2. Horseradish Dip with Crudités (page 108); 3. Bloody Mary Cocktail (page 56); 4. Seafood Cocktail (page 53); 5. Creole Gumbo (page 169)

curries and varieties of mixed spice contain a small proportion of poppy. Its function in curry is partially to thicken the liquid and add texture. The whole seeds are used in chutneys. The oil expressed from poppy seeds, which the French call *oillette*, is used for culinary purposes and is an acceptable substitute for olive oil. The European poppy variety, *Papaver rhoeas*, is used to make a syrup similar to that of rose hips, which is occasionally used in soups.

CHEMICAL COMPOSITION
The seeds yield 30–50 per cent of a fixed oil, of which the major constituents are oleic and linoleic acids; this is the French *oillette*. Opium, present only in the latex of the unripe Eastern buds, is an intricate complex of some two dozen alkaloids, morphine being the most important,

1. Daube Provençale (page 36); 2. Country Pâté (page 111); 3. Grilled Bass (page 91); 4. Snails with Garlic Butter (page 100)

followed by codeine and narcotine. Ripe poppy seed also contains minerals and proteins, but no alkaloids. The flowers of the Western variety have a hardly noticeable narcotic quality. Rhoeadic and papaveric acids, which are pigments, are responsible for the red colour. The seeds also contain protein, cellulose, pentosans and minerals.

ATTRIBUTED PROPERTIES
Western poppy syrup is an anodyne and expectorant. Eastern poppy is an anodyne and narcotic. Cough mixtures and syrups are also made from this variety, which is further used as a poultice with chamomile. An infusion of seeds is said to help ear and tooth ache. The seeds have appetising qualities. The use and dangers of poppy plant derivatives, such as morphine, heroin and codeine, are well known and this is not the place to elaborate on them.

PLANT DESCRIPTION
A glaucous hairless annual, reaching 30–120cm (1–4ft), the lobed leaves having a blue tinge. The flowers are white to purple; those of *Papaver rhoeas*, red. They grow up to 12cm (5in) in diameter. The Eastern wild varieties usually sport lilac-coloured blooms. Many wild species occur, such as the Corn Poppy (*P. rhoeas*), often seen in cornfields on the Continent and in Britain. Some varieties are grown ornamentally. When the flowers fade, a capsule remains, rounded and crowned with a star-shaped stigma. On drying, it splits, casting out myriad seeds in the winds. There are nearly one million seeds to the pound (0.5kg).

CULTIVATION
Poppies grow wild in warm lands and in the east of Britain. Wild varieties flower from June to August, cultivated varieties in July.
Aspect: Sunny.
Soil: Loamy.
Sow: Early spring, rows 30cm (1ft) apart. Poppies thrive with much watering, but must be well weeded. *Papaver somniferum*

grind, it requires a special machine. These hand-turned grinders are common in Austria and Germany but seldom seen in Britain. Poppy syrup is made from the flowers of the corn poppy or rose poppy, (*P. rhoeas*). It is used in cordials. This variety is also known as 'headache' – to smell it causes momentary dizziness. It is also the poppy of Poppy Day which is the emblem of the British and Commonwealth soldiers who perished in the Great War. Indian poppy seed – 'mawseed' – is a food for birds.

OTHER NAMES
Mawseed, Opium Poppy
French: pavot somnifère, oeillette
German: Mohn (samen)
Italian: papavero
Spanish: adormidera, amapola (Poppy)
Indian: kus-kus, khus(h)-khus(h), cus-cus
Tamil: kasakasa

may not be grown in Britain or the United States without a permit.

REMARKS
Papaver somniferum, the opium poppy, is native to the Middle East, but now grows also in China, Indo-China and India. An inert variety grows wild and is also cultivated in Europe and Britain. The oriental variety yields much opium, and it is grown expressly for this lucrative purpose. The Western plants yield little opium and the latex that provides the drug is absent by the time the flower ripens, the seeds of culinary use having none of the alkaloids that comprise the narcotic. Opium was known medically to the ancient Egyptians and the classical civilisations. The jockeyings and intrigues of the oriental opium warlords have made travellers' tales for centuries, and opium has been connected with literature since the days of De Quincey (1785–1859). Coleridge (1772–1834) wrote under the influence of laudanum, a tincture of opium (given even to babies in those days) and Baudelaire (1821–1867), an active member of the Hashish Club, admits gaining inspiration from it in *Les Paradis Artificiels*. Such inspiration is lacking in the poppy seed of culinary use. Being hard to

American Noodles (colour page 155)
Noodles make a quick, popular supper dish served with meat, fish or vegetables.

Serves 4

Imp	Metric	US
8oz noodles	225g	8oz
water		
salt		
1oz butter	30g	1oz
1 onion, finely chopped	1	1
1tsp Worcestershire sauce	5ml	1tsp
2tsp poppy seeds	2tsp	2tsp

1 Melt the butter and lightly fry the onion until soft. Stir in the Worcestershire sauce.
2 Cook the noodles in salted water, drain and add to the onion. Sprinkle with poppy seeds.
3 Place in a circle on a platter, fill the centre with minced meat, fish, shellfish or vegetables.

Poppy Seed Strudel
Poppy seeds add a lovely crunchy texture to this apple strudel. The pastry is available from delicatessen shops.

Makes 2 large strudels

Imp	Metric	US
1tbsp poppy seeds, previously covered with boiling water, allowed to stand for 1 hour and then crushed	1tbsp	1tbsp
1lb apples, coarsely grated	455g	1lb
1oz currants (optional)	30g	1oz
2½oz sugar	70g	2½oz
1tsp lemon rind, grated	1tsp	1tsp
¼tsp cinnamon, ground	¼tsp	¼tsp
4 strudel pastry leaves	4	4
2oz butter, melted	55g	2oz
3oz breadcrumbs	85g	3oz
icing sugar		

1 Mix poppy seed with the apple, currants, sugar, lemon rind and cinnamon.
2 Place one strudel leaf on a damp cloth, brush with melted butter and sprinkle with ¼ of the breadcrumbs.
3 Cover with a second strudel leaf and repeat brushing with butter and breadcrumbing.
4 Spoon half the apple mixture on to pastry leaving a 1in (25mm) border on all sides. Fold side edges over and roll up, lifting back cloth as you roll.
5 Repeat with the other strudel leaves and place the strudels seam side down on a greased baking sheet. Brush them with melted butter and bake in the oven Gas Mark 5, 375°F, 190°C for 40 minutes until golden.
6 Sprinkle with icing sugar and serve warm with cream.

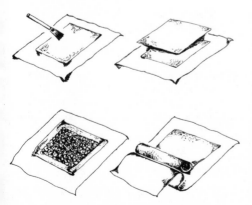

Folding a strudel

Safflower

Carthamus tinctorius
Fam Compositae

SPICE DESCRIPTION
The florets of a small plant, with tubular orange flowers about 13mm (½in) long, ending in five small teeth. The small light-grey seeds produce a golden-coloured cooking oil. The dried flowers are obtainable loose or pressed into cakes. Safflower yields a brighter yellow than saffron.
Bouquet Aromatic when fresh, leathery on keeping.
Flavour Somewhat bitter and pungent.
H Scale: 1

PREPARATION AND STORAGE
Fresh or dried florets may be added directly to the cooking pot, or infused like saffron to obtain a coloured liquid.

USES
The florets are used like saffron for colouring food, particularly in India, South America and the Middle East. In Poland, they are crushed and used in breads, bakery and confectionery. In Spain they are added to soups and other dishes. The leaves and young shoots may be eaten as well as the seeds, which should be lightly roasted. Safflower oil, extracted from the seeds, is commonly used in India. Because the oil is low in cholesterol, it is increasingly used by the health-conscious in the West.

CHEMICAL COMPOSITION
The flowers contain two colouring agents, carthamin, about 0.5 per cent, which is red, and safflor-yellow, 30 per cent, a yellow pigment. The red dye is extracted from the flowers by treating them with an alkaline solution and the yellow dye by repeated soaking in water. The seeds yield 20–35 per cent safflower oil which contains 75 per cent linoleic acid and 6–7 per cent saturated fatty acids.

ATTRIBUTED PROPERTIES
The flowers are diaphoretic, diuretic, emmenagogic and laxative. They are used in infusion in India in children's medicines for fevers and skin troubles; the dried flowers are used in jaundice. The seeds and oil are mild laxatives. Safflower oil is used for promoting *Imsak* – the holding of male orgasm. 'Take powdered root of Rui (gigantic swallow root), levigate it in oil of safflower-seed . . . [apply to the soles of the man's feet]' (*Ananga Ranga*).

PLANT DESCRIPTION
A herbaceous thistle-like annual, reaching 1.5m (5ft), stiff stemmed and densely branched. The leaves are 12cm (5in) long, spiny in some varieties. The bright yellow flowers consist of many spiky florets borne in a whorl of bracts. Some varieties bear orange or red flowers.

CULTIVATION
Safflower is usually cultivated on a commercial scale. It is propagated by seed. For dyes the full flowers are collected twice a week. For oil the plants are cut when the seeds are ripe, threshed and winnowed. It is possible to grow some varieties of safflower in northern climes, provided the position is sunny and the soil dry and poor.

REMARKS
Probably native to Egypt and Afghanistan, safflower is now grown in the Middle East, China, Indo-China, India, Australia, South Africa and southern Europe for oilseed. It is also a cheap saffron substitute and adulterant. It is used for dyeing silk and cotton and, mixed with talc, makes rouge. The seed oil is used for lighting in India. The Spaniards took safflower to Mexico and it is now cultivated on a major scale for its oil in California. In the paint industry, safflower oil is considered superior to linseed oil for its drying properties and the fact that it does not yellow with age.

OTHER NAMES
American Saffron, Bastard Saffron, Dyer's Saffron, Fake Saffron, False Saffron, Flores Carthami, Saffron Thistle
French: carthame, safran bâtarde
German: Färberdistel, Saflor
Italian: cartamo
Spanish: alazor, azafrán bastardo, cártamo
Arabic: kurtham
Chinese: hoang-tchi
Indian: kardai, kasumb(h)a, koosumbha, kurdi, kusum

Safflower Dressing
A light, mild and refreshing dressing for a lettuce or tomato and cucumber salad.

Makes about 1 cup

Imp	Metric	US
½tsp Dijon mustard	½tsp	½tsp
3tbsp orange juice	60ml	4tbsp
¼tsp pepper, freshly ground	¼tsp	¼tsp
¼pt safflower oil	140ml	9½tbsp
¼tsp salt	¼tsp	¼tsp
1 spring onion, chopped	1	1
1oz watercress leaves	30g	1oz
2tbsp wine vinegar	40ml	2⅔tbsp

1 Place all the ingredients in a blender for 5 seconds at maximum speed.
2 Refrigerate and stir well before use.

Saffron

Crocus sativus
Fam Iridaceae

SPICE DESCRIPTION
Saffron comes from the inner part of the flower of a small crocus. The part used consists of the three stigmas joined to the upper section of the style. The stigmas are delicate, thread like and extremely light. The whole section measures 2.5–4cm (1–1½in) in length. Its colour is a bright orange-red, and in genuine high quality saffron this is uniform. Saffron bearing white streaks or light patches is inferior, and such specks in its powdered form suggest adulteration. The spice is equally available whole or powdered. Also freely available are saffron substitutes which approximate the colour given to food by true saffron, though not its flavour. 'Cake saffron' is saffron and safflower pressed with honey into cakes. It is a cheaper commodity but lacks the distinctive characteristics of pure saffron.
Bouquet Strongly perfumed, with a penetrating 'honeyed' aroma.
Flavour A pungent bitter-honey taste. The delicacy of flavour in saffron dishes results from the use of tiny amounts.

H Scale: 0

PREPARATION AND STORAGE
Whole saffron can be prepared for culinary used in two ways. The first is to crush it into a fine powder which can be minimally and evenly distributed in the dish. It is necessary to use it evenly because the dye and flavour are so strong. Crushing the stigmas, however, is a tedious process. Easier, and equally acceptable, is to steep the saffron in hot water – a pinch to a cup. Good saffron should expand on contact with the water and freely diffuse its colour. The strained liquid will yield colour and flavour sufficient for 0.5kg (1lb) of rice. Powdered saffron, on the other hand, is added directly to the required ingredients. As with all colouring agents, keep out of sunlight and, as with all aromatics, keep airtight.

USES
When used as an infusion, saffron is often added towards the end of the cooking process. It is encountered mainly in Moorish, Mediterranean and Asian cookery and is no longer used extensively. Its most common function is to colour rice yellow as in *risotto milanese*, where its delicate flavour makes this the most famous of Italian rice dishes. Combining happily with fish and seafood, it is traditionally used in Spanish *paella*, Mediterranean fish soups and stews such as *bouillabaisse* and sauces to accompany shellfish. In Indian cookery, saffron is an essential ingredient in festive and elaborate *pilaus* and sweetmeats. Cornish saffron cake is now the best known use of the spice in England. This is a spicy yeast cake containing dried fruit and deriving its character from a small pinch of saffron. Saffron is commercially used in perfumes and dyestuffs. Do not confuse it with 'Indian saffron', which is actually turmeric.

CHEMICAL COMPOSITION
Saffron yields 0.5–1 per cent essential oil, of which the main ingredient is picrocrocin, responsible for the flavour and bouquet. The other active ingredient is crocin, the colouring agent. Their minute proportions

in a substance which is itself used in small amounts indicates the power of these chemicals. Saffron is a permitted colouring in the UK.

ATTRIBUTED PROPERTIES

Antispasmodic, diaphoretic, carminative, emmenagogic and sedative. Its diaphoretic action is strongest with children. It is used in the treatment of chronic uterine haemorrhage and in large doses as an abortifacient. A large dose is also believed to be aphrodisiac. Warning: large doses (24 grains, 1.56g) have been known to be fatal.

PLANT DESCRIPTION

A small attractive autumn-flowering ornamental crocus, flourishing in temperate and warm regions. It grows to a height of 15cm (6in). Its long, green chive-like leaves grow up around the lily-like flower, whose blue or violet colour contrasts with the protruding orange stigmas.

CULTIVATION

Aspect: Sunny.
Soil: Well tilled, well drained.
Plant corms 10–15cm (4–6in) apart in July. Pick when flower opens – around September. Transplant after third crop. Dry stigmas between papers in oven or over charcoal; or press into cakes.

REMARKS

Arguably a native of Greece or Asia Minor, saffron is now grown throughout the Mediterranean and in India, Turkey, China and Iran. It was valued as a spice, dye and medicine by the Greeks and Romans, as well as by the ancient Persians and Indians, its colour being prized as an epitome of beauty. It is called *karcom* in the Song of Solomon, and mentioned by Homer and other classical poets. The Moors introduced it into Spain and it was recorded in France in the sixteenth century. Widely used by those who could afford it in the English Renaissance, it had already a history of cultivation from the Middle Ages in Saffron Walden, whose

town arms include three saffron crocuses. It is the official colour of Buddhist robes (although turmeric is said to be a cheaper modern substitute).

This spice has always been at a prohibitive price. Hand-picked and very light, estimates vary around 200,000 stigmas to the pound. However, saffron is used sparingly, so a little lasts some time. The widespread adulteration of saffron has coloured the popular view of it as being neutral in flavour: recipes which require more than a pinch are misconceived. Valencia (Spanish) saffron is considered the best, French and Persian being inferior and giving less colour. The French culinary term *safrané* means 'coloured using saffron' as opposed to 'saffron-coloured'. The name comes from the Arabic *za'faran* meaning 'yellow'. As it is the world's most expensive spice, safflower (Mexican or bastard saffron) is sometimes used as a cheap substitute. 'Indian saffron' means turmeric, and confusions sometimes arise – see remarks for Turmeric.

OTHER NAMES

Alicante Saffron, Autumn Crocus (US), Crocus, Gatinais Saffron, Hay Saffron, Karcom, Spanish Saffron (US), Stigma Croci, Valencia Saffron, Zaffer
French: safran
German: Safron
Italian: zafferano
Spanish: azafrán
Indian: kesar, kesram, khesa, za(a)fra(a)n, zuffron, shahi zafran (stigma tip)
Tamil: kungumappa

Paella (colour page 34)

Spain's most famous dish.   Serves 6

Imp	Metric	US
12 mussels, fresh, scrubbed and bearded	12	12
¼pt white wine	140ml	9½tbsp
3–4tbsp olive oil	60–80ml	4–5⅓tbsp
8 chicken pieces	8	8
1 onion	1	1
2 garlic cloves	2	2
1tsp paprika	1tsp	1tsp

Imp	Metric	US
1 green pepper, sliced and seeded	1	1
7oz tomatoes, canned	200g	7oz
1 pimentos, small tin	1	1
salt and pepper		
½tsp saffron, powdered	½tsp	½tsp
¾-1pt stock, chicken	425-570ml	1¾-2½ cups
8oz peas, fresh or frozen	225g	8oz
1lb rice, *patna*	455g	1lb
2 *chorizos* (Spanish sausages), sliced (optional)	2	2
8 large prawns	8	8

1 Heat mussels in the white wine until they open. Remove, discarding unopened ones and reserve.
2 Heat oil and fry the chicken pieces until brown. Remove and reserve.
3 Fry onion, garlic, paprika and green pepper, until soft.
4 Add tomatoes with juice and pimentos. Stir and simmer for a few minutes.
5 Add the chicken pieces, mussel liquor, salt and pepper to taste.
6 Mix the saffron in some hot stock, then add to the pan with the remaining stock. Bring to the boil, then simmer for about 20 minutes.
7 Add peas and stir in the rice. Bring to the boil and simmer for 15 minutes uncovered.
8 Add sausages, stir, arrange the shell fish on the top, cover and simmer for 10 minutes.

Risotto alla Milanese

The best known *risotto* traditionally served with *osso buco* – see page 66. Serves 4

Imp	Metric	US
2oz butter	55g	2oz
1½oz beef marrow (optional)	70g	1½oz
1 onion, small, finely chopped	1	1
8oz Italian rice, *arborio* or *piedmontese* washed and thoroughly dried	225g	8oz
¼pt dry white wine	140ml	9½tbsp
1½-2pt stock, beef, veal or chicken	855-1140ml	3½-5 cups
⅛tsp saffron, powdered	⅛tsp	⅛tsp
2oz Parmesan cheese, freshly grated	55g	2oz
butter		

1 Melt the butter in a saucepan. Fry the marrow and onions until the latter are golden – do not brown.
2 Add the rice and stir until thoroughly coated. Cook for a few minutes.
3 Add the wine and a cup of stock infused with the saffron. Bring to the boil, stir and simmer for 5 minutes.
4 Add more stock cup by cup, stirring occasionally.
5 Cook until the rice is ready – *al dente* – when all the liquid should be absorbed.
6 Remove from heat, add a knob of butter, sprinkle with Parmesan cheese, stir and let stand for 2 minutes.
7 Serve with more cheese if desired.

Salt

Sodium chloride

SPICE DESCRIPTION
An inorganic substance, salt is not strictly a spice, rather a mineral. Today, its most common form is as table salt. Block salt, or kitchen salt, is table salt minus the chemical additives which cause it to flow freely, and comes in coagulated bricks or blocks. Less 'processed' than table salt, it is generally available in health food shops. Kitchen and table salt come from rock salt

– a rarer form is as untreated, separated crystals. Production of this has virtually stopped. The other form of salt is sea salt. This is growing in popularity. Sea salt, or bay salt, appears as small chunks or flakes, brittle enough to be powdered down easily. Saltpetre is chemically unrelated to common salt. It is used in preserving and pickling meats and is available from chemists. The following are some of the best known types of salt:

Bay Salt Bay salt is sea salt obtained by evaporation by sun and wind in coastal bays, possibly originally the Bay of Biscay – see sea salt.

Black Salt This is unrefined rock salt from Asia, available in attractive, crystallised lumps and coloured dark blue or red, due to various trace elements.

Block Salt Block salt is refined salt with no additives, available in block form, for kitchen use.

Common Salt Ordinary household salt available as coarse cooking salt or fine table salt.

Cooking Salt Cooking salt can be block salt but now more usually refers to fairly coarse, free running refined salt with added magnesium carbonate.

Fine Salt See table salt.

Freezing Salt A non-edible, coarse crystallised salt used for home freezing.

Grey Salt This is the same as black salt but of a grey appearance due to other trace elements.

Gros-sel The French name for coarse bay or sea salt.

Halite Halite is the scientific name for rock salt which occurs in layers from the evaporation of land-locked lakes and seas of past geological ages. Sometimes these layers rise up through the overlying sedimentary rocks to form salt domes which can act as oil traps. Halite is crystalline, transparent to translucent and of various colours such as yellow, red or blue (these are the grey and black salts of Asia). Rock salt is either mechanically or hydraulically mined.

Iodised Salt Salt with iodine added at the rate of 0.0025 per cent to supplement iodine-deficient diets (a lack of iodine causes thyroid problems). Sea salt contains iodine but this is lost during storage.

Kitchen Salt Another name for cooking salt.

Lump Salt Another name for rock salt (halite) or block salt (coarse kitchen salt).

Maldon Salt The finest English sea salt from Maldon, Essex. The crystals are small enough to be sprinkled directly on to food.

Monosodium glutamate (MSG) Strictly not salt, but a salt of glutamic acid which is added to foods to give a meaty and salty flavour. Very popular in China and with the Western food processing industry. MSG has been found to be dangerous in excessive quantities.

Pickling Salt Same as block and lump salt (refined rock salt) used for pickling because it is without additives that otherwise discolour the pickling liquid and make the pickles slimy.

Pretzel Salt A Mexican salt much used in the USA for *pretzels*. The crystals fuse during baking but retain a shiny and crystalline appearance.

Rock Salt The common name for halite. It is hard, crystalline and comes in large lumps. In the US the name 'rock salt' is used to describe freezing salt which is inedible.

Saltpetre Short for Chile saltpetre, potassium nitrate. Also called nitre, saltpetre acts as a meat preservative, usually used with salt; a small quantity only is required, otherwise it hardens the meat fibres. Saltpetre is responsible for the fine pink colour of bacon, hams, salamis, other preserved meats and pâtés.

Sea Salt Salt derived from sea-fed salt pans, obtained either by direct evaporation of sea water pans or factory finishing of saline concentrates from these pans. Sea salt sometimes contains traces of other salts and elements. However, any iodine present is lost during storage. Sea salt is considered the best salt because of its appearance, large pure crystals, and flavour. Commercially ground sea salt has magnesium carbonate added to aid flow and inhibit moisture absorption. Sometimes known as bay salt.

Sel Gris Coarse, grey coloured sea salt used in the kitchen in France.

Spiced Salt Also called seasoned salt. Salt with spices added such as ground celery seed, garlic or onion, being the most common. See Spice Mixtures.

Table Salt Any of the basic salts finely ground and with magnesium carbonate or another similar agent added to promote easy flow, used at the table.

Vegetable Salt Salts of vegetable origin.

Bouquet Normally odourless. However, sometimes sea salt has a faint smell of chlorine and some rock salts, especially from the East, have an unpleasant sulphurous smell.

Flavour Salty. Salt is one of the few basic flavours experienced by the taste buds. No domestically used salt is completely pure, so its flavour is always modified by the chemical traces it contains. Untreated rock salt is said to be best flavoured. Sea salt lacks the bitter aftertaste of table salt, but is more powerful. H Scale: 0

PREPARATION AND STORAGE

Kitchen and sea salts are powdered before use in cooking or as a condiment. For hard rock salt, a pestle and mortar or a mill are required. The more delicate sea salts can be crushed simply between thumb and finger. Less sea salt than rock salt is required in cooking. Temperature affects saltiness – the cooler a dish, the saltier it tastes. Steaks should be salted just prior to cooking, fish some time beforehand. Being non-organic, salt will keep indefinitely and does not always require airtight storage. But it absorbs moisture from the atmosphere and in humid climates will soon become damp and not flow, so silica gel or a few grains of rice will help keep it dry. Cooking salt may be kept handy in a stone crock or wooden box. Table salt, with its chemical additives, should not be used for freezing, salting or

pickling nor should it be kept for more than a day or two in silver cellars because chlorine attacks silver, discolouring it green.

USES

The use of salt is universal in savoury dishes, and even in sweet baking a small pinch is often useful to bring out other flavours. It is antiseptic and preservative in bacon, salt beef, herrings and kippers, foods which are prepared by curing with salt and brines. Salt has a toughening action which is why it is used initially in pickles for a crisp texture. It is also used to draw out bitter juices in such vegetables as courgettes and aubergines prior to cooking. Flavoured salts can be produced at home for use as required, by pounding the salt with other spices – garlic salt and celery salt are common. Often it is helpful to add some salt when pounding other spices in a mortar – garlic especially. For those compelled to reduce or restrict their intake of salt for medical reasons, the following spices may be added to recipes instead of salt: amchur, asafoetida, nasturtium, sumac, tamarind.

CHEMICAL AND PHYSICAL PROPERTIES

The chemical formula of salt is $NaCl$ (sodium chloride). Sea salt contains varying proportions of magnesium chloride, magnesium sulphate and calcium sulphate. Brine may contain in addition potassium sulphate and potassium chloride. Rock salt may include iron traces, other metals, soda, even arsenic. The main flow-promoting agent added to table salt is magnesium carbonate because of its whiteness and insolubility. Saltpetre is potassium nitrate, KNO_3. Commercial salt substitutes contain potassium salts.

ATTRIBUTED PROPERTIES

Salt is essential to life, regulating the osmotic tension of the tissues and blood. Salt deficiency can cause severe illness, and death. Conversely, too much can cause kidney failure and high blood pressure. Among its medical uses are the treatment of burns, saline drips and dialysis. Salt is said to induce labour and may be useful as an analgesic. Iodised salt is used in areas with endemic goitre, the malady often being reduced by 50 per cent. Saltpetre is toxic, but the amounts used for culinary purposes are too small to cause any damage.

REMARKS

Sodium chloride is called 'halite' or 'common salt' to distinguish it from other chemical salts. The importance of salt in the animal world is illustrated by salt licks, natural stretches of exposed rock salt which animals travel miles to visit. Its importance to human life, and its culinary value, have been recognised since the dawn of civilisation (as the earliest records show) and it has long been a prized commodity. One of the first major Roman roads was 'Salt Street', *via salaria*, linking the port of Ostia with important towns. Roman troops abroad received a salt ration, which eventually passed for cash payment and became 'salary'. Salt mixed with crushed ice in the proportion of 1:7 is used to freeze ice creams and puddings. In the West, the average daily salt consumption is about ten grammes; 90 per cent of this is artificially added to food by man and a similar amount is excreted. Since most natural salt in food is from meat, vegetarians will require more added salt in their regimen. Commercial uses of salt are: in curing hide, in the manufacture of baking and caustic sodas, and laboratory chemicals. Salt blocks, often vitaminised or medicated, are widely used in animal farming. 'Men catch Knowledge by throwing their Wit upon the Posteriors of a Book, as Boys do Sparrows by flinging Salt upon their Tails' (Swift, *A Tale of a Tub*, 1704).

OTHER NAMES

Kitchen Salt
French: sel de cuisine, sel gemme, sel gris
German: Kochsalz
Italian: sale di cucina
Spanish: salado (salt), sal de cocina, sal gema (rock salt)

Arab: malh
Chinese: yen
Indian: neemuch
Japanese: shio
Tamil: hoopoo
Table Salt
French: sel blanc, sel de table
German: Tafelsalz
Italian: sale fino
Spanish: sal de mesa
Sea Salt
French: sel marin, sel de mer
German: Meersalz
Italian: sale marino
Spanish: sal de mar

Fish in Salt

An unusual Spanish method of cooking fish. The flesh will be tender and succulent and not at all salty. Serve with wedges of lemon or green peppercorn sauce.

Serves 4

Imp	Metric	US
4–5lb salt, rock or sea	2–2.5kg	4–5lb
3lb bass, bream or grey mullet, neither cleaned nor scaled.	1.5kg	3lb

1 Put a ¾in (15mm) layer of salt in the bottom of a long narrow baking dish.
2 Dry the fish, place it on the bed of salt and cover it completely with the rest of the salt, patting down well.
3 Bake in a moderate oven Gas Mark 4, 350°F, 180°C, for one hour.
4 To serve, break off the salt and remove skin and innards. Save the salt for using again.

Sandalwood

Santalum album
Fam Santalaceae

SPICE DESCRIPTION

This spice comes in thin shavings or chips from the inner wood of a small Indian tree. These raspings average 6mm (¼in) in length and are hard and yellow to mid-brown. Sandalwood is available from herbalists and health food stores.
Bouquet Sweet and fragrant.
Flavour Aromatic, slightly woody.

H Scale: 0

PREPARATION AND STORAGE

Stored in airtight containers, sandalwood will keep almost indefinitely. To facilitate their removal from a liquid, sandalwood chips can be tied in a muslin bag.

USES

In cookery, the subtle fragrance of sandalwood can enhance a variety of dishes. In the past it was used to flavour English custards and jellies and even meat sauces. Milk infused with a few chips lends a delicate flavour to creams and rice puddings. Try adding a little in clear jellies such as crab apple to accompany roast lamb or game. Always remove the pieces before bottling. Small amounts may be tied in a muslin bag with mixed herbs to flavour soups and stews. Danish recipes for salted herrings sometimes call for sandalwood chips or shavings in the salting mixture. These are the herrings used in *glasmästarsill*, see page 19. In Indian cookery a few pieces of sandalwood can be included in festive *pilaus*. A little ground sandalwood mixed with water and rubbed over goose or duck is said to help reduce oiliness. The wood is left for a few hours and washed off before cooking.

CHEMICAL COMPOSITION

Sandalwood yields on distillation an essential oil that contains 2 per cent esters and some 90 per cent alcohols – santalols. Small quantities of unique aldehydes, ketones and other organic compounds are also present in the oil.

ATTRIBUTED PROPERTIES

The oil is used medicinally, being antiseptic, stimulant, expectorant, demulcent and diuretic. It eases chronic mucous infections such as those of the urogenital and respiratory systems. It is a urinary antiseptic, considered superior to cubeb, but dangerous side effects occur with excessive dosing.

PLANT DESCRIPTION

A densely branched tree reaching 10m (33ft), with grey fissured bark and many small greenish purple flowers. The pointed ovate leaves are about 7cm (2¾in) long, shiny on the upper surface. The fruit is a small, dark purple drupe. A curiosity of sandalwood is that it is semi-parasitic, having a multitude of hosts, and thus difficult to cultivate. Its roots attach themselves to those of the host, penetrating and absorbing nutrients from them. The heartwood is hard and termite-resistant.

CULTIVATION

The usually wild trees are felled and the trunks left some months while the outer sap wood disintegrates or is devastated by termites. The remaining heartwood, resistant to these depredations, is sawn into manageable blocks for joinery, carving and cabinet making or shaved for distillation and oil extraction.

REMARKS

Native to India and the Indonesian archipelago, sandalwood is now produced widely in India. The delicately scented oil is well known for its use in soaps, perfumes and cosmetics. The wood, hard and attractive, is ideal for ornamental carvings. The aromatic wood and oil have been used for centuries in the East for incense, in religious ceremonies and to waft the spirits of the dead to nirvana in an aura of sweet fragrance. A related East Indian species, red sandalwood (*Pterocarpus santalinus*), is used as a dyestuff.

OTHER NAMES
Sanders-wood
French: bois de santal, santal
German: Sandelholz
Italian: legno di sandalo
Spanish: sándalo
Indian: chandan, safed chandan

Sandalwood Creams

An Indian cream (sweetmeat) rather more exotically flavoured than our chocolate centres. Yields about 20 pieces.

Imp	Metric	US
4oz whole-milk powder	115g	4oz
1 cup water	285ml	1¼ cup
½tsp sandalwood shavings	½tsp	½tsp
4oz sugar, caster	115g	4oz
water		
2oz almonds, ground	55g	2oz
4 cardamom seeds, ground	4	4
1tbsp pistachio nuts, sliced	1tbsp	1⅓tbsp
vark, a few pieces		

1 Dissolve powdered milk in the water. Add the sandalwood and leave for one hour. Strain.
2 Heat the milk, simmer and stir until a thick paste is formed.
3 Dissolve the sugar in a little water and add to the milk. Stir.
4 Add the almonds and cardamom, stirring in well.
5 Turn the mixture into tins to a depth of about 1in (25mm). When cool cut into squares or diamond shapes, sprinkle with pistachios and decorate with vark.

Sassafras

Sassafras albidum
syn *S. varifolium, S. officinale*
Fam Lauraceae

SPICE DESCRIPTION
Sassafras is a common North American tree used for its leaves, aromatic root, root bark and pith. The sizeable woody roots are reduced into small chips varying in colour from brown to off-white. They are marked with concentric rings, and glisten from abundant oil cells. The root chips may be adulterated with grey stem or trunk chips. The root bark comes in irregular pieces, shiny and brittle when scraped of its corky lining. Its colour on oxidisation is off-white. The pith comes in thin, white, porous cylindrical pieces. These three forms of sassafras are differentiated in the United States, to which its use is largely confined; elsewhere they may not be. The leaves are also used in the United States and sold in powdered form, known as '*filé* powder'.
Bouquet Fragrant and aromatic, reminiscent of fennel.
Flavour Aromatic, sweet with an astringent undertone.   H Scale: 1

PREPARATION AND STORAGE
Filé powder is usually added to a dish for flavouring and thickening after cooking. For six portions add about one tablespoon of powder. Store roots and powder in airtight containers.

USES
Dried and powdered, the leaves may be used in sauces, soups, stews and casseroles, thickening and flavouring the liquid. This powder, called *filé* or *filet*, is mostly used in Creole *gumbos*. The leaves may also be eaten fresh in salads. Beers, beverages and cordials are made from the shoots of the tree, combined with other herbs and spices. Sassafras wood chips have long been used as a tea substitute; the deep rose-coloured drink used to be known in the nineteenth century in London as 'saloop'. Oil of sassafras is used to flavour fizzy drinks.

CHEMICAL COMPOSITION
The root contains 2–3 per cent volatile oil; the root bark up to 10 per cent. The main ingredients of this is saffrole – between 80 and 90 per cent. Also present are sassafrid (a derivative of tannic acid), gum, fixed oil, camphor, starch, resin, lignin, albumen, salts and wax. The pith and leaves contain a high proportion of mucilage.

ATTRIBUTED PROPERTIES
Sassafras is a mild aromatic stimulant and

carminative. It is alterative, rubefacient, diuretic, antiseptic and diaphoretic. It is given in rheumatism, gout, arthritis, and venereal and skin diseases. It is used also as a dental disinfectant. From the pith is prepared a demulcent, beneficial as an eyewash in inflammations and as a beverage in catarrh. Sassafras oil is used to disguise nauseous medicines. Excessively large doses may be poisonous, inducing narcotiform stupor and respiratory paralysis.

PLANT DESCRIPTION
A densely branched tree reaching up to 13m (43ft), with rust- or greyish-coloured bark. The small yellow-green flowers are borne in clusters. The fragrant oval leaves measure up to 17cm (7in) in length; sometimes these are three-lobed. The large roots are reddish-brown in colour, and the root bark soft but drying to a brittle texture. The fruits are deep-blue oval berries, in acornlike cups.

CULTIVATION
Sassafras is a widespread wild tree, thriving in sandy soils. It is sometimes grown as an ornamental tree in the United States.

REMARKS
Native to the eastern United States, sassafras grows along the length of America and into Mexico. The roots were first used by American Indians, who attributed

aphrodisiac properties to them. The first Westerners to discover sassafras were the Spanish, in Florida in the early sixteenth century, who identified most of its other medical properties. Records show that the tree was grown in England in the seventeenth century, but today it is known mostly in Europe only as a name. Its main use was as a substitute for tea, the leaves and bark being used as well as the roots. It is used commercially in the production of American soft drinks. The roots and berries are used in the manufacture of perfumes and soaps, and the flowers, wood and bark provide a dyestuff.

OTHER NAMES
Ague Tree, Cinnamon Wood, Sassafrax, Saxifrax
French: sassafras
German: Sassafras
Italian: sassafrasso
Spanish: sasafrás

Creole Gumbo (colour page 155)
Gumbo is the slave name for okra (lady's fingers) and Creole gumbo stews are traditionally flavoured and thickened with *filé* (dried and powdered sassafras leaves).

Serves 4

Imp	Metric	US
1oz butter	30g	1oz
2 onions, large	2	2
1 garlic clove	1	1
2oz ham, diced	55g	2oz
8oz okra, topped, tailed and sliced	225g	8oz
1 can tomatoes, drained	1	1
2oz green peppers, chopped	55g	2oz
1tsp parsley, chopped	1tsp	1tsp
1tsp thyme, crushed	1tsp	1tsp
½tsp chilli powder	½tsp	½tsp
1lb chicken meat, bite-sized pieces	455g	1lb
2pt stock, chicken	1135ml	5 cups
1tbsp sassafras (*filé*) powder or cornflour	1tbsp	1⅓tbsp
salt and pepper		

1 Melt butter in saucepan or casserole. Fry onion, garlic, ham and okra until light brown.

2 Add tomatoes, green peppers, parsley, thyme, chilli powder and stir well.
3 Add chicken and stock and stir. Cover and simmer for 30 minutes or until meat is tender.
4 Stir in sassafras until the stew is a good consistency.
5 Serve with rice.

Screwpine

Pandanus odoratissimus
syn *P. tectorius*
Pandanus odorus
Fam Pandanaceae

SPICE DESCRIPTION
Each of two varieties of the tropical tree screwpine yields a spice. The larger tree, *P. odoratissimus*, produces '*kewra*' – a clear, sweet fragrant essence or water distilled from the spathes of the male flowers. It is available in bottles from Indian shops.
Bouquet Exotic, sweet scented and slightly etheric.
Flavour Intensely flowery and perfumed.
H Scale: 0
The leaves of the smaller tree, *P. odorus*, are called '*daun pandan*'; the whole leaves, fresh or dried, are approximately 70cm (27in) long, 25mm (1in) broad, and bright green when fresh. The dried leaves are obtainable from some Asian food shops and the fresh leaves are available locally where the trees are cultivated.
Bouquet Reminiscent of newly cut grass.
Flavour Fragrant, but less scented than *kewra*. H Scale: 0

PREPARATION AND STORAGE
Kewra water is usually added to dishes by tablespoons, but *kewra* essence, which is far stronger, is added by drops. Care should be taken not to mistake one for the other. Good quality essence will keep indefinitely. Dried *daun pandan* is cut in pieces or strips before flavouring dishes. Carefully stored, it should retain its flavour for about three months. The fresh leaves are used to colour as well as flavour food

and may be pounded or blended to extract the green juice. When whole leaves are cooked, two or three can be tied together.

USES
Kewra is the vanilla of the East and used in Indian cookery, mainly in sweet dishes and ice creams. However, on festive occasions it flavours colourful rice dishes such as *korma pilau* and *biriani*. *Daun pandan* is widely used in Sri Lanka, Indonesia and Malaysia. In Sri Lanka it is known as *rampé* and spices many savoury recipes for rice and pulse dishes, and prawn, meat and vegetable curries, as well as pickles. It is popular in Indonesia and Malaysia in poultry dishes and desserts, scenting and colouring jellies, milk puddings and confectionery.

CHEMICAL COMPOSITION
The fruit contains about 80 per cent water. The remainder is mostly carbohydrate with small amounts of protein, fat and fibre, plus associated minerals and vitamins. Some varieties produce calcium oxalate in the fruit pulp. The leaves contain aromatic principles and, when crushed, smell of hay, suggesting the presence of coumarin. Essential oils, as yet unanalysed, occur in the leaves and flowers.

ATTRIBUTED PROPERTIES
Screwpine is restorative, antihydrotic, deodorant, indolent and phylactic, promoting a feeling of wellbeing and acting as a counter to tropical lassitude. A useful adjunct to oral hygiene as a breath sweetener, it is also used in local ritual, its sweetness symbolising man's better qualities.

PLANT DESCRIPTION
Pandanus odoratissimus is a tropical tree, liberally branched, and supported by a mass of adventitious aerial roots. The leaves are long blades, leathery and glaucous, up to 1.5m (5ft) in length and 4cm (1½in) broad, with barbs on the edges and underspine. The spadix of the male flowers is enclosed in a fragrant spathe.

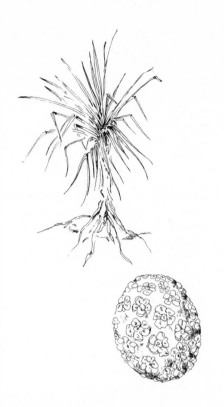

The red or yellow fruit, up to 25cm (10in) in diameter, resembles a large cone, sometimes mistaken for 'breadfruit'. *Pandanus odorus* is a smaller tree, reaching only 1.5m (5ft), with fragrant leaves whose barbs are less pronounced.

CULTIVATION
Cultivated only in the tropics, usually alongside water, *Pandanus* are propagated by suckers or cuttings and require a good annual rainfall.

REMARKS
The name 'screwpine' derives from the twisted appearance of the stems of the trees and the pineapple-like fruit. Screwpines, numbering some six hundred species, are native to the tropics of Africa and Asia. They are utility trees, all parts yielding useful products. The long swordlike leaves are woven into mats, umbrellas, hats and roofing materials. Fibre from the leaves and roots is spun into thread for various uses, especially those connected with fishing. Screwpines are planted along the banks of *klongs*, the dense root systems protecting and binding the soil. The fruit of some species are edible and oil is yielded from the seeds of others. The sweet smelling essence from the male flowers has provided the Indians with perfumes for centuries, and Swahili women have a predilection for scent from a local species. Preparations including screwpine flowers have 'a surpassing fragrance much affected by the voluptuous' (*Ananga Ranga*).

OTHER NAMES
Nicobar Breadfruit, Pandan, Umbrella Tree
French: pandan
German: Pandanus
Italian: pandano
Spanish: pandano
Indian: kedra, keora,i, ket(u)ki, kevara, kewara, kewda, kewra, keya, rampe
Indonesian: daun pandan, pandang
Malay: daun pandan
Sinhalese: rampé
Thai: bai toey

Kheer
A delicately flavoured Indian milk pudding.   Serves 4

Imp	Metric	US
1pt milk	570ml	2½ cups
1½oz rice, short grain	40g	1½oz
3 cardamom pods, bruised	3	3
2oz sugar	55g	2oz
1tbsp almonds, flaked	1tbsp	1⅓tbsp
2–3 drops *kewra* essence (screwpine)	2–3 drops	2–3 drops
vark (optional)		

1 Put milk, rice and cardamoms in a heavy saucepan and bring slowly to the boil.
2 Continue simmering, stirring frequently until the mixture begins to thicken (about 20 minutes).
3 Now add sugar and nuts and simmer until the mixture is the consistency of thick custard. Remove the cardamoms.
4 As the mixture cools, add the *kewra*, turn into serving dishes and serve chilled, decorated with *vark*.

171

Sesame

Sesamum indicum
syn *S. orientale*
Fam Pedaliaceae

SPICE DESCRIPTION

Sesame seeds are contained in the capsulate fruit of a tropical plant. They are tiny, flat and oblate, measuring about 3mm (⅛in) in length. Occasionally they may be red, brown, black or yellow, but commonly they are light brown or creamy white when husked. The pods contain many seeds. They are not sold themselves, but the seed is available dried, or ground to form a creamy-grey paste, *tahini*, resembling peanut butter.

Bouquet Nutty and earthy, the paste exuding a stronger aroma than the whole seeds.

Flavour Nutty, more pronounced when toasted.   H Scale: 0

PREPARATION AND STORAGE

The whole seeds are improved by lightly roasting before use. They are ready when they start to jump. Store in airtight containers. They can easily be ground to a moist powder with a pestle and mortar, food processor or liquidiser, but, since they are already dried, the result will not be as oily as the commercial paste. *Tahina* paste tends to settle – the oil floating over a very dry and tight-packed solid mass – so it needs a good hard stir before use. Store in leak-proof jars.

USES

The simplest culinary use of sesame is as whole part-roasted seeds sprinkled over cakes and breads, like poppy seeds. This use, characteristic of Greece and the Middle East, is now popular worldwide and especially in the United States. Sesame is a major constituent of *halva*, the Middle Eastern and Indian confection, the seeds ground and pressed into blocks with various bindings and sweet ingredients. Although sesame is eaten boiled as a substantial dish in Africa, its major use is in its ground paste form, commonly called *tahina* or *tahini*. This is the flavouring for *hummus bi tahini*, a spicy chick pea purée. Ubiquitous in the Middle East and eastern Mediterranean, *hummus* is used as a starter or a sauce for kebabs. *Tahini* itself is often mixed with lemon and garlic to make a bread dip – one of the most popular Arab pre-prandial snacks or *mezze*. A delicious Chinese canapé is made from fingers of toast spread with pounded prawns, liberally sprinkled with sesame seeds and deep fried. Sesame appears frequently in Japanese and Korean dishes; in China, and particularly in Mexico, the oil, *ajonjoli*, is widely used for cooking. Black sesame is used for coating Chinese toffee apples and is an ingredient of *gomasio*, the Japanese condiment, and other colourful Japanese seasonings.

CHEMICAL COMPOSITION

The seeds contain 45–60 per cent oil, tasteless and odourless in its pure state, composed of fatty oleic and linoleic acid glycerides. Contributing to the flavour and aroma are sesamin and myristin. Calcium, phosphorus and vitamins A and B_5 (niacin) are also present.

ATTRIBUTED PROPERTIES

Sesame has laxative, demulcent and antiemetic properties. 'Sesama stamped or beaten into pouder, and so taken in wine, restraineth immoderate vomits' (Pliny, trans. Holland, 1602). The leaves are used in bladder and kidney troubles and in Africa are administered to children for a variety of upsets including dysentery, diarrhoea and wind. Eye and skin lotions are also prepared from the leaves, which are believed detoxicant. Sesame oil is mildly laxative and in China and India is used as a dressing for burns. The seeds are used in poultices.

PLANT DESCRIPTION

A tropical herbaceous annual also grown in the sub-tropics, 1–2m (2–6ft) high. The plant has an unpleasant odour. Bushy and branchless varieties exist. The leaves are very variable, ovate to lanceolate, and are hairy on both sides. The flowers are foxglove-like, white, pink or lilac.

CULTIVATION

An annual of hot, dry tropical regions, sesame is grown from seed. It matures in 80–180 days when the stems are cut and hung upside down. The ripe seeds fall out and are collected on mats. Hand threshing and mechanical harvesting are also used.

REMARKS

A native of India, sesame is widely grown there and in China, Africa, Asia, Latin America and the southern United States, especially Texas, where it is naturalised. Said to be the oldest plant known for its seed use, it is still an oil seed of primary worldwide significance. It has been used in most climatically suitable regions for millennia. The Egyptians made a flour from it 3,000 years ago, at which time it was in use in China, where they also burned the oil to make soot for their inks. The Romans made a kind of *hummus* from sesame and cumin, and the ancient Persians knew of it. It has not declined – younger civilisations also use it. It is imported in bulk into Europe for margarine production and as a cooking oil, and in this latter capacity is used extensively in the Orient and universally in Mexico. Sesame oil, also called 'gingelly oil', has the advantage of being a non-drying oil, highly stable and slow to deteriorate in a hot humid environment. Among its non-culinary uses is its use as an ingredient in soap, medicines, lubricants and cosmetics. In southern India it is used to anoint the body and hair. The 'press-cake' remaining after the oil is extracted is highly nutritious and used widely as animal fodder and at times as a subsistence food.

OTHER NAMES

Bene Seeds (US), Beniseed, Benne, Gingelly, Gingili, Gingilly, Semsem, Simsim, Teel, Til
French: sesame

German: Sesam
Italian: sesamo
Spanish: ajonjoli, sesamo
Arabic: tahina, tahine, tahini
Chinese: chi(h) mah, hak chi(h) mah (black Sesame), ma yu (oil)
Indian: gingelly (oil), til(l)
Indonesian: wijen
Japanese: goma, goma abura (oil), kuro-goma (black Sesame)
Malay: bene, bijan, hijan
Sinhalese: thala

Hummus bi Tahini (colour page 33)

A traditional snack from the Middle East. Ideal also as a starter, cocktail dip or barbecue accompaniment. Can be made as spicy and hot as required by increasing the amount of red pepper. Yield: 1¾pt (1 litre)

Imp	Metric	US
8oz chick peas, dried, or 1lb	225/ 455g	8oz/1lb
cooked or canned chick peas	450g	16oz
3½tbsp lemon juice (2–3 lemons)	70ml	2.4fl oz
4 garlic cloves, minced	4	4
1tsp salt	1tsp	1tsp
6oz sesame paste (*tahini*)	170g	6oz
1–2tbsp olive oil	20– 40ml	1⅓–2⅔ tbsp
cayenne or paprika to taste	to taste	to taste
1tsp mint, dried	1tsp	1tsp

1 Wash dried chick peas thoroughly, picking out discoloured ones and impurities.
2 Cover well with cold water and soak overnight. The chick peas will swell to roughly double their original volume.
3 Drain the chick peas and wash well.
4 Add new water, bring to boil, simmer for about 1½ hours or until tender.
5 Allow to cool, drain off water, reserving about half the water and 5–10 whole chick peas.
6 Put half lemon juice, salt and all garlic into blender and blend for a brief spell.
7 Put handful of chick peas in blender and blend. Add more chick peas at intervals. As the paste thickens aid blending by adding more lemon juice, olive oil and the reserved water.

Blending must be watched carefully because if the mixture is too thick it will not circulate in the blender.

8 After all the chick peas have been reduced to a creamy texture add sesame paste and blend until a uniform colour is obtained.

9 Taste, and adjust flavour by adding more lemon juice or salt as necessary.

10 Spoon out into dish or plate with curved rim. Pour a little olive oil over top and then sprinkle pepper over – in a pattern if desired. Decorate with a few whole chick peas and a sprinkling of dried mint. Serve with *pitta* bread as a snack or dip.

Prawn Sesame Fingers
(colour page 52)

A flavoursome Chinese hot snack combining the soft light texture of pounded prawns with the crunchiness of toast and sesame seeds. They freeze well and may be reheated for 10 minutes in a moderate oven straight from the freezer.

20–30 fingers

Imp	Metric	US
8oz peeled prawns	225g	8oz
1in fresh ginger	25mm	1in
1 spring onion (scallion), chopped	1	1
1 egg	1	1
1½tsp cornflour	1½tsp	1½tsp
2tsp saki or dry sherry	10ml	2tsp
salt and anise-pepper or black pepper		
4–5 slices day-old white bread	4–5	4–5
4tbsp sesame seeds	4tbsp	5⅓tbsp
oil for deep-frying		

1 Liquidise (or chop and pound together) the first six ingredients to a smooth paste.

2 Season to taste with salt and anise-pepper. Use an ordinary peppermill for the anise-pepper.

3 Spread the paste thickly on one side of the bread.

4 Spread the sesame seeds on a flat plate and lightly press the bread paste-side down on to the seeds.

5 Heat the oil in a wide pan to a depth of about 1in (25mm) and fry the slices of toast for one minute each side as they float on the surface of the oil.

6 Drain on absorbent paper, cut into fingers and serve warm.

Soya

Glycine max
syn *G. soja, G. hispida, Soja max*
Fam Leguminosae

SPICE DESCRIPTION

Soya beans are the small round seeds formed in the bean pod of the soya plant. There is no standard size, but a multiplicity of varieties: the pods vary from 2.5 to 7.5cm (1–3in) in length, and may contain from 2 to 5 seeds. There may be anywhere between 2,500 to 3,500 seeds to the pound or 5,500 to 7,700 to the kilogram. The seeds have a smooth leathery skin and range in colour from pale yellow to black, some varieties being bichromatic or piebald – green and yellow, for example. Soya beans are available in the West, but are considered as a pulse, or a vegetable, rather than a spice. They are commonly sold dried, but may be found fresh, powdered or in paste form, either fermented or unfermented. *Tofu*, Japanese soya bean curd, or *dow foo*, Chinese bean curd, are unfermented, pale and custardy and available fresh in blocks or cubes. *Tofu* is also available as a powder. Japanese *miso* is a fermented soya bean paste, white, red or dark brown in colour and with varying degrees of saltiness. However, the primary Western manifestation of soya is as the flavouring 'soy sauce'. This is commonly a black or dark brown fluid, although light coloured varieties exist.

Bouquet Soy sauce and *miso* are both meaty and savoury.

Flavour Soy sauce and *miso* are salty and beefy, the saltiness more or less pronounced according to the manufacturer. Light soy sauce is sometimes saltier than the dark variety. H Scale: 1

PREPARATION AND STORAGE

The dried beans are steeped and cooked like other pulses. The curd or 'cheese' must be kept refrigerated in water and will keep for three days if the water is changed daily. The dried bean curd is in sticks or sheets and must be soaked before use. Soy sauce does not deteriorate if kept airtight; rather it is said to improve with age. *Miso*, available in tins or vacuum packs, can be stored in a refrigerator for up to a year.

USES

Soya pods may be eaten whole as a vegetable, and the beans are treated as a staple food in a variety of ways. Soya oil is widely used for cooking in the Orient, and soy sauce, made by fermenting the beans with flour, can be classed with the spices for its savoury taste. Soya bean curd, either dried or fresh, is an important ingredient of Chinese and Japanese cookery. *Miso* is used as a base for soups. Soy sauce has long been used in oriental cookery and enhances the flavour of most Eastern main courses, especially fish. Chicken and fish should be cooked with light soy sauce. In Chinese cookery, 'red-cooked' dishes are always simmered in liquid containing soy sauce, the main ingredients having first been fried. Mushroom and oyster-flavoured soy sauces are popular and numerous pastes and sauces, both sweet and savoury, are made with soya beans, perhaps the best known being *hoisin*, Chinese barbecue sauce. Soy sauce is used in various dips and accompaniments throughout Chinese, Japanese and South East Asian cookery. In Western dishes, it can be used like Worcestershire sauce – as a table sauce, sprinkled on meats and vegetables. It is used in marinades, barbecue sauces, sweet and sour sauces, salad dressings and with spare ribs.

CHEMICAL COMPOSITION

Dried beans contain 5–10 per cent moisture, 30–50 per cent proteins, 15–30 per cent carbohydrates and 13–24 per cent oil. Soya also contains calcium, iron, phosphorus, sodium and potassium. Vitamins, especially vitamin E, of which it is the commonest source, B_1, B_2 and B_5, are present along with vegelecithin. Soya beans contain more protein than all other pulses and nearly all other foodstuffs. The calorific value of 100g (3½oz) is between 380 and 400. Soya bean oil contains about 51 per cent linoleic acid, 30 per cent oleic acid and 6 per cent linolenic acid, and is classified as a semi-drying oil. The protein content of the seeds varies inversely with the oil content, for example the yellow-seeded varieties have high oil content and low protein and the black-seeded varieties vice versa.

ATTRIBUTED PROPERTIES

As soya is rich in unsaturated fatty acids and low in cholesterol and starch, it is a good food in heart disease and diabetes. An intravenous nutritional compound is prepared from the oil but this can have serious side effects. Lecithin is an emulsifying agent used in the processed food and other industries. Soya figures in the Chinese and Japanese pharmacopoeias. It is a hydrogue, tending to dehydrate body tissue. Prolonged use of soy sauce is said to affect the liver.

PLANT DESCRIPTION

An erect, branching annual bean-plant, reaching between 30cm (1ft) and 2m (6½ft) depending on variety. The deep polyramate tap roots give soya drought-resistant abilities, and the nodule-forming bacteria (rhizobia) on the roots produce part of the plant's nitrogen requirement.

The stems and the pale green trifoliate leaves of some varieties are hairy. Truncated racemes bear 8–16 flowers, small and purple or white, and bunches of pale brown pods grow on small stalks.

CULTIVATION

Soya is a sub-tropical plant that now grows as far north or south as 52°. Its climatic requirements are very similar to Indian corn, hence its widespread planting in the United States corn belt. It grows best in sandy loams, thriving in fertile soil. The plants mature in ten to thirty weeks depending on variety and are harvested when the leaves fall, usually by combine machines that reap and thresh simultaneously. The soya is an interesting plant in that it is a short day one, requiring cultivars to be developed for narrow latitude ranges.

REMARKS

Native to China, where it is known to have been in cultivation at least from the third millennium BC, soya is a foodstuff of major importance in the East, though in the West it has become popular only in the last hundred years, and only in one of its forms, as an oil for cooking and a margarine base. However, its high nutritional value and generally healthful nature are now recognised, and the beans themselves are beginning to find use in the Western kitchen, with the increasing interest in health foods and pulse and vegetarian cookery. The soya of commerce is an ancient hybrid, not found wild. A wide plethora of varieties now exists, growing in China, Japan, Korea, India, Africa, South America and the United States, which is the largest grower. As well as being a protein-rich foodstuff, soya provides a cooking oil widely used in the Orient, and as a meat substitute is now used to a great extent in the West. Soya bean meal is used as a cattle feed and a fertiliser. In industry it features in the manufacture of plastics and adhesives. The expressed oil is used in making chemicals, paints, waterproofing substances and lamp oil. The lecithin in the beans finds a use in commercial food stabilisers. Soy sauce is made by fermenting a mixture of the boiled beans, flour and salt in trays for a week. The beans are then placed in jars of brine which are left in the sun for several months. This process extracts the flavour from the beans and the 'sauce' is finally separated.

OTHER NAMES

Soja Bean, Soya Bean, Soybean, Soy Bean
French: extrait de soja, pois chinois, sauce piquant (de soya), soja, soya
German: Soja
Italian: soia
Spanish: soja
Chinese: ch'au-yau (soy sauce), cheong yaw, jiang yu, jiong yow (heavy soy sauce), lao ch'ou (soy sauce), lao tsou, lo tsow (dark soy sauce), sang tsow, sheng tsou (light soy sauce), shien tsow, sin tsou (table soy sauce), tofu (soya bean curd)
Indonesian: bumbu ketjap (spiced soy sauce), kecap manis (sweet soy sauce), ketjap manis (dark soy sauce), tahu (soya bean curd)
Japanese: hatcho-miso (pure soya bean

paste), koikuchi (dark soya sauce), miso (soya bean paste), sendai-miso (red soya bean paste), shoyu (soy sauce), tofu (soya bean curd), usukuchi (light soy sauce)
Malay: tauku (soya bean curd), tauyu (dark soy sauce)
Thai: taw hu (soya bean curd)

Chicken in Rice Paper (colour page 52)

Marinaded fingers of chicken wrapped in rice paper and deep fried. The entire parcel is eaten as part of an hors d'oeuvre. Makes about 30 pieces.

Imp	Metric	US
8oz chicken breasts, skinned and boned	225g	8oz
1tsp oyster sauce	5ml	1tsp
3tsp soy sauce	15ml	3tsp
½tsp sesame oil	2.5ml	½tsp
2tsp Chinese wine or dry sherry	10ml	2tsp
1tsp grated fresh ginger	1tsp	1tsp
½tsp salt	½tsp	½tsp
30 snowpeas (mangetout) or bean sprouts or slivers of cucumber	30	30
4 spring onions, shredded	4	4
1pkt rice paper	1	1
oil for deep frying		

1 Cut chicken meat into fingers about 1½–2in (4–5cm) and lay them in a dish.
2 Mix together the soy and oyster sauces, oil, wine, salt and ginger and thoroughly coat the chicken pieces.

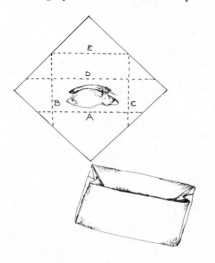

Leave for at least an hour.

3 Cut the rice paper into 5½in (14cm) squares and on each square lay a snow pea topped with a piece of chicken and a few shreds of spring onion. Use 4 or 5 bean sprouts or small fingers of cucumber if mangetout are not available.
4 Parcel up as illustrated, tucking the flap in neatly.
5 Deep fry a few at a time for about a minute in a wok or pan turning the parcels once or twice.
6 Drain well and keep warm until all are ready for serving. These parcels may be made with greaseproof, Bakewell or cellophane paper, when of course the paper is not eaten and the parcels are unwrapped at the table using chopsticks.

Cha Shao – Cantonese Roast Pork

Subtly spiced crispy pork equally good when served cold.   Serves 4–6

Imp	Metric	US
1½lb pork, fillet or boned belly	680g	1½lb
½tsp cassia, ground	½tsp	½tsp
½tsp five spice powder	½tsp	½tsp
2 garlic cloves, minced	2	2
1½tbsp hoisin sauce	30ml	2tbsp
1tsp salt	1tsp	1tsp
1½tbsp sherry	30ml	2tbsp
2tbsp soy sauce	40ml	2⅔tbsp
1tbsp sugar	1tbsp	1⅓tbsp
1tbsp oil	20ml	1⅓tbsp

1 Cut the meat lengthways into long strips 1½in wide, 1in thick (40mm × 25mm).
2 Mix together remaining ingredients and marinade meat in this mixture for at least 2 hours, preferably overnight.
3 Place meat on a wire rack above a baking tin half filled with water. Cook in the oven Gas Mark 6–7, 400–425°F, 200–220°C for 20 minutes. Turn, baste well with the marinade and cook for 15 minutes more. If using pork belly, reduce heat to Gas Mark 3, 325°F, 160°C and cook for a further 25 minutes.
4 Cut the meat diagonally across the grain

into ¼in (6mm) slices and arrange them overlapping on a serving dish.
5 Serve with noodles, plum sauce and Chinese spiced salt (see Spice Mixtures).

Star Anise

Illicium verum
syn *I. anisatum*
Fam Magnoliaceae

Star anise is the unusual fruit of a small oriental tree. It is, as the name suggests, star shaped, radiating between five and ten pointed boat-shaped sections, about eight on average. These hard sections are seed pods. Rough skinned and rust coloured, they measure up to 3cm (1¼in) in diameter. Each pod contains a shiny brown seed, 6–8mm (¼–⁵⁄₁₆in) long. The fruit is picked before it can ripen, and dried. The stars are available whole, or ground to a red-brown powder, both of which are easily obtainable in the West.
Bouquet Powerful and liquorice-like, more pungent and stronger than anise.
Flavour Evocative of a bitter aniseed, of which flavour star anise is a harsher version. Nevertheless, the use of star anise ensures an authentic touch in the preparation of certain Chinese dishes.

H Scale: 3

PREPARATION AND STORAGE
The whole stars can be added directly to the cooking pot; pieces are variously referred to as segments, points and sections. Otherwise, grind the whole stars as required. Small amounts are used as the spice is powerful. Stored whole in airtight containers, it has a lengthy shelf life, keeping for well over a year.

USES
Star anise is used in the East as aniseed is in the West. Apart from its use in sweetmeats and confectionery, where sweeteners must be added, it contributes to meat and poultry dishes, combining especially well with pork and duck. In Chinese red cooking, where the ingredients are simmered for a lengthy period in dark soy sauce, star anise is nearly always added to beef and chicken dishes. Chinese stocks and soups very often contain the spice. It flavours marbled eggs, a decorative Chinese hors d'oeuvre or snack. Mandarins with jaded palates chew the whole dried fruit habitually as a post-prandial digestant and breath sweetener – an oriental comfit. In the West, star anise is added in fruit compôtes and jams, and in the manufacture of anise-flavoured liqueurs, the best known being *anisette*. It is an ingredient of the mixture known as 'Chinese Five Spices' – see Spice Mixtures.

CHEMICAL COMPOSITION
The fruit yields around 3 per cent of essential oil, which contains mainly the strong aromatic anethole (80–90 per cent), the same active ingredient as in anise. There is 20 per cent fixed oil plus cellulose, minerals, protein and resin. The essential oil contains many organic substances including cineole, cymene, phellandrone, pinene, limonene and safrole.

ATTRIBUTED PROPERTIES
Like anise, star anise has carminative, stomachic, stimulant and diuretic properties. In the East it is used to combat

colic and rheumatism. It is a common flavouring for medicinal teas, cough mixtures and pastilles.

A small to medium evergreen tree of the magnolia family, reaching up to 8m (26ft). The leaves are lanceolate and the axillary flowers are yellow. The pods and seeds are described under Spice Description.

CULTIVATION
The tree is propagated by seed and mainly cultivated in China and Japan for export and home markets. The fruits are harvested before they ripen, then sun dried.

REMARKS
Native to China and Vietnam, star anise is today grown almost exclusively in southern China, Indo-China, and Japan. It was first introduced into Europe in the seventeenth century. The oil, produced by a process of steam extraction, is substituted for European aniseed in commercial drinks. A related variety of *Illicium* is *I. religiosum*, which is sometimes used to adulterate star anise. This darker fruit has a taste recalling turpentine or cardamom and is poisonous.

OTHER NAMES
Anise Stars, Badian, Badiana, Chinese Anise
French: anis de la Chine, anise étoilé, badiane
German: Sternanis
Italian: anice stellato
Spanish: anís estrellado, badián
Chinese: ba chio, ba(ht) g(h)ok, bart gok, pa-chiao, pak kok, peh kah (or anise)
Indonesian: bunga lawang
Malay: bunga lawang

Marbled Eggs (colour page 52)
A Chinese snack, these eggs have a lovely marbled appearance and a delicate flavour. Serve cut into quarters.   Serves 6–8

Imp	Metric	US
6 eggs	6	6
water		
½tsp salt	½tsp	½tsp
3tbsp soy sauce	60ml	4tbsp
2 star anise	2	2
1½tsp five spice powder	1½tsp	1½tsp
1½tbsp tea leaves	1½tbsp	2tbsp

1 Boil the eggs in water for 8 minutes.
2 Remove and tap the eggs all over with the back of a spoon giving them a crazed appearance.
3 Return eggs to the pan and cover with fresh water.
4 Add remaining ingredients and boil for 30 minutes.
5 Leave in the water for at least three hours.
6 Carefully remove shells and cut into quarters.

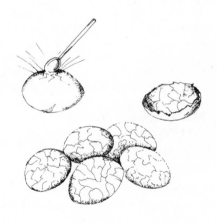

Red Cooked Beef
An oriental version of spiced beef.
Serves 4–6

Imp	Metric	US
2lb round or topside beef, well tied in one piece	1kg	2lb
1tbsp oil	20ml	1⅓tbsp
½pt soy sauce	285ml	1¼ cups
2tbsp Chinese wine or dry sherry	40ml	2⅔tbsp
1 garlic clove, bruised	1	1
2tbsp ginger, fresh, grated	2tbsp	2⅔tbsp
1 star anise (whole)	1	1
2tsp sugar, brown	2tsp	2tsp
water		

1 Brown meat in oil to seal.
2 Place meat in a saucepan, add remaining ingredients and enough water to cover.
3 Bring to the boil, simmer very slowly for about 1½ hours until the meat is tender. Allow the meat to cool in the liquid.
4 Remove meat, cover with a plate, weight down and chill. Reserve strained liquid for future use to enrich stocks.
5 Carve into very thin slices and serve as part of an hors d'oeuvre with Chinese sauces and dips.

Sumac

Rhus coriaria
Fam Anacardiaceae

SPICE DESCRIPTION

This spice comes from the fruits of a wild Mediterranean bush. The fruits are dried and crushed to form a coarse-grained purple-red powder. The whole fruit, borne in dense clusters, are small, round, 10mm (0.4in) in diameter, russet coloured and covered with hairs. The spice is obtainable in Middle Eastern food shops.
Bouquet Slightly aromatic.
Flavour Sour, fruity and astringent.

H Scale: 1

PREPARATION AND STORAGE

The dried seeds and berries can be ground and sprinkled into the cooking, or may be macerated in hot water and mashed to release their juice, the resulting liquid being used in place of lemon juice. Ground sumac keeps quite well if kept airtight.

USES

Sumac is used widely in cookery in Arabia, Turkey and the Levant, and especially in the Lebanese cuisine. In these areas it is a major souring agent, used where other regions would employ lemon, tamarind or vinegar. It is rubbed on to *kebabs* before grilling and may be used in this way with fish and chicken. The juice extracted from sumac is popular in salad dressing and marinades and the powdered form is used in stews and vegetable and chicken casseroles. 'The seed of Sumach eaten in sauces with meat, stoppeth all manner of fluxes of the belly . . .' (Gerard, 1597). A mixture of yoghurt and sumac is often served with kebabs. *Zather* is a blend of sumac and thyme used to flavour *labni*, a cream cheese made from yoghurt.

CHEMICAL COMPOSITION

Sumac contains a fixed oil, a little essential oil, protein, carbohydrate, ash, minerals, many tannins, resins and pigments. The astringency is due to the organic acids – malic, gallic and tannic. Red and yellow pigments give it its characteristic colour.

ATTRIBUTED PROPERTIES

The berries have refrigerant and diuretic properties, and are used in bowel complaints and febrile disorders. In the Middle East, a sour drink is made from them to relieve stomach upsets. The seeds are used as a styptic. All parts of the plant yield tannin and dyes which are used in the leather industry.

PLANT DESCRIPTION

A bushy shrub of the Anarcardiaceae family, reaching to 3m (10ft). It has light grey or reddish stems which exude a resin when cut. Young branches are hairy. The leaves are pinnate with up to eleven serrated elliptic leaflets, hairy on the underside. In autumn the leaves turn to a beautiful red. White flowers grow in dense panicles and are followed by conical clusters of fruit, each enclosed in a reddish-brown hairy covering.

CULTIVATION

Easily propagated by seed, sumac grows best in poor soils. In Sicily, where it is widely cultivated and grows wild in the mountains, its quality is found to increase proportionately the higher it is sited.

REMARKS

Sumac grows wild in all Mediterranean areas, especially Sicily and southern Italy,

1 Place the chicken pieces in a dish.
2 Mix the remaining ingredients together, pour over the chicken making sure the pieces are well coated.
3 Leave for several hours or overnight.
4 Grill or barbecue, turning 3 or 4 times and basting frequently with the marinade until the chicken is nicely browned.

Armenian Boats (colour page 33)

These little boats or *manti* have much in common with Chinese dumplings, *wonton*, and Italian *ravioli*. *Serves 6–8*

Imp	Metric	US
Filling		
8oz lamb, finely minced	225g	8oz
1 onion, minced	1	1
2tbsp parsley, finely chopped	2tbsp	2⅔tbsp
pepper to taste		
salt to taste		
1tbsp butter	1tbsp	1⅓tbsp
Dough		
8oz flour	225g	8oz
1tsp salt	1tsp	1tsp
1 egg	1	1
water		
1tbsp butter	1tbsp	1⅓tbsp
1tsp salt	1tsp	1tsp
pimento to garnish (optional)		
½pt yoghurt	285ml	1¼ cups
1tbsp sumac	1tbsp	1⅓tbsp

1 Mix meat with onion, parsley, pepper and salt and fry in the butter until brown all over. Set aside to cool.
2 Sift flour and salt together in a basin. Break the egg into the centre and mix to a firm dough adding water as necessary. Knead well, and leave to rest in a cool place for 30 minutes.
3 Roll out dough on a floured surface to ¹⁄₁₆in (1½mm) in thickness and cut into 2in (5cm) squares. A ruler makes this easier.
4 Place ½ teaspoon of the filling in the centre of each square and fold the corners inwards about ⅜ (1cm), lift up the corners and squeeze together to form a square 'boat'.

and parts of the Middle East, notably Iran. It is an essential ingredient in Arabic cooking, being preferred to lemon for sourness and astringency. Many other varieties of sumac occur in temperate regions of the world. In North America, *Rhus glabra* is well known for its use in the tanning industry and for its medicinal properties. Also in North America is the related *Rhus toxicodendron* – poison ivy – which on being touched causes severe skin disorders. Sumac is pronounced 'smark'.

OTHER NAMES
Elm-leaved Sumac, Sicillian Sumac, Sumach, Sumak, Summak, Tanner's Sumach
French: sumac
German: Sumach
Italian: sommacco
Spanish: zumaque
Arabic: sammak

Jujeh al Sammak

A favourite Arab grill. Serves 4

Imp	Metric	US
2 2lb chickens, quartered	2×1kg	2×2lb
1 onion, minced	1	1
2 garlic cloves, crushed	2	2
6tbsp olive oil	120ml	8tbsp
2tsp sumac	2tsp	2tsp
2in cassia bark	5cm	2in
pepper to taste		
salt to taste		

5 Melt butter in a large frying pan, pack the 'boats' tightly together and cook gently until the bases are golden.

6 Now slowly add enough boiling water to just cover the 'boats', add salt and cook for about twenty minutes, adding more boiling water if necessary.

7 Serve immediately accompanied by the yoghurt mixed with sumac and any remaining cooking liquid if desired.

Tade (Smartweed)

Polygonum hydropiper
Fam Polygonaceae

SPICE DESCRIPTION

'Tade' is the Japanese for the broad, wavy lance-shaped leaves of the smartweed, which are smooth and edged with hairs. The underside of the leaf is dotted with small glands, in which resides the flavour. Although tade features in Japanese cookery, and is commonly found wild throughout the West, it is as yet unknown as a Western culinary ingredient. In Japan the seedlings are widely marketed.

Bouquet No aroma.
Flavour Hot and biting.   H Scale: 5

PREPARATION AND STORAGE

The leaves may be used fresh and are usually chopped or grated. They may be preserved in vinegar.

USES

Tade is a common seasoning in the Japanese cuisine, featuring in *tade su*, a preparation of smartweed, vinegar and rice. It may also be ground and mixed into a paste with vinegar and *dashi* as a dipping sauce to accompany salted grilled fish, or for *tempura* – deep fried fish and vegetable pieces. The fresh leaves serve as a garnish for *sashimi* – sliced raw fish. The cotyledons or seed leaves are used with raw fish, or added to *sushi* with mackerel.

CHEMICAL COMPOSITION

The leaves contain an essential oil, cellulose, minerals, pigment, resin and tannin. Constituents of the essential oil include terpenes and the aldehyde tadeonal. The tannin content of the leaf is 3–4 per cent and the bioflavonoid rutin is also present.

ATTRIBUTED PROPERTIES

As one of its other names implies, smartweed is a remedy for haemorrhoids and it has been used thus for centuries. Counter-irritant, stimulant, diuretic, rubefacient, astringent and diaphoretic, it is beneficial in cases of colds, ulcers, rheumatism, toothache, gravel and diarrhoea.

PLANT DESCRIPTION

A herbaceous annual, related to buckwheat, ranging in height from 20 to 80cm (8–30in). The small white or off-pink flowers, appearing in autumn, are arranged in spikes. The lanceolate leaves have a pungent principle in glandular structures on the underside surface. The stalks are pinkish with many nodes (*poly*, many; *gonum*, knot, knee) from which the leaves and flowers grow. The leaves are odourless.

CULTIVATION

Smartweed thrives in damp conditions and is a common weed. However, several

varieties are cultivated in Japan. The fresh leaves are harvested when required, but the new leaves of seedlings are more favoured and are cut close to the ground just when they appear.

REMARKS

Native throughout Europe and the Orient, smartweed grows in damp marshy conditions. Although it enjoys culinary esteem in Japan it appears not to be used medicinally. Conversely, it has no culinary applications in the West, but was used extensively in folk medicine for centuries as a general counter-irritant and diuretic in Europe and the United States. It was known to the old herbalists and to Culpeper. The Japanese name is properly *yanagi tade*. There is a common cultivar, *matade*, and a variety, *P.h. fastigiatum*, *azabu tade*, is much prized by Japanese gourmets.

OTHER NAMES

Arcmart, Arsemart, Arsesmart, Arsmart, Arssmart, Biby Tongue, Biting Persicaria, Bloodwort, Ciderage, Culrage, Pepper Plant, Pepperwort, Red Knees, Smartass, Smartweed, Water Pepper
French: poivre d'eau, renouée poivrée
German: Wasser Pfeffer
Italian: pepe acquatico
Spanish: pimenta aquatica
Japanese: azabu-tade, matade, yanagi tade

Tade Sauce

Dashi flavoured with tade leaves and served with fish.
Mix 2 parts vinegar with 1 part *dashi* and add tade leaves according to taste.
To make *dashi* – Japanese basic stock – boil the seaweed for a few minutes, remove, add the fish shavings, bring to the boil then remove from heat. Let shavings settle, then strain.

Proportions:	Metric	US
For 5 pints of water use	2.81	12 cups
1oz *katsuobushi* (dried and shaved bonito-tuna)	30g	1oz
1oz *kombu* – seaweed	30g	1oz

Tamarind

Tamarindus indica
syn *T. officinalis*
Fam Leguminosae

SPICE DESCRIPTION

The spice comes from an irregularly curved brown bean-pod borne by the tamarind tree. The pod, dark brown when ripe, contains a sticky pulp enclosing one to ten shiny black seeds. It measures 15–20cm (6–8in) in length. On oxidising, the flesh turns a rusty brown. Tamarind is obtainable commercially in three varieties: West Indian – shorter pods containing around four seeds, usually preserved in syrup.
East Indian – the pods being skinned and partly dried.
Egyptian or Indian – most commonly available in Europe. This is a pressed brick of dried, partly broken pods, pulp and seeds, mottled white and brown with sticky texture. It is often spiced, and prepared syrups and pastes are also sold.
Bouquet Little aroma of itself, except for a faint sweetness.
Flavour Sour, but refreshing and tasty.
H Scale: 1

PREPARATION AND STORAGE

When a walnut-sized piece of dried tamarind is steeped in half a pint of hot water for about ten minutes, a dark sour juice can be squeezed out. Alternatively, tamarind paste can be made by soaking two to three ounces of pulp in a quarter pint of hot water overnight. Pass through a strainer. This paste may be kept up to a week in a refrigerator. Do not use metal containers. Dried tamarinds will keep their power indefinitely as they require maceration to release their juice. No special storage is necessary.

USES

Tamarind is used as a foodstuff in the East, but more commonly it is the juice or paste that is used as a souring agent, particularly in curries and chutneys (especially fresh chutneys), where its flavour is more authentic than that of vinegar or lemon juice. Occasionally it flavours pulse dishes. Another use is as an ingredient in sauces and side dishes for pork, fowl and fish, 'tamarind fish' being a prized relish in western India. Jams and jellies may often include tamarind due to its high pectin content. It commonly flavours guava jelly, and is a base for many fruit drinks. In India, the ground seed is used in cakes. A refreshing drink made from tamarind syrup is sold throughout the streets of Middle Eastern towns and is most welcome in the dry heat, resembling a still lemonade. Tamarind is a vital ingredient of Worcestershire sauce. Its extensive culinary use may be partly due to its medicinal properties and general wholesomeness.

CHEMICAL COMPOSITION
The sourness of tamarind pulp comes from the 10 per cent tartaric acid content. Other acids present are malic (10 per cent) and oxalic, and there is 8 per cent potassium bitartrate. Some authorities state that citric acid is also present. The pulp contains water (20–30 per cent), protein (3 per cent), fat (up to 1 per cent), sugars (40–70 per cent), fibre (3–5 per cent) and ash. The amounts of these constituents vary between the Asian, African and Caribbean varieties. Calcium, phosphorus, iron, sodium and potassium, and traces of vitamins A, B_1, B_2, B_5 and C occur, with potassium and vitamin B being the most important. The fruit is rich in pectin. The seeds contain starch (60 per cent), protein (15 per cent) and a pleasant smelling oil (5–20 per cent). The leaves contain a red and yellow dye, and the bark contains tannin. The food energy of the fruit is about 250 calories per hundred grammes.

ATTRIBUTED PROPERTIES
Tamarind is mildly laxative because of its acids and potassium bitartrate content, and it is used to relieve bilious upsets. In India, it is used in bowel disorders as an astringent, and in the West Indies for urinary troubles. The *Ananga Ranga* mentions the use of tamarind for enhancing sexual enjoyment by the female. Being highly acidic, it is a refrigerant – cooling in the heat – and febrifuge: '. . . it powerfully cooles and quenches thirst' (Gerard 1597). Its antiseptic properties are well recognised in the East, where a tamarind preparation is used as an eyewash and ulcer treatment. A tamarind paste is said to relieve rheumatism. It is used in many regions of Africa in similar ways. In Nigeria and the Ivory Coast it is included in leprosy remedies. In the United Kingdom an extract is utilised as a binding agent for tablets.

PLANT DESCRIPTION
A tropical evergreen tree, of the Caesalpiniaceae sub-family, medium to large, reaching up to 20m (66ft). The trunk is thick with grey bark; the leaves are pale green, odd-pinnate with 10–15 pairs of

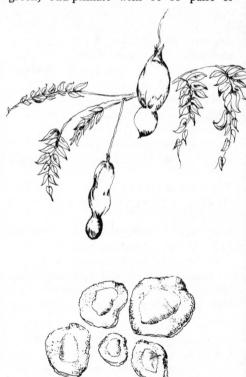

leaflets. Small clusters of yellow flowers with red stripes occur in terminal racemes. The brown curved pods grow up to 10cm (4in) and contain from one to ten seeds in a fibrous pulp. The pod shell is brittle, bulbous and usually constricted. The attractive seeds are about 13mm (½in) square and 6mm (¼in) deep with rounded edges. They are shiny and dark brown with a darker area on each face. In Africa and the West Indies the pods are usually riddled with insects.

CULTIVATION

The tree grows best in semi-arid tropical regions, and is propagated by seed, cuttings or budding. Little attention is required. Wild trees in Africa are often seen growing on or near anthills.

REMARKS

Believed to originate in east Africa, tamarind now grows wild throughout the Indian subcontinent and is cultivated in the tropics and subtropics. Being handsome and easily grown, it was common as a decorative tree in colonial gardens. Its major commercial use is as a base for fruit drinks. Although tamarind has been grown from antiquity in India, it is believed to emit acrid vapours harmful to nearby animal and vegetable life. Tamarind leaves are used in medical preparations – one a supposed vermifuge – and they yield red and yellow dyes. The very hard wood has many uses, takes a good polish and bends well. The fruits are used to clean brass and copper. Exploiting a local belief that malevolent demons inhabited the fresh pods, the British in Goa in Victorian times kept a tamarind in one ear when venturing into the native quarter to keep themselves free from harassment. This earned them the local nickname, '*Lugimlee*' or 'tamarind heads', and it has stuck to this day.

OTHER NAMES

Indian Date, Tamarindo
French: tamarin
German: Tamarine
Italian: tamarindo

Spanish: tamarindo
Indian: amyli (dried), chinch, im(a)li, imlee
Indonesian: asam
Lao: mal kham
Malay: asam, asam djawa
Sinhalese: siyambala
Tamil: pulee, puli
Thai: makahm, som ma kham

Tamarind Fish Relish

An unusual relish, adding a special authenticity to home-cooked Indian meals.

Serves 6

Imp	Metric	US
2oz tamarind brick	55g	2oz
¼pt vinegar, malt	140ml	9½tbsp
8oz white fish, skinned	225g	8oz
1tbsp mustard oil	20ml	1⅓tbsp
1tbsp coriander seeds	1tbsp	1⅓tbsp
1tsp cumin seeds	1tsp	1tsp
½tsp dill seeds	½tsp	½tsp
1tsp chilli powder	1tsp	1tsp
1 garlic clove, finely chopped	1	1
1tbsp ginger, fresh, grated	1tbsp	1⅓tbsp
1tsp sugar, brown	1tsp	1tsp
½tsp turmeric, ground	½tsp	½tsp
salt to taste		

1 Macerate tamarind in vinegar overnight, then mash and pass liquid and pulp through sieve.
2 Cut fish into slices about ½in (12mm) thick.
3 Lightly roast coriander, cumin and dill seeds, grind and add these to the tamarind vinegar.
4 Add the chilli powder, garlic, ginger, sugar, turmeric and a pinch of salt. Mix well.
5 Fry the fish in mustard oil until brown.
6 Pour the vinegar mixture into the pan with the fish, having first drained off surplus oil and cook gently for 5 minutes.
7 Serve fresh as a concomitant to curries or store in sterile bottles for later use.

Tamarind Chutney (colour page 103)

A spicy chutney to serve immediately or preserve.　　　　Makes 2 jars

Imp	Metric	US
4oz tamarind brick	115g	4oz
1–1½pt water	500–750ml	2–3 cups
½tsp chilli powder	½tsp	½tsp
¼tsp clove, ground	¼tsp	¼tsp
3in ginger, fresh, grated	7½cm	3in
2 onions, finely chopped	2	2
1tsp pepper, black, ground	1tsp	1tsp
4tbsp sultanas, soaked	4tbsp	5⅓tbsp
2tbsp sugar, brown	2tbsp	2⅔tbsp
2 tomatoes, skinned and finely chopped	2	2
salt to taste		
3tbsp vinegar, any	60ml	4tbsp

1 Break up the tamarind brick and soak in water for 30–45 minutes until softened. Work the tamarind with fingers to dislodge pulp. Pass firmly through a sieve, discarding seeds and fibre.
2 Mix the pulp with all the other ingredients apart from the vinegar and serve with curries, cold meats etc.
3 To preserve: add the vinegar, bring to the boil and simmer for 30 minutes or until all ingredients soft.
4 Warm sterilised jars in oven then fill, cap and label.

Tonka Bean

Dipteryx odorata
syn *Coumarouna odorata*
Fam Leguminosae

SPICE DESCRIPTION
A very dark brown almond-shaped seed, 25–40mm (1–1½in) in length. The skin is thin and papery and on the cured seed has longitudinal wrinkles often containing traces of a white crystalline substance – coumarin. It peels to reveal a dense, light coffee-coloured seed, also wrinkled. Good quality beans are pliable. They are available whole from spice shops and herbalists.
Bouquet Toffee-like and redolent of caramel. Newly mown hay has a similar scent owing to its coumarin content.
Flavour Raw seed is sharp and bitter, reminiscent of old-fashioned cough mixtures and cheap toffees.   H Scale: 0

PREPARATION AND STORAGE
The beans should be kept in airtight containers as their powerful aroma will quickly cling to other foods. A bean kept in a jar of sugar will provide a ready source of flavouring. After a tonka bean is infused in milk, it may be washed and carefully dried ready for further use. One bean infused for thirty minutes is sufficient to flavour half a pint of milk. To make tonka essence, cover two beans with alcohol (vodka or white rum), add a piece of cinnamon stick, cover and leave for two weeks.

USES
Tonka beans are used as a substitute for vanilla. Sugar or milk flavoured by infusion with the tonka beans is used in recipes requiring vanilla. However, bear in mind that they are much stronger. Many children prefer the taste of tinned rice pudding and the slightly malted flavour of the bean seems to emulate this product. Its stronger flavour may be preferred by some to the more delicate vanilla in home-made custards and ice creams, and in confectionery such as toffee, fudge and marshmallows. Tonka beans are used in bitters and to scent snuff, tobaccos and perfumes.

CHEMICAL COMPOSITION
The beans contain 25–35 per cent of a fixed oil (tonka butter), 8 per cent water and 3 per cent coumarin. Coumarin is the substance that gives tonka its characteristic bouquet and flavour, produced during the curing process by the reaction of an enzyme and glucoside. One part of coumarin is equivalent to three of vanilla, whence its use as a substitute for the latter. Coumarin is also manufactured synthetically.

ATTRIBUTED PROPERTIES
Coumarin is cardiac, tonic and narcotic and the fluid extract is used in whooping cough, but large doses cause paralysis of the heart. Coumarin derivatives are used as anti-coagulants.

186

PLANT DESCRIPTION

A tall, tropical leguminous tree up to 40m (130ft) in height, bearing egg-shaped fruits that enclose single seeds, the tonka beans. In cultivation the trees are lopped at 2m (6ft).

CULTIVATION

It is a tree of the South American tropical forest found along river banks, and is only cultivated on a commercial basis, mainly in Trinidad. The trees are propagated by seed and start to bear, depending on husbandry, any time between two and ten years of age. They usually crop annually but better crops occur every two or three years. The fallen fruits are dried and cracked open to obtain the beans, which are further dried. The dried beans are finally cured by soaking in 50 per cent alcohol or rum for a few days and then dried and sold.

REMARKS

The original name for the tree and its fruit is the Arawak Indian *cumeru*, whence Spanish *cumaru* and chemical 'coumarin'. Tonka is the Negro name for *cumeru*. The tree is indigenous to Brazil, Guyana and Venezuela and is now cultivated in the West Indies and Malaysia. Synthetic production of coumarin has reduced the need for the natural product. The extracted oil is like vanilla and was used as a substitute for that spice, but its use is now prohibited in several countries. In 1965 the UK Food Standards Committee recommended prohibition of coumarin because large doses caused liver damage in rats. However, eleven years later in 1976, the report on the review by the FACC (Food Additives and Contaminants Committee) recommended limiting the amount of coumarin to flavour alcoholic beverages to not more than 10mg per litre and 5mg per kilogram to flavour foodstuffs. Coumarin familiarly occurs also in melilot, meadowsweet, woodruff and vernal grass. It is present in small amounts in oil of cassia. The bark of the tonka bean tree exudes 'kino', a resin used in tanning.

OTHER NAMES

Coumarou, Cumaru, Tonga Bean, Tonqua Bean, Tonquin Bean
French: fève Tonka
German: Tonka
Italian: cumaru
Spanish: cumarú

Tonka Fudge

A lovely fudge with a caramel flavour.

Imp	Metric	US
1lb soft brown sugar	455g	1lb
1lb caster sugar	455g	1lb
2 tonka beans	2	2
½pt milk	285ml	1¼ cups
4½oz butter	130g	4½oz

1 Bring milk to boil with the 2 tonka beans, remove from heat and allow to infuse for about half an hour, or until sufficient flavour and aroma has been imparted to the milk.

2 While tonka beans are infusing, sieve sugars to remove lumps and impurities.

3 Remove tonka beans, wash and keep for further use.

4 Put sugar in saucepan and add milk. Stir thoroughly and leave for one hour.

5 Heat milk and sugar mixture until sugar dissolves. Do not boil.

6 Add butter, a small piece at a time, stirring until melted.

7 Bring to the boil and simmer until soft-ball stage is reached – 238°F, 114°C. Stir frequently to prevent sticking.

8 To test for soft-ball: drop a little into a cup of cold water. It is soft-ball when it coalesces and can be moulded into a ball with the fingers.

9 Remove from heat. Beat until creamy and just starts to thicken.

10 Pour into buttered tins. Pour rapidly to get a uniform layer in the tin, about ⅝in (15mm) in depth.

11 Mark into squares with knife, 1 × 1in (25 × 25mm) square, and let cool.

Trifala

Emblica officinalis
Fam Euphorbiaceae
Terminalia belerica, Terminalia chebula
Fam Combretaceae

SPICE DESCRIPTION
Trifala is listed as an ingredient of a well known English curry powder so it is worth while to pursue its origins, although it is not, as yet, obtainable as a spice outside India. Trifala means 'The Three Myrobalans', which are the trees listed above – the emblic, beleric, and chebulic myrobalans. Its use as a spice is probably as a mixture of the ground, dried pitted fruit from these sources; sometimes the bark is also included. Triphala *churna*, a yellow-brown powder, is available in Indian stores as a pharmaceutical preparation.
Bouquet Slightly sour.
Flavour Acidic and astringent.

H Scale: 1

PREPARATION AND STORAGE
As an ingredient of curry powder, keep in an airtight container.

USES
The fruits are all the fruits of the 'myrobalans' and are both acidic and astringent, so they have much the same uses as amchur and tamarind as souring agents in fish and meat curries; but little is known of these applications. The small fleshy fruits of the emblic myrobalan are used in preserves, and a refreshing drink is made by infusion. As stated above, trifala occurs as an ingredient of curry powders but there is some confusion between it and Badrang (page 30).

CHEMICAL COMPOSITION
Beleric myrobalan: the fruits contain 25 per cent tannins and a black dye.
Chebulic myrobalan: the fruits contain 20–40 per cent tannins, nearly 40 per cent fixed oil, 3.5 per cent chebulic acid, ellagic acid and a green oleoresin.
Emblic myrobalan: the fruits are one of the richest sources of vitamin C, and contain much tannin and a brown dye.
All the fruits contain protein, carbohydrates, fixed oil, minerals, cellulose and resin.

ATTRIBUTED PROPERTIES
Beleric myrobalan: the dried fruit is astringent and laxative. It is used in remedies for respiratory complaints and as a purgative.
Chebulic myrobalan: the fruits are mildly cathartic, astringent, tonic and stomachic. They are used in diarrhoea, piles and urinary disorders. The dried powdered fruit is effective in healing wounds.
Emblic myrobalan: the fruits are tonic, aperient, febrifugal and antiscorbutic.

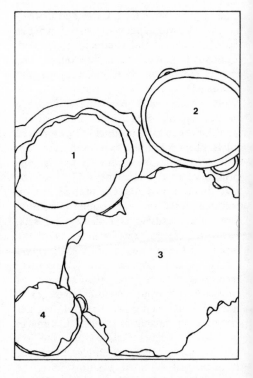

1. Spicy Potatoes (page 30); 2. Vindaloo (page 93); Hot and Spicy Grilled Chicken (page 114); 4. Pakoras (page 153)

The dried fruits are given in diarrhoea, venereal diseases and fevers.

The powder, trifala, made from the three myrobalans is cited in the ancient Hindu medical treatise, the *Ayurveda*, and is still used today. According to the *Ananga Ranga*, it is also an aphrodisiac imparting to the male 'the salacity of a sparrow, a bird which enjoys the female some ten or twenty times in succession'.

PLANT DESCRIPTION

Beleric myrobalan: a large buttressed tree with broad elliptic leaves. The flowers are yellow, in spikes, and emit an unwholesome smell. The fruit is small, 25mm (1in) in length, ovoid with a hard and fibrous stone.

Chebulic myrobalan: similar to the above with slightly smaller leaves and a larger black fruit, 50mm (2in) long.

Emblic myrobalan: a small deciduous tree with pinnate leaves and dense clusters of small yellow-green flowers. The fruit is 20mm (¾in) long, ovoid and dark with six indistinct grooves.

CULTIVATION

All three trees grow wild in the forests of India, Burma and Indo-China.

REMARKS

The trees are native to India and Pakistan. The woods are used as fuel and building material and for dyeing leather and silk, also as a basis for inks and hair dyes. The chebulic fruit produce black myrobalan – used as a mordant. Gerard describes the three myrobalans in *The Herball*, 1597.

OTHER NAMES

Emblic: Emblic Myrobalan, Indian Gooseberry
Beleric: Beleric Myrobalan
Chebulic: Chebulic Myrobalan, Triphala
French: trifala, myrobalan
German: Trifala
Italian: mirabolano, trifala
Spanish: mirabolano, trifala
Indian: beleric: bahera, barro, behada, vibhitaka
    chebulic: haritaki, harre, harro, hirda
    emblic: amala, amla, anvalli, dhatri
        emblic: amala, amla, anvalli, dhatri

Sandhurst Curry

A typically English mess curry, when those with a masochistic tendency may pile on the chilli powder!

Imp	Metric	US
2tbsp oil	40ml	2⅔tbsp
1 onion, chopped	1	1
2lb beef, cubed	1kg	2lb
2tbsp Bombay curry powder (see Spice Mixtures)	2tbsp	2⅔tbsp
¾pt stock	425ml	1¾ cups
1tsp salt	1tsp	1tsp
¼pt coconut milk	140ml	9½tbsp
2tsp sugar	2tsp	2tsp

1. Coleslaw (page 42); 2. Hungarian Goulash (page 147); Dill Pickle (page 88); 4. Swiss Spinach Pancakes (page 139); 5. French Onion Soup (page 142)

1 Heat oil in a large saucepan and fry onions until soft.
2 Add meat and brown, then add curry powder and stir for a minute.
3 Add stock and salt, bring to the boil, cover and simmer slowly for about 2 hours until tender.
4 Stir in coconut milk and sugar and serve with rice and side dishes such as sliced onions, tomatoes, apples, bananas, shredded coconut, chopped peanuts and chilli powder.

Turmeric

Curcuma domestica
syn *Curcuma longa*
Fam Zingiberaceae

SPICE DESCRIPTION

The rhizome or underground stem of a ginger-like plant provides this spice, which is available whole or ground. Ready ground turmeric is the most commonly available in the West. It is a deep yellow, fine powder. The whole turmeric is the rhizome, which is tuberous, and its skin is rough and appears segmented – characteristic rhizome features. It is yellowish-brown with a dull orange interior, yellow when powdered. The central rhizome measures some 2.5–7cm (1–3in) in length with a diameter of 2.5cm (1in); smaller tubers branch off it. It is always sold dried and smoothed, in rounded or elongated pieces from the central or lateral sections, known respectively as bulbs or fingers. This type is called 'Alleppy' or 'Madras'. A 'Bengal' (*C. aromatica*) type exists, in smaller cylindrical pieces, and is used as a dyestuff rather than for culinary purposes. Fresh turmeric root is also available.

Bouquet Woody, slightly acrid, redolent of a sawmill.

Flavour Warm and slightly aromatic with a bitter undertone.   H Scale: 3

PREPARATION AND STORAGE

Turmeric is always ground before use. Although the whole pieces provide a fresher powder, they are rock-hard and consequently difficult to grind at home. The powder, which is more convenient, will keep its colouring properties indefinitely if stored in an airtight container away from sunlight. The flavour of the powder will, however, diminish, so it is wise to buy in moderation.

USES

Turmeric is used extensively in the East and Middle East as a condiment and culinary dye. Care must be exercised in using it as a colouring agent, for its flavour is far from neutral. Nevertheless, in India it is used to tint many sweet dishes. Its colour may be perceived in chutneys and especially piccalilli, as may its flavour. It is also used in prepared mustards. Apart from its wide use in Moroccan cuisine to spice meat, particularly lamb, and vegetables, its principal place is in curries and curry powders. It is used a great deal in fish curries – possibly because it was the substance most successful at masking the rank ammoniac smell of decay. The Anglo-Indian breakfast dish of rice and fish known as kedgeree is always flavoured and coloured with turmeric. When turmeric is present in curry powder it is often one of the main ingredients, although too much of it will overpower and unbalance the mixture.

CHEMICAL COMPOSITION

The rhizome contains 1.5–5.5 per cent of a volatile essential oil, the principal ingredient being turmerone. The colouring agent contained in turmeric is curcumin. Also present are a fixed oil, protein, starch, cellulose, minerals etc. The essential oil also contains borneol, cineol, phellandrene, zingiberene etc.

ATTRIBUTED PROPERTIES
Turmeric is a mild digestive, being an aromatic, a stimulant and a carminative. An ointment based on the spice is used as an antiseptic in Malaysia. Turmeric water is an Asian cosmetic applied to impart a golden glow to the complexion. Formerly, turmeric was used to treat jaundice. Curcumin has been shown to be active against *Staphylococcus aureus* (pus-producing infections).

PLANT DESCRIPTION
A tropical perennial related to ginger – of the Zingiberaceae family. It grows to 60–100cm (2–3½ft). It bears long stemmed, bright green lily-like leaves which surround conical clusters of pale yellow flowers. Several varieties are in cultivation, one of which, *Curcuma angustifolia*, is the source of East Indian arrowroot.

CULTIVATION
Turmeric thrives in the tropics and sub-tropics where it requires a hot, moist climate and a fairly light soil. It is propagated by planting pieces of the rhizome. The roots are boiled, dried for over a week and then their rough skins are polished.

REMARKS
Turmeric is an ancient native of South East Asia, used from antiquity as a dyestuff and condiment. It is cultivated primarily in Bengal, China, Taiwan, Sri Lanka, Java, and more recently in Africa, Peru, Australia and the West Indies. It is still used in rituals of the Hindu religion, and as a dye for holy robes, being natural, unsynthesized and cheap. Turmeric is in fact one of the cheapest spices, a reason for its prominence in Indian cookery. Although as a dye it is used similarly to saffron, the culinary uses of the two spices should not be confused. Turmeric should never replace saffron in food dishes for it will introduce a flavour foreign to the original recipe. Unhelpfully, turmeric is also known as 'Indian saffron' and is often wrongly read as 'saffron' in Indian recipes. In doubtful cases remember that saffron is used sparingly to add a little flavour while turmeric adds a strong flavour to any dish in which it is used.

In chemistry a paper impregnated with turmeric is used as an alkali test: on contact with alkaline substances, it turns from yellow to brown, and dries to violet. Boric acid turns it a reddish-brown. The name derives from the latin *terra merita* – deserving earth. Former botanical names for turmeric are *Curcuma rotunda* and *Amomum curcuma*.

OTHER NAMES
Indian Saffron, Tumeric, Yellow Ginger
French: curcuma, saffron des Indes
German: Gelbwurz
Italian: curcuma
Spanish: curcuma
Arabic: kharkoum
Burmese: fa nwin
Chinese: wong geung fun
Indian: haldee, haldi, huldee, huldie
Indonesian: kunjit, kunyit
Malay: kunjit
Sinhalese: kaha
Tamil: munjal
Thai: kamin

Yellow Rice
Aromatic and brightly coloured, this Indonesian rice dish is served with curries and *sambals*.   Serves 2–4

Imp	Metric	US
8oz rice, washed	225g	8oz
¾pt water	425ml	1¾ cups
2tsp turmeric	2tsp	2tsp
2tsp salt	2tsp	2tsp
½pt coconut milk, hot	285ml	1¼ cups
1 screwpine leaf	1	1

1 Put the rice and water in a saucepan, bring to the boil, cover and simmer for

about 7 minutes until the water is absorbed.

2 Add turmeric and salt to the coconut milk and stir it into the rice.

3 Add the screwpine and simmer very gently until the milk is absorbed.

4 Turn out on to a serving dish and fluff up with a fork.

Piccalilli

A traditional mixed vegetable pickle, formerly known as Indian pickle.

Makes about 6lb

Imp	Metric	US
1lb pickling onions	455g	1lb
1 cucumber	1	1
1 cauliflower, small	1	1
8oz tomatoes, green	225g	8oz
8oz French beans	225g	8oz
4oz salt, cooking	115g	4oz
2oz flour, plain	55g	2oz
4oz sugar, granulated	115g	4oz
2oz mustard powder	55g	2oz
1oz turmeric, ground	30g	1oz
2pt vinegar, malt	1140ml	5 cups

1 Cut vegetables into small pieces (leave onions whole) and place in a glass or earthenware bowl. Sprinkle with salt, leave for 24 hours and drain.

2 Mix together the flour, sugar, mustard and turmeric and place in a saucepan. Blend to a paste with a little vinegar and gradually add the rest of the vinegar.

3 Bring slowly to the boil, stirring until thick.

4 Add the vegetables and simmer for 3 minutes.

5 Pack into hot jars, seal and store.

Vanilla

Vanilla fragrans
syn *Vanilla planifolia*
Fam Orchidaceae

SPICE DESCRIPTION

This flavouring comes from the seed capsule, known as a 'bean', of the vanilla plant. The prepared beans are very dark brown (Tahiti vanilla is a rust colour) 13–30cm (5–12in) long, averaging 20cm (8in), and slender wih a finely pleated appearance. At its best the bean is tough, though pliable, and frosted with a sugar-like crystal coating called *givre*. These crystals contain the active ingredient 'vanillin' responsible for the characteristic odour, and are produced, during the process of induced fermentation, by enzymatic reactions. Such pods are called 'fine vanilla'. Less common, and inferior, are 'woody vanilla' 13–20cm (5–8in) long, rust coloured and uncrystallised, and 'vanillons' 10–13cm (4–5in) long, opened, strong and slightly bitter. All beans contain thousands of tiny black seeds. Vanilla essence or extract is also available, and if of good quality is identical in flavour to the pods.

Bouquet True vanilla is highly fragrant, sweet and aromatic. Artificial vanilla flavouring, much cheaper than the essence, is harsh and leaves an aftertaste.

Flavour Agrees with the bouquet – rich, full and powerful. Tahiti vanilla is weaker and considered inferior. H Scale: 1

PREPARATION AND STORAGE

Vanilla, like the tonka bean, can with care be used repeatedly. Airtight storage is recommended however the pod is used, otherwise the aroma will dissipate and disappear. Vanilla essence, if good, is very powerful, a few drops sufficing for most uses. Using vanilla sugar is the most convenient and economical method of adding a vanilla flavour. A bean or two stored in a jar full of ordinary sugar will impart the characteristic flavour and aroma to the sugar which can then be used alone. A jar kept constantly filled with sugar gives a continuous supply of vanilla flavouring. At first, allow a month for the flavour to mature. After this, use vanilla sugar in place of ordinary sugar in sweet dishes and the vanilla balance will be correct. So kept, a good bean may remain potent for up to five years. Vanilla flavour can be imparted to a milk base for puddings by bringing the milk to the boil with one bean per pint, then steeping, allowing the preparation to cool for an hour. This process can be repeated a few times if the bean is washed directly after use, dried and kept airtight. Vanilla may also be ground for use in puddings and ices – half a bean per pint of liquid. When so used it is usual to leave the grounds in the dessert to indicate the authenticity of the flavouring.

USES

Vanilla has many uses, its delicate, mellow fragrance enhancing a variety of sweet dishes. It is as an ice cream flavouring that we know it best. We find vanilla in puddings, cakes, custards, creams and soufflés. Classic examples are crème caramel, pears Hélène, peach Melba and apple Charlotte. A deliciously subtle quality may be imparted to stewed fruits by the addition of a little vanilla and this is particularly apt with prunes and other dried fruits. Drinks, both alcoholic and non-alcoholic, and especially milk-based, are flavoured with vanilla. Home-made sweets and toffee are another favourite use. Vanilla flavour is detectable in many forms of chocolate and confectionery, and several liqueurs such as Crème de Cacao and Galliano taste strongly of vanilla.

CHEMICAL COMPOSITION

The fresh green beans consist of protein, sugars, cellulose, minerals, water, resin and oil. On curing, the water is reduced from 80 per cent to 20 per cent and enzymatic actions on glucosides, especially glucovanillin, produce vanillin and several other aromatic substances, alcohols, acids and aldehydes. These compounds give natural vanillin its unique fragrance which cannot be imitated by synthetic vanillin.

ATTRIBUTED PROPERTIES

Vanilla is supposedly a febrifuge – it was used to assuage fever – and a reviver. Workers handling vanilla continually are said to suffer from skin eruptions and headaches. However, its use is primarily as a flavouring, the attributed medical properties being incidental to its culinary use.

PLANT DESCRIPTION

A tropical climbing orchid. It has a long, green fleshy stem, which sprouts roots above the soil, clinging to other trees parasitically, but also delving into the earth. It sports bunches of typical orchidaceous flowers, which open for one day each, blooming one by one during the two month season. The leaves are about 13–18cm (5–7in) long and 5–8cm (2–3in) broad, fleshy and pale green.

CULTIVATION

This is a tropical crop and cannot grow naturally in temperate climates. When cultivated, these parasitic plants must be

trained using posts or support trees. As the aerial roots receive no nourishment, extra nutrients are provided. In nature they are pollinated only by Mexican bees; otherwise, they must be artificially fertilised using thin wooden skewers, like cocktail sticks. After pollination, bunches of pods begin to develop. They take about nine months to mature and are harvested when the tips begin to turn from yellow, being still unripe. The curing process is long and complex. First the beans are wrapped and subjected to high temperature and humidity in a special room to 'kill' the vegetative life. The next process involves alternate drying in the sun by day and sweating by night for a few days. The beans are now dark, oily and pliable and must be slowly dried in the shade for one to two months. They are then sorted and graded and placed in chests for a further conditioning period of one to two months, after which they are ready for market. Recently a method has been developed in Uganda that reduces the whole process to a few days.

REMARKS
Vanilla is native to Mexico, where it is still grown commercially. It is now cultivated in other tropical areas of the western hemisphere, especially in Malagasy and the Seychelles, and less importantly in Réunion, Indonesia and Tahiti, where the vanilla is said to be inferior. An allied species, *Vanilla pompona*, is grown in the West Indies. Vanilla was used by the Aztecs for flavouring their royal drink *xocolatl* – a mixture of cocoa beans, vanilla and honey. This was the original chocolate, and the beans and the vanilla were introduced to Europe by Cortés in the sixteenth century. Strangely, its now inseparable association with chocolate did not catch on here until the mid-eighteenth century, since when it has been used to flavour most forms of chocolate. Fresh vanilla is odourless, the active ingredient being formed during the curing process. The crystal frosting, *givre*, is an indication of quality, but is easy to counterfeit. Cheap vanilla is of suspect quality, whether frosted or not. Vanilla extract or essence, if genuine, is an acceptable alternative, being the result of the extraction of the essential oil by subjection to alcohol. Substances called 'vanilla flavour' etc are dubious, being synthesised from eugenol (oil of cloves), wood pulp waste, coal tar or 'coumarin', whose use is forbidden in several countries. Vanilla has many non-culinary uses, for example in commercial soft drinks, tobaccos and scents. The name derives from the Spanish for 'little pod', (*vaina*, pod).

OTHER NAMES
French: vanille
German: Vanille
Italian: vaniglia
Spanish: vainilla

Marble Sponge
An attractive cake originally from Denmark.

Imp	Metric	US
6oz butter or margarine	170g	6oz
6oz sugar, granulated	170g	6oz
3 eggs, separated	3	3
8oz flour, plain	225g	8oz
1tsp baking powder	1tsp	1tsp
¼pt milk	140ml	9½tbsp
1tsp lemon rind, grated	1tsp	1tsp
1tsp vanilla essence	5ml	1tsp
2tbsp cocoa	2tbsp	2⅔tbsp
caster sugar		

1 Cream together the butter and sugar until light and pale.
2 Add egg yolks gradually, beating well.
3 Sift together the flour and baking powder, add to the mixture, then add milk, beating well.
4 Whisk egg whites until stiff and gently fold in.
5 Take a third of the mixture and blend in the cocoa.
6 Put the mixtures in 5 layers into a greased *gugelhupf* mould, starting and ending with the vanilla.
7 Bake in a moderate oven Gas Mark 4, 350°F, 180°C, for 45 minutes. Remove tin from oven.

8 Allow to cool for a couple of minutes, turn out and sprinkle with caster sugar.

Peach Melba (colour page 138)

When made with fresh fruit this is one of the nicest summer desserts.   Serves 4–6

Imp	Metric	US
½pt water	285ml	1¼ cups
3oz sugar, granulated	85g	3oz
2tsp vanilla essence or 1 vanilla bean	10ml	2tsp
4 peaches, peeled and halved	4	4
8oz raspberries, sieved	225g	8oz
2oz icing sugar	55g	2oz
1¾pt vanilla ice cream	1 litre	3¼ cups

1 Put water, sugar and vanilla in a saucepan, bring to simmering point, stirring until sugar has dissolved.
2 Poach the peaches in the syrup for about 5 minutes until tender and allow to cool.
3 Gradually add the icing sugar to the raspberry purée until smooth and thick.
4 Take individual bowls and scoop in some ice cream, lay 1 or 2 peach halves on top and pour over the raspberry sauce.

Zedoary

Curcuma zedoaria (round)
Curcuma zerumbet (long)
Fam Zingiberaceae

SPICE DESCRIPTION
This spice, practically unknown in the modern West, is the large, fleshy underground stem of a plant resembling turmeric. The polyramate rhizome is rough skinned and hirsute. It is sold dried and sliced, presenting a grey surface with a yellow to grey-white interior, hard and tough. The pieces are in two forms: 'long', consisting of slices cut along the root, about 25mm (1in) wide and 6mm (¼in) thick; and 'round', consisting of small sections cut across the root. It is also sold as a powder in Chinese food shops.
Bouquet Musky, resembling ginger but redolent of camphor.

Flavour Warm, bitter, pungent, aromatic, gingery and camphorous.   H Scale: 4

PREPARATION AND STORAGE
Grind to a beige or yellow powder in a pestle and mortar or pulverise in a liquidiser. Store in airtight containers.

USES
Zedoary is used as a spice in South East Asia, as a condiment and an ingredient in curry powder. It quite often features in Indonesian seafood dishes. The root yields much starch, known as *shoti* starch. This is widely used as part of an Eastern regimen for the sick, weak or very young, being highly nutritious and easily metabolised. The leaves are used as a herb for flavouring Javanese dishes.

CHEMICAL COMPOSITION
Volatile and fixed oils are present, with some resin and a high proportion of starch. The volatile oil contains the colouring agent curcumin, as seen in turmeric.

ATTRIBUTED PROPERTIES
Zedoary is stimulant and carminative, used in flatulence, colic and dyspepsia. It is generally good for the digestive system. 'Zedwary, chawed "and swallowed" taketh awaye the grefe of the bely' (Lloyd, *Treasury of Health*, 1550). In its medical uses it is similar to but less active than ginger, and is a constituent of antiperiodic and urinary preparations. The leaves are

used to treat dropsy, and the root is chewed to relieve sore throats.

PLANT DESCRIPTION

Resembling turmeric, and related to ginger, growing in tropical and subtropical wet forest regions. The rhizome is large and tuberous with many branches. The leaf shoots reach 1m (3ft) in height. The light yellow flowers with white calyxes are enclosed in green or red-purple bracts.

CULTIVATION

Zedoary is commercially grown from parts of the rhizomes. It takes two years to mature. The roots are cut and dried when harvested.

REMARKS

Native to India and the Himalayas, zedoary grows also in Pakistan and China. The Arabs brought it into Europe in the sixth century, where it enjoyed great popularity in the Middle Ages, but today it is extremely rare in the West, ginger having replaced it. A substitute for arrowroot, it is used in Indian perfumes and in festive rituals. *Curcuma aromatica* (yellow zedoary or wild turmeric or cassumunar) is a close relative, growing wild in South East Asia. Its bright red to orange flesh is used in medicine and dyeing. Zedoary bears the same Indonesian name as lesser galangal, and this is a justifiable confusion because of the similarity of the rhizomes.

OTHER NAMES

Long Zedoary, Round Zedoary, Wild Turmeric, Zedoary
Dutch: kentjoer
French: zédoaire
German: Zitwer
Italian: zedoaria
Spanish: cedoaria
Indian: amb halad, gandhmul, ka(r)chur(a)
Indonesian: kentjur
Malay: kunchor
Tamil: soti

Rempah

Indonesian meat balls to serve hot or cold with drinks.

Imp	Metric	US
3oz desiccated coconut	85g	3oz
2tbsp hot water	40ml	2⅔tbsp
8oz beef, finely minced	225g	8oz
1tsp coriander, ground	1tsp	1tsp
½tsp cumin, ground	½tsp	½tsp
½tsp zedoary, ground	½tsp	½tsp
½tsp salt	½tsp	½tsp
1 egg	1	1
oil, for frying		

1 Moisten the coconut with the water and mix in a bowl with the meat.
2 Add the rest of the ingredients except for the oil and knead well with the hands for a few minutes.
3 Form into small balls about ¾in (20mm) and fry until golden brown.

Spice Mixtures

In most cases undimensioned proportions are given. For example, where the proportion figures are, say, 1, 2, 1, 4, this mean 'parts', eg teaspoons, grammes, whatever, can be used depending on the quantity required or the available measures. They can be scaled up or down as required, eg 10g, 20g, 10g, 40g for the above proportions. The same unit of measurement must, of course, be used throughout.

Mixture	Country of Origin	Spices and Proportions	Uses	Remarks
Apple Pie Spice	World	cinnamon, ground 4 cloves, ground 1 nutmeg, ground 1 (optional)	All types of apple pie, sauces, strudels and stewed fruit. Use ½–2tsp of spice mixture to 0.5kg (1lb) of fruit.	Proportions variable, to taste. Cinnamon and cloves may be used whole. Recipes may omit any one of the ingredients.
Barbecue Spice	World	black pepper to taste optional celery seed 2 chilli powder 1 garlic powder/granules 1 marjoram, dried 2 nutmeg, ground 1 onion powder 1 paprika 1 salt 1 sugar, soft brown 1	Barbecued meat, chicken, sausages, burgers etc. Make up mixture just before use. Rub on to meat during barbecuing, use as a condiment, or add to grills, dressings, cheese dishes and marinades.	Other spices, such as cumin, coriander, mustard and oregano, can be added or substituted.
Bengali Five Spices *see* Panch Phora				
Brine Mixtures	World	Brine mixture per litre (1¾pts) of water salt 135g (5oz) sugar 45g (1½oz) saltpetre 7g (¼oz)	Salted and cured pork or beef joints. Boil and skim brine. Add bag of spices and allow to cool. Strain into sterilised plastic or earthenware container. Add meat. Keep submerged with sterilised wooden weight. Leave for recommended time.	Nutmeg and cloves may replace allspice. Recipes for salting and curing should be followed carefully to avoid the meat spoiling.

[199]

Mixture	Country of Origin	Spices and Proportions	Uses	Remarks

Brine Mixtures	World	spice mixture:
		  allspice, whole 10
		  bay leaf, medium 1
		  juniper berries 10
		  peppercorns 20
		  thyme, sprigs 1		

Chat Masala	India	amchur powder 2 cardamom, ground 1 chilli, ground 1 coriander, ground 1 cumin, ground 1 fennel seed, ground 1 fenugreek, ground 1 mace, ground 1 nutmeg, ground 1 pepper, black, ground 1 pomegranate seeds, ground 2 salt, black 1	For flavouring pulses, okra, aubergines, potatoes, *dhals*, *bhajis*, stuffed vegetables and *samosas*.	This is not a curry powder but a hot, spicy and astringent mixture for vegetable and pulse dishes, originating from the Punjab.
Chicken Seasoning	World	Spit Roasting white flour 4tsp nutmeg, ground 1tsp lemon rind, grated 2tsp salt ½tsp pepper ½tsp Boiling mace, blade 1 celery seeds ½tsp peppercorns ½tsp small onion stuck with 3 cloves 1 bayleaf	Spit roasting: rub bird with butter and sprinkle mixture over skin. Boiling: add spices to the water.	The spit mixture can also be used for oven roasting. Start oven roasting with the chicken upside down, the body juices will baste the breast. Turn upside up half an hour before end of cooking time.

Mixture	Country of Origin	Spices and Proportions	Uses	Remarks
Chilli Seasoning	Mexico and US	chilli, ground 1–3 cumin, ground 1 garlic, granules 1 oregano, dried 1 coriander, ground 1 optional	Specifically for *chile con carne*, but may spice Mexican-style dishes, eggs, pasta and shellfish cocktail sauces.	Although associated with Mexico, *chile con carne* is a Texan dish often blisteringly hot.
Chinese Five Spices	China	anise-pepper, ground 1 cinnamon or cassia, ground 1 cloves, ground 1 fennel, ground 1 star anise, ground 1	Used in Chinese and Indo-Chinese cookery with chicken, pork, 'red-cooked' meats and spareribs.	The sweetness of anise predominates and this powder should be used with discretion. Also known as *heung lo fun, heung new fun, hung liu, ngung heung fun, ng hiong fun, zva hsiang fun.*
Chinese Spiced Salt	China	No. 1: salt, white, medium ground 1 anise-pepper, ground 1 No. 2: salt, white, medium ground 1 Chinese five-spice powder ¼	Roast mixtures for about one minute in a dry frying pan. Accompanies deep fried food, such as prawns and fried spareribs.	Known as *hua jiao yen* and served in small bowls as a dip.
Crab Boil	US	allspice, whole 1tsp 2 bay leaves 2 whole dried chillies cloves 1tsp coriander, whole 1tsp dill seed, whole 1tsp mustard seed, whole 2tsp peppercorns 1tsp	This mixture is suitable for 5 litres (1 gal) of salted water. For home cooking of fresh caught crabs and other crustaceans.	Also known as 'shrimp spice'.

Mixture	Country of Origin	Spices and Proportions	Uses	Remarks
(CURRY POWDERS)				
Bombay	India	chilli, crushed 1 cinnamon, stick 2 coriander seeds 8 cumin seeds 1 curry leaves, crushed 2 fennel seeds 1 fenugreek seeds 1 garlic powder ½ nagkeser, ground 1 optional trifala, ground 1 optional turmeric, ground 2	For beef and chicken curries all the spices except for curry leaves and garlic should be roasted before grinding.	Suitable for 'Anglo-Indian'-style curries. If nagkeser and trifala are unavailable, add two or three black kokums to the cooking pot.
Chinese	China	anise-pepper, whole 1 cassia, whole 1 chilli, whole ½ cloves, whole ½ coriander seeds, whole 6 fennel seeds 1 nutmeg, grated 1 star anise, ground ½ turmeric, ground 1	Chinese and Malaysian curries. Roast first six ingredients lightly before grinding and add to remaining spices.	This is a very sweet-smelling curry powder because of its anise-pepper content.
Kofta	India	cardamom, ground 1 cinnamon, ground 1 cloves, ground 1 coriander, ground 1 peppercorns, ground 1	Koftas – these spices are mixed with the minced meat. Cardamom is always better freshly ground.	These meat balls are made from very finely minced lamb or beef, onion, garlic and spices, cooked in a variety of curry sauces.

Mixture	Country of Origin	Spices and Proportions	Uses	Remarks
Korma	India	almonds, ground 2 or coconut, grated 4 cardamom, ground 1 chilli, ground ½ cinnamon, ground ½ cloves, ground ½ ginger, ground 2 or fresh 4 black pepper to taste salt to taste turmeric, ground 1	Curries of mutton, lamb, beef, chicken or duck.	The main characteristic of Korma curries is that the meat is marinaded in a mixture of sour curds or yoghurt, and spices. It is of Mogul origin. Sometimes spelt *kormah*, *krormah*, *quoorma* or *quormah*.
Madras	India	chilli, ground 1 coriander, ground 16 cumin, ground 8 ginger, ground 1 mustard, black, ground 1 turmeric, ground 2 black pepper, ground 1 curry leaves, whole 4 optional	Fish and meat curries.	Madras curries are medium hot to fiery depending on area. Madras is a main centre of southeast India where hotter dishes are preferred.
Sri Lanka	Sri Lanka	cardamom, ground 1 chilli, ground 2 cinnamon, ground 1 cloves, ground 1 *coriander, ground 16 *cumin, ground 8 curry leaf, crushed 8 *fennel, ground 4 *fenugreek, ground 1 *roast on low heat until dark before grinding.	For meat, fish, poultry and vegetable curries from Sri Lanka.	Distinct from Indian curries because of the dark roasting of some of the spices.

Mixture	Country of Origin	Spices and Proportions	Uses	Remarks
Tandoori	India	cardamom, ground ½ chilli, ground 1 cinnamon, ground ½ cloves, ground ¼ coriander, ground 4 cumin, ground 1 ginger, ground 2 black pepper, ground ¼ red colouring, powder ½	Grilled chicken, meat and fish. Marinade the meat or chicken for twelve hours in the spice mixture combined with yoghurt and lemon juice, first deeply scoring the skinned flesh.	'Tandoor' is the name for the clay oven in which this dish is traditionally spit roasted.
Tikka	India	chilli, ground ½ coriander leaves, ground 2 garlic granules ½ ginger, ground 1 black pepper ½ turmeric, ground 1 onion powder 1 garam masala 1 optional red colouring ½ optional	Cubed meat served on a 'sizzler'. Marinade meat for a few hours. Place on skewers for cooking.	Traditionally cooked in a tandoor. Served on a 'sizzler' (hot metal plate) the effect is quite dramatic. Other names are *tick-keah, tikia, tikkah.*
Vindaloo	India (Goa)	cardamom seeds, whole ½ chilli, ground 2 cinnamon, ground 1½ cloves, ground ¼ coriander, ground 2 cumin, ground ½ fenugreek, ground 1 fresh garlic or granules 1 ginger, ground 1 mustard powder 1 pepper, black, ground ½	Meat, fish, poultry and vegetable curries. Proportions are for ground spices but it is preferable to use whole spices, slightly roasted then ground. Pork is the best meat for the perfect vindaloo. Grind spices in blender. Add vinegar, re-mix. Marinade meat in spiced vinegar, for one day at least (use a non-metallic container). Agitate the marinade every few hours. Cook meat in mustard oil or *ghee.* Leave for a day. Reheat before serving.	Sometimes called bindaloo, the hotness of this curry can be varied to taste by changing the chilli proportion. A fairly hot version is best: between a Madras and a Pahl. Vindaloo is a curry variation created by the Portuguese during their annexation of Goa.

Mixture	Country of Origin	Spices and Proportions	Uses	Remarks
Dukkah Mix	Egypt	cinnamon, ground 1 coriander seeds 2 cumin seed 1 or mint, dried 1 sesame seed 4 salt to taste pepper to taste mixed with crushed hazelnuts 1 or cooked chick peas 1	Appetiser or dip for bread soaked in olive oil.	All the ingredients are coarsely ground in a blender. An Egyptian favourite.
Fish Seasoning	World	cayenne pepper ¼ fennel seeds, ground ½ lemon peel, grated 1 parsley, dried flakes 1	Fish soups, courts-bouillons, baked or poached freshwater or sea fish. Shellfish cocktails.	Use with discretion. Very amenable to variations.
French Dressing	World	Classic: olive oil 3 wine vinegar 1 pepper to taste salt to taste plus Dijon mustard ½ Variation I: salad oil 3 vinegar 1 sugar to taste garlic powder ⅛ mustard powder ¼ salt and cayenne pepper to taste	All types of salads, avocado pears etc.	To make the perfect dressing, spare the vinegar and be generous with the oil. For dressings with chopped ingredients it is convenient to mix everything in a blender.

Key to colour plate on facing page

1. Ajowan
2. Allspice
3. Amchur
4. Anise
5. Anise-pepper
6. Annatto
7. Asafoetida
8. Badrang
9. Caper
10. Caraway
11. Cardamom
12. Cassia buds
13. Cayenne
14. Celery seed
15. Chilli
16. Cloves
17. Coriander
18. Cubeb
19. Cumin
20. Dill
21. Fennel

22. Fenugreek
23. Laos powder
24. Ginger
25. Horseradish
26. Juniper
27. Sereh powder
28. Mahlebi
29. Mastic
30. Mint
31. Mustard
32. Mustard
33. Nigella
34. Papaya
35. Paprika
36. Pepper
37. Pepper
38. Pomegranate
39. Poppy
40. Saffron
41. Sesame
42. Sumac

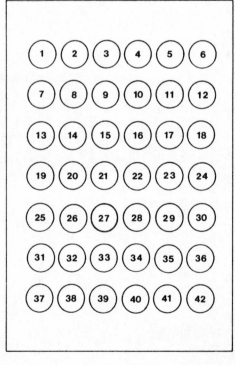

Key to colour plate on facing page

1. Amchur
2. Bay leaf
3. Black cardamom
4. Carob
5. Cassia bark
6. Cassia leaf
7. Chillies
8. Cinnamon
9. Tangerine peel
10. Lime leaves
11. Coconut cream
12. Curry leaf
13. Fenugreek leaves
14. Greater galangal
15. Lesser galangal
16. Garlic
17. Ginger

18. Pickled ginger
19. Kokum
20. Lemon grass
21. Liquorice
22. Mace
23. Nutmeg
24. Onion
25. Pepper
26. Rock salt
27. Sandalwood
28. Sassafras
29. Soy bean curd
30. Star anise
31. Tamarind
32. Tonka bean
33. Turmeric
34. Zedoary

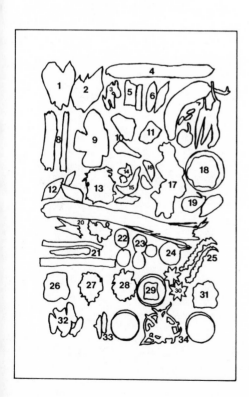

Mixture	Country of Origin	Spices and Proportions	Uses	Remarks
French Dressing	World	Variation II: olive oil 6 wine vinegar 1 celery seed ¼ chives ½ parsley ½ salt and pepper to taste Vinaigrette: Classic plus ¼ each of capers, chives, gherkins, nasturtium seeds, parsley and tarragon, all chopped plus a few drops of Worcestershire Sauce.		
Gado-Gado	Indonesia	garlic, dried, minced or powder 2 ginger, ground 1 chilli, powder 2 curry leaf, whole, per unit mix 2 peanuts, roasted, ground 16 shrimp extract, dried 2	Spices for the sauce accompanying gado-gado, which is an Indonesian vegetable dish. This peanut mix has many other uses, for example, with *sambals*, *kebabs*, barbecues, spreads, eggs, cheese, and so on. Mix dry ingredients with water as required to make sauce, boil then simmer for a few minutes until the right consistency is obtained.	Gado-gado sauce is easy to make and can be kept if properly bottled. Reduce the chilli content to taste.
Garam Masala	India	Basic Mixture: cardamom, ground 4 cinnamon, ground 1 clove, ground 1 cumin, ground 1 pepper, corns 1	For all savoury dishes from India, Pakistan and Bangladesh.	*Garam* means 'hot' and *masala* means 'spice'. Garam masala is best made up when required. Its function in Indian cooking is to add spiciness towards the end of cooking.

Mixture	Country of Origin	Spices and Proportions	Uses	Remarks
		Fragrant Mixture: Basic Mixture plus extra cinnamon 2 nutmeg, ground 1		This is one of the many variations of Garam masala.
Gomasio	Japan	black sesame seeds 10 salt 1 monosodium glutamate ½	A condiment for Japanese dishes. Gently roast the seeds before grinding together with the salts.	The Japanese word for sesame is 'goma'. It is ubiquitous in Japan.
Harissa	Tunisia	caraway seeds 2 chilli, ground 16 coriander, ground 1 cumin, ground 1 garlic, clove 1 salt to taste peeled and seeded tomatoes 16 or tomato purée 16 (let a tablespoon = 4)	Accompaniment to most main dishes, snacks, briks, kebabs and barbecues. Blend ingredients in liquidiser.	As can be seen from the proportions, this is a searingly hot sauce and is beloved by the peoples of Tunisia. It appears in a small dish alongside every meal and forkfuls of meat are dipped into this sauce with aplomb.
Hoisin Sauce	China	Constituents: chilli flour garlic ginger red rice salt sesame soya beans sugar vinegar	Traditional Chinese barbecue sauce. Applied to pork roasts, spareribs, crispy chicken and duck, shredded meats, hot salads, dips etc.	Hoisin makes European and American barbecued meats subtly different, uniting a gentle piquancy with sweet crispness. Usually pre-prepared, available in jars and tins.

Hua Jiao Yen see Chinese Spiced Salt

Mixture	Country of Origin	Spices and Proportions	Uses	Remarks
Italian Seasoning	World	basil, ground 1 bay leaves, ground 1 oregano, ground 1 paprika, ground ½ parsley, ground 1 pepper, ground 1 sage, ground 1 thyme, ground 1	All Italian savoury dishes, hamburgers and casseroles.	Commercial mixtures are available but it is preferable to make up your own.
Kashmiri Masala	India and Pakistan	black cumin seeds 1 black peppercorns 1 caraway seeds ½ cardamom seeds 2 cinnamon stick 1 cloves, whole 1 nutmeg, grated ½	Used particularly with prawn and lamb dishes. Lightly roast whole spices before grinding and blend well together with nutmeg.	Kashmiri cookery does not include beef, onions or garlic.
Khara Masala	India	bay leaves black peppercorns cardamom pods, whole chillies, dried cinnamon, stick cloves, whole apportion according to taste	Most popular in chicken and lamb dishes. Keep spices whole. Fry in oil before adding main ingredient.	'Khara' means whole, and the spices are served with the finished dish although not eaten. The mixture is sometimes varied by the addition of cumin, fennel, pomegranate or nigella seeds.
La Kama	Morocco	black pepper, ground 2 cinnamon, ground 1 ginger, ground 2 nutmeg, ground ¼ turmeric, ground 2	To flavour soups and stews.	This seasoning is particularly associated with Tangier, whilst the rest of Morocco favours *ras el hanout*, a mixture of twenty spices purported to give health, strength and virility.

Mixture	Country of Origin	Spices and Proportions	Uses	Remarks
Lamb Seasoning	Europe	coriander seed 1 ajowan seeds ¼ garlic, granules ¼ optional pepper, whole, black 1	Grind in a peppermill over joints for roasting.	The presence of a little ajowan is useful when fresh thyme, a traditional flavouring, is not available.
Lebanese Mix	Lebanon	cayenne pepper 1 cinnamon, ground 2 paprika 2	Used as a condiment or to flavour soups and stews.	The Lebanese are the gourmets of the Middle East and in happier times enjoyed a café life-style where spiced snacks were traditional.
Meat Tenderiser	World	No. 1: corn starch papain salt No. 2: bromelin seasonings salt	Commercial (but natural) products to tenderise steaks, chops or cuts of meat. Sprinkle on to meat using about one teaspoon per kilogramme (2.2lb) and leave for half an hour.	Papain and bromelin are enzymes extracted from papaya and pineapple respectively.
Mexican Mixture *see* Chilli Seasoning				
Mignonette	France	black peppercorns 1 white peppercorns 1	Coarsely grind together for a mixture, both hot and aromatic, to flavour steaks and *charcuterie*.	Also known as shot pepper, mignonette was the name for a bag of mixed spices – cinnamon, cloves, ginger, nutmeg, cayenne and coriander. This was dipped into the cooking pot to flavour food and used several times.

Mixture	Country of Origin	Spices and Proportions	Uses	Remarks
Mixed Spice	UK	allspice 1 cinnamon 1 cloves 1 ginger, ground 1 nutmeg 1	Grind whole spices and add to ginger and freshly grated nutmeg. Use in cakes, biscuits and puddings.	Also called pudding spice, the mixture can be varied with aniseed, cardamom, coriander or pepper.
Mukhwas *see* Pan				
Mulling Spice	Europe and US	Mulled wine or ale: peel of lemon 1 cinnamon 5cm (2in) stick 2 clove 6 nutmeg ½ sugar to taste Bishop: orange 1 cloves 10 allspice berries 10	The first mixture is for one litre (1¾pt) of red wine or ale. Brandy and water may be added to the wine, and whisky or other spirits to the beer. The second mixture is sufficient for one bottle of port and is known as the Bishop. For mulled wine, bring wine and 280ml (½pt) water slowly to just below boiling point with the lemon peel, cinnamon and cloves. Add 140ml (¼pt) brandy if desired, pour into glasses and top with grated nutmeg.	Always heat alcohol very slowly and never allow to boil. For the Bishop, stud the orange with cloves, wrap in foil and bake in a slow oven for an hour, then quarter it and add with the crushed spice to the warming port.
Mustard Mixtures *see* Mustard, page 126				
Nanami Togarshi *see* Shichimi-Togarashi				
Pan	India	areca nuts 4 cucumber seeds ¼ fennel seeds 2 sugar balls ½ all approximate proportions	Indian 'chew' and breath sweetener. Little red sugar balls are prominent in the mixture.	Also called *supari* or *mukhwas*. The areca nuts are sliced and crushed, coloured, sweetened and flavoured with various oils such as clove and cardamom. When areca nuts and bark are mixed with lime and wrapped in a betele pepper

Mixture	Country of Origin	Spices and Proportions	Uses	Remarks
				leaf, pinned with a clove, it is known as 'betel nut'. A characteristic red stain comes from the areca bark (*Areca catechu*). The mixture is an Indian favourite and now readily available in Indian foodstores. Also spelled *paan*.
Panch Phora	India	cumin seeds 1 fennel seeds 1 fenugreek seeds 1 mustard, black, seeds 1 nigella ½	Pan frying, stews, casseroles, vegetable dishes, mild curries.	Of Bengali origin, the mixture given is authentic, although variations do occur. In Hindustani, *panch* means 'five' and *phora* means 'seeds'. Available ready mixed from Indian shops. Sometimes called *panch puran* or *panch pora*.
Perfumery Spices	World	Soap mixture: clove oil 1 kewra oil 1 nutmeg powder 1 sandalwood powder 1 Incense mixture: cardamom, ground 1 cassia, ground 1 cloves, ground 1 sandalwood, ground 2	Perfumes, cosmetics, soaps, incense.	The essential oils of spices have been used for centuries for these purposes. There are countless variations.

Mixture	Country of Origin	Spices and Proportions	Uses	Remarks
Pickling Spices	World	**General Mix No 1** allspice, whole 1 chilli, small, whole, per jar 1 cinnamon, whole 1 cloves, whole 1 coriander, whole 1 ginger, dried or fresh, diced 1 mace, blade 1 mustard seed 1 peppercorns, black or white 1 **General Mix No 2** allspice, whole 1 chilli, small, whole, per jar 1 cinnamon, whole 1 cloves, whole 1 ginger, dried or fresh diced 1 mace, blade 1 peppercorns, black or white 1 **Dill Pickle Mix** allspice, whole 1 bayleaf, crumbled 3 chilli, small, whole, per jar 1 cloves, whole 1 coriander, whole 2 dill, seeds 4 or dill, sprigs, fresh 4 fennel or ajowan seeds ½ ginger, dried or fresh, diced 1 mustard seeds 6 peppercorns, black 1	Mixture Numbers 1 and 2 for pickling various vegetable or fruits. Dill Pickle Mixture for pickling small (ridge) cucumbers.	The spices can be adjusted to taste and do vary considerably from recipe to recipe. These mixtures are good general purpose ones.

Mixture	Country of Origin	Spices and Proportions	Uses	Remarks
Pilau Mixture	India	cardamom, ground 2 cinnamon, crushed 1 cloves, whole 1 nutmeg, ground ½ plus ½ saffron for coloured pilaus	*Pilaus.*	The spices may be either mixed freely in the rice during cooking or put in a bag.
Pork Seasoning	Europe	ginger ½ onion salt 1 orange peel ½ pepper ½ rosemary ½ sage 3	Sprinkle over joints, chops, add to casseroles and sausagemeat.	Commercial mixtures are commonly available.
Pudding Spice *see* Mixed Spice				
Quatre Epices	France, Middle East	cloves, ground 1 ginger, ground 3 nutmeg, ground 4 white pepper, ground 12	French *charcuterie* and Arab cookery. Sometimes cinnamon is substituted for ginger, and allspice for white pepper.	Literally 'four spices'. The proportions are infinitely variable.
Ras El Hanout	Morocco	A complex mixture of 20 spices including cardamom, chilli, cinnamon, cloves, coriander, cumin, ginger, nutmeg, pepper, salt, turmeric etc and possibly *za'atar*	Moroccan soups (*hareera*) and stews (*tagine*).	*Ras el hanout* means 'head of the shop' and is popular throughout the rest of Morocco whilst *la kama* is the favourite of Tangier. It allegedly promotes a sense of well-being and enhances sexual vigour, seemingly taking no chances on leaving out any spice that may have that property.

Mixture	Country of Origin	Spices and Proportions	Uses	Remarks
Salad Seasoning *see* French Dressing				
Sambal Mix	Indonesia	chillies, fresh 5 tamarind, water 2 or lemon juice salt ½	Very hot condiment to accompany Indonesian dishes, spring rolls etc.	This is a basic hot *sambal* sauce. The ingredients are blended together and once made and bottled can be kept in a refrigerator for three or four weeks. Other spices, such as ginger, galangal or garlic can be added to this preparation. Vinegar or sumac infusion can be substituted for the tamarind juice.
Sausage Seasoning	UK	cayenne, ground 2 cloves, ground 2 ginger, ground 2 mace, ground 1 nutmeg, ground 2 sage, ground 3 white pepper, ground 18 salt, fine, ground 70	Added to the sausage mix in the ratio of one of spice mix to thirty of sausage meat.	This seasoning, on the piquant side, combines the best of several English sausage seasonings.
Seasoning Salt	World	celery seeds, ground 1 white pepper, ground 1 cumin seed, ground 1 salt 10 plus cayenne pepper 1 optional or paprika 1 optional	Universal seasoning for canapés, soups, tomato juice, seafood cocktails, steaks, eggs, cheese dishes, chops, meat sauces, savouries etc.	This is another mixture amenable to variation. In fact many of the spices in this book can be added or substituted for the ones given here.

Mixture	Country of Origin	Spices and Proportions	Uses	Remarks
Sel Epicé	France	Basic: mixed spices 1 white pepper 1 salt, fine 5 Mixed spices: cassia 1 cloves ½ coriander 1 ginger 1 nutmeg 1	Stuffings, forcemeats and sausages.	Peculiarly French but affined to the seasoning and sausage spice mixtures. Allspice can be substituted for nutmeg, cloves and ginger.
Seven Flavour Spice *see* Shichimi-Togarashi				
Seven Seas Spice	Malaysia and Indonesia	cardamom, ground 1 cassia or cinnamon, ground 1 chilli or cayenne, ground 1 celery seeds, ground ½ cloves, ground ½ coriander seeds, ground 2 cumin, ground 1	Curries, *sambals*, soups, stews, casseroles and *kebabs*.	So called from the seven seas (Andaman, South China, Java, Celebes, Flores, Ceram and Sulu) washing the island shores of Indonesia and Malaysia.
Shichimi-Togarashi	Japan	chilli, ground 4 hemp seed, whole ½ poppy seed, whole ½ rape seed, whole ½ *sansho* (ground anise-pepper leaves) 3 sesame seed, black, whole 1 sesame seed, white, crushed 2 tangerine peel, dried, ground 3 (proportions can be varied)	Used as a condiment and seasoning for soups, noodles, *sukiyaki*, *tempura* etc.	Also known as seven-flavour seasoning, it is available in tins or bottles and varies in taste from mild to very hot and sharp. It sometimes includes mustard seed, perilla seed and crushed seaweed. *Nanami* means 'a number of things'.

Mixture	Country of Origin	Spices and Proportions	Uses	Remarks
Shichimi-Togarashi	Japan	A variation known as *nanami togarashi* consists of: chilli ground 4 seaweed, ground 1 sesame, white, ground 3 tangerine peel, dried, ground 3		
Spiced Beef Mixture	England	black peppercorns, ground 3tbsp cloves, ground 1tbsp juniper berries, crushed 3tbsp ginger, ground 1tbsp mace, ground 1tbsp salt, rock or sea salt 6oz saltpetre 1oz sugar, brown 6oz	A basic formula for dry-spicing 4½kg (10lb) of silverside of beef. Mix all ingredients together and rub into meat. Turn and rub daily for ten days, keeping covered in an earthenware crock. Remove spices and cook in a tightly covered dish with about ¼ litre (½pt) water in a very low oven for 6–7 hours. Weight down and refrigerate when cool.	There are numerous recipes for English spiced beef with varying spice mixtures. The spices should be freshly ground. Treacle is sometimes poured over the meat at the first rub.
Spiced Salt	France and India	French Mixture: salt, fine 7 pepper, black 1 pepper, white 1 *spice mix 1 *spice mix: bayleaf, ground 1 chilli powder 6 cinnamon, ground 1 cloves, ground 1 mace, ground 2 marjoram, ground 1 nutmeg, ground 1 rosemary, ground 1 sage, ground 1	French mixture: sausages, stuffings, rubbing on to meat, poultry etc. Indian mixture: added to vegetables and stews at end of cooking; rubbing on to meat joints and poultry for roasting, and for yoghurt based dishes.	Similar to sausage seasonings, seasoning salt and *sel épicé*.

Mixture	Country of Origin	Spices and Proportions	Uses	Remarks
		Indian Mixture: salt, crushed rock 16 asafoetida, powder ½ salt, Indian, crushed 1 *spice mix, ground 4 *spice mix (gently heat before grinding): chilli, crushed 1 coriander, seeds 1 cumin, seeds 1 mace, blade ¼ peppercorns black ¾		
Steak Spice *see* Barbecue Spice				
Tabil	Tunisia	caraway, ground 1 coriander, ground 1 garlic, crushed 1 chilli, dried crushed 1	Mix well together and use in lamb stews and vegetable dishes.	About one tablespoon of *tabil* spices a dish for four people if no extra hot seasoning is specified.
Taklia	Arabia	coriander, ground 1 garlic, crushed 1	Fry together in a little oil. For meat, pulse and green vegetable dishes.	*Taklia* is added at the end of the cooking period and is a very popular Middle Eastern flavouring.
Tsire Powder	Nigeria and West Africa	chilli powder 1 *mixed spice, ground 2 peanuts, ground 4 salt, to taste *any commercial mixed spice is suitable or Mixed Spice above.	*Kebab* coating and accompaniment to grilled meat. (Dip *kebabs* in oil or beaten egg then into the tsire powder).	A tasty and satisfying barbecue sauce, *tsire* is the classic dressing for the West African *kebabs* variously known as *tsire agashe* (Nigeria), *chachanga* (Togo) and *chichinga* (Ghana).

Mixture	Country of Origin	Spices and Proportions	Uses	Remarks
Tsire Powder	Nigeria and West Africa	Ground cinnamon or cassia also serve adequately. Roast peanuts before grinding.	The powder is also served separately with slices of meat.	
Virgin Islands Spice	Virgin and Leeward Islands	celery seeds, whole ½ cloves, crushed 1 garlic, granules 1 mace, crushed ½ nutmeg, crushed ½ parsley, dried, crushed ½ peppercorns, ground 1 salt, sea, medium 1	Soups, tomato juice, fish, shellfish, beef stews, steaks, chops, cheese, eggs and salad dressings.	Obtainable as a proprietary brand. Evocative of the sunny, balmy Caribbean.
Yakhni Spice	India	bayleaves 2 cardamom pods 5 cinnamon stick 50mm (2in) cloves, whole 5 coriander seeds, whole 2tsp fennel seeds 2tsp garlic cloves, bruised 3 ginger, whole, green 50mm (2in) onion, whole 1 peppercorns 1tsp	A flavouring for lamb or chicken stock (yakhni) using 0.5kg (1lb) meat on the bone and 2 litres (3½pt) water. See Cardamom for Festive Pilau recipe.	This mixture is the Indian equivalent of bouquet garni and the stock is used in pilaus and birianis.
Zathar	Middle East	sumac 1 thyme 1	A sour and aromatic seasoning popular with labni, a cream cheese made from yoghurt.	Zathar should not be confused with za'atar, a Moroccan wild herb.
Zhug	Yemen	caraway, seeds 1 cardamom, seeds 1 chilli, ground 2 coriander, seeds 2 garlic, cloves 1	Grind all spices together. Use as condiment.	Was popular with British troops in Aden to liven up dull army rations.

Chilli Guide

The taxonomy of the genus *Capsicum* is a nightmare. There are some one hundred and fifty varieties of chilli in Mexico alone. Capsicums have been cultivated and interbred for so long that there is confusion as to even the broadest distinctions between varieties, and as to which species and cultivars may be legitimately recognised. Thus, there are several different 'authoritative' systems, all of which disagree. Capsicums may be broadly distinguished by size, shape, pungency and colour. In size, it generally holds that the smaller the chilli, the hotter it will be. In colour, the darker ones are usually the hottest. Colour is also an indication of ripeness, as unripe capsicums are green, ripening often to red or yellow, or a darker colour – purple or black. Chillies are generally milder before they ripen. Chillies may also be distinguished by species – the broadest classification being that of *Capsicum annuum* and *Capsicum frutescens*. *C. frutescens* usually provides the hottest chillies, while *C. annuum* species are generally larger and less pungent. One variety of *C. annuum, C. a. grossum*, deserves special consideration. It is the sweet or bell pepper, mild compared to other capsicums and often eaten as a vegetable. It is easily distinguishable by its larger size and angular, often squarish, shape. A further distinction between chillies is whether they are fresh or dried. Dried chillies are usually wrinkled, darker and brittle. They are generally hotter than their undried counterparts.

The Pungency of Chillis

The pungency, or hotness, of chillies (*Capsicum*) is dependent on the amount of capsaicin present. Several methods have been developed to determine this. The Scoville method, designed in 1912 and improved upon over the years, is one of the best known, although, being a subjective method, its accuracy and consistency between tests is not completely reliable. In the method 1 per cent of capsaicin is equivalent to 150,000 Scoville Heat Units. The table below gives the Scoville heat values of several chillies calculated from the capsaicin content of their oleoresins (oleoresins are mixtures of the essential oils and non-volatile resinous materials of spices extracted by various solvents and used in the food manufacturing industry in place of raw spices). This table gives a clear impression of the great variation in pungency of several well known and less well known chillies. Capsaicin is an incredibly powerful substance; human taste can detect one part of capsaicin in one thousand.

Scoville Values of Chilli Oleoresins

Variety (Origin)	Scoville Heat Units	Variety (Origin)	Scoville Heat Units
Uganda (Uganda)	127,000	Carolina (USA)	39,000
Mombassa (Kenya)	120,000	Mundu (India)	34,000
Mombassa (Kenya)	78,600	Cayenne Long Slim	
Bahamian (Bahamas)	75,000	(Mexico)	30,670
Hontaka (Japan)	52,150	Anaheim M (Mexico)	18,000
Santaka (Japan)	51,500	College 64L (USA)	16,500
Sannam (India)	49,500	Abyssinian (Ethiopia)	11,100
Usimulagu-Bird Chilli		Turkish (Turkey)	11,000
(India)	42,000	Long Thin Cayenne (USA)	7,670

Recognised Species of Cultivated Capsicum

C. a.: *Capsicum annuum*
C. f.: *Capsicum frutescens*

Average lengths given

C. a. abbreviatum:
5cm (2in)

oval
oval-elongate
pungent
various colours

Wrinkled Peppers

C. a. accuminatum:
10cm (4in)

carrot shaped
pungent
various colours

Chilli

C. a. cerasiform:
1–3cm (⅜–1¼in)

spherical
pungent
red, yellow,
purple

Cherry Peppers

C. a. conoides:
3cm (1¼in)

coniform
very pungent

Cone Peppers

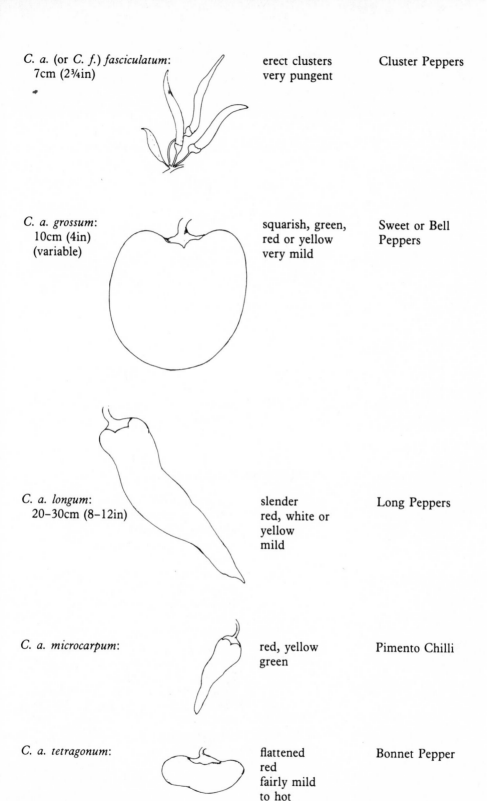

C. a. (or *C. f.*) *fasciculatum*:
7cm (2¾in)

erect clusters
very pungent

Cluster Peppers

C. a. grossum:
10cm (4in)
(variable)

squarish, green,
red or yellow
very mild

Sweet or Bell
Peppers

C. a. longum:
20–30cm (8–12in)

slender
red, white or
yellow
mild

Long Peppers

C. a. microcarpum:

red, yellow
green

Pimento Chilli

C. a. tetragonum:

flattened
red
fairly mild
to hot

Bonnet Pepper

C. f. syn *minimum*: 2–3cm (¾–1¼in)		erect clusters red very pungent	Bird Chillies
C. f. baccatum: 1cm (⅜in)		spherical	Cherry capsicums
C. f. pendulum:		large red black seeds very hot	Roqueto (South America) (Tabasco)
C. frutescens: 10–15mm (⅜–⅝in)		small, red or black capsular very hot	African

Mexican Chillies

Some typical shapes:
Pasilla

Mulato

Ancho

Major varieties:
Ancho: (*accuminatum*) large, brown, mild, heart-shaped
Chipotle: dark red, very hot
Fresno: fairly hot
Guero: Californian, green-yellow, medium hot
Hontaka: wrinkled, small, red, very hot (Japanese)
Jalapeño: fairly hot
Malagueta: green or red, small, very hot
Mulato: brown, large, hot
Pasilla: brown, quite hot
Piquin: small, dark-green, very hot
Poblano: ('popular') large, dark-green, mild
Serrano: small, very hot

African Chillies

Congo, Mombas(s)a and Zanzibar: rust coloured, 10–15mm (³⁄₈–⁵⁄₈in) wrinkled and very hot
Nigerian: red, 1–3cm (³⁄₈–1¼in) wrinkled, hot
Ethiopian: red, very mild
West African: red, smooth, capsular, 10–15mm (³⁄₈–⁵⁄₈in), very hot

Japanese Chillies

Honka or Hontaka: orange or red, wizened, 2–5cm (¾–2in) pungent
Santaka: deep red, erect, hot

United States Chillies

Louisiana: Domestic Sports Pepper, 2–6cm (¾–2³⁄₈in) orange to red, very pungent

Indian Chillies

Guntur: deep red, compressed base, short, stalk and calyx easily removed
Kovilpatti: high yielding, pest resistant
Kalyanpur: high yielding, pest resistant
Kesanakurru: high carotene content
Mundu: deep red, short and stout, mild
Warangal: similar to Ethiopian varieties
Lanka: similar to Ethiopian varieties
Usimulagu: Bird chilli, mild to hot, not very red
Sannam: red, medium hot

Common and Scientific Names of Chillies

Bell Pepper	*C. a. grossum*
Bird chilli	*C. frutescens* syn *minimum*
Bird Pepper	*C. f. baccatum*
Birds' Eye Pepper	*C. f. baccatum*
Bonnet Pepper	*C. a. tetragonum*
Bull-nosed Pepper	*C. a. grossum*
Cayenne Pepper	*C. f. minimum* (or *baccatum*)
Cherry Pepper	*C. a. cerasiform*
Cherry Capsicum	*C. f. baccatum*
Cone Pepper	*C. a. conoides*
Cluster Pepper	*C. a. fasciculatum*
Devil Pepper	*C. frutescens* (var)
Goat Pepper	*C. fruticosum*
Green Pepper	*C. a. grossum* (unripe)
Guinea Pepper	*C. annuum* (var)
Indian Pepper	old term for hot capsicums
Long Pepper	*C. a. longum*
Lunan Pepper	*C. a. tetragonum*
Mexican Chilli	*C. a. accuminatum*
Paprika	*C. a. tetragonum*
Pimento	*C. annuum* (*accuminatum*) or *microcarpum*
Red Pepper	*C. a. grossum* (ripe)
Roqueto	*C. f. pendulum*
Scotch Bonnet	*C. a. tetragonum*
Spanish Pepper	*C. a. tetragonum*
Spur Pepper	*C. annuum* (var)
Sweet Pepper	*C. a. grossum*
Tabasco	*C. a. conoides*
Turkish Pepper	*C. a. tetragonum*
Wrinkled Pepper	*C. a. abbreviatum*

Many of the correspondences listed above are less than rigorous. For instance, cayenne (or paprika) may signify not merely one *capsicum* variety but a variety of related strains. Some of these names are unfamiliar but are listed to aid identification.

Juniper

Mediterranean

Caper
Coriander
Fennel
Mint
Mustard
Onion

Trade

Sassafras

Vanilla

Allspice
Annatto
Grapefruit

Allspice
Annatto
Capsicum Chilli
Cocoa
Papaya

Melegueta
pepper

Coconut

Cayenne

Tonka Bean

Nasturtium

Salt

World Map Showing Origin of Spices

S. Europe
alery
II
enugreek
orseradish
iquorice
igella

Juniper

Tade

Saffron
Bay Leaf
Caraway
Garlic

Safflower   Onion   Dill

Asafoetida   Anise—Pepper
Dill
Garlic   Orange
                  Mandarin
                  Tangerine
                  Sesame

Sumac Sumac Nigella
Pomegranate

lebi

Trifala   Badrang   Seville Orange

Liquorice   Amchur   Star Anise
Poppy   Cassia
                           Lemon
            Pepper
            Cardamom   Pepper

Mustard   Kokum
(Juncea)
        India

        Ajowan   Ginger
        Amchur(mango)   Lemon Grass
        Calamus   Screwpine
        Curry Leaf   Cinnamon   Amchur   Tumeric
        Fenugreek   Curry Leaf
        Sandalwood   Lime
        Sesame   Nutmeg & Mace
        Zedoary
                           Galangal
Tamarind
                                    Clove
                              Nutmeg & Mace   Coconut

                        Cubeb
                        Sandalwood

229

Appendices

TASTE – HOW IT FUNCTIONS

Taste is the sense by which we distinguish the qualities and flavour of a substance. There are four basic sets of taste and these are selected by taste buds which are mainly located in the upper surface of the tongue and to a lesser extent in other parts of the mouth:

Taste	Part of the Tongue	Example	Temperature Influence
Sweet	tip	sugar	reduced by cold
Sour	back, sides	vinegar	reduced by cold
Bitter	back	quinine	
Salt	tip, back and sides	salt	increased by cold

All other types of taste, such as metallic and astringent, are a combination of these, except for hotness which can also be considered as pain.

The sense of smell is equally important since many tastes are in fact smells. We all know this, as when suffering from a cold some things become tasteless. In this case the smell receptors, located high in the nasal cavity, are prevented by nasal secretions from being stimulated.

Only minute quantities of substances are needed to stimulate the senses of smell and taste. This is illustrated in the former case by the fact that a male bumble bee can detect the smell of a female bumble bee five miles away, and in the latter, as little as one part in a thousand of capsaicin, the 'hot' constituent of chilli, can be detected by taste in humans.

USEFUL WEIGHTS AND MEASURES

1 *Ounces (oz) to Grammes (g) and vice versa*

oz	g	to nearest 5g	g	lb	oz(¼)
1	28	30	5		¼
2	57	55	10		¼
3	85	85	20		¾
4	**113**	**115**	30		1
5	142	140	40		1½
6	170	170	**50**		**1¾**
7	198	200	60		2
8	**227**	**225**	70		2½
9	255	255	80		2¾
10	283	285	90		3¼
11	312	310	**100**		**3½**
12	**340**	**340**	200		7
13	369	370	300		10½
14	397	395	400		14
15	425	425	500	1	1¾
16 = 1lb	**454**	**455**	600	1	5¼
2		905	700	1	8¾
3	1.36kg		800	1	12¼
4	1.81		900	1	15¾
5	2.27		**1000** = 1kg	**2**	**3¼**
			1kg	2.2	

2 *Pinches* (for dry powders etc)
   small pinch   2g
   pinch   5g   ⅛ teaspoon (tsp)
   good pinch   7g

3 *Spoons*

	Imperial	Metric	US
(approx ⅕ fl oz)	1 teaspoon (tsp)	5ml	1 teaspoon (tsp)
	3 teaspoons	15ml	1 tablespoon (tbsp or T) = ½fl oz (US)
4 tsp =	1 tablespoon (tbsp)	20ml	1⅓ tablespoon
		240ml (237)	16 tablespoons (tbsp or T) = 1 cup (US)

(dessertspoons (dsp) are not recognised but if come across 1 dsp ≃ 2 tsp (imp))

4 *Cups* (with useful approximations)

	Imperial	Metric	US
1 cup ≡	10 fl oz (imp) ≡ ½pt (imp)	285ml	1.2 cup (US) ≡ 9.6 fl oz (US)
0.88 cup ≡	8.8 fl oz (imp)	**1 cup** = 250ml	1.1 cup (US) ≡ 8.5 fl oz (US)

			240ml	**1 cup** $\equiv$ 8 fl oz (US)
0.84 cup $\equiv$ 8.4 fl oz (imp)			(235)	$\equiv$ ½pt (US)

NB The symbol $\equiv$ means 'equivalent to'

Oven Temperatures

	Gas Mark	Electric °F	Electric °C
		200	90
very cool	¼	225	110
	½	250	120
slow	1	275	135
	2	300	150
moderate	3	325	160
	4	350	180
fairly hot	5	375	190
hot	6	400	200
	7	425	220
very hot	8	450	230
	9	475	250
		500	260

An easy method of converting from °C to °F

For example 260°C

1 Double the °C	$\times 2 =$	520
2 Subtract $\frac{1}{10}$		-52
		468
3 Add 32		$+32$
		500°F

Spice Measures

Allspice	35–40 berries per teaspoon
Anise-Pepper	50 'cases' per teaspoon
Annatto	100 seeds per teaspoon
Capers (non-pareilles)	20–25 per teaspoon
Cardamom	15 pods yield ½ teaspoon of seeds
Cinnamon	10cm (4in) yields about 1½ teaspoons of coarse ground powder
Clove	25 cloves per teaspoon
Coriander	130 seeds per teaspoon
Fenugreek	300 seeds per teaspoon
Juniper	10–12 berries per teaspoon
Lemon	1 small lemon yields 4 tablespoons of juice and 4 teaspoons of grated rind
Mace	1 blade yields about ¼ teaspoon ground mace
Onion	large onion weighs 170g (6oz)
	medium onion weighs 115g (4oz)
	small onion weighs 55g (2oz)
Papaya	50 dried seeds per teaspoon
Pepper	50 peppercorns per teaspoon
Turmeric	25mm (1in) yields about ½ teaspoon powder

INDIAN VOCABULARY

(Tam = Tamil)

aab ghosh (Tam)	lamb boiled in milk
aam, am	mango
aam choor, aam chur	dried mango (or powder)
aam papar	dried mango sheets
aata, ata, atta	wholewheat flour
achar, achchar	pickle
adrak, adruk	ginger, green
ahtoo koottee (Tam)	lamb, sheep
ajmoda	celery
ajwa(i)n, ajvini	ajowan
akoori, ekuri	scrambled eggs (Parsi), spiced with ginger and coriander
alebele	pancakes (Goa) and coconut filling
aloo, alu	potato
aloo chat	potato slices
aloo-ki-tikiya	potato patties
am	mango
am(a)la	emblic myrobalan
amb halad	zedoary
amchoor, amchur	dried mango (or powder)
amphulia	baked mango with rice
amyli	dried tamarind
anar	pomegranate
anardana	pomegranate seeds
anda	eggs
anda ki kai	egg curry
annanas	pineapple
anvalli	emblic myrobalan
appam, appum	rice flour pancake (southern India)
arachee,i (Tam)	rice
arbi, arvi	yam
ardrakh	green ginger
arhar dal	pigeon pea
arnar	pomegranate
arv	peach
at(t)a	whole wheat flour
bacha	calamus
badam	almond
badami roghan josh	rich lamb and almond dish
badhak, budhuk	duck
baghar	spices cooked in hot oil then added to meat dishes
baida	eggs
baigan	*brinjal,* aubergine

baison, besan	chick pea flour
bajre	millet flour
bakarknani	thin, crisp bread
bakra	goat
balushahi	doughnuts, sugar coated
banarsi rai	black mustard
bandakoi (Tam)	okra
bandh gobi	cabbage
barakalinjan	greater galangal
barfi	condensed milk sweet with silver leaf
baris	ground lentil lumps
barisaunf	fennel and lentil
basmati	superior type of long grain rice
bath, buth	rice (western and southern India)
bathak	duck
beebeek	coconut cake
behada	beleric myrobalan
be(h)ndi(kai)	okra
belatee byngun	tomato
besan	chick pea flour
betel	chewing nut, *Areca catechu*, commonly with leaf of *Piper betle*, spices, seeds and lime
beveca	rice pudding, coconut flavoured
bhaji	greens, vegetables
bhajia, bhajya	fritter, spiced
bhapa doi	Bengali sweet steamed yoghurt
bharta	purée
bhatura	Punjab fried bread using eggs and baking powder
bhindi	okra
bhoota	corn
bhugia	vegetable, spiced
bhujiya	vegetable fritters
bhuna, i	fried
bhuna gosht	dry curry (beef or lamb)
bhurta	purée
bhustrina	lemon grass
bindaloo	*vindaloo*
biriani, biryani	rice *pilau*, rich and yellow with twice as much meat as rice
bommalde machee	Bombay duck
boortha	purée
boti kabab	marinaded meat kebab
brinjal, brinjel	aubergine
buckra	lamb, sheep
budhuk	duck
buffado	cabbage, potato dish
bundi	small *jalebis*
burra budhuk	goose
burra nimbu	lemon

burra teetur	guinea fowl, partridge
burruf	ice
byngun	aubergine
cachumbar	salad; spiced (chilli) onion salad
chai	tea
chan(n)a dal	chick peas
chandan	sandalwood
chap(p)ati	circular unleavened bread
chasnidarh	sweet and sour
chat	snacks
chat masala	hot spice mixture
chatni	chutney
chaval	rice
chawal	rice
cheenee	sugar
cheeregum (Tam)	cumin seed
chenna	(lentil) chick peas
cheroonjee	*chironji*
chhoti elachi	cardamom
chinaconee (Tam)	shrimp
chinch	tamarind
chironji	*chironji* nut (almond substitute)
cholum (Tam)	maize, Indian corn
chota butter	quail
chota ginga	shrimp
chota hazri	early light breakfast (Anglo-Indian)
chota peg	short drink (Anglo-Indian)
chuckeray (Tam)	(palm) sugar
chukunda	beetroot
choona	white lime paste
chunda	hot mango chutney (Gujerat)
churbee	dripping, fat
comlong	vegetable marrow
copra kana	rice cooked in coconut milk
cuddalay (Tam)	chick pea
cus-cus	poppy
dahi	curds, yoghurt
dahi bath	rice and yoghurt (western and southern India)
da(h)l	pulse(s), from 'split' = *dal*
dal bath	rice and lentils (western and southern India)
dal(-)chini	cinnamon, cassia
dalim	pomegranate
dam	*dum*
darchini	cinnamon
degh	pot, casserole
degi mirich	mild red chilli
dhai	curds, yoghurt

dhall cheene	cinnamon, cassia
dhan(y)ia, dhuniah	coriander (seed)
dhania patta(r), dhania sabz	coriander leaf
dhansak	meat and vegetable casserole (Parsi)
dhokla	pulse and rice batter
dhum	*dum*
dhuniah	coriander
dhup	Indian juniper
dhye (Tam)	curds (*tyre*), yoghurt
diliya dosa	oat pancake
do pyaza	meat and fried onions dish
dosa	lentil and rice pancake bread
dubbul roti	European bread
dudh pera	*barfi* balls
d(h)um	steaming between two fires
eelachie, elaichi	cardamom
eeral (Tam)	liver
ekuri	scrambled eggs (Parsi), spiced with ginger and coriander
ela(i)chi	cardamom
elam (Tam)	cardamom
falsa	blackberry juice
faluda	tapioca milk
firni	ground rice pudding
foogath, fugath	vegetable savoury with *masala*
gagar, gagur, gajjar	carrot
gandhmul	zedoary
garam	hot
garam masala	spice mixture (see Spice Mixtures)
gart gobee	cabbage, cauliflower
ghai ka gosht	beef
ghandhtrina	lemon grass
ghee	clarified butter
ghol	buttermilk
ghuchhi	black mushrooms
ghurmasalah (Tam)	*garam masala*
ghurm mussala, masala	mixed spices
ginga	prawn
ginga patia	prawns, Parsi style
gingelly	sesame
ginikori (Tam)	guinea fowl
gobee, gobi	cabbage, cauliflower
gobi mhaans	cauliflower and meat
golgappas	fried wafers with chick peas
(gol) mirich	black pepper
gooda	marrow
goor	*jaggery* (palm sugar)
goorda	kidney

gosh(t)	meat
gosht do pyaza	meat and onions
gosht ka salun	Deccan meat curry
goshtaba	Kashmiri lamb and curd meatballs
gram	chick pea
guda	marrow
gudumba	spiced mango drink
gulub jaman, jamun	small batter balls in syrup
guranthor alu	sweet potato
gurda	kidney
haldee,i	turmeric
halva, halwa	vegetable or fruit sweet
hara dhania	coriander leaves
hari mirchi	green chillies
hasina kebab	lamb kebab
hazri	breakfast
heeng	asafoetida
hing(u)	asafoetida
hirda	chebulic myrobalan
hisa(a)b	bill (account)
hoopoo (Tam)	salt
huddi	bone
huldee,ie	turmeric
hur(r)an ka gosht	venison
illaichi	cardamom
im(a)li	tamarind
imlee	tamarind
indad	Goan pork curry
ingee (Tam)	ginger
jaffatry	mace
jaggery	palm sugar
jaiphal, jaiphul	nutmeg
jal	water
jalebi	fried batter spirals in syrup
jal jeera	cumin, tamarind and mint drink
japatri (Tam)	mace
jathikkai	nutmeg
jauphull	nutmeg
javanee	ajowan
javatri, jawatrie	mace
jeeb	tongue
jeera(ka)	cumin (seed)
jeera pani	cumin, tamarind and mint drink
jellabie	fried batter twirls in syrup
jethi madh, madhuka, mithi lakdi	liquorice
jhinga	prawns
jira	cumin
jowari	barley

kaafi	coffee
kabab	1 roast meat
	2 skewered meat/vegetables
	3 fried mince patties
kabab cheene	allspice
kaboothur	pigeon
kab(u)li channa	chick peas
kachori	stuffed pastry ball, spiced lentil or potato
kachumbar	salad
ka(r)chur(a)	zedoary
kadhinim(b)	curry leaves
kadoo,u	pumpkin
kaduhennai (Tam)	mustard oil
kafi(i)	coffee
kahwa	sweet tea, coffee
kaju	cashew nuts
kakadi	cucumber
kala	black
kala chana	small black chick pea
kala mirchi	black pepper
kala zeera, zira	black cumin
kala zeera, zira, kalajira	nigella
kaleja,i	liver
kali mirchi, mirich	black pepper (corns)
kalkal	semolina-coconut milk cake
kalonji	black cumin, nigella
kama-i-anguza (Afghan)	asafoetida
kanji	carrot pickle
karavhat (Tam)	salt fish
karbooza	melon
kardai	safflower
karhai	wide deep frying bowl similar to *wok*
karhi	chick pea flour and buttermilk dish
kari (Tam)	Tamil spiced sauce, curry. Origin of the English word 'curry'
karipatta(r), kari phulia	curry leaves
karudari (Tam)	partridge
karuvapadai (Tam)	cinnamon
karuvepila (Tam)	curry leaves
kasakasa (Tam)	poppy seed
kasta	crisp, crusty
kasumb(h)a	safflower
kathal	jackfruit
katnim	curry leaf
katori	individual metal bowl
kat(t)ha	the characteristic red (*catechu*) paste with *betle* leaves
kayla	plantains
kedra	screwpine
keema	minced meat

keeray (Tam)	greens
kekra	crab
kela	banana, plantain
keora,i	screwpine
kervai	stuffed banana balls
kesar	saffron
kesram	saffron
ket(u)ki	screwpine
kevara	screwpine
kewara	screwpine
kewda	screwpine
kewra	screwpine
keya	screwpine
khara	abbreviation for meat prepared with bruised whole spices
khara masala	mixed whole spices (see Spice Mixtures)
khargosh	hare, rabbit
kharnub	carob
khawa	sweet tea, coffee
kheema	minced meat, raw or cooked
kheer, ir	creamed rice (with gold and silver leaf – *vark*)
kheera, ira	cucumber
khesa	saffron
khewa	coffee
khi(t)chhari	see *kitcheri*
kho(i)a,ya	thick condensed milk, unsweetened
khumb(i)	mushrooms
khus(h)-khus(h)	poppy seeds
kimcea	brown mustard
kismis	raisins, sultanas
kitchelly pullum (Tam)	orange
kitcheri,(e)e	jumble, mixture; especially rice and lentils; origin of English 'kedgeree'
kitcheri unda	scrambled eggs
kitha neem	curry leaves
kochikai (Tam)	fresh red chilli
koela	charcoal
kofta(h), kooftah, koaftah	meatball, croquette
kokam, kokum	kokum
kookarch, urh	chicken
koosumbha	safflower
korma	curd based curry
kothamilee (Tam)	coriander
kothimbir	coriander
kotimear	coriander
kotimli	coriander
krishna	long pepper
krishnajiraka	nigella (*krishna*, Sanskrit, lit. dark, black)

kuddoo	pumpkin
kudoo (Tam)	black mustard
kulanjan	greater galangal
kulfi	Indian ice-cream with nuts
kulkuls	semolina and coconut milk cake
kulmie darchini	cinnamon
kungumappa (Tam)	saffron
kurdi	safflower
kurghosh	hare, rabbit
kurlleachi kari	crab curry
kurva teil	mustard oil
kus-kus	poppy seeds
kusum	safflower
kutta	sour, acrid
laddoo	sweet, fried chick pea flour balls in syrup
lal mirchi,ee, mirich	chillies (red)
lao(o)ng, laung, lavang	clove
lavungam (Tam)	clove
las(s)an, lashuna, lassoon, lus(s)on	garlic
latkhan	annatto
lob(h)ia dal	black-eyed peas
lombia	black-eyed peas
long	clove
luchchi	Bengal white flour bread like *puri*
mach(ch)(l)i	fish
madhuka	mastic
madhurika	fennel
madoo (Tam)	beef
Madrasi	of Madras
makhan	butter
malai	cream from boiled milk
malpua	pancakes in syrup
marakkari (Tam)	vegetables
masala(h)	ground mixed spices
masoor,ur	red lentil
mat(t)an	lamb, mutton
mathulam param (Tam)	pomegranate
mattar	peas
mayti	fenugreek
meen (Tam)	fish
meetha neem	curry leaves
memna pilau	lamb *pilau*
methee,i	fenugreek
mhaans	meat
milagutannir (Tam)	pepper water, origin of 'mulligatawny'
min	fish
mirchi	chilli

misht nim, mitha neem	curry leaf
mithi lakdi	mastic
Mog(h)lai	Mogul (style)
molee	1 south Indian dish based on coconut milk
	2 radish
moloo (Tam)	black pepper
mo(o)lo(o)ga(h) (Tam)	chilli
moong, mung	yellow lentil, mung bean
mooraba	preserve, jam
moorg(h)ee	fowl (chicken)
moorhabi	(wild) duck
moosa	lentil (variety)
mootay molee	south Indian egg curry
muchlee	fish
mulligatawny	Anglo-Indian hot meat soup
munjal (Tam)	turmeric
murg(h)	chicken
murghabi	duck
murg(h) massalam	spiced whole chicken casserole
mussor	lentil (variety)
mutter	peas
mydah	white flour
myhee	fish
na(a)n	a puffy Punjabi leavened bread baked in *tandoor*
nagkesar, nagkeser	cassia buds
nareul, nareal	coconut
nargisi kofta	Indian 'scotch egg'
narikel, nariyel	coconut
narrangee	orange
nar(r)ul	coconut
neemuch	salt
neemuch muchlee	salt fish
nethali	dried fish
nimboo, nimbu	lime or lemon
ooloonthoo (Tam)	lentil
oorukai (Tam)	pickle
oothappam	south Indian rice and lentil flour pancake
pa(a)n	leaf of betel pepper (*Piper betle*) filled with areca nuts ('betel nuts'), lime and spices
pa(h)l	extremely hot curry
pakora,i	spiced fritter or batter
palak	spinach
palandu	onion
panch	five

panch phora	five spice seeds powdered
panch puran	five seeds
paneer,ir	curd cheese
pani	water
papar	*pappadum*
papaya, papeeta, papita	papaya
pappadum, poppadum, puppadum	round crispy spicy wafer of chick pea flour about 25cm (10in) diameter
para(a)t	(south India) round tray for kneading bread
paratha	flaky wholemeal bread cooked with *ghee*
parval	small green marrow-like vegetable
patrani	banana leaves
patta(r)	leaf, curry leaf
pe(e)az, piaz, pyaz	onion
perunka(m) (Tam)	asafoetida
phal	fruit
phaluda	tapioca milk
phari rai	brown mustard
phirni	ground rice pudding
phulgobi, phoulgobee	cauliflower
pilau, pollau, pullau	rice cooked in *ghee* then water, often with a specified vegetable or meat ingredient
pip(p)al, pipel, pippli	long pepper
pista(ch)	pistachios
podina, pudina	mint
poori	deep fried wholemeal 'bread'
pootheena, puthina (Tam)	mint
pulee, puli (Tam)	tamarind
purpoo (Tam)	lentil
rai	mustard (seed)
raita	vegetable (cucumber or onion) yoghurt salad
rajma	red kidney beans
raktapurka	kokum
rampe	screwpine
rasam	tamarind soup, pepper water
rasgollahs	flour balls in syrup
roghan josh	spiced lamb dish, rich and red
roti	bread
sabz(i)	vegetables
sabz mirich	green chilli
sadah	mutton
saf(e)d	white
safed chandan	sandalwood
sag(h)	spinach, cress
sambal, ol, sumbol	side dish, sauce, condiment

sambar	spiced lentils and vegetables
same	green beans
samo(o)sa	triangular pastry stuffed with spicy minced meat or vegetables, deep fried
sarota	betel nut cutter
saunf	anise
savia	deep fried, sweet *besan* 'vermicelli'
sayoo	apple
seek	1 rolls of minced meat 2 skewer
seena	ribs
seer	one kilogram (2.2lb)
seetful	allspice
sendri	annatto
sera	lemon grass
sev	deep fried spiced *besan* 'vermicelli'
shahi zafran	saffron (stigma tip)
shalgam	turnip
shami	shaped spiced mince with lentils fried in *ghee*, chillies, mint and onions
sharbat, shurbut	fruit drink
sheek	same as *seek*
shoorva	soup
shukur	(brown) sugar
shur	Indian juniper
sompf	anise
sonf	fennel
sont(h)	dried ginger
soojee, suji	semolina
sooka, sookhe	dried
sooka mirchi	dried red chillies
soorthee	lentil (type)
soowar ka gosht	pork
soti (Tam)	zedoary
souf	aniseed
suara	anise
sufaid	white
saufaid zeera	white cumin
sulgum	turnip
supari	mixture of seeds and spices for chewing – see Spice Mixtures
surva	Indian dill
taaza	green
taiphal	nutmeg
taipmal	nutmeg
tali	fried
tamatar	tomato
tandal	cauliflower stalks

tandoor	clay oven
tandoori	of *tandoor*
tarka	*baghar*
tavitri	mace
teesri	mussels, clams
teetur	partridge, game bird
tejpat(tar)	cassia leaf
thainga	coconut
thuckaley (Tam)	tomato
thurkajee	vegetables
tick keah, tikia, tikka(h)	diced meat barbecued, sometimes served on hot iron plates (sizzlers)
til(l)	sesame
tisrya	mussels, clams
tithar	partridge, game bird
toor, tur	lentil (type)
tyre (Tam)	curds
udru(c)k	green ginger
uduth	lentil (type)
unda(h)(y)	eggs
ur(e)d, urhad	black pea, also yellow lentil
urulaikkirangu (Tam)	potato
vacha	calamus
vadees	*baris*
var(a)k	gold and silver leaf
vellai-milahu (Tam)	allspice
vendhyam (Tam)	anise
vellaypoondoo (Tam)	garlic
vellum	*jaggery*
venthium	fenugreek
vindaloo,u	very hot Portuguese (Goa) curry
vungium (Tam), vunguim	onion
yakhni	meat stock for cooking rice – see Spice Mixtures
yamani	ajowan
yellumshikai (Tam)	lemon or lime
za(a)fra(a)n	saffron
zeera, zira	cumin
zuffron	saffron

SOUTH EAST ASIAN VOCABULARY

B = Burmese, I = Indonesian, L = Lao, M = Malaysian, P = Philippine,
S = Sinhalese, T = Thai

abba (S)	black mustard
abon daging (I)	shredded meat
acar (M)	vinegar
acar kuning (M)	pickled vegetables
achuete (P)	annatto
adas (I)	fennel
ajam (I)	chicken
alba (M)	fenugreek
aliah (I)	green ginger
amu miris (S)	green, chilli
asam (M, I)	tamarind
asam babi goreng (I)	fried pork with tamarind
asam djawa (I)	tamarind
asinam (I)	raw vegetable salad
atjar (I)	pickles
ayam (M)	chicken
ayam kichup (M)	spiced chicken
bai mak nao (L)	lemon grass
bai toey (T)	screwpine
bamee (T, M, I)	noodles
bamee goreng (T, M, I)	fried noodles
bawang merah (M, I)	onion
bawang goreng (M, I)	fried onion
bawang puteh, putih (M, I)	garlic
beehoon (M)	Chinese vermicelli
begedel (I)	patties
bene (M)	sesame
bijan (M)	sesame
biji sawi (M)	mustard seed
blachan (I)	shrimp paste, block
blatjan (I)	*blachan*
buah pala (M)	nutmeg
buah pelaga (M)	cardamom, candlenut
bumbu ketjap (I)	spiced soy sauce
buncis (I)	beans
bunga chingkek, bunga c(h)ingkeh (M)	cloves
bunga lawang (M, I)	star anise
cabai hijan (M)	green chilli
cengkeh (I)	cloves
chabai (M)	chillies
char (M)	fried

245

cheeregum (S)	cumin
chilli (M)	chilli
chyet-thon-phew (B)	garlic
cumi-cumi (I)	squid
dadar (I)	,melette
daun bawang (M, I)	spring onion
daun kari (M)	curry leaves
daun kes(s)om (M, I)	mint
daun ketumbar (M, I)	coriander leaf
daun pandan (M, I)	screwpine
daun pudina (M)	mint
daun sala(a)m (I)	curry leaves
daun seladri (M)	celery
dendeng ragi (I)	crisp fried meat
djahe (I)	green ginger
djeruk nipis (I)	citrus fruit
djeruk perut (I)	citrus leaves
djinten (I)	cumin seeds
enasal (S)	cardamom
enduru (S)	dill
fan taeng (T)	stuffed marrow
fa nwin (B)	turmeric
forng tawhu (T)	dried bean curd
gado-gado (I)	cooked salad with peanut sauce
gahn plu (T)	cloves
gaju (M)	cashew nut
gajup (T)	water chestnut
gammiris (S)	black pepper
gin (B)	ginger
grawahn (T)	cardamom
gulai ayam (M)	chicken curry
gulai daging lembu (M)	beef curry
gulai ikan (M)	fish curry
gulai kambing (M)	mutton curry
gula jawa (I)	palm sugar
gula melaka (M)	palm sugar or sago pudding
gule (I)	curry
halia (M)	green ginger
hang kathi (T)	thin coconut milk
hati (I)	liver
hed hunu (T)	cloud ear fungus
hijan (M)	sesame seed
horapa (T)	basil
hua horm (T)	onion
hua kathi (T)	thick coconut milk

ikan ayer (M)	tuna
ikan bandeng (I)	baked fish
ikan bilis (I, M)	dried fish
ikan bumbu santan (I)	fish dried with coconut milk and spices
ikan kacang (I)	fish with peanut sauce
ikan panggang (I)	grilled fish
inguru (S)	ginger
ingurupiyati (S)	lesser galangal
itek (M)	duck
jahe (I)	green ginger
jang (T)	highly seasoned grilled pork or beef
jathikkai (T)	nutmeg
jeera (S)	cumin
jintan manis (M)	fennel
jintan puteh (M)	cumin seed
jinten (I)	cumin seed
kachang hijan (M)	green *gram*
kachang tanah (M)	peanut
kaeng (T)	a dish with gravy
kaeng phet (T)	curry
kaeng phet kai (T)	chicken curry
kah (T)	greater galangal
kaha (S)	turmeric
kaju manis (I)	cinnamon
kamin (T)	turmeric
kao pot ping	barbecued corn ears
kapi (T)	*blachan*
kapulaga (I)	cardamom
karabu (S)	cloves
karapincha (S)	curry leaves
kari-kari (P)	oxtail stew with annatto
karupillay (M)	curry leaves
katjang hidjan (I)	green *gram*
katjang tanah (I)	peanut
kayu manis (M, I)	cinnamon
kecap manis (I)	sweet soy sauce
kelapa (M)	coconut
kemangi selaseh (M, I)	basil
kemiri (M, I)	candlenut
kencur (I)	lesser galangal
kentjur (I)	lesser galangal, zedoary
ketimun (I)	cucumber
ketjap (manis) (I)	dark soy sauce
ketumbar (M, I)	coriander seed
ketupat (M)	pressed rice cakes
kha (T, L)	greater galangal
khao kluk kapi (T)	rice with shrimp paste
khao suey (T)	steamed rice

kinchay (P)	coriander
k(h)ing (T)	green ginger
kottamalli (S)	coriander
kottamalli kolle (S)	coriander leaves
kluey chap (T)	deep fried green bananas
krachai (T)	lesser galangal
krathiem (T)	garlic
kravan (T)	cardamom
krung kieng (T)	curry paste
krupuk (udang) (I)	prawn cracker
kuali (or kwali) (M, I)	*wok*
kunchor (M)	lesser galangal, zedoary
kung (T)	prawn
kung haeng (T)	dried prawns
kunjit (M, I)	turmeric
kunyit (I)	turmeric
kuping djamu (I)	cloud ear fungus
kuping tikus (M)	cloud ear fungus
kurundu (S)	cinnamon
kway teow (M)	rice noodles
lada (M, I)	pepper
lada hitam (M)	black pepper
laksa (M)	Chinese vermicelli
languas, lenguas (M)	greater galangal
laos (I)	greater galangal powder
lember (I)	filled rice balls
ley-nyin-bwint (B)	cloves
limau kestum (M)	lime
limau nipis (M)	citrus fruit
limau purut (M)	citrus leaves
lombok (I)	fresh red chilli
lonbokhijan (I)	green chilli
look jun (T)	nutmeg
luk nua (T)	meat balls
maduru (S)	fennel
mah tai (M)	water chestnut
mak phet kunsi (L)	fresh red chilli
makahm (T)	tamarind
makrut (T)	citrus fruit
makrut bai (T)	citrus leaves
mal kham (L)	tamarind
malu miris (S)	mild fresh chilli
manis djangan (I)	cinnamon
ma now (T)	lime
ma row (T)	lime
mee (I, M, T)	noodles
mee goreng (I)	fried noodles
mee krob (T)	crisp noodles
meenchi (S)	mint

merica hitam (I)	black pepper
meritja (I)	pepper
mu wan (T)	sweet pork
nam plu (T)	fish sauce
nam prik (T)	'hot' sauce
nannambin (B)	coriander leaves
nannamzee (B)	coriander seed
nasi kuning lengkap (I)	yellow festival rice
nasi kunyit (M)	yellow rice
nasi goreng (I)	fried rice
nasi gurih (I)	coconut rice
nasi pitih (I)	white rice
nasi uduk (I)	rice in coconut milk with spices
nga-youk-kaun (B)	black pepper
nil thee (B)	fresh red chilli
nil thee sein (T)	green chilli
nor my (T)	bamboo shoots
nua tang (T)	sweet mince
nyiur (M)	coconut
op cherry (T)	cinnamon
otak otak (M)	'hot' kedgeree
pacari (I)	pineapple and coconut chutney
pakah (T)	deep fried lima beans
pak chi bai (T)	coriander leaf
pak chi farang (T)	celery
pak chi met (T)	coriander seed
pak chi rahk (T)	coriander root
pak hom ho (L)	mint
pala (I)	nutmeg
pandang (I)	screwpine
pange (I)	sour stew
pange ikan (I)	fish stew
panggang (I)	barbecued or grilled
petis (I)	shrimp paste
phak hom pom (L)	coriander
phak si (L)	dill
phalazee (B)	cardamom
phik noi (L)	black pepper
pilus (I)	sweet potato rissoles
pindang telur (I)	eggs in soy sauce
pipian (P)	chicken and pork with annatto
pisang (I)	banana
pla (T)	fish
plasroi (T)	dried fish
plattod (T)	fish with tamarind
prik chee pha, prik ki fa(h) (T)	red chilli
prik ki nu (T)	chilli
prik ki tai (T)	pepper

pyi-naw-thein (B)	curry leaf
rampe (S)	screwpine
rathu miris (S)	fresh red chilli
rebong (M)	bamboo shoot
rebung (I)	bamboo shoot
rempah (I)	meat and coconut balls, or *rempeh*
rempeh (M)	mixture of spices and flavourings
rempeyek (I)	crackers or fritters
roti jala (M)	lacy pancakes
rudjak (I)	ritual dish of fruit, vegetables, fish sauce, chilli and sugar
sadikka (S)	nutmeg
sajur (I)	vegetable broth
sajur lemeng (I)	vegetable curry
sambal (I)	basic seasoning of chilli, garlic and shrimp paste; chutney-like condiment
sambal goreng (I)	fried with chilli
samouk-saba (B)	fennel
santan kental (M)	coconut milk
satay, sate (M, I)	kebabs with a curry sauce
satay bumbu	spicy *satay*
satay manis	sweet *satay*
satay udang	skewered grilled prawns
saus kecang (I)	peanut sauce
sayer (I)	stir fried vegetables
selamat makan (I)	*bon appétit!*
selaseh (M)	basil
sel(e)dri (I)	celery
semur daging (I)	beef in soy sauce
sera (S), serai (M)	lemon grass
sere(h) (I)	lemon grass
serundeng (I)	mixed garnish of peanuts, coconut and spices dry fried
sheingho (B)	asafoetida
siyambala (S)	tamarind
som ma kham (T)	tamarind
soon (I)	Chinese vermicelli
sothi (M)	coconut milk soup
soto (I)	soup
sotong (M)	squid
su(du)duru (S)	cumin
sudulunu (S)	garlic
tahu (I)	soya bean curd
tahu poug (I)	bean curd omelette
takrai (T)	lemon grass
tangeh (M)	beansprouts
taoge (I)	beansprouts
tauko ikan (I)	fish in brown bean sauce

tauku (M)	soya bean curd
tauyu (M)	soy sauce (dark)
taw hu (T)	soy bean curd
telo dardeh (M)	omelette with chilli
telor (I)	eggs
telor berwarna (I)	marbled eggs
terung (I)	egg plant
terung loteh (I)	egg plant and prawn soup
thala (S)	sesame
thit-ja-boh-gauk (B)	cinnamon
thua khiaw (T)	green *gram*
thua lisong (T)	peanuts
thua ngork (T)	beansprouts
thua thorng (T)	green *gram*
tjabé (I)	chilli
tjabé djawa (I)	cubeb
tjengkeh (I)	cloves
tom yam (T)	spiced soup
ton horm (T)	spring onions
tord mun kung (T)	fried prawn balls
trasi (I)	*blachan*
tumis (I)	stir fried vegetables
ukoy (P)	shrimps and sweet potato fritters
uluhaal (S)	fenugreek
urap (I)	vegetables cooked with chilli, coconut and garlic
utang kering (M, I)	dried prawns
wajan (I)	*wok*
wasa-vasi (S)	mace
wijen (I)	sesame seed
wun sen (T)	Chinese vermicelli
yam (T)	salad
yira (T)	cumin or fennel
zedoary (M)	lesser galangal

CHINESE VOCABULARY

ajinmoto	msg – monosodium glutamate
bahk gwoah	ginko nut
baht ghok	star anise
bak choy	Chinese green cabbage
ban sai si	Peking salad (with anise-pepper)
bo ping	Peking pancakes
buck ging ngap	Peking duck

ch'ao	stir fry
chao gwoo	straw mushroom, a delicacy
ch'ao mien	boiled noodles, stir fried with meat and vegetables
ch'ao tan	fried rice
cha-ts'ai	salted vegetables, quite hot
ch'au-yau	soy sauce
cha yeh dan, cha yip dahn	hard-boiled eggs simmered in aniseed water, tea eggs (marbled eggs)
cheong yow	soya
cheung, chiang	ginger
chi(h) mah	sesame
chiu yim ha	prawns in spiced salt
choong	onions
chuan-chiao, chun-chiu, chun-tsin	anise-pepper
dahn min	egg noodles
dao foo	bean curd
ding heung	clove
doong gwoo	dried mushrooms, a delicacy
dow see	salted black beans
dung shung	bamboo shoot
fa-chiu, faah-jiu, faah-jew	anise-pepper
fan chiew	chilli
fooh jook	dried bean curd
fu yu	soy bean cake
fu-yung	omelette often filled with meat or vegetables
gom pei	dried tangerine peel
ha	shrimp
hak chi(h) mah	black sesame
hao-yu	oyster sauce
heung lo fun, heung new fun, heung neu fun	Chinese Five Spices, also *wu hsang fen*
hoang-tchi	safflower
ho fun	rice noodles
hoisin cheung	*hoisin* sauce
ho lan dow, ho lan dau	snow peas – *ordan* (*mangetout*)
hsang tsai	coriander
hsia	shrimp/prawn
hsiao	fresh salted meat
hsia-su	prawn crackers
hsiang su ya	succulent duck
hsien-mi	fresh rice
hsun dan	boiled eggs marinaded in soy sauce
hua-chan	steamed rolls
hua-chiao, hua jiao	anise-pepper
hua chiao yen	roasted anise-pepper and salt

hui chou	a hotpot
hun-fun	stuffed pie with fluffy edges
hung liu	Chinese Five Spices

For words beginning with 'j', see under 'ch'

kai choy	Chinese cabbage
kaoliang-chiang	galangal
kim chiam	lily buds
kung po ha	Peking prawns in a hot sauce

la chiang	hot chilli sauce
lao ch'ou	soy sauce
lap cheong	dried pork sausages
leong-goo	tree mushroom
lien ngow	lotus root
lob bahk	giant white radish
lung hsia	lobster

mantou	steamed raised bread
ma tai	water chestnut
ma yu	sesame oil
ma yung bao	sweet steamed bun
mei-chien	msg – monosodium glutamate
mi fun	rice vermicelli

ngap	duck
ngau	beef
ngung heung (fun)	Chinese Five Spices

paat-kok, pa-chiao, peh kah	anise, aniseed, star anise
pai-tsai	green cabbage
pao-ping	thin pancake
pao-tzu	steamed bun with filling
pok pang	mandarin pancakes

sa leung geung	lesser galangal
sang keong	green ginger
shu-kua	papaya
siew mai	steamed prawn dumpling
suehn	bamboo shoot
suen tau	garlic
sung chow	light soy sauce

ta-liao	'Great Spice' – anise-pepper
taukau	nutmeg
t'ien la	sweet chilli sauce
tim suen gheung	sweet and sour sauces
tofu	bean curd
tou-nga	bean sprouts
tze bao gai	chicken fried in paper

wok	a shallow curved pan
wong geung fun	turmeric
wonton	small dumplings, savoury
wooi heung	fennel
wu hsiang fen	Chinese Five Spice powder, also *heung neu fun*
yen	salt
yen-sui	coriander
yook gway	cinnamon
yuanshih chiang	bean sauce
yu chiap	fish sauce
yu-yu	squid

JAPANESE VOCABULARY

aburage	deep-fried bean curd
aji-n(o)-moto	monosodium glutamate
aonoriko	powdered seaweed used as a herb
azabu-tade (asabu-tade)	smartweed, see *tade*
bancha	coarse green tea
beni(-)shoga/u	red pickled ginger
budoshu	wine
daikon	large white radish, *Raphanus sativus*
daizu	soya beans
dashi	soup stock
ebi	prawn, lobster, shrimp
goma	sesame seed
goma abura	sesame oil
gomairi hatagorashi	a relish of sesame seed and leaf and red pepper
gomas(h)io	a seasoning of black sesame seed, salt and monosodium glutamate
hakka	field mint
hanagatsuo	dried bonito fish shavings
hanayuzu	evergreen orange, *Citrus junus*
hatcho-miso	pure soya bean paste
hatsu-take	mushroom
ika	cuttlefish, squid
inaka-miso	beige-coloured *miso*
karashi	mustard
karasumi	salted mullet or tuna roe
katsuobushi	dried bonito, basic ingredient of *dashi*

kikurage	wood fungus, a delicacy
kinkam	cumquat
kinome	dried prickly ash leaf (anise-pepper), a garnish and seasoning
koikuchi	dark soya sauce
kosho	peppers, capsicums
koyadofu	dried bean curd
kurogoma	black sesame
kuwai	water chestnut
matade	a *tade* cultivar
menrui	noodles
mikan	tangerine, orange
mioga	Japanese ginger
mirin	rice wine, for cooking
miso	soya bean paste
miso shiru	red bean paste, a soup thickener
moyashi	beansprout
myoga	*mioga* ginger
naganegi	spring onions
namasu	raw fish salad
negi	onion
ninniku	garlic
nira	chive
nitsuke	simmering in soy sauce and sugar
nori	dried seaweed
orenji	orange
piman	green pepper, capsicum
ponzu	soy-and-sour-orange sauce
rakkyo	Chinese onion
remon	lemon
renkon	lotus root
sansho	a spice, powdered prickly ash leaf (see Anise-Pepper)
sendai-miso	red soya bean paste, highly salted
seto fuumi	seasoning consisting of dried seaweed, sesame, tuna and monosodium glutamate
shichimi-togarashi	7 flavour seasoning: poppy, mustard or rape, hemp or chilli, sesame, tangerine peel and *sansho* (see Spice Mixtures)
shio	salt
shiro-miso	white soya bean paste
shobu	sweet flag, calamus, *Acorus calamus*
shoga	ginger

shoyu	soya sauce
soba	buckwheat noodles
somen	thin, wheat flour noodles
su	vinegar
su-mi-re	citron and orange liqueur
sushi	snacks with rice base served in lacquered boxes
tachibana	clementine
tade	*asabu-tade*, smartweed, *Polygonum hydropiper*
tade su	*tade*, vinegar and rice
tamago	egg
tamanegi	onion
teriyaki	basting with soy sauce and *mirin* during cooking
tofu	soya bean curd
togarashi	chilli or cayenne pepper
usukuchi	light soya sauce
uzu	evergreen orange, *Citrus juncus*
wakame	lobe-leaf seaweed
yakidofu	grilled soya bean curd
yakimono	grilled foods
yakumi	spice
yanagi tade	smartweed, see *tade*
yodofu	boiled soya bean curd
yuzu	citron

ARABIC VOCABULARY

ahwa	coffee
arni filfit	chilli
aza	mastic (Persian)
azaf	caper
badunis	parsley
bedinjan mahshi	stuffed eggplant
bharout	carob
borghul, bourghol, burghul	parboiled cracked wheat
dawoud basha	minced lamb dish
dolmas	lit. 'wrapping', usually rice and meat in vine or cabbage leaves
döner kebab	sliced lamb packed round a spit for roasting
dukkah	crushed nuts and spices dry dip
eggah	Arab omelette thick with vegetables
falafel	hot spicy balls of chick pea

fattoush	Lebanese mixed salad
feta	Greek cheese
filfil	pepper
habiba	chicken and tomatoes, cold
halva	sesame sweet
hareera	soup
harissa	hot chilli sauce (Tunisian)
helbeh	fenugreek (Egypt)
hommous, hommos, hummus	chick pea or chick pea and sesame paste dip
karawya	caraway
kemoun, kamman, kammun	cumin
khalanjan	galangal
kharkoum	turmeric
kharub	carob
kibib	Egyptian anise liqueur
kizbara	coriander
kurtham	safflower
laban	yoghurt
lahem muqaddad	skewered lamb
la kama	Moroccan fragrant spice mixture
maamoul	stuffed pastries
malh	salt
maz(z)a	Mediterranean hors d'oeuvre
meshwi	grilled foods
raki	Turkish anise liqueur
ras el hanout	Moroccan 20 spice mix
rigani	wild marjoram
samak	fish
sammak	sumac
shahwe(a)rma, shawirmah	sliced lamb on vertical spit
shashlik	skewered lamb
ta'amia	Egyptian for *falafel*
tabil	Tunisian spice mixture: caraway, coriander, garlic and chilli
tahina, tahine, tahini	sesame seed paste
taklia	ground coriander fried with crushed garlic
tas kebab	lamb stew
toom	garlic
uran filfil	chilli
zathar, zather	mixture of sumac and thyme
zhug	seasoning of garlic, chilli, cardamom, caraway and coriander

GLOSSARY OF TECHNICAL TERMS

Abortifacient, inducing abortion.

Acetic acid, a pungent, vinegary liquid found in certain fruits. $CH_3 COOH$.

Achene, a non-succulent, indehiscent fruit containing a loose, single seed.

Adulterant, an inferior substance added to 'bulk-out' or debase a product.

Adventitious, growing unusually, eg roots from a trunk above ground.

Albedo, the white mesocarp of citrus fruits.

Aldehyde, a chemical compound, de-hydrogenated alcohol.

Alkali, compounds known as bases, highly soluble in water; neutralising acids forming a salt and water and turning litmus blue.

Alterative, restorative; inducing the return to health.

Alternate, of leaves: each placed further along, and opposite to its neighbour.

Anaesthetic, causing loss of sensation.

Analgesic, pain-relieving.

Anodyne, pain killer.

Anthelmintic, clearing worms from the intestines, etc.

Anticoagulant, delaying or preventing blood clotting.

Antihydrotic, anti-perspirant.

Anti-inflammatory, reducing swelling.

Antimicrobial, killing germs.

Antinauseant, preventing or relieving vomiting.

Antiperiodic, beneficial in recurrent illnesses.

Antiscorbutic, anti-scurvy.

Antiseptic, destroying or preventing germ growth.

Antispasmodic, preventing or relieving muscular cramps and convulsions.

Aperient, gently laxative.

Aphrodisiac, encouraging sexual appetite.

Appetitive, encouraging appetite.

Aril, a fleshy structure connected to or embracing various seeds.

Ascorbic acid, a crystalline substance in fruits and vegetables, vitamin C.

Astringent, causing living tissue to contract; stopping bleeding.

Atonic, relaxing, especially of muscle.

Axil, the angle between leaf and stem.

Axillary, borne in axils.

Bacteriostatic, preventing bacterial development.

Berry, a fruit with a fleshy pericarp containing more than one seed.

Biennial, having a life span of two years.

Bioflavonoid, crystalline substances, present in some fruits, affecting blood capillaries.

Blanch, to grow white, excluding chlorophyll by lack of sunlight.

Bract, a leaf whose axil bears a flower.

Brine, a strong mixture of salt and water.

Bulbil, a small bulb, or a bulbous reproductive structure growing above ground.

Calyx, the protective covering of a bud composed of individual or fused sepals.

Capsule, a moistureless fruit that splits open to cast its seeds.

Carbohydrates, organic compounds containing hydrogen, oxygen and carbon. The group includes sugars and starch.

Cardiac, of, or beneficial to, the heart.

Carminative, relieving or expelling gas in the alimentary canal.

Carpel, the female element of a flower – the stigma, style and ovary.

Cathartic, cleaning out the bowels, purgative.

Cellulose, the dominant substance in cell walls in plants, a polysaccharide.

Chaemonucleolysitic, breaking down the nucleus of cells by chemical action.

Cholesterol, a waxy, insoluble steroid alcohol present in all body tissue, an excess of which is linked to heart disease.

Citric acid, an acid present in citrus fruits, useful in the metabolism of carbohydrates.

Comfit, a sugar-covered nut or seed.

Coniferous, bearing cones.

Coriacious, leathery.

Cortisone, a hormone, which can be synthesised, used against leukaemia, arthritis, skin diseases etc.

Cotyledon, a seed leaf in the embryo of certain plants.

Cyanide, a highly poisonous acid salt.

Deciduous, shedding all foliage yearly.

Dehiscent, opening spontaneously to cast pollen, seeds etc.

Demulcent, soothing the skin.

Diaphoretic, inducing perspiration.

Digestive, promoting healthy digestion by stimulating production of saliva and gastric acids.

Dioecious, having separate male and female flowers on separate plants.

Diuretic, stimulating the flow of urine.

Drupe, a single-seeded, indehiscent fruit with a stony endocarp.

Elliptical, shaped like a flat circle.

Emetic, inducing vomiting.

Emmenagogue, encouraging menstruation.

Emollient, soothing the skin.

Endocarp, hard inner pericarp.

Endosperm, the matter in a seed that protects and feeds the embryo.

Enzyme, complex proteins produced by living cells that act as catalysts in bodily processes.

Essence, the substance in a plant containing its characteristic qualities in concentrated form, usually oil, glycoside or alkaloid.

Essential oil, the odorous principles of a plant in the form of a volatile oil, usually containing esters and terpenes.

Ester, a substance resulting from the interaction between an alcohol and an acid; in plants often an aromatic liquid.

Expectorant, clearing the chest by expelling moisture from lungs and windpipe.

Family, a level of botanic classification: subdivision of an order, a group comprising plants with similar characteristics including one or more genera.

Febrifuge, a medicine that combats fever.

Fixed oil, vegetable or animal non-volatile oil.

Floret, a small flower.

Freeze-dried, dried by elimination of liquid after quick freezing in a partial vacuum.

Fructose, a crystalline fruit sugar.

Fumigant, a substance from which smoke or fumes are used to treat contamination or purify the air.

Fungicide, that which kills fungus.

Galactogogue, that which stimulates lactation.

Germicide, germ killer.

Glabrous, smooth, hairless.

Glaucous, bloomy, waxy or powder-covered.

Glucose, a crystalline sugar, important energy source in metabolism.

Glucoside, a glycoside that hydrolises to produce glucose.

Glyceride, a solid ester derived from glycerol.

Glycoside, a dehydroxylated monosaccharide.

Gum, a gluey substance issuing or tapped from certain plants, hardening on oxidisation.

Hardy, surviving the winter outdoors.

Herbaceous, fleshy; not woody.

Hermaphroditic, combining male and female reproductive elements in the same flower or plant.

Hesperidium, any citrus fruit.

Homogenise, to make into a uniform mixture.

Hydragogue, removing accumulations of water or serum, causing water discharges.

Hypoglycaemic, with abnormally low blood sugar.

Indehiscent, not splitting open to cast seeds.

Indolent, causing no pain.

Inflorescence, arrangement of flowers in plants.

Infusion, a liquid with the properties or

flavour of the substance soaked in it.

Insectifuge, repelling insects.

Irritant, over-stimulating, inflaming.

Lanceolate, slender and pointed at both ends: lance-shaped.

Laterite, a tropical clay deposit containing oxides of iron and aluminium.

Latex, a milky liquid present in many plants.

Laxative, loosening the bowels, encouraging voiding of faeces.

Legume, a pod-producing vegetable.

Linear, thin and straight.

Linoleic acid, a fatty acid common in natural oils, used to manufacture soaps etc; vitamin F.

Linolenic acid, a fatty acid present in natural oils. Less common than linoleic acid. Used in paints.

Lithontriptic, suppresses or reduces urinary calculi (stones).

Lyrate, lyre-shaped.

Macerate, to soak until soft or broken.

Mesocarp, the central portion of the pericarp, usually fleshy.

Minerals, a group of natural inorganic substances many of which are essential for health.

Mordant, a substance used to fix colours in the dyeing process.

Mucilage, sticky carbohydrates present in various plants.

Mulch, soft vegetable matter laid over soil to enrich it or protect plants.

Narcotic, a stupor-inducing drug.

Niacin, nicotinic acid, part of vitamin B complex, B_5.

Node, a swelling; the junction of a branch etc with the main stem.

Oblate, shaped like a flattened sphere.

Obovate, egg-shaped, with smaller end at base.

Odd-pinnate, pinnate with a single leaflet at end of stalk.

Oleic acid, an unsaturated oily acid, a glyceride, present in most fats.

Oleic glyceride, oleic acid.

Oleoresin, resin and essential oil in combination. Extracted from plants.

Ovate, egg-shaped.

Ovoid, egg-shaped.

Oxidation, reaction with oxygen causing formation of an oxide.

Panicle, a multiple raceme.

Paripinnate, pinnate with no single end leaflet.

Pectin, acid carbohydrates present in fruits, which jellify when heated with sugar.

Pentosans, a series of polysaccharides present in plants.

Perennial, enjoying a life span of three or more years.

Pericarp, the element of a fruit that surrounds the seeds.

Pharmacopoeia, a list of drugs in official use.

Phenol, carbolic acid, a weak acid derived from benzene. Used as an antiseptic.

Phylactic, acting as a charm.

Phytonicide, destroying plant cells.

Pigment, any colouring agent present in living tissue.

Pinene, Alpha or Beta, two terpenes present in certain essential oils.

Pinnate, consisting of opposing leaflets.

Pinnatifid, lobed, the divisions reaching more than half way to the middle of the leaf.

Placenta, ovary part to which seeds are attached, eg the white internal matter of capsicum, papaya etc.

Protein, the building blocks of life, nitrogen-bearing substances based on amino acid chains.

Prussic acid, a highly poisonous weak acid, hydrocyanic acid.

Pulse, edible seed of leguminous plants.

Purgative, emptying the bowels.

Raceme, a formation where stalked flowers grow along a main stem, the oldest at the bottom.

Refrigerant, cooling, combating fever.

Resin, solid or semi-solid waste products exuded from certain plants.

Restorative, pick-me-up.

Rhizome, underground stem, from which new plants grow.

Riboflavin, Vitamin B_2.

Rootstock, rhizome.

Rubefacient, reddening the skin.

Rutin, formerly vitamin P, see bioflavonoids.

Schizocarp, dry fruit splitting into single-seeded parts when ripe.

Sedative, calming.

Sepal, the leaf-like parts of a calyx.

Sessile, stalkless.

Set, seedling, cutting etc ready for planting.

Sheath, a leaf etc encasing a part of a plant.

Sodium, an alkaline metal essential to life but harmful in excess.

Soporific, sleep-inducing.

Spadix, a flower spike with a fleshy stem, enclosed in a spathe.

Spathe, a large bract wrapped around the flower spike of certain plants, or two or more bracts enclosing a flower cluster.

Specific, a medicine with a particular use.

Spike, inflorescence with sessile flowers arranged along a single stem.

Stamen, male organ of flower, bearing the pollen-producing anther.

Starch, a glucose-based polysaccharide common in vegetable tissue as the principal reserve food store.

Stearic acid, a waxy fatty acid, used to make candles etc.

Stigma, the tip of the style, where pollen is collected.

Stimulant, encouraging physiological action.

Stipule, a small double leaf-like growth at the base of a leaf or stalk.

Stolon, a runner, a side-stem trailing along the ground producing nodal roots.

Stomachic, beneficial to the stomach; increasing gastric activity.

Style, a thin cylindrical structure extending from the ovary, bearing the stigma.

Sucker, a new shoot or one growing from a root or rhizome.

Sucrose, sugar, a saccharine carbohydrate.

Sulphide, a sulphurous compound.

Synonym, a taxonomic name that has been replaced.

Taenifuge, anti tape-worm.

Tannic acid, plant-produced derivatives of gallic acid used in tanning, dyeing etc.

Tannin, tannic acid.

Tap root, the main vertical root of certain plants.

Tartaric acid, a crystalline acid common in fruits, used in beverages, confectionery etc.

Taxonomy, classification of animals and plants.

Terpenes, a group of hydrocarbons common in essential oils.

Terpineol, a lilac-scented alcohol of the terpene class.

Thiamine, vitamin B_1, occurring in the husks of rice and other grains.

Tincture, an alcoholic solution of a drug.

Toxic, poisonous.

Umbel, a flower formation where all the stalks grow from one point.

Umbelliform, umbel-shaped.

Vermifuge, an agent that expels worms from the intestines.

Vitamin A, retinol, an alcohol present in green vegetables and egg yolks. Deficiency leads to night blindness.

Vitamin B complex, a group including the following: B_1 thiamine, B_2 riboflavin essential in metabolism of carbohydrates, B_5 niacin, nicotinic acid.

Vitamin C, ascorbic acid, necessary to prevent scurvy.

Vitamin D, a vitamin present in dairy products. Necessary to prevent rickets.

Vitamin E, alpha-tocopherol, a vitamin present in some vegetables and in egg yolk. A deficiency is believed to impair human reproduction.

Vitamin P, rutin, bioflavonoid.

Vitta, an oil channel in some fruits.

Volatile, vaporising readily.

Volatile oil, essential oil.

BOTANICAL INDEX

NB Taxonomic synonyms are scientific names now invalidated or replaced. They appear here prefixed with an asterisk.

Acorus calamus	calamus	37
Aframomum melegueta	melegueta pepper	122
Allium cepa	onion	140
Allium sativum	garlic	97
Alpinia galanga	galangal (greater)	94
Alpinia officinarum	galangal (lesser)	94
Amomum cardamomum	cardamom	43
Amomum granum paradisii	grains of paradise	123
Amomum melegueta	melegueta pepper	122
Amomum zingiber	ginger	100
Anethum graveolens	dill	84
Apium graveolens dulce	celery	54
Armoracia lapathifolia	horseradish	106
Armoracia rusticana	horseradish	106
Bergera koenigii	curry leaf	82
Bixa orellana	annatto	26
Brassica alba	mustard (white)	126
Brassica juncea	mustard (brown)	126
Brassica nigra	mustard (black)	126
Capparis spinosa	caper	38
Capsicum annuum	capsicum (chilli, cayenne, paprika)	145
Capsicum frutescens	capsicum (chilli, cayenne, paprika)	49, 56
	(see Chilli Guide for other forms)	
Carica papaya	papaya	143
Carthamus tinctorius	safflower	159
Carum ajowan	ajowan	16
Carum carvi	caraway	40
Carum copticum	ajowan	16
Caryophyllus aromaticus	clove	66
Ceratonia siliqua	carob	45
Chalcas koenigii	curry leaf	82
Cinnamomum cassia	cassia	47
Cinnamomum zeylanicum	cinnamon	60
Citrus spp	citrus	63
Cochlearia armoracia	horseradish	106
Cocos nucifera	coconut	72
Coriandrum sativum	coriander	75
Coumarouna odorata	tonka bean	186
Crocus sativus	crocus (saffron)	161
Cuminum cyminum	cumin	79
Curcuma domestica	turmeric	192
Curcuma longa	turmeric	192

Curcuma zedoaria	zedoary (round)	197
Curcuma zerumbet	zedoary (long)	197
Cymbopogon citratus	lemon grass	113
Dipteryx odorata	tonka bean	186
Elettaria cardamomum	cardamom	43
Emblica officinalis	trifala (3)	188
*Eugenia aromatica	clove	66
*Eugenia caryophyllata	clove	66
Eugenia caryophyllus	clove	66
*Eugenia pimenta	allspice	17
Eugenia polyantha	*daun salam*	83
Ferula assafoetida	asafoetida	28
Ferula foetida	asafoetida	30
Ferula narthex	asafoetida	30
Ferula rubricaulis	asafoetida	30
Foeniculum vulgare	fennel	89
Garcinia indica	kokum	111
Glycine max	soya	174
*Glycine hispida	soya	174
*Glycine soja	soya	174
Glycyrrhiza glabra	liquorice	115
*Illicium anisatum	star anise	178
Illicium verum	star anise	178
Juniperus communis	juniper	109
Kaempferia galanga	galangal (Kaempferia)	94
*Kaempferia pandurata	galangal (Kaempferia)	94
*Kaempferia rotunda	galangal (Kaempferia)	94
Languas galanga	galangal (greater)	94
Languas officinarum	galangal (lesser)	94
Laurus nobilis	bay leaf	32
Mangifera indica	mango (amchur)	20
Mentha spp	mints	123
Mesua ferrea	nagkesar	112
Murraya koenigii	curry leaf	82
Myristica fragrans	nutmeg and mace	116, 134
*Nasturtium indicum	nasturtium	130
Nigella sativa	nigella	132
Pandanus odoratissimus	screwpine	170
Pandanus odorus	screwpine	170
*Pandanus tectorius	screwpine	170

Papaver rhoeas	corn poppy	157, 158
Papaver somniferum	poppy	154
Papaya carica	papaya	143
Peucedanum graveolens	dill	84
Pimenta dioica	allspice	17
Pimenta officinalis	allspice	17
Pimpinella anisum	anise	22
Piper cubeba	cubeb	78
Piper longum	pepper (long)	148
Piper nigrum	pepper (black, white, green)	148
Pistacia lentiscus	mastic	120
Polygonum hydropiper	tade (smartweed)	182
Polygonum hydropiper fastigiatum	azabu tade	183
Prunus mahaleb	mahlebi	118
Ptychotis ajowan	ajowan	16
Punica granatum	pomegranate	152
Rhus coriaria	sumac	180
Santalum album	sandalwood	167
Sassafras albidum	sassafras	168
Sassafras officinale	sassafras	168
Sassafras varifolium	sassafras	168
Schinus terebinthifolius	pepper (pink)	148
Sesamum indicum	sesame	172
Sesamum orientale	sesame	172
Sinapis alba	white mustard	126
Soja max	soya	174
Syzygium aromaticum	clove	66
Tamarindus indica	tamarind	183
Tamarindus officinalis	tamarind	183
Terminalia belerica	trifala (1)	188
Terminalia chebula	trifala (2)	188
Theobroma cacao	cocoa	69
Trachyspermum ammi	ajowan	16
Trigonella foenum-graecum	fenugreek	92
Tropaeolum majus	nasturtium	130
Tropaeolum minus	nasturtium	130
Vanilla fragrans	vanilla	194
Vanilla planifolia	vanilla	194
Xanthoxylum piperitum	anise-pepper	24
Zanthoxylum alatum	badrang	31
Zanthoxylum budrunga	badrang	30, 31
Zanthoxylum limonella	badrang	31
Zanthoxylum piperitum	anise-pepper	24, 31
Zanthoxylum rhetsa	badrang	30, 31
Zingiber officinale	ginger	100

INDEX OF BOTANICAL FAMILIES OF SPICES

Alliaceae: garlic, onion; *relative* chive

Anacardiaceae: amchur, mastic, pink pepper, sumac; *relatives* cashew, pistachio

Araceae: calamus; *relatives* arum lily, cuckoo pint

Bixaceae: annatto

Caesalpiniaceae: see Leguminosae

Capparidaceae: caper

Caricaceae: papaya

Combretaceae: trifala (beleric and chebulic myrobalans); *relatives* buttonwood, Indian almond

Compositae: safflower; *relatives* artichoke, daisy, lettuce

Cruciferae: horseradish, mustard; *relatives* cabbage, turnip, wallflower, watercress

Cupressaceae: juniper; *relatives* cedars

Euphorbiaceae: trifala (emblic myrobolan); *relatives* cassava, castor oil, poinsettia

Gramineae: lemon grass; *relatives* rye grass, wild barley, wild oat

Guttiferae: kokum, nagkeser; *relatives* bitter cola, mammey apple, mangosteen

Iridaceae: saffron; *relatives* iris, yellow flag

Labiatae: mint; *relatives* marjoram, nettle, rosemary, sage, thyme

Lauraceae: bay leaf, cassia, cinnamon, sassafras; *relative* avocado

Leguminosae:

  Caesalpiniaceae: carob, tamarind; *relatives* brazil nut, flamboyant, senna

  Papilionaceae: fenugreek, liquorice, soya, tonka bean; *relatives* beans, indigo, lentil, lupin, peas

Magnoliaceae: star anise; *relatives* magnolia, tulip tree

Myristaceae: mace, nutmeg

Myrtaceae: allspice, clove; *relatives* eucalyptus, guava, myrtle

Orchidaceae: vanilla; *relatives* orchids

Palmae: coconut; *relatives* palms

Pandanaceae: screwpine; *relative* Nicobar breadfruit

Papaveraceae: poppy; *relatives* corn poppy, greater celandine

Papilionaceae: see Leguminosae

Pedaliaceae: sesame

Piperaceae: cubeb, pepper

Polygonaceae: tade; *relatives* buckwheat, dock, rhubarb, sorrel

Punicaceae: pomegranate

Ranunculaceae: nigella; *relatives* buttercup, columbine, traveller's joy

Rosaceae: mahlebi; *relatives* apple, apricot, sloe, strawberry

Rutaceae: anise-pepper, badrang, citrus, curry leaf; *relative* rue

Santalaceae: sandalwood; *relatives* bastard toadflax, quadong

Solanaceae: cayenne, chilli, paprika; *relatives* aubergine, deadly nightshade, potato, tomato

Sterculiaceae: cocoa; *relative* cola

Tropaeolaceae: nasturtium; *relative* watercress

Umbelliferae: ajowan, anise, asafoetida, caraway, celery seed, coriander, cumin, dill, fennel; *relatives* carrot, lovage, parsley

Zingiberaceae: cardamom, galangal, ginger, melegueta pepper, turmeric, zedoary; *relatives* lilies

SPICE SUPPLIERS

Spices under many brand names are now readily available throughout the United Kingdom in most food shops and supermarkets. Listed below are some mail-order sources for those without local suppliers, together with a few addresses for obtaining the less common spices. Most of the spices in this book are available in local Indian and Chinese retailers.

Chun Yin Supermarket
63 Cambridge Street
Glasgow C3
Chinese spices and provisions.

Culpeper
21 Bruton Street
London W1X 7DA
Spices and herbs. Branches also in Hampstead, Covent Garden, Bath, Brighton, Cambridge, Guildford, Norwich, Oxford, Salisbury and Winchester.

The Curry Club
P.O. Box 7
Haslemere
Surrey GU27 1EP
Mail order spices and spice mixtures for members.

Loon Fung Chinese Emporium
39 Gerard Street
London W1
Chinese and Indonesian supplies.

Mikadoya
250 Upper Richmond Road
London SW15
Japanese spices and provisions.

Nippon Food Centre
483 Finchley Road
London NW3
 and
193 Upper Richmond Road
London SW15
Japanese spices and provisions.

Osaka Ltd
17A Goldenhurst Terrace
London NW6
Japanese spices and provisions.

Patak (Spices) Ltd
Park Lane
Abram
Wigan WN2 5XJ
Indian spices and pickles by mail order.
Retail branches in major UK towns.

Patel Brothers
187 Upper Tooting Road
London SW17
Large range of Indian spices and provisions.

Patels
33 Fife Road
Kingston-upon-Thames
Surrey
Spices and general provisions.

Further Reading

The Book of Spices, F. Rosengarten Jr (Livingstone Publishing Co, Penn. USA, 1969)

Chinese Herbs, John D. Keys (Charles E. Tuttle, Vermont USA, 1976)

The Complete Book of Herbs and Spices, Claire Loewenfeld and Philippa Back (David & Charles 1978)

Culpeper's Complete Herbal (W. Foulsham & Co Ltd 1952)

A Guide to Spices, Ivan and Isabelle Day (The Herb Society 1978)

Handbook on Japanese Herbs, Plants & Gardens (Brooklyn Botanic Garden, New York, 1976)

The Herbal or *General History of Plants*, John Gerard 1597 (Dover, New York, 1975)

Herbs of Greece, Alta Dodds Niebuhr (Herb Society of America 1970)

Herbs, Spices and Flavourings, Tom Stobart (Penguin Books 1977)

A Modern Herbal, M. Grieve (Penguin Books 1980)

Nouveau Larousse Universel Vols I & II (Librairie Larousse, Paris, 1948)

Potter's New Cyclopaedia of Botanical Drugs and Preparations, R. C. Wren (Health Science Press 1975)

Spices Vols I & II, John W. Parry (Chemical Publishing Company Inc, New York, 1969)

Spices Vols 1 & 2, J. W. Purseglove, E. G. Brown, C. L. Green & S. R. J. Robbins (Longman 1982)

Spices & Condiments, J. S. Pruthi (National Books, Delhi)

Sturtevant's Edible Plants of the World, Ed. U. P. Hedrick (Dover, New York, 1972)

The Vegetable Book, Yann Lovelock (George Allen and Unwin 1972)

Acknowledgements

We would like to thank the members of our families and the many friends who have helped in a multiplicity of ways to create this book. Their efforts and enthusiasm have been invaluable and are deeply appreciated.

We express special thanks to Mick Clark, our research and literary assistant, for his work, erudition and wit; to Doreen East who has typed the manuscript with patience and good humour throughout; to Charles Pocklington for his painstaking photography and to Ann Collingridge for her excellent line drawings.

For their interest and assistance we are particularly grateful to Barrie Collingridge, Victor Hardingham, Brenda Jackson, Marie Kalfayan, Maggie Paish and Ariadne Vraila.

We are indebted to the following for information or samples of spices: Culpeper's Ltd; Hansens Laboratory Ltd; Larkhall Laboratories; the Royal Botanic Gardens, Kew; the Tropical Products Institute; Patak (Spices) Ltd; English Provender Company; and the America Spice Trade Association.

Index

Page numbers in italics refer to illustrations

Absinthe, 23, 90
Achiote, 28
Africa(n) Pepper, 59
Agi, 59
Ague Tree, 169
Ajave, 17
Ajonjoli, 172
Ajwa(i)n, 17
Akvavit, 41, 43, 90, 122
Albert sauce, 107
Ale, Mulled, 214
Alga(r)oba (Bean), 47
Alligator Pepper, 123
Amchur Fish Kebabs, 21
Ameos, 17
American Noodles, 158, *155*
American Pepper, 59
American Saffron, 160
Ananga Ranga, 16, 76, 112, 115, 160, 171, 184, 191
Anardana, 152
Anesone, 22, 115
Anise Acre, 81
Anise Cakes, 23
Anise Liqueur, 23
Anisette, 22
Annotto Chicken and Pork, 28, *51*
Aploppas, 28
Apollo, 35–6
Apple Pie Spice, 199
Applemint, 123–5
Apples, Baked, 68
Arabian Nights, 44
Arcmart, 183
Armenian Boats, 181, *33*
Aromatic Ginger, 96
Arra(c)k, 22, 73
Arsemart, 183
Autumn Crocus, 162
Aztec Pepper, 59

Badian, 179
Baked Apples, 68
Barbecue Spice, 199
Bass, Grilled, 91
Bastard Cinnamon, 49
Bastard Saffron, 160, 162
Beans, *see* Pulses and Vegetables
Beef, *see also* Meat; Carbonnade, 30; Daube provençal, 36
Beer, 110, 116, 127; Beef in, 127;

Chill-proof, 144; Mulled (ale), 214
Belladonna, 58
Bell Pepper, 59
Benedictine, 18
Bene Seeds, 173
Bengali Five Spices, 199
Bengal Root, 105
Betel pan, 43, 150
Betel Pepper, 150
Biby Tongue, 183
Bird's Beak, 53
Bird's Eye Pepper, 59
Bird's Foot, 93
Biscuits, *see* Cakes
Bishop, The, 214
Bishop's Weed (Candy, True), 17
Biting Persicaria, 183
Black Cumin, 133
Black Sugar, 116
Bloodwort, 183
Bloody Mary, 56, *155*
Blume, 59
Bombay Curry Powder, 202
Bonnet Pepper, 59
Bouquets garnis, 32, 64, 113
Bread: Caraway, 42; Cinnamon toast, 62; Greek Brioche, 119; Naan, 132, 134; Pitta, 174
Brine Mixtures, 199
Butter: Garlic, 98, 100; Green Peppercorn, 151; Home production, 26; Horseradish, 108

Cacao, 71
Cacauatl, 71
Cakes and Biscuits: Anise, 23; Carob, 47; Gingerbread, 106; Mahlebi Biscuits, 120; Marble Sponge, 196
Camel's Hay, 114
Canary Creeper, 132
Canel, 49
Capper, 40
Capsaicin, 50, 57, 58, 146, 147, 223, 224, 230
Capsicum, 59
Capuchin, 132
Caraway Bread, 42
Carbonnade of Beef, 130
Carob Cake, 47

Carom, 17
Carouba, 47
Carvies, 42
Cassumunar, 198
Celeriac, 55
Cha Shao, 177
Chachanga, 221
Charlock, 129
Chartreuse, 18
Chat Masala, 200
Cheese: Liptauer, 40; Straws, 54
Cherry Pepper, 59
Chicken in Rice Paper, 177, *52*
Chicken Seasoning, 200
Chicken, *see also* Poultry and Game; Creole Gumbo, 169; Jujeh al Sammak, 181
Chile Con Carne, 81, *51*
Chilli Guide, 223
Chilliepin, 53
Chilli powder, 53, 56–9
Chilli Seasoning, 58, 201
China Root, 96
Chinese Anise, 179
Chinese Cinnamon, 49
Chinese Curry Powder, 202
Chinese Drumsticks, 49
Chinese Five Spices, 201
Chinese Ginger, 96
Chinese Parsley, 77
Chinese Pepper, 31
Chinese (Brown) Pepper, 25
Chinese Spiced Salt, 201
Chocolate, 69–71
Chocolate Leaves, 71
Chutney, *see also* Condiments; Tamarind, 183–5
Ciderage, 183
Cilantro, 77
Cinnamon Toast, 62
Cinnamon Wood, 169
Citronella Grass, 114
Clove Oil, 61
Clove Pepper, 19
Clown's Treacle, 99
Cochin Grass, 114
Cockspur Pepper, 59
Cocktails, *see* Drinks
Cocoa substitutes, 46
Coconut Sambal, 74, *86*
Cocum, 112

269

Coleslaw, 42, *190*
Colic Root, 96
Condiments, *see also* Chutney; Country Mustard, 130; Horseradish Relish, 108; Piccalilli, 194; Tamarind Fish Relish, 185
Cone Pepper, 59
Confectionery: Chocolate Leaves, 71; Marzipan, 23; Mastiha Gliko, 121; Sandalwood Creams, 168; Tonka Fudge, 187
Congo Pepper, 59
Coumarou, 187
Country Mustard, 127, 130, *137*
Country Pâté, 111, *156*
Crab Boil, 201
Crab Curry, 84
Crème de Menthe, 124
Creole Gumbo, 169, *155*
Cress, Indian, 132
Crudités, 40
Culrage, 183
Cumaru, 187
Curry: Crab, 84; Egg, 31; Fish, 112; Sandhurst, 191; Vindaloo, 93
Curry Pak, 83
Curry Powders, 202–4

Damascena, 133
Daphne, 35
Daube Provençale, 36, *156*
Daun pandan, 170
Delicatessen (paprika var), 147
Desserts, *see* Puddings
Devil-in-the-Bush, 133
Devil Pepper, 59
Devil's Dung or Durt, 30
Dhal, 94
Dill Pickle, 88, *190*
Dips: Horseradish, 108; Hummus bi Tahini, 173; Liptauer Cheese, 40
Dizzycorn, 77
Dolmades, 125, *33*
Dried Fruit Salad, 116, *137*
Drinks: Anise liqueur, 23; Bishop, 214; Bloody Mary, 56; Mulled wine or ale, 214; Piña Colada, 74
Duck, *see* Poultry and Game
Dukkah Mix, 205
Dyer's Saffron, 160

East Indian Catarrh Root, 96
East Indian Pepper, 105
East Indian Root, 96
Edesnemes (paprika var), 147
Egg Curry, 31
Egg(s): Curry, 31; Marbled, 179
Embalming, 19, 62, 121
English Caper, 132
English Spice, 19
Erös (paprika var), 147
Ethiopian Cumin, 17

Fagar, 25, 31
Fake Saffron, 160
Falafel, 77, *33*
False Saffron, 160

Félédes (paprika var), 147
Fennel Flower, 133
Festive Pilau, 44, *103*
Filé Powder, 168
Fish: Amchur Kebab, 21; Curry, 112; Glasmästarsill, 19; Grilled Bass, 91; Lemon Trout, 66; Paella, 162, *34*; in Salt, 166; Soup, 91; in Soy Sauce, 97
Fish Curry, 112
Fish in Salt, 166
Fish Seasoning, 205
Fish in Soy Sauce, 97, *86*
Fish Soup, 91
Flores Carthami, 160
Food-of-the-Gods, 30
Forester's Venison, 69, *137*
French Dressing, 205, 210
French Onion Soup, 142, *190*
Fruit: Baked Apples, 68; Compôte, 38; Peach Melba, 197; Poppy Seed Strudel, 158; Salad, Dried, 116
Fruit Compôte, 38
Fudge, Tonka Bean, 187

Gado-Gado, 210
Garam Masala, 210
Gargaut, 96
Gatinais Saffron, 162
Geranium Grass, 114
Gingelly, 173
Gingerbread, 106, *137*
Gingergrass Oil, 114
Ginny Grains, Pepper, 123
Gith, 133
Glasmästarsill, 19
Goat's Horn, 93
Goat's Pepper, 59
Gomasio, 172, 211
Goulash, Hungarian, 41, 145
Graines, 123
Grains of Paradise, 44, 123
Great Raifort, 108
Greater Cardamom, 123
Green Peppercorn Butter, 151
Green Peppercorn Sauce, 151
Gremolata, 64
Grenadier, 153
Grenes, 123
Grilled Bass, 91, *156*
Gros-sel, 164
Groundnut Chop, 59, *51*
Guinea Grains, 123
Guinea Pepper, 53, 59, 123
Guinea Seeds, 123
Gulé Lamb, 79
Gum Asafoetida, 30

Habas à la Asturiana, 148
Halite, 164, 166
Hangover cures, 41
Harissa, 211
Hay Saffron, 162
Helbeh, 93
'Hippocras', 123
Hoisin Sauce, 211
Honey Locust, 47
Horse Plant, 108

Horseradish: Butter, 108; Dip, 108, *155*; Relish, 108; Sauce, Hot, 108
Hot and Spicy Grilled Chicken, 114, 189
Hungarian Goulash, 147, *190*
Hungarian Pepper, 147

Imsak, 160
India Root, 96
Indian Bay, 36
Indian Cress, 132
Indian Date, 185
Indian Gooseberry, 191
Indian Pepper, 53, 59
Indian Saffron, 193
Indian Verbena, 113
Italian Seasoning, 212

Jamaica Pepper, 18, 19, 105
Japan Pepper, 25
Japanese Parsley, 77
Japanese Pepper, 31
Japanese Steaks, 26, *85*
Java Chicken, 96
Japan Pepper, 25
Java Pepper, 79
John's Bread, 49
Jollof Rice, 123
Jujeh al Sammak, 181
Juniper Pork Chops, 110

Kaempferia Galangal, 94
Kaffir Lime, 63
Kama Sutra, 102, 115
Karcom, 162
Kashmiri Masala, 212
Kewra, 170
Khara Masala, 212
Kheer, 171
Kibib, 22
King Cumin, 91
Kino, 187
Kinome, 24, 25
Kofta Curry Powder, 202
Kokum Butter Tree, 112
Koran, 153
Korma Curry Powder, 203
Krona Pepper, 147
Különleges (paprika var), 147
Kümmel, 41, 80

La Kama, 212
Lamb, *see also* Meat; Armenian boats, 181; Sheek Kebab, 45, *103*
Lamb Gulé, 79, *86*
Lamb Seasoning, 213
Large Cumin, 91
Laser (picum), 30
Laurel, 35, 36
Lebanese Mix, 213
Lemon Lamb, 62, *138*
Lemon peel, 113
Lemon Trout, 66
Lentil Dishes, 140; Dhal, 94
Lentisk, 121
Lettuce Soup, 132, *137*
Lime, 63
Lion's Head, 105, *52*

Liptauer Cheese, 40
Liqueurs, *see* Drinks
Lobhia, 134, *104*
Lobster, 22
Locust Bean, Seed, 47
Long Pepper, 148
Long Pepper (chilli), 59
Louisiana Sport Chilli, 59
Lovage, 17
Love-in-a-Mist, 133

Mad Pepper, 53
Madras Curry Powder, 203
Mahlebi Biscuits, 120
Ma Ho, 99, *85*
Malabar Grass, 114
Mamaeiro, 144
Mangosteen, 21; Oil, 112; Oil Tree, 112
Maniguetta Pepper, 123
Márathon, 91
Marbled Eggs, 179, *52*
Marbled Sponge, 196
Marinade, Papaya, 144
Marzipan, 23
Mastiha Gliko, 121
Mawseed, 158
Meat: Annatto Chicken and Pork, 28; Carbonnade of Beef, 130; Cha Shao, 177; Chile Con Carne, 81; Country Pâté, 111; Daube Provençale, 36, *156*; Hungarian Goulash, 147; Japanese Steak, 26; Juniper Pork Chops, 110; Lamb Gulé, 79; Lemon Lamb, 62; Lion's Heads, 105; Meat Loaf, 118; Osso Buco, 66, *34*; Pork with Coriander, 77; Red Cooked Beef, 179; Shabu-Shabu, 142; Steak au Poivre, 151; Steak Kebab, 59
Meat Loaf, 118
Meat Tenderiser, 213
Melanthion, 133
Melissa Oil, 113
Melon Tree, 144
Methi, 93
Mexican Mixture, 213
Mexican Turkey, 71
Mignonette Pepper, 148, 149, 213
Mixed Spice, 214
Molee, 74
Molinillo, 70
Mombassa Chilli, 59
Mongolian Firepot, 142
Monosodium Glutamate, 164
Mossoia Bark, 49
Motia, 113, 114
Mountain Radish, 108
Mukhwas, 214
Mulled ale, 214
Mulled Wine, 214
Mulling Spice, 214
Mustard Mixtures, 127
Myrobalans, The Three, 188, 191
Myrtle Pepper, 19

Naan Bread, 134, *104*

Nagkeser, 112
Nanami Togarashi, 214
Nepal Pepper, 53, 59
Nicobar Breadfruit, 171
Nim (Leaf), 83
Noodles, *see* Pasta
Nutmeg Flower, 133

Oil Plant, 114
Ojen, 22
Oliver's Bark, 49
Oman, 17
Onion Soup, 142
Opium, 157, 158
Orange Blossom Water, 65, 120
Oregano, 57, 58
Orellana, 28
Orlean(a), 28
Osso Buco, 66, *34*
Our Lady's Mint, 125
Ovid, 39

Paella, 162, *34*
Pakoras, 153, *189*
Palmarosa Oil, 114
Pan, 104, 214, 215
Panch Phora, 215
Pandan, 171
Papaya Marinade, 144
Papaya Vinaigrette, 145, *51*
Paradise Grains, Nuts, 123
Pasta: American Noodles, 158; Armenian Boats, 181; Pomodoro Sauce for, 56
Pastis, 22, 23
Pâté, *see* Meat
Pawpaw, 144
Peach Melba, 197, *138*
Pennyroyal, 123–5
Pepper Eyes, 25
Pepper Plant, 183
Peppermint, 123–5
Pepperwort, 183
Perfumery Spices, 215
Pernod, 22
Persian Silphium, 30
Piccalilli, 194
Pickles: Dill, 88; Piccalilli, 194
Pickling Spices, 216
Pilau, *see* Rice
Pilau Mixture, 217
Pimenta, 18, 19
Pimento Dram, 19
Pimento Pepper, 147
Pimenton, 59
Piña Colada, 74, *51*
Pink Pepper, 148
Pistachio Tree, 121
Pod Pepper, 59
Pomodaro Sauce, 56, *34*
Poor Man's Treacle, 99
Poppy Seed Strudel, 158
Porcupine Wood, 73
Pork, *see also* Meat; Cha Shao, 177; Lion's Heads, 105
Pork Chops, Juniper, 110
Pork with Coriander, 77
Pork Seasoning, 217
Potted Shrimps, 118, *138*

Poultry and Game: Annatto Chicken and Pork, 28; Chicken in Rice Paper, 177; Chinese Drumsticks, 49; Creole Gumbo, 169; Forester's Venison, 69; Groundnut Chop, 59; Java Chicken, 96; Jollof Rice, 123; Jujeh al Sammak, 181; Mexican Turkey, 71; Spicy Chicken, 114; Szechwan Duck, 25
Prawn Molee, 74, *104*
Prawn Sesame Fingers, 174, *52*
Prickly Ash, 24, 25
Puddings: Baked Apples, 68; Kheer, 171; Peach Melba, 197; Poppy Seed Strudel, 158; Pumpkin Pie, 19
Pudding Spice, 217
Pulses: Dhal, 94; Falafel, 77; Hummus bi Tahini, 173, *33*; Lobhia, 134
Pumpkin Pie, 19

Quatre Epices, 78

Rabbit, *see* Country Pâté
Ras El Hanout, 217
Red Cluster Pepper, 59
Red Cole, 108
Red Cooked Beef, 179
Red Knees, 183
Relish, *see* Condiments
Rempah, 198
Ricard, 22
Rice: Dolmades, 125; Festive Pilau, 44; Jollof, 123; Kheer, 171; Paella, 162; Risotto alla Milanese, 163; Yellow, 193
Ripiena, 135
Risotto alla Milanese, 163
Rocambole, 141
Roman Coriander, 133
Roqueto Pepper, 58, 59
Rosha Grass, 114
Rosza, (paprika var), 147

Saffron Thistle, 160
Safflower Dressing, 160
Sage of Bethlehem, 125
St John's Bread, 47
St Lucie's Cherry, 120
Salad: Coleslaw, 42; Taboulleh, 126
Salad Dressing: Papaya, 145; Safflower, 160
Salad Seasoning, 218
Saloop, 168
Saltpetre, 164–6
Sambal, Coconut, 74
Sambal Mix, 218
Samosa, 81, *103*
Sandalwood Creams, 168
Sanders-wood, 168
Sandhurst Curry, 191
Sansho, 24, 25
Satay Sauce, 59, *85*
Sauces: Green Peppercorn, 151; Horseradish, 108; Molee, 74; Pomodoro, 56; Satay, 59; Tade, 183; Tartare, 40

Sauerkraut, 88
Sausage Seasoning, 218
Saxifrax, 169
Scotch Bonnet Pepper, 59
Scoville heat units, 224
Seafood Cocktail, 53, *155*
Seasoning Salt, 218
Sel Epicé, 219
Semsem, 173
Sereh powder, 113, 114
Sesame Prawn Fingers, 174
Sev, 17, *103*
Seven Flavour Spice, 219
Seven Seas Spice, 219
Shabat, 46
Shabu-Shabu, 142
Sheek Kebab, 45, *103*
Shellfish: Crab Curry, 84; Lobster,
  22; Paella, 162; Potted Shrimps,
  118; Prawn Molee, 74; Prawn
  Sesame Fingers, 174; Seafood
  Cocktail, 53; Snail Butter, 100
Sherry with Chillies, 57
Shichimi-Togarashi, 219-20
Shot Pepper, 148
Shrimp Spice, 201
Shrimps, Potted, 118
Siamese Ginger, 96
Simsim, 173
Smallage, 55
Smartass, 183
Smartweed, 183
Smörgåsbord, 19
Snacks: Cheese Straws, 54;
  Chicken in Rice Paper, 177;
  Cinnamon Toast, 62; Dolmades,
  125; Falafel, 77; Hummus bi
  Tahini, 173; Liptauer Cheese,
  40; Ma Ho, 99; Marbled Eggs,
  179; Pakoras, 153; Prawn
  Sesame Fingers, 174; Rempah,
  198; Samosas, 81
Snails with Garlic Butter, 100
Sofia, 114
Soja Bean, 176
Soups: Fish, 91; French Onion,
  142; Lettuce, 132
Spanish Juice, 116
Spanish Pepper, 59
Spanish Saffron, 162

Spearmint 123-5
Spice Mixtures, 199-222
Spiced Beef, 220
Spiced Beef Mixture, 220
Spiced Salt, 220, 221
Spicy Potatoes, 30, *189*
Spur Pepper, 59
Sri Lanka Curry Powder, 203
Steak, *see also* Meat; Japanese, 26;
  au Poivre, 151; Shabu-Shabu,
  142
Steak Spice, 221
Stigma Croci, 162
Stinking Gum, 30
Sugar Pod, 47
Sumac with Yoghurt, 181, *33*
Suterberry, 25
Sweet Cane, 38
Sweet Cumin, 23, 91
Sweet Flag, 38
Sweet Grass, 38
Sweet Pepper, 147
Sweet Sedge, 38
Sweetroot, 116
Sweetwood, 116
Swine's Bread, 47
Swiss Spinach Pancakes, 139, *190*
Szechwan Pepper, 24, 25
Szechwan Duck, 25

Tabasco (chilli), 59
Tabasco Sauce, 57, 58
Tabbouleh, 126, *33*
Tabil, 221
Tade Sauce, 183
Tahina, 172
Tailed Cubebs, 79
Tailed Pepper, 79
Taklia, 18, 221
Tamarind Chutney, 185, *103*
Tamarind Fish Relish, 185
Tandoori Curry Powder, 204
Tangerine Peel, 64
Tartare Sauce, 40
Teel, 173
Tikka Curry Powder, 204
Til, 173
Tobacco, 68, 114, 116, 186, 196;
  Chewing, 58; Snuff, 96
Tom Thumb, 131

Tonga Bean, 187
Tonka Fudge, 187
Tonqua, Tonquin Bean, 187
Toothache Bark, Tree, 25
Tree Melon, 144
Trout, Lemon, 66
Tsire Agashe, 221
Tsire Powder, 221
Turkey, *see* Poultry and Game
Turkish Delight, 120

Umbrella Tree, 171

Vampirifuge, 98
Veal, 66
Vegetables: Dhal, 94; Dolmades,
  125; Habas à la Asturiana, 148;
  Lobhia, 134; Pakoras, 153;
  Sauerkraut, 88; Spicy Potatoes,
  30; Swiss Spinach Pancakes, 139
Vindaloo Curry, 93, *189*
Vindaloo Curry Powder, 204
Vinegar: Garlic, 98; in Horse-
  radish Sauce, 107, 108;
  Nasturtium, 131
Virgin Islands Spice, 222

War Paint, 28
Wasabi, 106-8
Water Pepper, 183
Wild Cumin, 42
Wild Onion Seed, 133
Wild Turmeric, 198
Wine, Mulled, 214
Witches, 41, 88
Wrinkled Pepper, 59

Xocolatl, 71, 196

Yakhni Spice, 222
Yellow Ginger, 193
Yellow Rice, 193
Yellow Wood, 25
Yoghurt: with Coriander, *104*;
  with Sumac, 181, *33*

Zaffer, 162
Zanzibar Pepper, 59
Zathar, 222
Zeera pani (a beverage), 80
Zhug, 222